The Role of Tradition in Japan's Industrialization

JAPANESE STUDIES IN ECONOMIC AND SOCIAL HISTORY

Edited by Osamu Saito and Kaoru Sugihara for the Socio-economic History Society of Japan

The Role of Tradition in Japan's Industrialization

Another Path to Industrialization

VOLUME 2

Edited by
MASAYUKI TANIMOTO

OXFORD
UNIVERSITY PRESS

OXFORD

UNIVERSITY PRESS

Great Clarendon Street, Oxford OX2 6DP

Oxford University Press is a department of the University of Oxford.
It furthers the University's objective of excellence in research, scholarship,
and education by publishing worldwide in

Oxford New York

Auckland Cape Town Dar es Salaam Hong Kong Karachi
Kuala Lumpur Madrid Melbourne Mexico City Nairobi
New Delhi Shanghai Taipei Toronto

With offices in

Argentina Austria Brazil Chile Czech Republic France Greece
Guatemala Hungary Italy Japan Poland Portugal Singapore
South Korea Switzerland Thailand Turkey Ukraine Vietnam

Oxford is a registered trade mark of Oxford University Press
in the UK and in certain other countries

Published in the United States
by Oxford University Press Inc., New York

© Oxford University Press, 2006

The moral rights of the authors have been asserted
Database right Oxford University Press (maker)

First published 2006

British Library Cataloguing in Publication Data

Data available

Library of Congress Cataloging in Publication Data

Data available

Typeset by Newgen Imaging Systems (P) Ltd., Chennai, India
Printed in Great Britain
on acid-free paper by
Biddles Ltd., King's Lynn

ISBN 0-19-829274-0   978-0-19-829274-6

PREFACE

This is the second volume of the series "Japanese Studies in Economic and Social History", edited under the auspices of the Socio-economic History Society of Japan.

It is a well-known story that Japan's modern economic growth started in the last quarter of the nineteenth century, transplanting the advanced technologies and institutions from industrialized western countries. Recent studies on economic history of modern Japan, however, have claimed the importance of the aspects other than the transplantation from west to realize the feature of the Japan's economic development. The indigenous factors, which we call "tradition" in the broad sense in this volume, should be pointed out to account for the cause of Japan's modern economic development. This recognition was already expressed as a concept of "balanced economic growth" from the viewpoint of macro economic analysis in the 1970s. Inspired by this argument, many economic historians in Japan have considered the role of indigenous industries, executing micro-based analysis of the industrial histories from the 1980s onwards. The principal aim of this volume is to provide the English reading academics with the fruits of this field, compiling the recent representative works. The volume also intends to clarify the existence of "indigenous development" in Japan's economic development that would shed new light on the conventional concept of "the dual economy" in the industrialized economies as well as for the developing countries.

It was impossible to complete the volume without the invaluable assistance of many people. We are most grateful to Linda Grove and Patricia Sippel for their devoted efforts to improve the English-language presentation of the chapters. Hiroki Ichinose and Kei Saito helped us as well with the English translation for some chapters. Osamu Saito has given us advice and many suggestions from the beginning of this project. Some of the editorial work was helped by Hidetoshi Miyachi. The CIRJE (Center for International Research on the Japanese Economy, affiliated with the Graduate School of Economics, the University of Tokyo) generously gave us financial support. We would like to express our gratitude to them all for their contributions.

Masayuki Tanimoto

CONTENTS

viii   *Contents*

LIST OF FIGURES

LIST OF TABLES

LIST OF MAPS

Sea of Japan

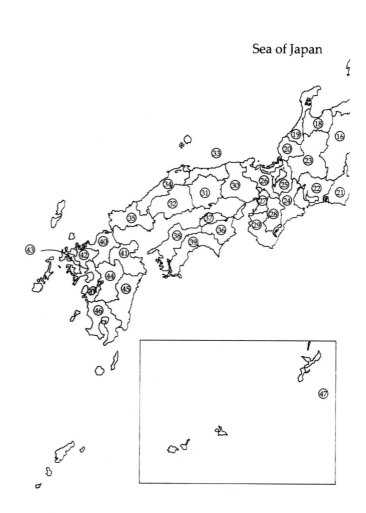

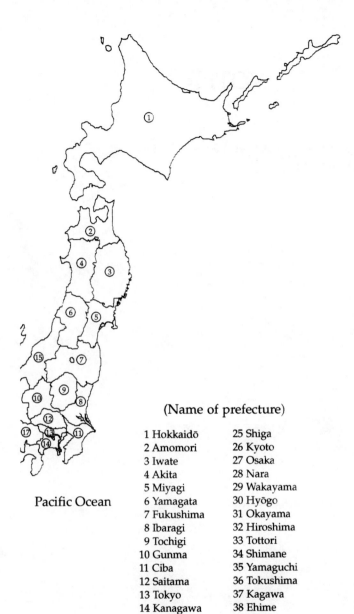

(Name of prefecture)

1 Hokkaidō	25 Shiga
2 Amomori	26 Kyoto
3 Iwate	27 Osaka
4 Akita	28 Nara
5 Miyagi	29 Wakayama
6 Yamagata	30 Hyōgo
7 Fukushima	31 Okayama
8 Ibaragi	32 Hiroshima
9 Tochigi	33 Tottori
10 Gunma	34 Shimane
11 Ciba	35 Yamaguchi
12 Saitama	36 Tokushima
13 Tokyo	37 Kagawa
14 Kanagawa	38 Ehime
15 Niigata	39 Kōchi
16 Nagano	40 Fukuoka
17 Yamanashi	41 Ōita
18 Toyama	42 Saga
19 Ishikawa	43 Nagasaki
20 Fukui	44 Kumamoto
21 Shizuoka	45 Miyazaki
22 Aichi	46 Kagoshima
23 Gifu	47 Okinawa
24 Mie	

Pacific Ocean

NOTES

Japanese names are expressed in Western order, that is, first name followed by family name.

LIST OF CONTRIBUTORS

Masayuki Tanimoto, Graduate School of Economics, University of Tokyo, Tokyo

Takanori Matsumoto, Faculty of Economics, Seikei University, Tokyo

Johzen Takeuchi, School of Economics, Zhejiang University, Hangzhou

Satoshi Matsumura, Faculty of Economics, Kanagawa University, Kanagawa

Jun Sasaki, Faculty of Economics, Ryukoku University, Kyoto

Jun Suzuki, Graduate School of Humanities and Sociology, University of Tokyo, Tokyo

Kazuhiro Ōmori, Faculty of Economics, Surugadai University, Saitama

Masaki Nakabayashi, Graduate School of Economics, Osaka University, Osaka

Takehisa Yamada, Faculty of Business Administration, Tezukayama University, Nara

Hisami Matsuzaki, Junior College, Urawa University, Saitama

Futoshi Yamauchi, Faculty of Economics, Kyoto Sangyo University, Kyoto

PART I
Introduction

1

The Role of Tradition in Japan's Industrialization: Another Path to Industrialization

MASAYUKI TANIMOTO

1. Statement of the Problem

This volume explores the role of "indigenous development" in Japan's industrialization, focusing on what may be identified as "traditional" or "indigenous" factors. In this volume we will use the words "tradition" and "indigenous" with rather broad meanings. In general, "tradition" and "indigenous" are used to indicate goods, technology or institutions whose origins were other than "modern" or "transplanted", but the definition of the words often depends on the contexts. The essential point is to indicate the existence of a particular industrialization process that is different from the factory-based industrial process, that is usually seen as the essence of what is viewed as "modern industry" or industries based on technology transfer.

The papers in this volume tackle this issue from the perspective of industrial history. Since our interest is focused on alternatives to factory-based industrialization, these papers do not deal directly with the industrial sectors that are commonly identified as the driving force of industrialization such as cotton spinning, railroads, or the iron and steel industries. Rather these papers argue that "traditional" or "indigenous" production systems in small-scale industry also played a significant role in the industrialization of Japan.

In making this statement, we do not deny that technology transfer from industrialized western countries played a major role in Japan's early industrialization. Technology transfer, which included the transplanting of factory-based production systems, was a major pillar of the Meiji government's development strategy. Government leaders viewed the importation of the workshop equipped with modern machinery, that is, the "factory system of organization," as one of the fastest ways to "catch up with and overtake" Western industrialized nations. The Meiji government actively promoted a variety of industrial sectors in the early 1870s. Government efforts focused not only on defense-related industries such as munitions and shipbuilding, but also on industries designed to produce consumer goods and inputs for both the domestic and export markets, including such industries as cotton spinning, silk-reeling, cement, glass and beer. These government-established factories were equipped with machinery imported from industrialized countries and employed foreign engineers and skilled workers who were paid high salaries to instruct Japanese workers in the manufacturing the most up-to-date technologies and techniques.

During the 1880s, the Meiji government faced serious budget deficits and was forced to sell many of the factories it had established to the private sector. Many of these ex-government factories eventually developed into major business operations, as exemplified by Mitsubishi Shipbuilding in Nagasaki and Kawasaki Shipbuilding in Hyōgo (Kōbe), and some then became core units of what later became known as the "zaibatsu" group of capitalists. The factories were acquired at quite favorable terms by Japan's leading capitalist entrepreneurs with the purchase prices considerably below what would have been the start up costs for investment from scratch. The only early factories that remained under government control were munitions factories. Under a similar scheme, what was to become Japan's largest steel mill, the Yahata Steel Mill, was launched in the early twentieth century as a government operation. In all of the above cases the government assumed the initial risk, and all of these cases fall in the category of industries based on the transfer of technology and production systems from more advanced industrialized countries.

A similar pattern of technology-transfer-based development can be found in the mechanized cotton spinning industry, although private entrepreneurs—rather than government bureaucrats—took the initiative. While the first government-sponsored cotton-spinning mill was equipped with only one British spinning machine with the capacity of 2,000 spindles, one of the pioneering private cotton spinning companies—Osaka Spinning Company (*Osaka Bōseki Kaisha*)—started operation in 1883 with more than 10,000 spindles, and became the first commercially successful cotton spinning company in Japan. During the late 1880s and 1890s, many more cotton spinning companies with tens of thousands of spindles were established as a great boom in investment in cotton spinning swept the nation. The newly-founded spinning mills drove English and Indian imported yarn out of the domestic market, and started to export to foreign markets, primarily Korea and China, as early as the late 1890s. The accounts I have given to this point stress what has often been regarded as Japan's main path to industrialization—that is, the development of modern industry based on technology transfer from the West. This path seems to represent a major break with the indigenous industrialization process, since Japanese domestic textile production in the 1870s had made use of hand-spun cotton yarn produced by peasant households as a sideline industry.

There is still a question, however, as to whether the story of Japanese industrialization can be adequately covered by a focus only on technology transfer and the development of the modern factory system. One way to approach this question is to consider the relative contribution of the modern industrial sector to overall Japanese production. Since it is difficult to estimate the relative weight of the modern sector in value-added terms, we will use the contribution to employment as a way to approach this problem. The first national census of population was carried out in 1920, thirty years after the boom in the establishment of modern cotton spinning mills. Table 1.1 shows the proportion of the working population employed in different production units at the time of this census. The total working population engaged in manufacturing sectors was approximately 4,560,000. The breakdown of the total was 3,168,000 employed as workers, 236,000 as salaried workers, and 1,162,000 as "employers". Official statistics of private factories (*Kōjō Tōkei Hyō*) in 1920, using a definition of "factory" as a workshop employing more than 5 workers, estimated that 1,486,000 people were working as "factory" workers. Therefore, regarding employees in government-run factories, approximately 160,000, as "factory" workers, 1,522,000 workers (3,168,000–1,486,000–160,000) might have been employed in small workshops which would not usually be regarded as factories. Adding to this, the greater part of those classified as "employers" should be considered as "self-employed workers" working in non-factory workshops, since these statistics suggests that there were only 45,806 "factories". Even assuming that all salaried workers were employed in units that can be classified as "factories", 62.9 percent of the total working population engaged in the manufacturing sector was working in non-factory workshops. The number of workers in the factories that employed more than ten employees was still smaller.

How do these numbers compare with other industrializing nations? According to Kinghorn and Nye, the proportion of workers in factory units that employed one to five workers was 37 percent in France and 33 percent in the United States around 1910 (Kinghorn and Nye 1996, pp. 106).[1] France is usually regarded as one of the industrialized nations in which small-scale production played a major role (O'Brien and Keyder 1978). As we can see from these statistics, the proportion of small workshop workers in Japan was higher than that of France. From this we can see that the western style factory system played a comparatively limited role in the process of Japan's industrialization.

This evidence suggests that we need to look more closely at the role of small scale and indigenous industry in Japan's industrialization. Recent research on Japan's pre-modern (Tokugawa era) economic history has shown that economic development had already started before the

Table 1.1. Structure of labor in manufacturing sector (1920)

(%)

	Occupied population A	(Breakdowns)			Factory with > 5 employees		Ratio of occupied population at the workshops < 5 employees (B + C − E + D − F)/A
		Wage worker B	Salaried worker C	Employer D	Wage worker E	Number of factories F	
Manufacturing Sector Total	4,565	3,168	236	1,162	1,647	45,806	62.9
Breakdowns							
Textiles	1,381	1,107	55	219	819	18,098	39.4
silk reeling	381	345	14	22	299	3,461	20.5
spinning	217	202	13	2	186	331	14.0
weaving	474	351	13	109	262	10,333	42.4
Metal, Machinery and Tools	815	618	65	132	366	6,245	54.4
Chemicals	432	314	35	83	165	5,509	60.5
Foods and Drinks	536	313	40	183	134	7,771	73.6
Miscellaneous	1,309	753	38	517	140	7,838	88.7

Sources: Naikaku Tōkei Kyoku [The Cabinet Statistical Bureau] (1920a,1920b). Nōshōmushō [Ministry of Agriculture and Commerce] (1920).

Note: A to E: thousand persons.

beginning of technology transfer from the west. Studies of price history have identified the long term, downward trend in price levels in the eighteenth century, and have shown that, with the re-coinage by the Tokugawa government, this downward trend was reversed, with an upward trend in prices beginning in the late 1820s and continuing to the end of Tokugawa period. According to these studies, the re-coinage marked the beginning of sustainable economic development, initiated under the conditions of inflation. Another study, based on an examination of estimated real money balances during the period, has claimed that there was continued economic growth, defined as the continuous increase in output, from the end of eighteenth century to the middle of the nineteenth century. These evaluations have argued that there was macro-economic development in the late Tokugawa period (Hayami, Saito, Toby 2004).

Numerous micro historical case studies have supported these views. Thomas C. Smith's books (Smith 1959, 1988), well known in the English reading world, are among the representative studies on these issues. Not a few Japanese scholars also have eagerly pointed to the evidence of industrial development—the development of commercial agriculture and non-agricultural production—in the late Tokugawa period.[2] Table 1.2, based on the earliest production statistics on a national level compiled by the Meiji government, "Fuken Bussan-hyō (Table of industrial products by prefecture)", illustrates the achievement of these developments. It should be pointed out that the data in "Fuken Bussan-hyō" were presented not in value-added terms, but in terms of the value of production output. Consequently, they may overestimate the weight of industrial production, as the values of industrial products included many agricultural goods that were used as inputs. Despite this bias toward industrial products, it should still be recognized that Table 2 suggests that "industrial" production occupied a significant portion of total production activity, when compared to the number of people engaged in industrial production shown in the demographic statistics by occupation (Table 1.2(b)). As a matter of fact, a regional historical archive of the Bōchō district in the 1830s, a relatively economically advanced region in western Japan, indicates that the ratio of non-agricultural income reached more than 50 percent in not a few farming villages, calculated from data in value-added terms (Smith 1988, Nishikawa 1987).

How should we understand these seemingly contradictory facts, namely, industrial development in the Tokugawa era and the limited use of the western style factory system in modern Japan? As we have already seen, modern factories trace their origins to the direct transplantation of western technologies and production know-how. This means that there does not seem to be any direct line of development from pre-Meiji industrial activities to the foundation of the modern factory system.

Masayuki Tanimoto

Table 1.2(a). Agricultural and non-agricultural products in Japan (1874)

Field of industry	Sum of production (Thousand yen)	(%)
Agricultural products	227,287	61.0
Manufacturing products	111,892	30.0
(Breakdown of manufacturing products)		
Textiles	30,994	
fabrics	17,159	
raw silk	6,165	
Foods and drinks	46,945	
breweries	34,326	
Other industries	33,953	
(over 2 million yen)		
oil	5,443	
paper	5,167	
machinery and tools	3,061	
fertilizer	3,057	
pottery	2,092	
Forestry products	14,565	3.9
Stock farm products	7,478	2.0
Fishery products	7,276	2.0
Mining products	3,809	1.0
Total	372,307	100.0

Source: Naimushō [Ministry of the Interior] (1874).

Table 1.2(b). Number of gainful workers by industry and occupation (1874) (Classified by the Meiji government)

Occupation	Number of workers (Thousand people)	(%)
Agriculture	15,657	77.2
Miscellaneous	1,922	9.5
Commerce	1,358	6.7
Manufacturing	749	3.7
Employee	418	2.1
Fishery	27	0.1
Others	152	0.7
Total	20,283	100.0

Source: Yamaguchi (1956: 37–8).

The orthodox view, based on general theories of the development of capitalism, has assumed that the transfer of the modern factory system led to the collapse of indigenous systems of production. A typical argument along this line can be seen in the historical research on the cotton weaving industry. The reason why the development of weaving industries in the late Tokugawa era resulted mainly in a putting-out system, not in the factory system, was attributed to the severe competition caused by the influx of cheap British cotton goods after the opening of the ports in 1859 (Takamura 1971, Ishii 1986). Since these theories regard the putting-out system as a stage in the development process (a stage that prepared for the transition to the factory system), retaining of the putting-out system meant the failure of the transition. The application of proto-industrialization theory to the Japanese case may share the same frame with these interpretations, since the failure to develop the factory system in the process of industrialization could be considered as de-industrialization or pastoralization.

A comparison of the predictions of what we would expect to happen, based on theory, and the actual experiences of the Japanese economy have raised a number of questions about how to interpret Japan's early industrialization. One of the first things we note is that the weaving industry revived and increased its production swiftly after the opening of the ports, as weavers began to make use of imported cotton yarn (Tanimoto 1992). Moreover, when we also consider the expansion of export markets, there is no question that the opening of the ports benefited the Japanese economy, at least at the macro level (Huber 1971).In fact the development of the raw silk export industry played a significant role in supporting the development of the weaving industry, by extending the domestic textile market at a time when Japan was faced with the influx of imported cotton goods (Saito and Tanimoto 1989/2004).

A second set of concerns is related to general theories of proto-industrialization, which offer explanations on the links between proto-industrial development and demographic growth. Franklin Mendels' well-known arguments about the growth mechanism of proto-industry, based on his study of Flanders (Mendels 1972), suggested that proto-industrialization usually led to earlier marriage and an increase in the population. But historical demographic studies of the Tokugawa era have not found this in rural villages during the Tokugawa era. Furthermore, it has been shown that while rural industries did not accelerate population growth, grain-cropping agriculture did contribute to population growth (Saito 1983).

When we put all these facts together—growth in the rural weaving industry after the opening of ports, the stimulus from new export markets for the products of "traditional" industries, and the fact that proto-industry did not produce the same effects in Japan that it had in Western Europe—it becomes clear that we must find new explanations for Japanese modern industrial growth that incorporate the small scale industrial sector. It is not enough to just look at the heritage of proto-industrialization as the foundation of the factory system. It is necessary to place the non-factory production system on the extended line of economic development linking developments in the late Tokugawa and the Meiji era.

The concept of "balanced growth" proposed by Takafusa Nakamura was the first attempt to try to incorporate these considerations (Nakamura 1971/1983). Nakamura divided the industries developed in modern Japan into two types, "modern industry" and "indigenous industry". Nakamura's work emphasized the large proportion of the workers engaged in the indigenous industries and their significant role in producing the relatively high growth rate of Japanese GDP during the late nineteenth and the early twentieth centuries. As his work concentrated mostly on an analysis of the quantitative macro level data, the process of industrial development itself was not fully investigated. However, inspired by his work, various monographs based on detailed case studies of "indigenous industries" have been published since the 1980s. These monographs showed that various "indigenous industries" had continued to develop even in the late nineteenth and early twentieth centuries. There has been much discussion of the roles of government policies and institutions in the development of these industries. The essays included in this volume grow out of this richly developed research tradition. Building on this research, this book brings together studies with a rich empirical base, focusing on small-scale industry as a central feature of Japan's industrialization process. As this pattern was based on "traditional" or "indigenous" factors, we call this pattern of development "indigenous development". This indigenous development pattern co-existed alongside the development of the transplanted western style factory system, and it was this combination that is characteristic of the modern Japanese economy.

The theoretical framework used in this volume draws on a comparative historical perspective. On the one hand, it aims to compare the history of industrial development in Japan with that of other developing countries. The fact that the direct importation and use of the Western factory system partly drove the industrialization of Japan may suggest the existence of a dual economy divided between "modern" and "traditional" sectors, similar to those that can be seen in contemporary developing countries. It should, however, be noted that the "duality" emphasized in this volume does not refer to the conventional theoretical framework that sees the division between the modern industrial sector and the traditional agricultural or so-called informal sectors[3] (Boeke 1953, Lewis 1954, etc.), but rather to duality existing between the "implanted" sectors and other "indigenous" sectors within the non-agricultural sectors (or formal sector that is separate from the concept of informal sector). The focal point of these papers therefore lies in the development of non-agricultural, industrial sectors in response to the market economy. Though small in scale, productive activities in these sectors were maintained as business operations, and should not be identified simply as an informal sector. This exploration of the Japanese industrialization process and its internal logic should also shed new light on our understanding of the industrialization process in other non-Western, developing countries in which both the dual economy and the formation of informal sectors have been observed.

On the other hand, the recent re-evaluation of Britain's Industrial Revolution has argued that the extent of the factory system was rather limited even in the British industrialization process (Crafts 1985). This re-evaluation suggests that a quantitative analysis of macro level data is not enough to argue for the special characteristics of an industrialization process. In fact, the role of various production forms other than the factory has been pointed out through the controversy over this revision (Berg 1994, Hudson 2004). That is, a simplistic comparison of the industrialization processes solely focused on the emergence of the factory system has gradually lost its ground. At the same time, there is another line of research that focuses on the regional industrialization process based on small-scale business in Continental Europe. These studies examine the industrialization process of small-scale business in comparison to American or British "mass production" systems, and look at the case studies of Japanese industrial development as exemplifiers of the former style of development (Piore and Sabel 1984). In these studies, the existence of production systems other than "mass production" is seen as characteristic of the Japanese industrialization process. Since it is our intention not only to note the similarities of the production forms but also to deepen the comparison to the patterns of industrialization, it is necessary to investigate the inner logic and conditions for industrial development based on the consideration of specific industries on a micro level. With such diverse views on what is supposed to be "advanced" industrialization process in Europe and the United States, in addition to the comparisons with attention to the specific characteristics of developing stages, the theoretical perspective of industrial history needs to construct a framework that deals with typological differences of industrialization processes.

In this introductory essay, I will describe the typical indigenous development process by looking at a case study of one rural weaving district. The third section of this essay will discuss the institutions supporting development, and the last section tries to place the implications of the argument in a far broader perspective.

2. Production Organization of Small Businesses: from a case study of the Weaving Industry

2.1. The role of the industrial district in Japan's weaving industry

British cotton industrial districts around Manchester were characterized by a concentration of mechanized factories not only in cotton spinning, but also in other branches of the textile industries such as weaving and processing. As we have already noted, a similar production pattern can be observed in the cotton *spinning* industry in Japan. But, when it comes to the cotton *weaving* industry, producers were divided into two different categories. One category included the weaving mills attached to cotton spinning companies. Such companies were equipped with British power looms and employed many young female workers, just as in the cotton spinning mills. This type represents the factory system directly trans-planted from western countries. It should, however, be noted that this production system produced, at maximum, only about one-third of the total value of cotton fabric in 1914. The rest of the cotton weaving was carried out in regional industrial districts ("sanchi") where clothiers and other manufacturers worked together in areas characterized by a highly concentrated presence of merchants dealing in a single type of product and materials (Abe 1989: 24). Table 1.3 shows the number of workers in the weaving industry in 1905. The number of workers in "factories"— production units employing more than 10 employees—took up only about 12 percent of the total number of workers in the whole industry. The table also shows that 30 percent of the workers were employed at workshops with less than 10 workers, and that 50 percent of the workers were work-ing in workshops organized under the putting-out system. On top of this, the average number of workers at these workshops was less than two. As similar industrial structures could also be found in prefectures such as Osaka and Aichi which were regional centers for mechanized cotton spin-ning and weaving, it may therefore be assumed that many of cotton cloth producers in the regional industrial districts operated in small-sized workshops. Indeed, even in 1914, the power loom ratio (the number of power looms divided by the total number of looms) remained as low as 16 percent (Abe 1989: 46). Since we can identify continuity in both technology and production systems, the weaving industry can be seen as a typical rep-resentative of the pattern of indigenous development. The following brief case study will explore the logic of this pattern of industrial development.[4]

2.2. *Adoption of the putting-out system*

As was indicated in Table 1.3, the largest category among workers in the weaving industry in the early twentieth century was *chin'ori*, namely "wage-weavers". "Wage-weavers" were workers organized by the cloth-iers through such means as supply of raw materials. Putting-out seems to have been the major production system in the weaving industry during this period.

The putting-out system is often seen as the classic form for organiza-tion of production in the age of proto-industrialization (Mendels 1972), and there is little question that it can be found in some form in the cotton

Table 1.3. Production forms of the weaving industry in Japan (1905)

		Number of working population of weaving					Ratio of female labor Total (%)
		Total	Factory	Domestic workshop	Clothier	Wage-weaver	
Total	(person)	767,423	91,279	229,446	58,591	388,107	95.3
	(%)	100.0	11.9	29.9	7.6	50.6	
Sum of twelve prefectures*	(person)	512,115	65,219	115,421	45,931	285,544	94.7
	(%)	100.0	12.7	22.5	9.0	55.8	
Kyoto	(person)	44,374	12,458	12,468	6,201	13,247	63.9
	(%)	100.0	28.1	28.1	14.0	29.9	
Fukui	(person)	25,820	9,111	13,431	374	2,904	97.8
	(%)	100.0	35.3	52.0	1.4	11.2	
		(Average number of working population per each working place)					
Total	(person)	1.7	29.5	1.7	4.1	1.3	
Sum of twelve prefectures	(person)	1.8	37.4	1.8	5.1	1.3	
Kyoto	(person)	5.1	35.3	4.6	23.3	2.4	
Fukui	(person)	4.9	20.5	6.3	1.8	1.2	

Source: Nōshōmushō [Ministry of Agriculture and Commerce] (1905).

Notes: * "Twelve prefectures" includes the prefectures that had more than twenty thousands of working population of weaving. The name of twelve prefectures in order of the number of weaving population are as follows: Aichi, Ehime, Wakayama, Kyoto, Saitama, Osaka, Gunma, Tochigi, Nara, Niigata, Fukui, Fukuoka.

weaving districts in the late Tokugawa period. Recent studies, however, show that the putting-out system came to play a dominant role in Japan's weaving industry only after the 1880s (Abe 1999 surveys such studies). The primary form for organization of production in the weaving district in Iruma, Saitama Prefecture, which we will take up in the following section, into the 1870s was the *kaufsystem*. In this system, rural factors bought the fabrics produced by peasants as sideline work, and sold them to local wholesalers at the local distributing center for fabrics. From the 1880s, some of the factors were transformed into putters-out (clothiers). These clothiers started to buy cotton yarn—imported yarn at the beginning, and domestic, machine-made yarns later—from the cotton yarn merchants in the distributing center, then had the yarn dyed and warped, and supplied the warped yarn to wage-weavers.

This transformation from the *kaufsystem* to putting-out was triggered by competition in the market. The market shrank through the recession in the early 1880s (the so-called Matsukata deflation), intensifying competition among the weaving districts. Although the market began to expand again in the late 1880s, the fierce competition continued with new districts entering the market. At the same time, the economic boom during the period increased income levels so that more and more consumers were able to exercise their more sophisticated demand for products (Tamura 2004). Since cost reduction through the introduction of power looms was not a feasible choice because imported power looms were too expensive, it became vital for clothiers to enhance their competitive edge through the improvement of the quality of their products. Under such circumstances, the putting-out system based on the supply of yarn served to improve the quality through the use of standardized materials. Adding to that, the clothier was able to provide the wage-weavers with detailed market information such as texture and design of the fabric through the supply of dyed, warped yarn, which played a pivotal role in the evaluation of product quality. The introduction and implementation of the putting-out system should then be seen as an adaptation strategy to emerging market conditions.

2.3. Wage-weavers and the peasant household

How did the clothier relate to the wage-weaver in the putting-out system? For Stephen Marglin, who argued that the emergence of the factory system represented a form of organization based on control of laborers who had been "deskilled" as a result of changes in the division of labor, the putting-out system was based on a similar principle: the weaver, who had formerly been an independent producer, was now organized and controlled by the clothier virtually as a laborer. This was the case of the wage-weavers in Iruma district whose weaving skill levels were not so high as to be able to operate as independent weavers. However, this does not mean that the clothier could freely mobilize the wage-weavers according to his needs. Fig. 1.1 shows the output figures (as indicated by the number of orders placed) and wages for the wage-weavers subcontracted by a prominent clothier of the Takizawa family in Iruma. The remaining documents about Takizawas' business activities, including various account books, enable us to analyze the transactions between clothier and wage-weavers. The data in Fig. 1.1 suggest that there were significant seasonal fluctuations in the volume of output and the wages provided by the clothier. While the subcontracted volume drastically fell during the period from May to July, it increased during the periods from March to April and from September to January. On the other hand, the wages paid at piece rates decreased in winter to the extent that the wage in January was less than half of that in June. If the demand for weaving labor determined the wage, the wage level should have increased in winter, one of the peak periods of production. Fig. 1.1, however, shows that the highest wage was recorded in the slack period of production, that is, in June. It follows that the labor demand in this region was influenced largely by factors other than those inherent to weaving labor.

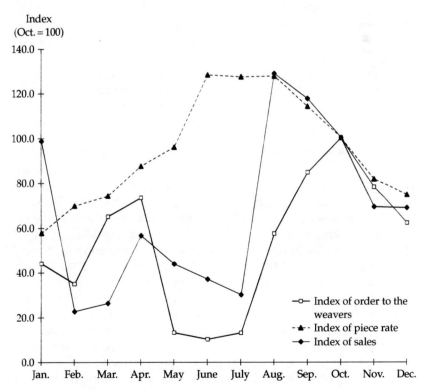

Fig. 1.1. Order, sales and piece rate in the putting-out system (Case of the Takizawas, 1897).

Source: Archives of the Takizawas.

In Iruma, the period from May to June coincides with the peak period of barley harvesting, tea making and sericulture. During these months female labor within the household of the wage-weaver tended to be allocated to agriculture-related activities, which consequently reduced the available labor supply for weaving. At the same time, this was a period when the clothier attempted to increase the volume of cloth. Since market competition positioned the fabrics of Iruma as winter clothing, the sale of fabric by the Takizawa family was heavily concentrated in autumn as we can see from Fig. 1.1. Thus for the clothier, it was desirable to increase production during this period in preparation for autumn sales. The high level of labor demand for weaving and the seasonal nature of labor demand on the one hand, and the seasonal shrinking of labor supply on the other, caused the relative hike in the wage rate during this period. The wage-weaver, therefore, should not be deemed as a source of labor freely mobilized at the will of the clothier. Indeed, Fig. 1.1 shows that the subcontracted volume of the clothier exceeded that of sales in the period of March to April. As it was difficult to increase orders to the wage-weavers during the summer, the clothier had to do that earlier, which resulted in a heavy financial burden placed on the clothier.

Thus, within the peasant household we can assume that the level of labor supply for wage weaving was determined in relation to that of labor demand for agricultural activities. A detailed look at the mechanism can be seen in the case of a peasant household in the Izumi district—a weaving district where the putting-out system was widely practiced. As we can see from Table 1.4, the head of the household was fully occupied in agricultural production. To cope with the labor demand for agriculture during the two peak periods, he also had to mobilize the labor of his "wife" and "old mother." As a result, a limitation was placed on the amount of time the wife could allocate to weaving. This is vividly illustrated by the fact that the amount of labor of both the "wife" and the "daughter" allocated to weaving production added up only to the labor-days equivalent to 1.5 years. At the same time, it should be noted that there was a mechanism that served to increase the amount of labor devoted to weaving. The labor of the "old mother" relieved the burden of agricultural labor required of the "daughter," which then enabled the "daughter" to devote all her available labor (except for necessary housework) to weaving. Even in housework, the "old mother" could cover a relatively heavy burden of "cooking" and reduce the labor demands for the "wife" and the "daughter." Moreover, the "old father," over seventy years old, was mobilized to participate in yarn reeling, and an eleven-year-old son was also assigned a portion of housework: baby-sitting. Thus the members of the household who were least suitable for full-time labor in agriculture or industrial production—and this category includes both the elderly and younger children—were assigned auxiliary tasks including housework so that more labor increasingly could be spared for weaving.

Table 1.4. The apportion of labor within a peasant's household (1901, in Senboku-gun, southern part of Osaka Prefecture)

Cultivated acreage	7 hectares odd			
Holding	under 6 hectares			
	Apportion of labor			
	agriculture	housework	weaving	straw work, etc.
Old father (75)			yarn winding	
Old mother (59)	part time	cooking, sewing, washing		
Householder (38)	full time			part time
Wife (35)	part time	sewing, washing	part time	
Daughter (14)		sewing, washing	full time	
Son (11)		baby-sitting		
Son (9)				
Daughter (5)				
Daughter (3)				
Total amount of labor	239.1(persons)*		540 days	
Total amount of woven fabrics			2,160 pieces	

Source: Osaka-fu Nōkai [Agricultural Organization of Osaka Prefecture] (1904).

Notes:* one day work by one person = one person.
The number in parenthesis is an age.

2.4. A solution of the managerial problems

As described above, the adoption and the duration of the putting-out system can be regarded as the clothier's adaptation to the fabric market and the labor market. Because the wage levels of wage-weavers were relatively lower than those of factory workers,[5] the adoption of the putting-out system also could reduce labor costs. However, because of the dispersed nature of the workshops, managerial problems were more or less inherent in the putting-out system. David Landes and others have suggested that the difficulties of controlling the outworkers might have lead to the decline of this system (Landes 1969, etc.). In fact, these problems appeared in the forms of "embezzlement of raw materials" and "delay in delivery terms" in the Iruma district, and the clothiers had to cope with them. Were the clothiers able to overcome such managerial problems?

Figure 1.2 shows data concerning "the embezzlement of raw materials". From 1902 to 1917, the yield rate of weaving production at the clothier (Takizawa), measured by the product weight divided by the weight of yarn supplied as raw materials, showed a reverse correlation to the volume of the production. That is, the yield rate went down at times of boom, and went up at times of recession. This meant that the clothier had to hand extra materials to the wage-weavers when the competition to contract

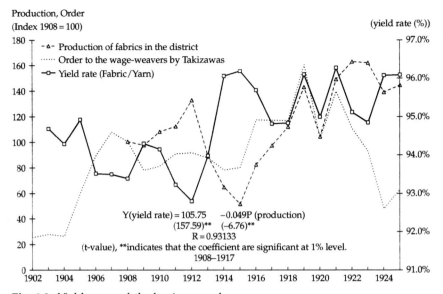

Fig. 1.2. Yield rate and the business cycle.

Source: Tanimoto (1998). Original date sources are Archives of the Takizawas and production data of trade association.

weavers became severe. It may therefore be assumed that the weavers' practice of "reserving yarn" was done with the knowledge of the clothier.

When we think about the problem "the embezzlement of raw materials" in this way, we can see "embezzlement" as a kind of negotiation strategy on the part of the weavers; the problem was eventually resolved with the introduction of a system of "payment in kind". A downward trend was also found in "the days required for weaving," that is, "the delivery terms." Thus the behavior of Takizawa may exemplify the methods used by putting-out masters who were trying to solve, at least temporarily, the inherent "managerial" problems of the putting-out system of production.

One of the features that made such a solution of managerial problems possible was the effort to build a close relationship between the clothier and the wage-weavers. From 1896 to 1925, Takizawa placed production orders with a minimum of 60 wage weavers, and a maximum of just under 200 weavers per year. It can be seen that Takizawa repeatedly hired and fired the weavers in response to market fluctuations. However, we should also note the presence of a group of core wage weavers who continuously received orders from Takizawa for more than five years. Such repeated transactions may have put limits on the morale hazard of the wage-weavers.

Further, although the Takizawa's business grew in scale, the geographic coverage of his order list tended to concentrate in specific localities. While there is no written evidence indicating the motivation behind this narrowing down of suppliers, we may assume that it was designed to allow close communication with core suppliers, thereby ensuring that the delivery terms would be met. This would also have allowed them to be assured that his core suppliers would continue to work for him in a situation characterized by severe competition for wage workers. In the case of the Takizawa firm these strategies—continuous transactions and geographical concentration—incorporated in the firm's putting-out system may have served to overcome the managerial problems inherent to the system, and to sustain a relatively long, and prosperous period for the putting-out system in the region.

3. The Institutional Basis of the "Indigenous Development"

As I noted earlier, the putting-out system played a dominant role in the indigenous weaving industry in modern Japan. This production organization was composed of the wage-weaver and the clothier. The wage-weaver was the supplier of labor and the clothier was the one who coped with the fabric market. It was the combination of the work of these two that gave birth to the particular pattern of industrial development in Japan. In the following sections, we will elaborate on the points discussed above and consider the institutional basis of "indigenous development".

3.1. Labor supply in small businesses

As was seen in the typical case of wage weavers above, the putting-out system depended on domestic work, that is labor utilized within the household unit. This labor force usually consisted of the head of the household (employer) and his family. An international comparison shows that modern Japan had a higher percentage of its work force involved in such domestic work than any of the other countries in the comparison.

Table 1.5 shows an international comparison of self-employment ratios—the estimated number of self-employed workers divided by the total number of workers—in each country, based on the assumption that the sum of "employer," "working on own account" and "family worker" was equivalent to the total self-employed laborers.[6] The table suggests that Japan had conspicuously higher ratios than other countries. It is true that these higher ratios could be attributed to the large agricultural population—a typical form of self-employment—in Japan. It should, however, be noted that the proportion of the agricultural population in Japan was about the same as that of Italy around 1930, and was lower by 10 percent than that of Mexico. When compared with countries with similar per capita GDPs such as Hungary in the 1930s and Mexico and Portugal in the 1950s, Japan is still seen to have had higher self-employment

Table 1.5.1. Ratio of self-employed workers ("employers", "workers on own account", + family employees) to total workers

Country (around 1930)	Year	Ratio of Self-employed Workers					Distribution of Workers			GDP per capita (1990 price, dollars)	
		All industries	Agriculture	Non-Agriculture	Manufacturing	Commerce	Agriculture	Non-Agriculture	Manufacturing		
JAPAN	1930	**67.6**	**95.1**	**40.8**	**39.6**	**68.8**	**49.4**	**50.6**	**16.0**	**1,780**	1930
POLAND	1931	**64.7**	**84.7**	**27.7**	**30.1**	**67.4**	**65.0**	**35.0**	**16.9**	**1,994**	1930
ITALY	1936	48.4	72.2	26.3	22.6	63.3	48.2	51.8	28.6	2,854	1930
FRANCE	1931	44.6	72.0	25.7	24.9	48.0	36.3	63.7	31.2	4,489	1930
HUNGARY	1930	**42.1**	**60.9**	**20.8**	**25.3**	**41.5**	**53.0**	**47.0**	**23.2**	**2,404**	1930
CZECHOSLOVAKIA	1930	36.4	70.5	15.2	14.0	44.2	38.3	61.7	34.3	2,926	1930
GERMANY	1933	32.9	71.7	17.1	13.9*		28.9	71.1	40.4*	4,049	1930
U.S.A.	1930	29.2	71.3	17.3	6.0	27.0	22.0	78.0	29.4	6,220	1930
U.K.	1931	13.7	40.3	11.9	8.5	27.7	6.4	93.6	38.3	5,195	1930
(around 1950)											
JAPAN	1950	**60.7**	**94.1**	**29.2**	**21.8**	**64.0**	**48.5**	**51.5**	**15.9**	**1,873**	1950
MEXICO	1950	**53.5**	**70.3**	**30.1**	**31.9**	**74.3**	**57.8**	**42.2**	**11.7**	**2,085**	1950
ITALY	1955	41.1	74.4	23.1	23.2	35.2	35.2	64.8	22.1	3,425	1950
FRANCE	1954	35.3	77.0	19.3	13.6	42.9	27.7	72.3	26.2	5,221	1950
WEST GERMANY	1950	29.2	77.9	14.5	12.7	37.8	23.2	76.8	30.8	4,281	1950
PORTUGAL	1950	26.8	38.6	15.7	17.6	43.5	48.4	51.6	18.8	2,132	1950
SWITZERLAND	1950	25.0	76.3	14.9	13.2	25.4	16.5	83.5	38.2	8,939	1950
SWEDEN	1950	23.2	70.2	11.2	9.1	22.1	20.3	79.7	31.5	6,738	1950
U.S.A.	1950	17.8	72.3	10.2	4.6	19.1	12.2	87.8	26.8	9,573	1950
U.K.	1951	7.4	32.9	6.0	2.3	16.8	5.0	95.0	37.6	6,847	1950
(around 1970)											
THAILAND	1970	85.4	96.9	35.1	34.2	79.8	81.4	18.6	3.2	1,596	1970
INDONESIA	1971	62.9	76.8	40.1	47.2	86.2	62.2	37.8	7.4	1,239	1970
MEXICO	1970	37.7	51.0	29.0	23.2	52.5	39.2	60.8	16.7	3,774	1970
POLAND	1970	35.0	87.3	2.1	2.7	1.7	38.6	61.4	24.9	4,428	1970
JAPAN	1970	**34.9**	**95.1**	**20.7**	**15.4**	**36.9**	**19.1**	**80.9**	**25.5**	**9,448**	1970
ITALY	1972	**28.1**	**62.4**	**20.9**	**15.7**	**55.1**	**17.5**	**82.5**	**31.1**	**9,508**	1970
SPAIN	1970	24.9	55.4	14.8	8.5	39.3	24.8	75.2	25.5	7,291	1970
FRANCE	1972	19.9	80.4	11.5	5.7	29.8	12.3	87.7	26.3	11,558	1970
WEST GERMANY	1971	16.1	87.2	9.7	5.8	19.7	8.2	91.8	38.8	11,933	1970
SWEDEN	1972	10.6	66.7	5.9	2.9	11.8	7.7	92.3	28.5	12,717	1970
U.S.A.	1972	9.2	61.8	6.9	1.3	10.4	4.2	95.8	23.6	14,854	1970
U.K.	1966	7.1	42.1	6.0	1.3	13.3	3.1	96.9	34.7	10,694	1970

Sources: International Labour Organization (1939, 1956, 1973), Maddison (1995).

Notes: Agriculture includes forestry and fishery industry.
Bold letters indicate the countries whose per capita GDP level are similar to those of JAPAN.
* includes mining.

ratios. Similar traits can be found in the high self-employment ratios of Germany and France in comparison to those of the United Kingdom and the United States. This international comparison should suggest that the self-employment ratio does not only reflect the degree of economic development, but also mirrors a specific employment pattern in each country.

The comparison of specific industrial figures tells us that the Japanese industrial structure was characterized by its overwhelming ratio of self-employment in the agricultural sector. Japan is the only country in the table that recorded more than a 90 percent self-employment ratio in that sector in around 1930 and 1950. The United Kingdom exemplifies the extreme opposite with an agricultural sector in which self-employed workers occupied only 30–40 percent. In the United States, Germany, France, Italy and Mexico, the agricultural ratio in each country reached up to the order of 70 percent, which indicates that the agricultural labor in those countries was supplied primarily by self-employed labor. Even in those countries, however, about one-fourth of the total agricultural labor was supplied by employed labor.

It is widely known that the landlord system achieved rapid development in modern Japan, and that more than 40 percent of cultivated land in the early twentieth century was under tenancy, that is, the land was managed by those other than the landowner (Waswo 1977). It should then be clear that the possession of the land was monopolized by a small number of landowners. While land ownership was concentrated, land management was not. When we examine the size of managerial units, we can see that the average size of the land lot remained as small as less than 1 ha, and only 15 percent of the total farming households cultivated land lots larger in size than 1.5 ha. In other words, in the agricultural sector in Japan, there were almost no large-scale agricultural enterprises based primarily on hired labor. The sector was characterized by the prevalence of small-sized farming households of both owners and tenant farmers. Moreover, the dispersion of farm size gradually contracted, that is, peasant households with land lots of about 0.5 to 1.5 ha increased in proportion in the twentieth century.

This trend, which is called "the standardization of middle-sized farming" in the field of Japanese agricultural history, should then be seen as a developmental trajectory of the peasantry that combined owned and tenanted lands (Numata 2001). While responding to changes in the market, the peasantry did not dissolve into farmers and wage laborers, but developed into a sophisticated form of the peasant household. This is exemplified by the fact that the development of commercial agriculture and sericulture, and the increased agricultural income that included these sectors, functioned to confine the family labor within the household (Saito 1998). It should also be pointed out that there were some tenanted peasants that invested their non-agricultural income in their agricultural activities (Nishida 1997).

"Domestic industry" and other sideline business opportunities should then have been integrated into the maintenance and development strategy of the peasantry. Since the household needed to guarantee access to a supply of seasonal agricultural labor, "domestic industry" was one way of doing that by providing other income-generating opportunities at times when the labor was not employed in agriculture. At the same time, because the job opportunity incorporated within the household created a variable form of work, "reproductive labor" (such as housework) could be allocated easily within the household. The incorporation of "domestic industry" within the peasant household should then be seen partly as a "rational choice" of job opportunities. However, it should be noted that this behavior was rational only as long as one assumed that preservation and the reproduction of the peasant household was a central goal. The always present possibility of the peasantry shifting to non-agricultural household employment cannot be ruled out since industrial development in modern Japan produced many opportunities for non-agricultural work.

The Japanese pattern of development seems quite different from what we know about European development. In fact, the literature on European proto-industrialization often notes that there was a division between households that chose specialization in agricultural and those that chose non-agricultural pursuits. The emergence of full-time small-scale weavers, who specialized in non-agricultural work, has also been reported in the development process of a contemporary Indonesian weaving district (Mizuno 1996, 1999). In the Japanese case, the location of non-agricultural activities within the peasant household was based on the strong determination of Japanese peasants to preserve the farming household.

When peasant households became involved in non-agricultural activities, overall labor input of the family increased. This feature has been identified in discussion of the the so-called labor intensiveness of the Japanese peasant household. Akira Hayami has argued that the Japanese peasant experienced an "Industrious revolution" during the period of peasant formation in the Tokugawa era (Hayami, A. 1979/2001).[7] The increase in work intensity was not confined to the Tokugawa era; the total number of hours of work in peasant households continued to increase during the pre-World War II period in spite of the increase of income (Saito 1998). Thus the concept of "the standardization of the middle-sized farming" was also based on the assumption of the labor intensity of the peasant household. Since it is assumed that the tenant-peasants were striving to accumulate savings to purchase the land they were leasing, intensive labor input of the household members must have been seen as a way to accumulate the funds for purchase of land. In this context, it is clear that Chayanov's well-known theory of peasants' economic behavior in which he assumed an equilibrium of labor inputs and consumption and believed that there would be a decline in labor inputs in proportion to the decline of the consumption unit, cannot be used to explain the behavior of Japanese peasants (Chayanov 1925/1986).

These points suggest the need to investigate the factors that shaped peasants' behavior from a different analytical frame. Sociological studies on the rural community, which paid strong attention to the family system called *ie*, suggest one approach to this problem. For instance, Kizaemon Ariga, a leading sociologist in this field, characterized the Japanese peasant family as the stem-family with the single inheritance custom of lineal male descendant. Ariga argued that this system was well suited to a system which placed high value on the succession of the *ie* as an independent unit (Ariga 1972). The fact that the number of farming households had remained constant around 5.5 million from the 1890s to the 1930s suggests the correctness of this assumption (Namiki 1955). If the *ie*—rather than the individual or the nuclear family unit—was established as the subject of inheritance, a choice to sell lands and to abandon farming could not be made by a single generation. As a result, the household gave first priority to farming and the labor supply to non-agricultural work was determined in view of the labor input to agricultural work. This argument can be applied to landless tenants as we recall to mind the long-term stability of the relationship between the landowners and the tenants in modern Japan (Sakane 1999). The structure of the division of labor among the household members should also be noted. As we saw earlier when we looked at the gender division of labor, managerial work was usually assigned to men and manual labor to women, with the householder holding the power and authority to allocate a certain kind work to a certain member of his "labor force", even in opposition to the preferences of individual members. If we assume that this power was guaranteed by social consent, the peasant household cannot be regarded simply as the set of individualistic economic subjects. That is, the Japanese peasant household was an institution with very specific characteristics, integrating a particular form of the family system, the *ie*, and a division of labor by gender. The development of domestic industries must be understood within the framework of this particular form of the peasant household.

Since not all small-scale, indigenous industry was located in the countryside, we must next ask if it is possible to extend this argument to the non-agricultural sectors such as urban small business. Table 1.5, which we have referred to before, provides a clue for answering this question. In the manufacturing sector in Japan, slightly less than 40 percent of the work force was categorized as self-employed during the 1930s, which was the highest figure among the countries listed in the table. The ratios in the United Kingdom and the United States during the same period fell to under 10 percent. In France and Germany, the figures were around 20 percent. Around 1950, the ratios in West Germany and France were around 12–13 percent, and those in the United Kingdom and the United States were less than 5 percent. This means that the workers in those manufacturing sectors in other countries were primarily composed of those hired as laborer. Similar patterns of decline in the self-employed ratio can be found in other countries. During the same period, the ratio in Japan fell to approximately 20 percent, about the same figure as that of Italy. When looking at the long-term shift until 1970, however, we can identify distinctive trajectories of industrial structures among these countries. As is shown in Table 1.5.2, Japan's self-employment ratio in the non-agricultural sector (including manufacturing) increased 1.67 times (1.7 times in the manufacturing sector only). On the other hand, the ratios in Germany and France decreased during the same period, and that of Italy only slightly increased. Indeed, recent international comparisons of generational social mobility show that Japan's inward mobility ratio from other forms of employment to self-employed during the 1970s and 1980s is significantly higher than those in other countries in Europe and the United States. Based on these findings, Hiroshi Ishida argues that non-agricultural, self-employed labor in Japan is characterized by its distinctive generational stability and self-reproduction (Ishida 2001).

Micro level approaches to non-agricultural small or petty-scale businesses are also included in this study. Chapter 3 (Takeuchi) shows that it was small or petty-scale businesses which engaged in the manufacturing sundries after the breakdown of the early factories in that industry. Chapter 6 (Suzuki) describes the activities of small-scale machine manufacturing workshops, which were run by skilled mechanics. The quantitative overview of non-agricultural small businesses can be seen in Chapter 2 (Matsumoto). These studies suggest that "non-employed" labor, such as the employer or members of his family, played a significant role in labor supply in small-scale businesses even in the non-agricultural, urban sectors. In fact the analysis of the municipal population census of Tokyo has revealed that the ratio of workers in petty manufacturing workshops (workshops employed not more than 4 workers), including workshop

Table 1.5.2. Sectorial transition of self-employed workers

(1950 = 100)

Country	Year	All Industries	Agriculture	Non-Agriculture	Manufacturing	Commerce
Mexico	1970	110	77	219	162	124
Japan	1970	86	60	167	170	159
Italy	1972	65	39	109	90	n.a.
France	1972	64	53	82	47	79
West Germany	1971	67	48	97	70	98
United States	1972	77	43	109	36	107
United Kingdom	1966	108	91	113	57	101

Source: Same as Table 5.1.1.

masters, reached 69 percent of all gainfully employed workers in the manufacturing sector in 1908 and the number of petty manufacturing workshops and retail shops increased from 1908 to 1920 (Tanimoto 2002). The development of small manufacturing businesses in Tokyo in the Interwar period has also been investigated (Tanimoto 2005). The characteristics of the workforce in these non-agricultural activities seem to have been more similar to the peasants' household than to the typical factory workers. The pattern of indigenous development based on the household economy and the *ie* therefore can be assumed to have existed in fields unrelated to the agricultural sectors.

3.2. The institutions supporting small and petty-scale businesses

Did small and petty-scale businesses also engage in distinctive managerial practices? Let us consider the managerial practices of the entrepreneurs such as putters-out. Japanese putters-out tended to remain as small size enterprises. In the weaving industry, for example, it was often the case that the clothiers, who were equivalent to putters-out, lived in the farming village where they organized the wage-weavers who resided in the same or neighboring villages. They sold the fabrics they had gathered to the wholesale merchants in the local distributing center. Compared to the typical cases described in the proto-industrialization literature on European experiences in which the organizers of the weavers were prominent urban merchants, the size of Japanese clothiers could be characterized as small businesses. Keeping the scale of the enterprises in mind, our studies examine the significance of the institutions and policies that supported the development of the industries.

First, we can point to some measures executed by the government in this context. The Ministry of Foreign Affairs, together with the Ministry of Agriculture and Commerce, actively surveyed overseas markets. Outcomes were summarized as ministry reports and widely distributed for use by enterprises of all scales (Tsunoyama (ed.) 1986). The Meiji government, which had participated in international exhibitions in the 1860s and 1870s, opened the first large-scale domestic exposition as early as 1877, recognizing the positive effects of exhibitions for promoting industries. From that time onward to 1903, the central government held five domestic expositions with tens to hundreds of thousands of exhibits. In addition to these nationally-sponsored exhibitions, local governments and non-government organizations held numerous exhibitions and trade fairs. As experts examined exhibits and commented on them from the technological point of view, the exhibitions are presumed to have had considerable effects on the distribution of technological information together with the promotion of technological development (Kiyokawa 1995). Such exhibitions were particularly significant for indigenous industries whose capacity for technological development was supposed to be limited.

Along with the programs supporting production, the industrial schools (Jitsugyō Gakkō) also played significant roles. In the weaving districts, for example, the clothiers' sons gained knowledge and skill of weaving or dyeing processes through the schools and this contributed to advance the technological level of the weaving districts (Takeuchi 1982, Hashino 2000). Chapter 9 (Yamada) shows that various types of schools, from polytechnic to vocational schools, functioned to absorb and adapt western technology in the traditional pottery industry. Experimental stations and laboratories run by local governments for the development and marketing of products also played important roles, as we can see from a number of detailed case studies (Yamazaki 1969, Abe 1989, Sawai 1999). These and similar measures, planned and financed by central and local governments, can be regarded as the construction of the "informational infrastructure" (Sugihara 1995). This infrastructure formed a favorable environment for the entrepreneurs who promoted indigenous development.

However, it should be pointed out that these measures only had their intended effects because of the systematic efforts from the industry side to take advantage of the opportunities created by such efforts. In fact, local industrial circles played an important role in founding the industrial schools, and the activities of the experimental station were strongly linked to those of the local association in the same trade. These associations often executed undertakings to support industries. Joint purchasing of raw materials like yarn were common undertakings among weaving districts and some of then eventually operated joint factories for the finishing process (Abe 1989). Chapter 7 (Ōmori) is a detailed analysis of these activities, such as common purchase and sales, taking examples from the pottery industry and the straw works industry.

Still, we should be aware that the original purpose of founding trade associations (*dōgyō kumiai*), the principal executer of these undertakings, was to regulate the activities of traders concerned. In the beginning, the Meiji government made a negative assessment of such regulation based on the principle of "the freedom of trade". The 1872 order to dissolve the *kabu-nakama*, a kind of guild from the Tokugawa era, was based on this principle. As the traders, however, often complained about market disorder, the government enacted the law permitting the revival of organizations of traders in a similar line of business in 1884 and revised the law in 1900 to strengthen the enforcement power to eliminate outsiders.[8] Our attention here is on what we might call the latent functions of this regulatory policy. There is no question that these regulations may have functioned to distort the distribution of profits. The control of wage rates by the clothiers' association was an example that might have led to exploitation of wage-workers (Ōshima 1985). However, in the case of Iruma, the weaving district discussed above, wage control did not function as well as the successful measures to prevent wage-workers' embezzlement of raw materials (Tanimoto 1998). Since the latter measure was crucial to the quality control problem, it was one of the major issues the trade association tackled. Ōmori shows that product inspections conducted by the trade associations were essential to control the quality of products. His paper also introduces a trial, undertaken by the pottery association, to restrict design imitation by endowing exclusive rights to original designers. This measure, which put the brakes on production of inferior goods and also stimulated the development of designs and techniques to maintain the reputation of product brands, was indispensable to restricting the opportunistic activities of traders. Thus, the regulation measures of trade associations included factors that may have served as the basis of industrial development.

3.3. *Industrial districts and regional society*

Lastly, let us consider the *place* in which industries operated. From the viewpoint of industrial location, it is notable that many of the industries discussed above were located in relatively concentrated spaces, forming a kind of cluster. For example, in the weaving district of Iruma, which we discussed in the previous section, the actors in the industry such as local wholesalers, clothiers, and wage-weavers resided within a radius of ten kilometers of the distributing center of Tokorozawa. However, this centripetal structure had not yet formed when market oriented production had started in the late Tokugawa era. Fabrics produced in villages were shipped to various towns such as Hachiōji, Ōme and Kawagoe, all of which were located further than ten kilometers from Tokorozawa. In the case of the clothier Takizawa, a fairly representative putting-out master in this district, sales routes to Ōme maintained a certain ratio until the latter half of 1890s. However, Takizawa's sales came to concentrate in Tokorozawa around 1900. By 1900, almost all the local wholesalers of fabrics, who sold products in a nationwide market through the wholesalers in central distributing centers such as Tokyo and Osaka, and the distributors of raw materials who mediated the sale of yarn between clothiers and yarn merchants in Tokyo, had settled in this town. The wholesalers became the leaders of the district and even founded a bank to cover the financial needs of the industry. Tokorozawa thus established its position as the distributing center for this district. On the other hand, the clothiers still resided in the countryside and maintained close relationships with the wage-weavers in peasant households. These clothiers had been trying to form an association together with the merchants in Tokorozawa, and this trial, which entailed a controversy over what geographical areas should be covered by the agreement, was eventually settled at the beginning of the twentieth century. The final agreement included the whole area neighboring Tokorozawa. The fabrics inspected by the trade association had begun to be recognized as special products produced in the Tokorozawa region. This was certainly a process in which the Tokorozawa region was located as an industrial district providing goods to a nationwide market.

According to Alfred Marshall's well-known description, it is natural for traders in a common commodity to gather together in concentrated geographical regions since such clusters of economic activities generate positive externality (Marshall 1920). However, industrial districts should be distinguished from the general geographical concentration of economic activity. The industrial district is a unit participating in market competition and that unit would not be workable without the characteristic structures of production and distribution. The structure was based on organized activities such as the putting-out system or trade associations. The putting-out system can be characterized as the vertical organization of the subjects located at different levels of the structure of the division of labor, the trade association as the horizontal organization of the leading actors in the production and distribution system who are located at similar levels.[9] As the chapters of this volume indicate, indigenous industries tended to form industrial districts, and those industrial districts became the units that joined together to market products that came to be associated with a specific regional industrial district. These phenomena can be understood when we remember that the small scale of individual businesses was a central feature of these industries. In other words, the formations of industrial districts, as well as the organization of cooperative organizations, were distinctive features of indigenous development. Thus, it is important to evaluate the function of industrial districts in the process of industrial development in comparison with other forms of production systems, such as the large-scale factory system or the clusters of strongly independent artisans. The latter comparison may relate to the typology of industrial clusters since the artisans' workshops also were inclined to concentrate within small geographical areas. Some chapters in this volume discuss issues related to this problem.

At the same time the reasons why quite a lot of industrial districts in Japan could be organized well is also an important question from the point of view of comparative history. Generally speaking, it is not the easy way to construct the order favorable to the collective interest since each economic subject pursues its own interest. It might have been more difficult in the circumstance where the participants were small and the transactions were complicated. Therefore, the industrial districts, where small traders and workshops concentrated, might have turned to the nests of conflicts and opportunistic behaviors. Recognizing the complexity of these problems, studies on industrial districts in contemporary Italy have been conscious of the social foundations that have lead to industrial successes in the districts (Brusco 1982, Lazerson 1990, Putnam 1993).

As a matter of fact, these phenomena can also be observed in the industrial districts in Japan. The existence of managerial problems in organizing wage-weavers (vertical organization) has already been mentioned. The opposition to regulatory measures, introduced by the associations, also suggest that conflicts sometimes arose as a result of differences between individual and collective interests. The joint enterprises run by associations may also have contributed to conflicts among the members over the costs that had to be shared. How could they overcome the private interests of individual firms to secure collective goals promoted by the association? By asking questions about the place where industrial districts developed we may be able to find clues that will help us answer this question. Industrial districts did not develop in vacuums, but in regional societies that had distinctive historical backgrounds. How did the specific characteristics of a given regional community influence the development of an industrial district?

"Saving transaction costs" is a factor that should be considered as one of the economic functions of the region. If we look at recent theories in development economics, we discover the idea that one of the functions of the community was to restrict the morale hazard of individual members (Hayami 1997, Aoki and Hayami 2000). Akihiko Ohno and Masao Kikuchi have applied this framework to contemporary weaving industries in Asian countries and insist that the existence of the community had a positive effect on the deployment of the putting-out system (Ohno and Kikuchi 1998). In fact, it has been the common understanding in the field of rural history that Japanese villages, even in the modern period, could be characterized by the intensity of human relations. Yoshihiro Sakane compared the tenant system of agriculture in modern Japan to that of contemporary Bangladesh and concluded that the long-term relationships between tenant and landowner characterize the Japanese tenant system. In contrast, frequent turnovers of tenants undermined the tenant system itself in Bangladesh. Sakane attributed this difference to trust among the inhabitants of the local community and added that this frame could be applied not only to the tenant system but also to the putting-out system deployed in industrial districts (Sakane 1999). The web of ties that characterized regional society in modern Japan may have enhanced the organizational capability of industrial districts through the alleviation of "internal contradictions of the (putting-out) system" (Landes 1969: 58).

Another point is that the existence of "regional community" may have affected industrial development by providing the entrepreneur or the man of property with motivations besides profit maximization. Chapter 11 (Yamauchi) provides an example in which the association of the silk weaving industry heavily depended on the wealthy farmers for both finance and management of the associations. Although they were not engaged in the weaving industry, they were urged to devote funds or energy to the industry because of the assumption that men of a certain social status should be responsible for the development of regional community. Chapter 10 (Matsuzaki) also argues that the behavior of certain economic actors in the regional community—such as wholesalers in a local distributing center, clothiers, and local banks—utilizing the the concept of "social capital" which existed within the region. According to Robert Putnam, "social capital" refers to features of social organization, such as trust, norms, and networks that can improve the efficiency of society by aiding in the coordination of the activities of different actors (Putnam 1993: 167). Matsuzaki, however, also points out the negative aspects of social capital, and tried to evaluate the function of social capital in concrete industrial history. The argument about the characteristic investment activities of such individuals in Chapter 12 (Tanimoto) shows a similar understanding. In spite of the high risks and low expectations for returns, the men of property in the region tended to invest their funds in enterprises that had some connection to the regional community. Tanimoto assumes that the motivation for this investment had come from the desire to acquire a higher reputation in the region.

Certainly, it is not easy to measure the effects of the favorable functions of regional community on industrial development. It might have been possible to prevent the embezzlement of raw materials through tighter managerial control exercised by the clothiers: for example, they could have chosen to limit the number of wage-weavers who worked for them. As for the "peculiar motivation", Matsuzaki himself also shows us an example in which adherence to the "communitarian principle" led to the failure of the business in market competition. The arguments above, however, at least show us the existence of the vector from regional community to industrial development. Although the tighter managerial control was a result of a business method that involved repeated business dealings between a clothier and a contracted weaver, the effect of repeated transactions may also have been enhanced by the low mobility among peasant households, which was a general characteristic of peasant households in Japanese villages (Nojiri 1943). Thus peasant households had every reason to expect that they would continue to work in the same community, and this may well have discouraged behavior that might harm their reputation. Profit motives were often not enough in the case of risky investment in new business opportunities that were unfamiliar and uncertain. Under the conditions of imperfect information, genuine *homo-economicus* often fails to capture the promising opportunities. The regional community, which was still characterized by many traditional factors, may have functioned to complement the market economy that generated industrial development. In that sense, regional society was one of the institutional bases of indigenous development.

4. The Features and the Implication of "Indigenous Development"

The discussion thus far has focused on one of the important features of indigenous development the organization of peasant or small business through the putting-out system. If we take this discussion as the starting point, we next need to ask where other systems of production stand in the overall picture of industrial development.

For instance, Table 1.3 showed that in the Kyoto Prefecture the total number of workers belonging to "factory" and "workshop" units was twice as large as those classified as "wage-weavers" under the putting-out system. The fact that there were equal proportions of male and female workers was also a feature that distinguished Kyoto from other prefectures. This was a reflection of the production system in Nishijin, which had been the major producer of high quality silk fabrics since the Sixteenth century. Nishijin organization was based on an apprentice system, in which young male workers were trained to become skilled weavers under the supervision of a master. Thus, the master, skilled weavers and apprentices worked together in workshops with several scores of workers (Yamaguchi 1974, Nakaoka *et al.* 1988). Individual workshops were able to maintain their independence in part because of the scarcity of highly skilled weavers. A similar production system was seen in the metal processing or machine-making industries. As Suzuki's paper in this volume shows, workshops with several to scores of workers played a significant role in these industries (Chapter 6, also see Table 1.1). Since the workers in such industries were already using machine tools, the links with traditional skills were somewhat different from those for the Nishijin weavers. However, there was a similarity in the forms of organization since the metal working industries used a quasi-apprentice system, in which the members of the work force were recruited at a young age and were trained on the job (Hyodo 1971, Gordon 1985). Since metal-working also required relatively high levels of skill this led to the use of organizational forms analogous to those of the traditional artisan.

On the other hand, Table 1.3 shows that the ratio of wage-weavers under the putting-out system was only slightly more than 10 percent in the Fukui prefecture, which specialized in the production of a plain-woven silk fabric called *Habutae*. The level of skill required to weave Habutae was not as high as that required for other fabrics. However, since the fabric was utilized as an intermediate good in the United States, which was the largest market for Japanese Habutae, uniform quality was demanded (Kandatsu 1974). The demand for uniform quality also was seen in the case of the silk-reeling industry. The silk-weaving industry in the United States, which provided the largest market for Japanese raw silk, shifted very rapidly to power looms after the 1880s. Since the uniformity of the raw silk affected productivity on the power looms, weaving enterprises demanded a uniform product. It was the Japanese silk reeling firms—especially those in the Suwa district—that developed a production system for meeting this demand (Chapter 8, Nakabayashi). The keys to Suwa's success included concentrating juvenile female labor in a workplace where their work could be closely monitored, and making use of standardized raw materials, especially cocoons, and unified working environments. The development of this combination of managerial practices allowed the Suwa silk reeling enterprises to produce raw silk of a uniformly high quality, while still using techniques that derived from handiwork techniques in which the quality of the product depended on the skill-level of individual workers.

From the above examples, we can see something of the variety of organizational patterns that were used in various indigenous industries, and the factors related to the nature of the product and the skill needed for its production that influenced the choice of organizational pattern. The uniformity of products required the concentrated workshop, while the high-skilled workers tended to form independent workshops. How can we position the putting-out system in this context?

In the case of the Iruma weaving district, which we have referred to several time, weavers produced a wide variety of finished goods. However, the level of weaving skill was far lower than in Nishijin, so it was still possible to train workers within the household workshop. Mothers passed on the weaving skills to their daughters within the peasant household, and one of the main paths for the transfer of weaving skills between households was marriage.[10] Thus we can see that the putting-out system was adopted in weaving districts whose product did not require either high levels of weaving skill or consistent uniformity of the product. It is important to note that these kinds of products targeted the domestic mass consumption market whose volume of demand was the largest. In fact, the number of workers in Nishijin or Fukui was not large, as can be seen from Table 1.3. When we consider these and numerous other examples together, a pattern emerges that suggests that the use of independent artisanal workshops or concentrated workplaces was relatively rare in the case of industries which continued to use indigenous techniques and were little affected by the transplanting of machinery or management styles from abroad. Even in the case of Nishijin, which is one of the classic examples of artisanal organization styles, the introduction of the power loom in the 1920s led to a lowering of skill levels and the emergence of a considerable number of wage-weaver households with one or two power looms, using female family labor (Hareven 2002). In the field of heavy industry as well, the putting-out system could be seen in industries manufacturing relatively simple products such as certain kinds of metal processing (Tokyo Municipal Office 1936).[11] A certain level of skill formation was implemented in the workshops without a formal apprenticeship system (Tanimoto 2005). The range of activities for the classical artisanal workshops was rather small.

Similar things can be said with regard to the organization of work within concentrated workplaces. Although raw silk was commonly used as an intermediate good, raw silk for the European market continued to be produced within the putting-out system during the late nineteenth and into the early twentieth century. Even in the Suwa district, which specialized in the production of standardized quality raw silk for the American market, we can see small and medium size raw silk enterprises alongside the large scale factories, together with the sideline reeling workers who were organized under a putting-out system which targeted the domestic market (Chapter 4, Matsumura). The concentration of silk reeling factories in Suwa district represented one of the rare examples of the transformation from domestic production to a factory system in a continuous development process in Japan. However, large-scale factory production only developed in the case of production of raw silk for the specialized market of the United States, where consistent quality control was important.

The fate of the factories established in the early stages of technology transfer is also interesting in this context. The transplantation of cotton spinning factories was apparently very successful. The development of a modern pottery company described in Chapter 9 (Yamada) might be seen as an example of factory-based development observed even in a traditional industry. However, many of the factories established during the early stages of transplantation later failed. Takeuchi referred to these factories as "the early factory". While he recognized the significant role these factories played in transplanting knowledge and technology, he argued that many of these factories were overcome by the evolution of another production form similar to the putting-out system (Chapter 3). Not only traditional industries, but also a number of other types of industry eventually came to use non-factory production systems.

Some scholars have assumed that one of the reasons for this pattern was the continued preference for traditional products (Nakamura 1971/1983). Fabrics, for example, were usually tailored for Japanese style clothing (*kimono*), until the 1930s. Pottery, porcelain and brewed products such as sake and *shoyu* (soy sauce) were also linked to the traditional Japanese life style. Thus, a view that traditional patterns of consumption functioned as the basis of the continuity of indigenous production forms certainly contains some truth. According to Takeuchi, however, various export-oriented industries adopted the putting-out system centered in small-scale businesses. Therefore, considering the fact that Western markets were significant markets for those various industries, we should refrain from attributing too much to traditional life styles, even though

there may be room to argue for the similarity of demand between traditional Japanese markets and the Asian region (Kawakatsu 1994, Sugihara
1996).

Thus, factors on the demand side are not a sufficient explanation for
the development patterns we have seen. A wide range of products were
produced in these systems based on small-scale production units. We can
also not explain these developments with arguments about the levels of
manufacturing skills or with arguments about the differences in intended
use of the intermediary or finished products. The argument of this chapter stresses factors besides the characteristics of demand or product that
formed the basis for indigenous development. In my view, another important consideration is the logic of labor supply: namely, the existence of the
household economy practicing a "rational" labor allocation strategy
among household members within the framework of the traditional institution of the *ie*. In addition, policies and institutions established by the
central and local governments supported the organization and market
adaptation on the management side. Regional community also functioned
to stabilize the relation between labor and management. All these factors
worked to construct the system that has been identified in the papers in
this volume. Since each of the factors, including the intensity of labor
inputs with relative low wages within peasant and small business households, a certain level of skill formation within the household, and the benefits from a division of labor generated by this style of organization,
contributed to competitiveness in the market, this system could function
as the basis of indigenous development.

Starting from this standpoint we can identify similarity and differences
between the Japanese cases described to this point and what has been said
about the role of small-scale business in the industrialization process in
Western countries. Arguments about the Western cases have used the concept of "flexible specialization", primarily focusing on examples from
Continental Europe, to describe craft production that had the ability to
respond to a differentiated and changing market conditions (Sabel and
Zeitlin 1985, 1997). As we can sense from the common use of the term
"craft" in these arguments, these arguments stressed skill as the decisive
factor in the production system. Recalling the importance of skilled workers in Nishijin or in the machine making workshops, it is obvious that the
role of skilled labor cannot be denied in the Japanese case.

However, as we have seen in the discussion of the Japanese experience,
there were other crucial factors besides skill that account for the existence
of indigenous development. These other factors include the managerial
ability of putters-out and merchants, labor allocation strategies of peasant and urban small business households, the undertakings of the central
and local governments, and the existence of regional community. As they
all functioned, in various combinations, to create production forms other

than the factory system, the indigenous development model can be expanded to a wide range of industries. In other words, social institutions such as the *ie* and community, together with the capability of management side and governments, played key roles in determining the form of industrial development. On the basis of this understanding, it is obvious that the simple application of the "flexible specialization" argument is not sufficient to explain the Japanese case.

Similarly, although the arguments that deal with the development of various production forms during the British industrial revolution proposed a common view in terms of the existence of small workshops and businesses (Berg 1994, Hudson 2004), we should carefully look at the social foundation behind the similarity in production forms. Admittedly the role of the peasant household in the Japanese case, in contrast to the relatively small role assigned to the peasant system in British agriculture might suggest different foundations from Japanese case. We need to compare the socio-economic background of the small workshops and businesses to identify the role of this production form in the whole economy.[12]

In addition to the flexible specialization arguments, there are a number of studies that have examined the development of non-agricultural and non-transplanted industries in contemporary developing countries (Mizuno 1996, 1999, Kikuchi 1998, Ohno 2001). In this field, the Japanese experiences of indigenous development have often been referred to for clues to analyze the data from empirical research (Hayami (ed.) 1998, Francks 2002). Through these studies, both points in common and points of difference have been revealed. The existence of various production forms is commonly observed, while the social structures—even among Asian countries—sometimes show great divergence. A clear understanding of the logic of indigenous development is required for this field as well. This volume intends not only to introduce the argument in the context of Japanese economic history, but also to provide materials for future comparative study.

At the same time, the specific features we have observed have provided a fundamental framework for understanding the economic and social structures of contemporary Japan. To take one example, in the weaving industry the system of domestic manufacturing organized under the putting-out system went into sharp decline during the 1920s, and power-loomed, mechanized manufacturing spread even into the rural industrial districts. This shift may be viewed as the beginning of the shift to full-scale industrialization. It should not, however, be judged as a process in which the pattern of indigenous development simply faded away, and was totally replaced by a unified pattern of "modern" industrial development. With regard to the pattern of labor supply, Sasaki has shown that in the factories built near farming villages, the supply of wage labor was still influenced by the farming cycle and/or housework in the peasant household (Chapter 5). Even in a factory, we can identify an organizational pattern of labor that had links to the patterns of "domestic production" examined in this paper.

It was pointed out in another study that rural factories were generally small or medium sized, and that the managerial development of these businesses was manifested as a sophisticated form of the industrial district (Abe 1989). The progress of mechanized manufacturing in these cases, therefore, should be seen as the mechanization of small and medium scale firms, not of large ones. The proliferation of small urban workshops, both mechanized and non-mechanized, was also seen in the Inter-war period. In the case of Tokyo, such small workshops began to form the prototype of urban industrial clusters (Tanimoto 2005). This phase of industrialization can be seen as the pre-history of the economic growth of the post-Second World War period that was heavily dependent on the thick accumulation of small- and medium-scale manufacturing firms. There seems little doubt that these inheritances from the pattern of indigenous industrial development formed an important foundation for the economic growth of the post-Second World War period. At the same time, as indigenous development based on "traditional" social institutions, it functioned to preserve the "tradition" even in the industrialization process. In this sense, indigenous development played a key role in forming the particular character of the economic and social structures of contemporary industrialized Japan.

5. Structure and Content of this Volume

The introductory part of this volume includes two chapters, this essay and an essay by Matsumoto. The aim of Chapter 2 (Matsumoto), "The development of traditional industries in modern Japan: a statistical exposition", is to assess the quantitative position of "traditional" or "indigenous" industries in the whole economy, including the commercial and service sectors, important areas that are not discussed in independent chapters in this volume.

In Part II, five chapters discuss diverse processes of industrialization. Chapter 3 (Takeuchi), "The role of 'early factories' in Japanese industrialization", deals with the manufacture of products newly introduced from western countries after the opening of the treaty ports. These goods include brushes, buttons, matches, knitting goods and soap. Takeuchi shows that although the modern factories founded to manufacture these goods played significant roles in the early stage of industrialization, they eventually went into decline in spite of the development of the industries. Based on this factual discovery, Takeuchi claims that the combination of modern technology and traditional skills formed another route to industrialization in modern Japan. Chapter 4 (Matsumura), "Dualism in the silk reeling industry in Suwa from the 1910s to the 1930s", argues that there was a substantial diversity in the forms of production in the silk reeling industry. Although it is true that export growth led to the development of this industry, the domestic market for raw silk was also important in accounting for increases in total demand after the first decade of the twentieth century. The existence of this large domestic market is a major factor in explaining why domestically oriented manufacturers did not adopt the factory system of production, but rather used various forms of production such as independent operation, subcontracting to small-scale factories and putting-out. Chapter 5 (Sasaki), "Factory girls in an agrarian setting circa 1910", looked into the reality of the working process in a rural weaving factory. Sasaki's analysis of attendance books showed that the days and hours actually worked by female workers in the factory were still influenced by the labor demand from agriculture and housework, concluding that the introduction of machines into rural factories in the early twentieth century did not mark the major divide that is commonly assumed by economic historians. Chapter 6 (Suzuki), "The humble origins of modern Japan's machine industry", shows the importance of artisan workshops in the development process of the machine manufacturing industry. Export-oriented industries such as silk reeling and coal mining were supplied by these workshops with low price boilers and pumps; these links are a representative example of the way in which positive linkages worked in the industrialization process of modern Japan. Similar kinds of interconnections contributed to the establishment of modern machine manufacturing factories by providing training for skilled workers and by forming markets for machinery. Chapter 7 (Ōmori), "How local trade associations and manufacturers' associations worked in pre-war Japan", focuses on the pottery industry and the straw goods industry, two typical traditional industries. Ōmori investigates the various activities of the trade association and manufacturer's association in these two industries, and argues that they made important contributions to the development of traditional industries, especially the industries dominated by small manufacturing firms.

Part III of this volume includes two papers that emphasize the modernization process of silk reeling and pottery. Although the product and technology originated in pre-modern period, there were some firms that developed the new style of production. The papers in this section pursuit their trajectories, and provide the useful benchmark for the comparison of the industrialization processes that lead to the clearer understanding of the particularity of the indigenous development. Chapter 8 (Nakabayashi), "The rise of a factory industry: silk reeling in the Suwa district", attributes the rapid growth of silk reeling firms in Suwa to the establishment of an efficient factory system. Detailed investigation of marketing, labor management, the financial system and so on reveals the foundation for the strong competitiveness of these firms in the expanding raw silk market in the United States. Chapter 9 (Yamada), "The export-oriented industrialization of Japanese pottery: the adoption and adaptation of overseas technology and market information", also pays attention to the development of newly established modernized pottery firms. The paper focuses on the introduction and adaptation processes of advanced technology from western countries, together with the utilization of overseas market information.

Factories and firms were the promoters of modernization. However, the regional communities within which their activities took place can be identified as places where traditional practices were reproduced. Chapters in Part IV turn to the role of tradition by looking at the relationships between industry and community. Chapter 10 (Matsuzaki), "The development of a rural weaving industry and its social capital", demonstrates that the activities of traders in the Isezaki weaving district were strongly influenced by motives embedded in the regional community. Matsuzaki identifies both positive and negative effects of the industry–community relationships for the development of the industrial district. While it deals with a weaving district, Chapter 11 (Yamauchi), "Communal action in the development of regional industrial policy: a case study of the Kawamata silk weaving industry", looks at practices and actions by local leaders and government officials. Yamauchi argues that their practices and actions were based on the understanding that the notables in the region had to take responsibility for the development of the regional economy. Chapter 12 (Tanimoto), "Capital accumulation and the local economy: brewers and local notables", looks at the role brewers played in financing new businesses in the 1880s and 1890s. Together with the development of the brewing industry that raised funds, Tanimoto claims that the desire to keep their reputations as notables in the regional communities motivated the brewers to invest in businesses that were highly risky but nonetheless strategically important for the development of the regions.

Notes

1. The numbers are calculated by combining population census data and industrial statistics. These were the earliest data available in western industrialized countries.
2. Such research interests originated in the controversy over "manufacture" in the early 1930s. The controversy included speculations about the historical conditions under which Japan, unlike India and China, was able to establish a nation-state and achieve capitalistic development in the late nineteenth century, when many of other Asian states and regions came to be incorporated into the empires as colonies. The debate was initiated by the writing of Shisō Hattori (Hattori 1933). In the late Tokugawa period, Hattori argued, Japan had already

reached the stage that Marx termed the period of "manufacture," and this provided the conditions for Japan's full-fledged capitalization. Up until around the 1960s when there were active debates on the "manufacture" controversy, many of the "Marxist" economic historians produced papers that claimed the relatively high stage of economic development in the late Tokugawa period. From this point of view, it is not a balanced view to claim that the "Marxist" perspective sees the Japanese economy under the Shogunate system solely as a period of stagnation (Hanley and Yamamura 1977, Chapters 1 and 2).

3. Non-agricultural works done for self-sufficient purpose are included here as well.
4. The historical data referred to in this section is extracted from several chapters in Tanimoto (1998).
5. Several studies provide the wage data that confirm the lower wage level of wage weavers (Oshima 1985, Matsuzaki 1997, Tanimoto 1998).
6. As the statistical coverage of family employee varies in each country, it is difficult to carry out accurate comparison on these figures. It should be noted that the figures used here are rough indications, and leave room for more statistically accurate comparisons in the future.
7. The ideological basis of peasants' morale was clarified by Yoshio Yasumaru's works (Yasumaru 1974). His recent paper applied this argument to urban small businesses (Yasumaru 1999).
8. Differing from the traditional guild, Kabu-nakama, trade association could not legally limit membership. The way to eliminate outsiders was to have all the traders concerned under the control of the association. To strengthen the validity of mandatory participation in the association was the measure to accomplish this purpose.
9. It is notable that the clothiers in the villages and local wholesalers in Tokorozawa formed the united trade association.
10. There were also cases in which the skill of wage-weavers was formed during years of employment in a centralized workshops or factory in such silk weaving districts as Kiryū, whose products were ranked as upper medium level in quality (Ichikawa 1996).
11. This investigation included reports about several metal related industries as follows. Tin toy, electric bulb, radio, bicycle parts.
12. Sokoloff and Dollar (1997) discussed the production form in England in relation to the agricultural structure. In the studies of Continental Europe, the relationship between the peasant household and the supply of labor was often discussed in the context of proto-industrialization (Medick 1976, Braun 1978, Pfister 1989, 1992). However, the attempts to enhance the perspective of these arguments to the age of industrialization seem to be limited (Quataert 1988, Kriedte, Medick and Schlumbohm 1993).

References

Abe, Takeshi, *Nihon niokeru Sanchi Men'orimonogyō no Tenkai* [The Development of Rural Cotton Weaving Districts in Japan] (Tokyo, 1989).
——, "The development of the putting-out system in modern Japan", in Odaka, Kōnosuke and Minoru Sawai (eds), *Small Firms, Large Concerns* (New York, 1999).

Aoki, Masahiko and Yujiro Hayami (eds.), *Communities and Markets in Economic Development* (New York, 2000).

Ariga, Kizaemon, *Ie* [The Family] (Tokyo, 1972).

Berg, M. "Factories, workshops and industrial organisation", in Floud, R. and D. McCloskey, *The Economic History of Britain since 1700*, Vol. 1 1700–1860 (2nd edn) (Cambridge, 1994).

Boeke, J. H., *Economics and Economic Policy of Dual Societies as Exemplified by Indonesia* (New York, 1953).

Braun, R., "Early industrialization and demographic changes in the canton of Zurich", in Tilly, C. (ed.), *Historical Studies of Changing Fertility*, (Princeton, 1978).

Brusco, S., "The Emilian model: productive decentralisation and social integration", *Cambridge Journal of Economics* 6–2 (Cambridge, 1982), 167–84.

Chayanov, A. V., *The Theory of Peasant Economy* (Madison, Wisconsin, 1986, Originally published in Moscow in 1925).

Crafts, N. F. R., *British Economic Growth during the Industrial Revolution* (Oxford, 1985).

Francks, P., "Rural industry, growth linkages, and economic development in nineteenth-century Japan", *The Journal of Asian Studies* 61–1 (2002), 33–55.

Gordon, A., *The Evolution of Labor Relations in Japan: Heavy Industry 1853–1955* (Cambridge, Massachusetts, 1985).

Hanley, S. B. and K. Yamamura, *Economic and Demographic Change in Preindustrial Japan 1600–1868* (Princeton, 1977).

Hareven, T. K., *The Silk Weavers of Kyoto: Family and Work in a Changing Traditional Industry* (Berkeley and Los Angeles, 2002).

Hashino, Tomoko, "Orimonogyō niokeru Meiji-ki 'sosei ranzō' mondai no jittai" [Technology and the quality problem of the weaving industry in the Meiji period], *Shakaikeizaishigaku* 65–5 (2000), 45–64.

Hattori, Shisō, "Meijiishin no kakumei oyobi han-kakumei" [The revolution and the counterrevolution of Meiji Restoration], in *Nihon Shihonshugi Hattatsushi Kouza*, Vol. 1 *Meijiishin* (Tokyo, 1933).

Hayami, Akira, "Kinsei nihon no keizai hatten to 'Industrious Revolution'" [Industrious Revolution and the economic development of early modern Japan], in Shinbo, Hiroshi and Yasukichi Yasuba (eds), *Kindai Ikō-ki no Nihon Keizai* (Tokyo, 1979).

——, "Industrial Revolution versus Industrious Revolution", *Journal of Japanese Trade and Industry*, 20–6 (2001).

Hayami, Akira, Osamu Saito and Ronald Toby (eds), *The Economic History of Japan*, Vol. 1 *Emergence of Economic Society in Japan 1600–1859* (Oxford, 2004. The Japanese original version was published in 1988/9).

Hayami, Yujiro (ed.), *Toward the Rural-Based Development of Commerce and Industry: Selected Experiences from East Asia* (Washington, 1998).

——, *Development Economics: From the Poverty to the Wealth of Nations* (Oxford, 1999).

Huber, J. R., "Effect on prices of Japan's entry into world market after 1858", *The Journal of Political Economy*, 79–3 (1971), 614–28.

Hudson, P., "Industrial organisation and structure", Floud, R. and P. Johnson (eds), *The Cambridge Economic History of Modern Britain* Vol. 1 (Cambridge, 2004).

Hyōdō, Tsutomu, *Nihon niokeru Rōshi Kankei no Tenkai* [The Deployment of the Industrial Relations in Modern Japan] (Tokyo, 1971).

Ichikawa, Takamasa, *Nihon Nōson-kōgyōshi Kenkyū* [A Study on the History of the Rural Industry in Japan] (Tokyo, 1996).

International Labour Organization, *Year Book of Labour Statistics* (Geneva).

Ishida, Hiroshi, "Industrialization, class structure, and social mobility in postwar Japan", *British Journal of Sociology* 52–4 (2001), 579–604.

Ishii, Kanji, "Ishin henkaku no kiso katei" [The Basic Process of the Meiji Restoration], *Rekishigakukenkyū* 560 (1986), 138–148.

Kandatsu, Haruki, *Meijiki Nōson Orimonogyō no Tenkai* [The Development of Rural Weaving Industry in Meiji Japan] (Tokyo, 1974).

Kawakatsu, Heita, "The emergence of a market for cotton goods in East Asia in the early modern period", in Latham A. J. H. and Heita Kawakatsu (eds), *Japanese Industrialization and the Asian Economy* (London, 1994).

Kikuchi, Masao "Export-oriented garment industries in the rural Philippines", in Hayami, Yujiro (ed.), op.cit. (1998).

Kinghorn, J. R. and J. V. Nye, "The scale of production in western economic development", *The Journal of Economic History* 56–1 (1996), 90–112.

Kiyokawa, Yukihiko, *Nihon no Keizai Hatten to Gijutsu Fukyū* [The Spread of Technology in Japan's Economic Development] (Tokyo, 1995).

Kriedte, P., H. Medick and J. Schlumbohm, "Proto-industrialization revisited: demography, social structure, and modern domestic industry", *Continuity and Change* 8–2 (1993), 217–52.

Landes, D. S., *The Unbound Prometheus* (Cambridge, 1969).

Lazerson, M. H., "Subcontracting in the Modena knitwear industry", in Pyke, F., G. Becattini and W. Sengenberger (eds), *Industrial Districts and Inter-firm Co-operation* (Geneva, 1990).

Lewis, W. A., "Economic development with unlimited supplies of labor", *Manchester School of Economic and Social Studies*, 22 May (1954), 139–91.

Madison, A. *Monitoring the World Economy 1820–1992* (Paris, 1995).

Marglin, S. A., "What do bosses do?: the origins and functions of hierarchy in capitalist production", *The Review of Radical Political Economics*, 6–2 (1974), 60–112.

Marshall, A., *Principles of Economics* (8th edn) (London, 1920).

Matsuzaki, Hisami, "Naraken nōson orimonogyō no suitai katei" [The collapse of rural weaving industry in Nara prefecture], *Shakaikeizaishigaku* 52–6 (1987), 32–61.

Medick, H., "The proto-industrial family economy", *Social History*, 3 (1976), 291–315.

Mendels, F., "Proto-industrialization: the first phase of the industrialization process", *The Journal of Economic History* 32–1 (1972), 241–61.

Mizuno, Kōsuke, *Rural Industrialization in Indonesia, A Case Study of Community-based Weaving Industry in West Java* (Tokyo, 1996).

——, *Indonesia no Jibasangyō* [The Regional Industry in Indonesia] (Kyoto, 1999).

Naikaku Tōkei Kyoku [The Cabinet Statistical Bureau], *Dai-ikkai Kokusei Chōsa* [The First National Census of Population] (Tokyo, 1920a).

——, *Dainihonteikoku Tōkei Nenkan* [The Annual Statistics of Imperial Japan] (Tokyo, 1920b).

Naimushō [Ministry of the Interior], *Meiji 7 nen Fuken Bussann Hyō* [Table of Industrial Products by Prefecture] (Tokyo, 1874).

Nakamura, Takafusa, *Economic Growth in Prewar Japan* (New Haven, 1983. The original Japanese version was published in 1971).

Nakaoka, Tetsuro *et al.*, "Textile history of Nishijin: East meets West", *Textile History* 19–2 (1988).

Nagano, Hiroko, *Nihon Kinsei Gender-Ron* [Gender Issues in Early Modern Japan] (Tokyo, 2003).

Namiki, Shōkichi, "Nōgyō-jinkō no sengo 10 nen" [Population of farming households during ten years after the Second World War], *Nōgyōsōgōkenkyū* 9–4 (1955), 1–46.

Nishida, Yoshiaki, *Kindai Nihon Nōmin-Undōshi Kenkyū* [The Study on the Movement of Peasants and Farmers in Modern Japan] (Tokyo, 1997).

Nishikawa, Shunsaku, "The economy of Chōshū on the eve of industrialization", *Economic Studies Quarterly*, 38–4 (Tokyo, 1987).

Nojiri, Shigeo, *Nōmin Rison no Jisshōteki Kenkyū* [The Empirical Research on the Emigration of Peasants] (Tokyo, 1943).

Nōshōmushō [Ministry of Agriculture and Commerce], *Kōjō Tōkei Hyō* [The Statistical Charts of Factories] (Tokyo, 1905).

——, *Nōshōmu Tōkei Hyō* [Statistical Charts of the Ministry of Agriculture and Commerce] (Tokyo).

Numata, Makoto, *Ie to Mura no Rekishiteki Isō* [The Historical Phases of the Family and the Village] (Tokyo, 2001).

O'Brien, P. and C. Keyder, *Economic Growth in Britain and France 1780–1914* (London, 1978).

Ohno, Akihiko, "Market integrators for rural-based industrialization: the case of the hand-weaving industry in Laos", in Aoki, Masahiko and Yujiro Hayami (eds), op. cit. (2000).

—— and Masao Kikuchi, "Organizational characteristics of rural textile industries in East Asia", in Hayami, Yujiro (ed.), op. cit. (1998).

Osaka-fu Nōkai [Agricultural Organization of Osaka Prefecture], *Nouka Keizai Chōsa* [Economic Investigation of Peasant's Household] (Osaka, 1904).

Ōshima, Eiko, "Kenmen-kōshokumono sanchi no keisei katei" [The emergence of the weaving district specialized in silk-and-cotton fabrics], *Shakaikeizaishigaku* 50–5 (1985), 1–29.

Pfister, U., "Work roles and family structure in proto-industrial Zurich", *The Journal of Interdisciplinary History*, 20–1 (1989), 83–105.

——, "The proto-industrial household economy: towards a formal analysis", *Journal of Family History* 17–2 (1992), 201–32.

Piore, M. J. and, C. F. Sabel, *The Second Industrial Divide: Possibilities for Prosperity* (New York, 1984).

Putnam, R. D., *Making Democracy Work* (Princeton, 1993).

Quataert J. H., "A new view of industrialization: "protoindustry" or the role of small-scale, labor-intensive manufacture in the capitalist environment", *International Labor and Working-Class History* 33 (1988), 3–22.

Sabel, C. and J. Zeitlin, "Historical alternatives to mass production", *Past and Present* 108 (1985), 133–76.

—— (ed.), *World of Possibilities* (Cambridge, 1997).
Saito, Osamu, "Population and the peasant family economy in proto-industrial Japan", *Journal of Family History*, 8–1 (1983), 30–54.
——, "The rural economy: commercial agriculture, by-employment, and wage work", in Jansen, M. B. and G. Rozman, (eds), *Japan in Transition: from Tokugawa to Meiji* (Princeton, 1986).
——, *Chingin to Rōdō to Seikatsusuijun* [Wage, Labor and Standard of Living] (Tokyo, 1998).
Saito, Osamu and Masayuki Tanimoto, "The re-organization of indigenous industries", in Hayami, Akira, Osamu Saito and Ronald Toby (eds.) op. cit. (2004, The original Japanese version was published in 1989).
Sakane, Yoshihiro, "Nihon niokeru jinushi kosaku kankei no tokushitsu" [The characteristics of tenant-landowner relationship in Japan], *Nōgyōshikenkyū* 33 (1999), 20–28.
Sawai, Minoru, "The role of technical education and public research institute in the development of small and medium enterprises", in Odaka, Konosuke, Minoru Sawai (eds), op. cit. (1999).
Smith, T. C., *The Agrarian Origins of Modern Japan* (Stanford, 1959).
——, *Native Sources of Japanese Industrialization 1750–1920* (Berkeley and Los Angeles, 1988).
Sokoloff, K. L. and D. Dollar, "Agricultural seasonality and the organization of manufacturing in early industrial economies: the contrast between England and the United States", *The Journal of Economic History*, 57–2 (1997), 288–321.
Sugihara, Kaoru, "Keiei hatten no kiban seibi" [The equipment of the basis of business development], in Miyamoto, Matao and Takeshi Abe (eds), *Nihon-Keieishi 2 Keiei Kakushin to Kōgyōka* (Tokyo, 1995).
——, *Asia-Kan-Bōeki no Keisei to Kōzō* [The Formation and the Structure of Intra-Asian Trade] (Kyoto, 1996).
Takamura, Naosuke, *Nihon Bōsekigyōshi Josetsu* [The Introduction to the History of the Cotton Spinning Industry in Japan] Part 1.2 (Tokyo, 1971).
Takeuchi, Johzen, "Tsuru senshoku gakkō" [Tsuru school of weaving and dyeing], in Toyoda Toshio (ed.), *Wagakuni Ririku-Ki no Jitsugyō Kyōiku* (Tokyo, 1982).
——, *The Role of Labour-intensive Sectors in Japanese Industrialization* (Tokyo, 1991).
Tamura, Hitoshi, *Fasshion no Shakai-keizaishi* [The Socio-economic History of Fashion] (Tokyo, 2004).
Tanimoto, Masayuki, "The evolution of indigenous cotton textile manufacture before and after the Opening of the Ports", *Japanese Yearbook on Business History* 9 (Tokyo, 1992), 29–56.
——, *Nihon niokeru Zairaiteki Keizai Hatten to Orimonogyō* [The Weaving Industry and the Indigenous Economic Development in Japan] (Nagoya, 1998).
——, "Kindai Nihon no toshi shōkeiei" [Urban petty businesses in modern Japan], in Nakamura, Takafusa and Nobuyuki Fujii (eds), *Toshika to Zairaisangyō* (Tokyo, 2002).
——, "Senkanki Nihon no toshi shōkōgyō" [Urban small manufacturing industries in interwar period, Japan], in Nakamura, Satoru (ed.), *Higashi Ajia Kindai Keizai no Keisei to Hatten* (Tokyo, 2005).

Tokyo-shi [Tokyo municipal office], *Tonya-Sei Shōkōgyō Chōsa* [Industrial Investigation on Small Manufacturing and Processing Workshops under the Putting-out System] (Tokyo, 1936).

Tsunoyama, Sakae (ed.), *Nihon Ryōji Hōkoku no Kenkyū* [The Historical Study on the Japanese Consular Reports] (Tokyo, 1986).

Waswo, A., *Japanese Landlords* (Berkeley and London, 1977).

Yamaguchi, Kazuo, *Meiji-Zenki Keizai no Bunseki* [The Analysis of the Japanese Economy of Early Meiji Period] (Tokyo, 1956).

——, "Nishijin orimonogyō no hattatsu" [The development of Nishijin weaving industry], in Yamaguchi, Kazuo (ed.), *Nihon Sangyō Kinyūshi Kenkyū, Orimono Kin-yū Hen* (Tokyo, 1974).

Yamazaki, Hiroaki, "Ryō-taisenkanki niokeru Enshū men-orimonogyō no kozō to undō" [The structure and the movement of Enshū cotton weaving industry in interwar period], *Keieishirin* 6–1. 2 (1969), 95–152.

Yasumaru, Yoshio, *Nihon no Kindaika to Minshū Shisō* [The People's Thoughts in Japanese Modernization] (Tokyo, 1974).

——, " 'Tsūzoku dōtoku' no yukue" [The future of Japanese "popular morality"], *Rekishikagaku* 155 (Osaka, 1999).

2

The Development of Traditional Industries in Modern Japan: A Statistical Exposition

TAKANORI MATSUMOTO

1. Aim of Essay

The aim of this essay is to analyze quantitatively the development process of traditional industries in pre-war Japan. In doing so, it seeks to address two limitations in current studies of Japanese traditional industry. The first is that most analyses are concentrated on certain types of manufacturing, such as the textile industry, while hardly any attention has been paid to the commerce and service industries that played an important role in the traditional economy.[1] Second, studies to date have not yet fully clarified how traditional industries developed on a nationwide scale in the modern era.[2] Accordingly, this essay will move beyond the current focus on small and medium-sized manufacturers and attempt to elucidate the reality of traditional industry. In other words, it will consider the development of traditional industries in quantitative terms, with commerce and service industries as the main focus of analysis.

2. The Number of Gainfully Occupied Workers in Traditional Industries

2.1. Changes in the total number of workers in traditional industries

First, we need to clarify our definition of traditional industry. In principle, traditional industries may be defined as small-sized manufacturing, commerce or service industries that have produced, distributed or provided traditional commodities and services since pre-modern times, and are managed by family laborers or a small number of employees. This definition focuses on scale of establishment rather than on type of industry because of limitations in statistics. It considers traditional industry to comprise small-scale manufacturing managed in a workroom rather than a factory or in a factory that employs no more than five workers.

Also included are civil construction, transportation businesses that use rickshaws, wagons, cows or horses and any other small-scale retail or wholesale businesses. Of course, it is possible that traditional industries might include big businesses that use large amounts of capital and employ dozens of employees. However, large-scale traditional industries are relatively uncommon in modern Japan. Accordingly, in this chapter we have adopted for convenience a definition that focuses on smallness of scale.

Table 2.1 compares the percentages of gainfully occupied workers in traditional industries with the total number of workers in all industrial sectors in pre-war Japan. It shows that the total number of workers in modern industries increased rapidly, from 920,000 in the period 1886–90 to 5,360,000 in the period 1931–35. This increase represented an average annual growth rate of 3.6 percent. The percentage of workers in modern industries compared with all workers rose from 4.1 percent to 17.7 percent in the same period. On the other hand, the number of workers in traditional industries grew slowly, from 6,520,000 in 1886–1990 to 10,380,000 in 1931–35. This increase represents an average annual growth rate of 1.0 percent, hardly keeping pace with that of modern industries. Yet it is worth noting that, for the half-century from 1886 to 1935, the number of workers in traditional industries, even excluding those engaged in primary industry, continued to account for more than 30 percent of the total number of workers. Although modern industries showed rapid development, the number of gainfully occupied workers in the modern sector did not surpass the number of workers in traditional industries in the period up to 1935. Therefore, one may argue that in the pre-war era, traditional industry accounted for the largest number of gainfully occupied workers outside agriculture, forestry and fisheries. It was a sector that continued to develop steadily and to provide work opportunities.

2.2. Changes in the number of workers in commerce and in service industries

Traditional industry, which in the pre-war era accounted for the largest number of gainfully occupied workers outside agriculture, forestry and fisheries, included many small-sized businesses and was characterized by its remarkable diversity. As shown in Table 2.1, traditional industry consisted primarily of commerce and services.[3] The percentage of workers in traditional commerce and services compared with the total number of workers engaged in traditional industries increased from 50 percent in the period 1886–90 to over 65 percent from 1931–35. Traditional commerce and services included: domestic commerce; day laborers in the construction industry; transportation using rickshaws, wagons, cows or horses; carpenters, plasterers, painters and thatchers; and other construction workers. All of these were male occupations. Female occupations included domestic service, waitressing at restaurants and bars, dressmaking by housewives, and even prostitution and geisha services.

Table 2.1 illustrates the following four important facts about traditional industry. First, the number of gainfully occupied workers in commerce grew steadily, from 2,300,000 in the period 1886–90 to 5,430,000 in 1931–35, giving an average annual growth rate of 1.7 percent. During this period, the percentage of workers in traditional commerce compared with the total number of all gainfully occupied workers also increased, from 10.2 percent to 17.9 percent. In the same period, the percentage of workers in traditional commerce compared with the total number of workers in traditional industry increased from 35 percent to 50 percent. It may be argued that commerce was the sector of traditional industry that showed the most remarkable development. Within the commercial sector, product sales accounted for the highest percentage. The number of workers in this category more than doubled within the 50-year period from 1886 to 1935, from 1,340,000 to 2,940,000. As shown in Table 2.1, product sales continued to provide opportunities to more than 20 percent to 30 percent of the workers engaged in traditional industries, including male and female workers. One might conclude that product sales were the most worthy of attention among the various traditional industries.

The second fact that emerges from Table 2.1 is that the number of gainfully occupied workers in service industries grew steadily, from 910,000 in 1886–90 to 1,510,000 in 1931–35, giving an average annual growth rate of 1.0 percent. During this period, the percentage of service workers compared with the total number of workers increased from 4.0 percent to 5.0 percent. The percentage of service workers compared with the total number of workers engaged in traditional industries remained at 15 percent. Within the service industry, domestic service showed especially notable development, growing steadily from 530,000 in 1886–90 to 850,000 in 1931–35. Domestic service continued to provide work opportunities, especially for female workers.[4]

Third, Table 2.1 shows that, within traditional industries, construction included a high percentage of one-person firms, with the exception of Shimizu-gumi (present-day Shimizu Construction Corporation) and Kajima-gumi (Kajima Construction Corporation). The number of workers in construction tripled in the 50-year period from 1886 to 1935, from 360,000 to 990,000. Among traditional industries, construction continued to provide remarkable work opportunities for male workers.

Finally, Table 2.1 shows that transportation using rickshaws, wagons, cows and horses grew steadily, from 180,000 in 1886–90 to 490,000 in 1931–1935, giving an average annual growth rate of 1.8 percent. As a traditional industry, transportation played an important role in filling the gaps in the modern transportation networks of railroads and shipping.

Table 2.1. Changes in the number of gainfully occupied workers in the entire traditional industrial sector

Period	All Gainfully Occupied Workers	Primary Industries	Secondary and Tertiary Industries	Modern Industries					Subtotal of Traditional Industries
				Subtotal of Modern Industries	Manufacturing (Managed in a Factory Employing over Five Workers)	Transportation and Communication (Railroad, Shipping and Communication)	Public Service (Public Servants and Armies)	Others (Mining, Gas, Electricity, Water Service, and so on)	
	(1)	(2)	(3)	(4)	(5)	(6)	(7)	(8)	(9)
	=(2)+(3)		=(4)+(9)	=(5)+(6)+(7)+(8)					=(10)+(13)+(14)+(15)+(18)+(21)
1886–1890	22,601	14,862	7,739	922	517	30	289	87	6,518
(%)	100.0	65.8	34.2	4.1	2.3	0.1	1.3	0.4	28.8
1891–1895	23,355	14,774	8,581	965	528	68	253	116	6,831
(%)	100.0	63.3	36.7	4.1	2.3	0.3	1.1	0.5	29.3
1896–1900	24,008	14,817	9,191	1,192	514	150	379	149	7,190
(%)	100.0	61.7	38.3	5.0	2.1	0.6	1.6	0.6	29.9
1901–1905	24,614	14,780	9,834	1,620	672	261	484	203	7,416
(%)	100.0	60.0	40.0	6.6	2.7	1.1	2.0	0.8	30.1
1906–1910	25,124	15,364	9,761	2,208	978	398	560	272	7,553
(%)	100.0	61.2	38.8	8.8	3.9	1.6	2.2	1.1	30.1

1911–1915	25,756	15,405	10,351	2,585	1,232	425	599	330	7,766
(%)	100.0	59.8	40.2	10.0	4.8	1.6	2.3	1.3	30.2
1916–1920	26,764	14,864	11,900	3,806	2,067	538	733	468	8,095
(%)	100.0	55.5	44.5	14.2	7.7	2.0	2.7	1.7	30.2
1921–1925	27,844	14,481	13,363	4,545	2,555	703	872	415	8,818
(%)	100.0	52.0	48.0	16.3	9.2	2.5	3.1	1.5	31.7
1926–1930	29,075	14,629	14,446	4,881	2,668	670	1,089	455	9,565
(%)	100.0	50.3	49.7	16.8	9.2	2.3	3.7	1.6	32.9
1931–1935	30,313	14,573	15,740	5,361	3,011	675	1,313	362	10,380
(%)	100.0	48.1	51.9	17.7	9.9	2.2	4.3	1.2	34.2

Source : Matsumoto and Okuda (1997: Part 1), Matsumoto (1996), Umemura *et al.* (1988).

Notes : Number is the mean value in the period concerned.

Because some number of gainfully occupied workers between 1886 and 1905 are estimated, there is a small gap between actual and number estimated. However, the gap has not adjusted because of data restrictions.

"Others" in Commerce includes Finance, Insurance, and Hotel and Restaurant businesses.

"Professional Services" in Service Industries means Educational Service, Religion, Medical Service, etc.

On the estimation of gainfully occupied workers in Commerce and Service Industries in traditional industry, see Matsumoto above. On the estimation of gainfully occupied workers in Manufacturing Industries, see also footnote 6.

Table 2.1. (*Continued*)

	Manufacturing		Construction	Transportation and Communication	Commerce			Service Industries			Other Traditional Industries
Subtotal of Manufacturing Industries (10) =(11)+(12)	(Extremely Small-sized Manufacturing Industry Managed in a Very Petty Workroom that isn't Regarded as a Factory) (11)	(Manufacturing Industry Managed in a Factory Employing Five Workers or Fewer) (12)	(13)	(Traditional Transportation Business with Riksha, Wagons, Cows or Horses) (14)	Subtotal of Commerce (15) =(16)+(17)	(Retail Sales) (16)	Others (Wholesale and so on) (17)	Subtotal of Service Industries (18) =(19)+(20)	(Professional Services) (19)	(Domestic Service) (20)	(21)
2,604	2,398	205	360	182	2,304	1,341	962	907	378	529	161
11.5	10.6	0.9	1.6	0.8	10.2	5.9	4.3	4.0	1.7	2.3	0.7
2,655	2,446	210	403	157	2,422	1,411	1,011	1,024	427	598	170
11.4	10.5	0.9	1.7	0.7	10.4	6.0	4.3	4.4	1.8	2.6	0.7
2,590	2,385	204	590	183	2,514	1,480	1,034	1,137	474	663	176
10.8	9.9	0.9	2.5	0.8	10.5	6.2	4.3	4.7	2.0	2.8	0.7
2,539	2,301	239	575	190	2,651	1,549	1,102	1,275	529	746	186
10.3	9.3	1.0	2.3	0.8	10.8	6.3	4.5	5.2	2.2	3.0	0.8
2,280	1,953	327	644	324	2,799	1,624	1,176	1,353	545	808	152

9.1	7.8	1.3	2.6	1.3	11.1	6.5	4.7	5.4	2.2	3.2	0.6
2,190	1,787	404	737	298	3,017	1,804	1,214	1,357	533	824	167
8.5	6.9	1.6	2.9	1.2	11.7	7.0	4.7	5.3	2.1	3.2	0.6
2,135	1,456	679	788	389	3,257	2,074	1,183	1,339	518	821	187
8.0	5.4	2.5	2.9	1.5	12.2	7.7	4.4	5.0	1.9	3.1	0.7
2,171	1,332	838	860	398	3,960	2,272	1,687	1,272	582	690	158
7.8	4.8	3.0	3.1	1.4	14.2	8.2	6.1	4.6	2.1	2.5	0.6
2,049	984	1,066	979	455	4,736	2,573	2,163	1,266	608	658	79
7.0	3.4	3.7	3.4	1.6	16.3	8.8	7.4	4.4	2.1	2.3	0.3
1,882	606	1,277	992	491	5,433	2,940	2,494	1,508	657	850	74
6.2	2.0	4.2	3.3	1.6	17.9	9.7	8.2	5.0	2.2	2.8	0.2

Traditional transportation developed as a complement to the modern transportation industry.[5]

2.3. Changes in the number of workers in traditional manufacturing industries

Let us now turn to the development of traditional manufacturing industries. Manufacturing may be divided into three sectors: (1) extremely small-sized manufacturing industries managed in a small workroom that could not be regarded as a factory; (2) manufacturing industries managed in a factory that employs five workers or fewer; and (3) manufacturing industries managed in a factory that employs five workers or more. We may assume for convenience that (1) and (2) constitute traditional manufacturing industries, while (3) is a modern manufacturing industry.[6]

As shown in Table 2.1, the number of workers in modern manufacturing industries increased six-fold within the 50-year period from 1886 to 1935, from 520,000 to 3,010,000, giving an average annual growth rate of 3.6 percent. During this period, the percentage of workers in modern manufacturing compared with all workers also increased, from 2.3 percent to 9.9 percent. We can confirm that modern manufacturing industry grew rapidly. On the other hand, combining (1) and (2), we find that the number of workers in traditional manufacturing industries decreased, from 2,600,000 in 1886–90 to 1,800,000 in 1931–35, giving an average annual growth rate of −0.6 percent. The percentage of workers in traditional manufacturing compared with all workers also declined, from 11.5 percent in the period 1886–90 to just over 6.2 percent in 1931–35.

If, however, we distinguish between (1) and (2), a rather different picture emerges, as follows. The number of workers in (1) decreased rapidly, from 2,400,000 in 1886–90 to 610,000 in 1931–35, giving an average annual growth rate of −2.7 percent. The percentage of workers in very small workrooms compared with the total number of workers also decreased, from 10.6 percent in 1886–90 to over 2.0 percent in 1931–35. The manufacturing sector (1) was thus reduced in scale. The spread of motorization after the Russo–Japanese war (1904–05) gave an impetus to the reduction of such small-scale work groups. One should note, however, that sector (1) provided remarkable employment opportunities to over 2 million workers in the period before the Russo–Japanese war. By contrast, the number of gainfully occupied workers in sector (2) increased six-fold, from 210,000 in 1886–90 to 1,280,000 in 1931–35, giving an average annual growth rate of 3.7 percent. The number of workers in sector (2) increased slowly after the Russo–Japanese war, and rapidly in the 1920s. Japanese economic growth had replaced manufacturing sector (1) with sector (2).[7]

It was noted above that, as the Japanese economy developed, growth in sectors (2) and (3) contrasted sharply with the decline in sector (1).

Nevertheless, the traditional manufacturing industry, especially sector (1) before the 1920s and sector (2), provided remarkable work opportunities, especially to younger and female workers, although its contribution fell short of that offered by traditional commerce and traditional service industries.[8]

2.4. Traditional industry as a "buffer"

Let us next consider the area in which area workers were employed, comparing the marginal contribution rate of each category against the increase in the total number of workers.

Table 2.2 shows that much of the increase in the total number of workers was absorbed by traditional industries in the period 1891–95, in the pre-First World War depressions of (1906–10 and 1911–15), and also in the post-First World War recessions of the 1920s (1921–25 and 1926–30, including the Shōwa depression). In the first two of these periods, the process of industrialization had not fully taken place and the modern industrial sector could not absorb all of the available labor force. It can be considered that the figures for these periods were high because traditional industries were more able than modern industries to absorb new labor. Further, figures in Table 2.2 show that during the recession after the First World War, most of the additional workers obtained employment in traditional industries. In long-lasting recessions, many workers who could not find work in the modern industrial sectors were not able to return to farming because the capacity of farming villages to absorb more labor was limited. Such workers finally found work in traditional industries (especially in commerce and in the domestic service industry). Thus traditional industry contributed to the promotion of "full-employment" in Japan, by absorbing the surplus labor that could not be taken in by modern industries or by farming, On the other hand, Table 2.2 also shows that, in the post-First World War boom era of 1916–20, when modern industries were growing, enormous amounts of labor were transferred from traditional industry to the modern industrial sector. (Of the approximately 147 percent increase in the number of workers in modern industries, 47 percent was supplied from traditional commerce.) In other words, traditional industry functioned as a "buffer," supplying workers to, and absorbing workers from, the modern industrial sector according to changing economic currents (Odaka 1984, Ch. 4).

3. The Nationwide Development of Traditional Commerce

The following section will examine by prefecture the development on a nationwide scale of traditional commerce and service industries, which were the most important parts of traditional industry.

Table 2.2. Marginal contribution rate of each category against the increase in the total number of workers

Period	Total %	Primary industries	Modern industries	Traditional industries Subtotal	Traditional industries Commerce	Traditional industries Service industries	Traditional industries Domestic service
1886–1890	—	—	—	—	—	—	—
1891–1895	100.0	−16.9	24.6	92.6	27.8	12.0	16.8
1896–1900	100.0	3.7	48.9	47.6	7.8	6.8	9.5
1901–1905	100.0	−19.8	144.5	−24.4	8.1	4.6	13.0
1906–1910	100.0	−25.5	42.1	83.4	61.7	−9.3	−7.1
1911–1915	100.0	−37.5	56.9	80.6	43.3	1.9	6.4
1916–1920	100.0	−38.6	147.4	−8.9	−47.0	−9.1	−21.5
1921–1925	100.0	−42.1	33.4	108.6	61.8	4.3	9.0
1926–1930	100.0	29.6	5.2	65.2	41.0	−2.0	18.3
1931–1935	100.0	8.2	83.1	8.7	26.3	1.4	10.7

Source: Table 2.1.

3.1. Nationwide trends in traditional commerce

What were the main trends in the nationwide development of traditional commerce? In order to show how traditional commerce developed on a nationwide scale in modern Japan, it is useful to examine statistics on Business Tax,[9] using principal component analysis. The results are shown in Fig. 2.1. The parameters of the two functions in this figure show that the first principal component (the horizontal axis) represents the scale of traditional commerce, and the second principal component (the vertical axis) represents the growth rate of traditional commerce.

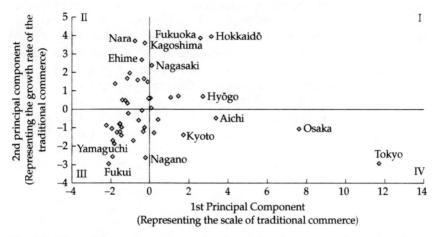

Fig. 2.1. Plots of the nationwide trends of traditional commerce in modern Japan by the Principal Component Analysis.

Function of 1st Principal Component:
$$F_1 = 0.95696 \cdot Z_1 + 0.94614 \cdot Z_2 + 0.97726 \cdot Z_3 + 0.95010 \cdot Z_4 + 0.96601 \cdot Z_5 + 0.89188 \cdot Z_6$$
$$+ 0.21875 \cdot Z_7 + 0.16725 \cdot Z_8 + 0.15101 \cdot Z_9 + 0.26430 \cdot Z_{10} + 0.24153 \cdot Z_{11} + 0.72461 \cdot Z_{12}$$
Contribution Rate of 1st Principal Component = 0.51243

Function of 2nd Principal Component:
$$F_2 = -0.19477 \cdot Z_1 - 0.20944 \cdot Z_2 - 0.14103 \cdot Z_3 - 0.20032 \cdot Z_4 - 0.21818 \cdot Z_5 - 0.03647 \cdot Z_6$$
$$+ 0.86748 \cdot Z_7 + 0.80281 \cdot Z_8 + 0.66168 \cdot Z_9 + 0.47064 \cdot Z_{10} + 0.90492 \cdot Z_{11} + 0.26091 \cdot Z_{12}$$
Contribution Rate of 2nd Principal Component = 0.26117

Total Contribution Rate = 0.77360

Z_1 = Number of Commercial Business Managers Z_2 = Value of Wholesale
Z_3 = Value of Retail Z_4 = Value of Building Leases
Z_5 = Number of Employees Z_6 = Population
Z_7 = Growth Rate of Number of Commercial Business Managers
Z_8 = Growth Rate of Value of Wholesale
Z_9 = Growth Rate of Value of Retail
Z_{10} = Growth Rate of Value of Building Leases Z_{11} = Growth Rate of Number of Employees
Z_{12} = Growth Rate of Population

I: Industry size is big; growth of industry is rapid.
II: Industry size is small; growth of industry is rapid.
III: Industry size is small; growth of industry is slow.
IV: Industry size is big; growth of industry is slow.

Source: Ōkurashō Shuzeikyoku Tōkeinenpō [Annual Statistical Report of National Tax Administration Agency of Ministry of Finance].

First, one can note that Tokyo and Osaka, the two prefectures with the largest urban areas, appear in the fourth quadrant, providing an obvious indication that product sales in those two cities were organized on a huge industrial scale. Second, one can discern that, next to Tokyo and Osaka, product sales were conducted on a large industrial scale in Aichi and Hyōgo. Third, Fukuoka and Hokkaidō also attract the analyst's attention. In those two prefectures, product selling was organized on a large scale, second after Tokyo, Osaka, Aichi and Hyōgo, and it was growing at an incredible pace. Fourth, Nara, Kagoshima, Ehime, Nagasaki and other prefectures of the Kinki, Kyūshū and Shikoku regions characteristically appear in the second quadrant. This placement shows that product sales in those regions, though comparatively small-sized, showed remarkable development. On the other hand, prefectures that are placed in the third quadrant, such as Yamanashi, Nagano and Fukui, belong to the Tōzan, Hokuriku and Tōhoku regions. This placement suggests that in the Tōzan, Hokuriku and Tōhoku regions the scale of product sales was small and the pace of development was slow.

In short, one can conclude that the industrial scale of product sales in prefectures containing major cities was large. Outside of those prefectures, the development of product sales was noteworthy in Kinki, Kyūshū and Shikoku, while it was relatively slow in Tōzan, Hokuriku and Tōhoku.

3.2. *Prefectural trends in traditional commerce*

Table 2.3 lists the numbers of retailers by prefecture who operated product-sales businesses in modern Japan. The data is based on the Business Tax imposed on both wholesalers and retailers. Because the Business Tax was imposed on commercial and industrial businesses according to their capital, sales and the number of employees, the data in Table 2.3 include big businesses that used large amounts of capital and employed dozens of employees. However, big business in the area of traditional commerce was relatively rare in modern Japan. Accordingly, we can assume that the Business Tax data mainly represent small-sized wholesalers and retailers who deal in traditional commerce. Further, since the data of the table include both wholesalers and retailers we use the terms "product sellers" or "product sales" in this section.

First, one can note that, in all years listed, product sellers in the top 10 prefectures were responsible for around 50 percent of total product sellers. Moreover, this percentage showed a steady rising trend, from 46.5 percent in 1899 to 50.0 percent in 1925. The nationwide distribution of product selling thus clearly indicates a tendency towards concentration. Second, one should note that Tokyo and Osaka always occupied the first and second positions respectively, while Aichi maintained a high ranking.

Table 2.3. Prefecture-specific changes in the number of persons operating retail sales

		1899				1905	
Rank	Prefecture	Persons operating retail sales	Percentage	Rank	Prefecture	Persons operating retail sales	Percentage
1	Tokyo	29,826	11.0	1	Tokyo	34,700	11.1
2	Osaka	19,602	7.2	2	Osaka	23,803	7.6
3	Aichi	13,196	4.9	3	Aichi	17,522	5.6
4	Kyoto	11,816	4.4	4	Kyoto	11,677	3.7
5	Hyōgo	10,022	3.7	5	Hyōgo	11,546	3.7
6	Nagano	9,076	3.4	6	Nagano	10,238	3.3
7	Shizuoka	8,453	3.1	7	Hiroshima	9,690	3.1
8	Niigata	8,159	3.0	8	Niigata	8,950	2.9
9	Hiroshima	8,054	3.0	9	Shizuoka	8,825	2.8
10	Okayama	7,877	2.9	10	Chiba	8,688	2.8
Total of top 10 prefectures		126,081	46.5	Total of top 10 prefectures		145,639	46.7
National total		270,914	100.0	National total		312,091	100.0

Source: Ōkurashō Shuzeikyoku Tōkeinenpō [Annual Statistical Report of National Tax Administration Agency of Ministry of Finance].
Notes: Figures are given in the numbers of persons and in percentages.
Figures operating retail sales have been taken from the original data without alteration.

Table 2.3. (*Continued*)

	1910				1915		
Rank	Prefecture	Persons operating retail sales	Percentage	Rank	Prefecture	Persons operating retail sales	Percentage
1	Tokyo	41,055	10.1	1	Tokyo	25,085	10.3
2	Osaka	29,072	7.2	2	Osaka	19,951	8.2
3	Aichi	22,010	5.4	3	Aichi	14,048	5.8
4	Hyōgo	17,127	4.2	4	Hyōgo	10,996	4.5
5	Kyoto	16,098	4.0	5	Kyoto	10,324	4.2
6	Fukuoka	15,360	3.8	6	Fukuoka	9,880	4.1
7	Hiroshima	12,979	3.2	7	Hokkaidō	7,648	3.1
8	Shizuoka	11,826	2.9	8	Shizuoka	7,185	2.9
9	Niigata	11,180	2.8	9	Niigata	7,122	2.9
10	Nagano	11,017	2.7	10	Nagano	6,183	2.5
Total of top 10 prefectures		187,724	46.3	Total of top 10 prefectures		118,422	48.6
National total		405,535	100.0	National total		243,606	100.0

Table 2.3. (*Continued*)

		1920				1925	
Rank	Prefecture	Persons operating retail sales	Percentage	Rank	Prefecture	Persons operating retail sales	Percentage
1	Tokyo	57,042	10.8	1	Tokyo	80,360	9.9
2	Osaka	41,064	7.7	2	Osaka	72,466	9.0
3	Aichi	26,182	4.9	3	Hyōgo	46,898	5.8
4	Fukuoka	25,879	4.9	4	Aichi	42,744	5.3
5	Hyōgo	25,760	4.9	5	Fukuoka	37,583	4.6
6	Kyoto	19,053	3.6	6	Kyoto	29,555	3.7
7	Shizuoka	15,640	2.9	7	Hokkaidō	25,648	3.2
8	Hokkaidō	15,274	2.9	8	Shizuoka	24,115	3.0
9	Hiroshima	15,000	2.8	9	Hiroshima	23,471	2.9
10	Okayama	14,262	2.7	10	Niigata	21,035	2.6
Total of top 10 prefectures		255,156	48.1	Total of top 10 prefectures		403,875	50.0
National total		530,396	100.0	National total		808,240	100.0

This probably reflected the concentration of population in the largest cities. On the other hand, we should also note, third, that, whereas Kyoto gradually fell in the ranking (fourth in 1899 and sixth in 1925), Hyōgo was on the rise (fifth in 1899 and third in 1925). Those results probably reflected both the fall in Kyoto's relative standing among large cities in Japan and the economic expansion of Hyōgo. Fourth, one may notice that the number of product sellers increased rapidly in Fukuoka. After rising to sixth place from eleventh in 1910, Fukuoka held fourth place in 1920 and fifth in 1925. The development of product sellers in the Kyūshū region in the modern era has already been discussed in the foregoing section on the principal component analysis. However, the growth of product sales in Fukuoka was outstanding. Fifth, one can see that Hokkaidō, too, experienced a rapid increase in the number of product sellers. It moved from eleventh place to seventh in 1915; from then, it continued to hold seventh or eighth place. Hokkaidō already had a large number of brokerage wholesalers who dealt in products from the northern sea. But Table 2.2 suggests that product sellers also increased rapidly in Hokkaidō from the Taishō era; it also suggests a widespread presence of sellers who dealt in products from outside the region. Although conclusive data is not available, one may suppose that this growth reflected the expansion of distribution networks in Hokkaidō as the region developed.

It is, therefore, possible to argue that the fluctuations in the product sales sector in modern Japan reflected the economic development of each region. In prefectures that included large cities such as Tokyo, Osaka, Aichi or Hyōgo, there was a large-scale sales organization. Rapid development was also seen in Fukuoka, where the economy was showing remarkable growth, and in fast-developing Hokkaidō.

3.3. The structure of traditional commerce: size, number, complexity and productivity

As a means of analyzing the structure of traditional commerce, distribution-related indexes have calculated and the shifts presented in Table 2.4. First, let us consider smallness in scale, a characteristic feature of traditional commerce. Table 2.4, which shows the number of workers employed by each product seller, indicates a declining tendency over time. This suggests, further, that the scale of product sales in modern Japan was steadily being reduced. This process was especially rapid in the latter part of the post-First World War boom and in the subsequent recession. The number of product sellers, on the other hand, shows the completely opposite tendency. Figures for the number of sellers per 1,000 people demonstrate a consistent increase; again, the rise was particularly rapid in the latter part of the post-First World War boom and in the subsequent recession. The changes in those two sets of figures explain that, although the scale of

Table 2.4. Distribution-related indexes

Year	Small scale Number of employees per operating retail sales	Competitiveness Number of persons operating retail sales per every 1,000 people of the population	Complexity Amount of wholesale price/ Amount of retail price	Productivity Amount of wholesale price and retail price per person operating retail sales
1900	2.294	3.478	2.193	19,358
1905	2.297	3.604	2.255	17,015
1910	2.171	4.408	2.549	18,401
1915	2.113	4.587	3.024	17,777
1920	1.824	9.491	5.892	23,377
1925	1.715	13.530	3.312	15,601

Source: Matsumoto and Okuda, op. cit.

Notes: Figures are given in the numbers of persons and in yen. Due to the limitation in available materials, no reliable data can be obtained on retail sellers whose annual sales were less than 2,000 yen. Therefore, the figures in the table show those retail sellers who sold 2,000 yen or more yearly.

enterprise was reduced, competition among the increasing number of product sellers was intensified, particularly in the post-World War I boom and subsequent recession.

Let us next consider the distribution system. The index of complexity (multi-layered tendency) is calculated by dividing the wholesale price by the retail price; a higher result indicates a more complex system of distribution. The index rose rapidly during the boom period that followed the First World War; after the boom, it dropped rapidly. Aside from this fluctuation, however, the indexes show a long-term rising tendency, indicating that the distribution system of modern Japan was gradually becoming more complex (and had longer distribution channels).

As for the productivity of the sales business, except for the boom period after the First World War, the index of complexity stayed more or less within the range of 16,000 yen to 18,000 yen. There were some small fluctuations and a slight decreasing tendency. This finding, in conjunction with the prefectural data, indicates that the rapid expansion of the workforce was not random, but that it stopped when productivity became stabilised. One can conclude, therefore, that in the product sales business, which continued to expand throughout the modern period, competition among smaller-sized sellers became fiercer and the distribution system grew more complex. Despite all of those tendencies, however, productivity inproduct sales was in reality maintained at the same level nationwide.

4. The Nationwide Development of Traditional Service Industry

4.1. Nationwide trends of traditional service industry

Among traditional service industries, we have adopted traditional civil construction contracting industry as a typical example. Fig. 2.2 presents the results of principal component analysis in order to examine the nationwide development of the civil construction contracting industry in modern Japan in the same way as shown in Section 3.1. The first

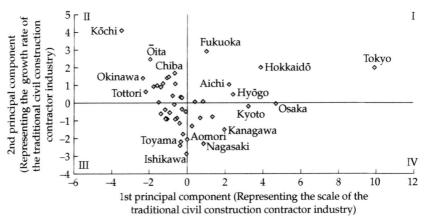

Fig. 2.2. Plots of the nationwide trends of the traditional civil construction contractor industry in modern Japan by the Principal Component Analysis

Function of 1st Principal Component:
$$F_1 = 0.93910 \cdot Z_1 + 0.93739 \cdot Z_2 + 0.92542 \cdot Z_3 + 0.83829 \cdot Z_4 - 0.53520 \cdot Z_5 - 0.36812 \cdot Z_6$$
$$- 0.54765 \cdot Z_7 + 0.73621 \cdot Z_8$$

Contribution Rate of 1st Principal Component = 0.57295

Function of 2nd Principal Component:
$$F_2 = 0.23666 \cdot Z_1 + 0.27025 \cdot Z_2 + 0.20644 \cdot Z_3 + 0.28443 \cdot Z_4 + 0.77987 \cdot Z_5 + 0.77097 \cdot Z_6$$
$$+ 0.75046 \cdot Z_7 + 0.28134 \cdot Z_8$$

Contribution Rate of 2nd Principal Component = 0.26219

Total Contribution Rate = 0.83514

Z_1 = Number of Civil Construction Contractors Z_2 = Value of Contracts
Z_3 = Number of Employees Z_4 = Population
Z_5 = Growth Rate of Number of Civil Construction Contractors
Z_6 = Growth Rate of Value of Contracts Z_7 = Growth Rate of Number of Employees
Z_8 = Growth Rate of Population

  I : Industry size is big; growth of industry is rapid.
 II : Industry size is small; growth of industry is rapid.
III : Industry size is small; growth of industry is slow.
IV : Industry size is big; growth of industry is slow.

Source: Same as Figure 2.1.

principal component of this figure represents the scale of the traditional civil construction contracting industry, and the second principal component represents the growth rate of the traditional civil construction contracting industry.

The first characteristic feature of the figure is that prefectures such as Tokyo, Osaka, Hokkaidō, Kyoto, Hyōgo, Aichi, Kanagawa and Fukuoka appear in the first and fourth quadrants. This indicates that, in prefectures that had large-scale economies, the activities of contractors were also organized on a large scale to meet the heavy demand for civil construction works. In particular, the prefectures in the first quadrant (Tokyo, Hokkaidō, Aichi, Hyōgo and Fukuoka) not only had large-scale industry but also characteristically showed rapid growth. A second feature of Fig. 2.2 is that prefectures in the Kinki, Chūgoku and Kyūshū regions are located in the second quadrant. Among them, Kōchi, Ōita, Okayama, Tottori, Chiba and Okinawa present typical examples. One can see that, although such prefectures were small in size, there was active contracting for civil construction works and growth was remarkable. Third, one can note that many prefectures in the Hokuriku and Tōhoku regions, including Ishikawa, Toyama and Aomori, characteristically appear in the third quadrant. This suggests that contracting businesses for civil construction works in these regions were small in scale and were developing slowly in comparison to other prefectures.

In summary, it can be argued that contracting businesses for civil construction works were organized extensively in major prefectures such as Tokyo, Osaka, Hokkaidō, Hyōgo, Aichi and Fukuoka, where the scale of economy was large and there was active demand for civil construction works. Contracting businesses showed remarkable growth in many parts of the Kinki, Chūgoku and Kyūshū regions, but in the Hokuriku and Tōhoku regions, civil construction contracting was small in scale and development was slow. In other words, as a general tendency, the nationwide development of contracting businesses for civil construction works in modern Japan was "high in the west and low in the east".

4.2. Prefectural trends in the traditional service industry

Let us examine prefectural trends in the contracting business for civil construction works in Table 2.5 in order to consider the nationwide development of traditional industry. It should be noted that, as a result of an amendment to the Business Tax Law in 1911, the civil construction contracting industry and contract labor were put together under a new category called the contracting industry.

First, one can see that contracting businesses were concentrated in the top ten prefectures, which included 50 to 70 percent of the total number of persons who operated such businesses nationwide. Second, the

Table 2.5. Prefecture-specific changes in the number of persons operating businesses in the contracting industry (civil construction contracting industry and contracting labor)

		1899				1905	
Rank	Prefecture	Persons operating business in the contracting industry	Percentage	Rank	Prefecture	Persons operating business in the contracting industry	Percentage
1	Tokyo	935	16.0	1	Tokyo	1,184	14.8
2	Kyoto	593	10.2	2	Kyoto	661	8.3
3	Osaka	542	9.3	3	Osaka	499	6.3
4	Kanagawa	287	4.9	4	Hokkaidō	382	4.8
5	Hokkaidō	264	4.5	5	Kanagawa	372	4.7
6	Hyōgo	246	4.2	6	Aichi	326	4.1
7	Hiroshima	212	3.6	7	Hyōgo	315	3.9
8	Aichi	194	3.3	8	Hiroshima	257	3.2
9	Gunma	148	2.5	9	Tochigi	230	2.9
10	Nagano	138	2.4	10	Fukuoka	202	2.5
	Total of top 10 prefectures	3,559	61.0		Total of top 10 prefectures	4,428	55.5
	National total	5,830	100.0		National total	7,982	100.0

Source: Same as Table 2.3.

		1910				1915	
Rank	Prefecture	Persons operating business in the contracting industry	Percentage	Rank	Prefecture	Persons operating business in the contracting industry	Percentage
1	Tokyo	1,571	12.2	1	Tokyo	1,886	13.8
2	Kyoto	922	7.2	2	Osaka	1,146	8.4
3	Hokkaidō	693	5.4	3	Kyoto	1,024	7.5
4	Osaka	632	4.9	4	Aichi	885	6.5
5	Aichi	627	4.9	5	Hokkaidō	773	5.7
6	Hyōgo	565	4.4	6	Hyōgo	707	5.2
7	Fukuoka	531	4.1	7	Fukuoka	598	4.4
8	Hiroshima	456	3.5	8	Tochigi	392	2.9
9	Kanagawa	444	3.4	9	Shizuoka	387	2.8
10	Niigata	354	2.7	10	Kanagawa	379	2.8
Total of top 10 prefectures		6,795	52.7	Total of top 10 prefectures		8,177	59.9
National total		12,893	100.0	National total		13,652	100.0

Table 2.5. (*Continued*)

		1920				1925	
Rank	Prefecture	Persons operating business in the contracting industry	Percentage	Rank	Prefecture	Persons operating business in the contracting industry	Percentage
1	Tokyo	6,033	17.2	1	Tokyo	13,415	16.8
2	Osaka	4,412	12.6	2	Osaka	11,857	14.8
3	Aichi	2,493	7.1	3	Kyoto	5,982	7.5
4	Hyōgo	2,247	6.4	4	Hyōgo	5,866	7.3
5	Kyoto	2,139	6.1	5	Aichi	4,885	6.1
6	Hokkaidō	1,573	4.5	6	Fukuoka	3,137	3.9
7	Fukuoka	1,542	4.4	7	Hokkaidō	3,007	3.8
8	Shizuoka	1,347	3.8	8	Kanagawa	2,635	3.3
9	Kanagawa	889	2.5	9	Shizuoka	2,455	3.1
10	Hiroshima	773	2.2	10	Hiroshima	1,866	2.3
Total of top 10 prefectures		23,448	66.7	Total of top 10 prefectures		55,105	68.8
National total		35,141	100.0	National total		80,059	100.0

consistency of Tokyo, Kyoto and Osaka in occupying prominent positions suggests that the demand for civil construction works and labor were huge in large cities and that contracting businesses operated actively in those three prefectures. The appearance of prefectures such as Hyōgo, Aichi, Fukuoka and Hokkaidō after this top group is probably due to the provision of infrastructure, causing an increase demand for contracting business. Third, one can note that Kanagawa and Hiroshima are continually located in the top ten. The provision of harbor facilities and civil construction works for military purposes is the likely reason for the high ranking of both prefectures. Prefectures such as Gunma, Nagano and Tochigi also appear in the ranking, although briefly, possibly prompted by civil construction projects for dam or mine construction. Moreover, in various areas, the start and completion of railway construction are reflected in rising and falling tendencies.

Overall, a substantial number of contracting businesses operated in Tokyo, Osaka and other prefectures that contained large cities. Business spread through the country in response to the necessity of creating infrastructure for military and industrial purposes.

4.3. The structure of the traditional service industry: size, numbers, complexity and productivity

In order to analyze the structure of the traditional service industry, the contracting business has been taken as an example. Management indexes have been calculated and the changes are shown in Table 2.6. First, let us consider changes in the size of business. The figures in column 1 represent the average number of workers employed by each contractor at five-year

Table 2.6. Change in management indexes of contracting industry in Japan

Year	Small scale Number of enployees per contractor	Competitiveness Number of contractors per every 10,000 people of the population	Productivity Actual amount of compensation per contractor in yen
1900	2.177	1.775	9,598
1905	1.801	2.262	9,505
1910	1.754	3.122	11,204
1915	2.497	4.266	9,156
1920	3.314	10.437	3,775
1925	2.750	22.244	4,870

Source: Same as Table 2.3.

Notes: Management indexes have been calculated using estimates of contractors whose annual compensation exceeds 1,000 yen. Figures of compensation have been deflated using the deflator of the construction industry.

intervals between 1900 and 1925. The number dropped in the period 1900 to 1905 and remained at roughly the same level until 1910. Although the number rose again rapidly in the prosperous days of the post-First World War era, it dropped with the recession of the 1920s. The contracting business was, indeed, small-sized: the average business had only two or three employees. But many people owned such small-scale businesses. Even restricting the count to those who paid Business Tax, one reaches a total of 7,000 independent contractors in 1900 and 80,000 in 1925. As shown in column 2 of Table 2.6, the index of excessive numbers, which reflects competitiveness among the relevant contractors, rose continuously. The rise was particularly remarkable from the latter part of the post-First World War boom into the recession years of the 1920s. With regard to the productivity of the contracting business (the actual annual payment received per contractor), although the figure stayed at the 10,000 yen level up to the outbreak of the First World War, it fell rapidly during the recession at the end of the war. This finding suggests that, particularly in the First World War boom era and in the recession that followed, there was a sharp increase in the number of small contracting business owners, among whom competition intensified continuously. At the same time, the productivity of their businesses declined and contractors were forced to run their businesses in difficult conditions.

5. Summary

First, the characteristic features of traditional industry, as seen in terms of changes in the number of gainfully occupied workers, may be summarized as follows:

1) Traditional industry, which accounted for the largest number of gainfully occupied workers, developed steadily in the modern era and continued to provide opportunities to those workers whom the modern industrial sector could not absorb.
2) Of the various traditional industries, commerce and service industries had the largest number of gainfully occupied workers. These industries provided opportunities to the largest number of workers, male and female.
3) There was a decline in the number of manufacturing industrial workers who operated in extremely small-scale workrooms that are not regarded as factories. On the other hand, there was an increase in number of manufacturing industrial workers who operated in factories employing five workers or fewer. Traditional manufacturing industries of this type continued to provide working opportunities, especially for younger or female workers.

4) Traditional industry, with a large number of gainfully occupied workers, functioned as a "buffer" that could supply and absorb labor according to the fluctuations of the economy.

Second, one can summarize as follows the findings on the nationwide development of traditional commerce, as part of the traditional industrial sector:

1) The results of principal component analysis suggest that product sales in prefectures that contained major cities was organized on a large industrial scale. In addition, the growth of product sales was remarkable in Kinki, Kyūshū and Shikoku but slow in Tōzan, Hokuriku and Tōhoku.
2) One could argue that product selling in modern Japan fluctuated in accordance with the economic development of each particular region. While it was organized extensively in prefectures such as Tokyo, Osaka, Aichi or Hyōgo, that contained large cities, it also developed rapidly in Fukuoka, which had a growing economy, and in fast-developing Hokkaidō.
3) In retailing, which continued to expand throughout the modern era, competition intensified among sellers whose business scale was gradually reduced. Furthermore, it can be concluded that the distribution system became increasingly complex; in other words, distribution channels became longer. Yet, despite these tendencies, the actual productivity of product selling was maintained more or less at the same level throughout the country.

Finally, the contracting industry was examined as an example in order to trace the nationwide development of the traditional service industry, which forms the other major part of the traditional industrial sector. The main findings are summarized below.

1) The results of principal component analysis indicate that contracting businesses for civil construction works were organized on a large scale in major prefectures such as Tokyo, Osaka, Hokkaidō, Hyōgo, Aichi and Fukuoka, where there was a highly-developed economy and much demand for civil construction. Moreover, the civil construction contracting industry also showed remarkable development in prefectures of the Kinki, Chūgoku and Kyūshū regions. By contrast, in Hokuriku and Tōhoku, the contracting industry was small-scale and the pace of development was rather slow. One can conclude, therefore, as a general tendency that the civil construction contracting industry in modern Japan was "high in the west and low in the east".
2) Civil construction and other contracting businesses were prominent in Tokyo and Osaka, the prefectures that contained Japan's large cities.

But they also spread throughout the nation in response to the need to provide infrastructure for military and industrial purposes.

3) During the First World War boom era and the recession that followed, the number of small-sized contractors grew rapidly and competition intensified consistently. Productivity declined and contractors were forced to run their business in severe conditions.

Notes

1. On the nationwide development of commerce and service industries, which were the most important areas of traditional industry, see the pioneering work of Matsumoto and Okuda (1997) and Matsumoto (2004a). For a detailed analysis of commodity retailers, see Matsumoto (1996).
2. For representative works that have demonstrated the nationwide development of traditional industry, see Chapter 2 of Nakamura (1971). See also Chapter 8 Nakamura (1985).
3. For the estimation of gainfully occupied workers in commerce and service industries in traditional industry, see the two works by Matsumoto above.
4. According to Ōhara Shakai Mondai Kenkyūjo (1922) (Ch. 4), 44 percent of female workers engaged in commerce in Aichi, Kanagawa and Hyōgo, were involved in "retail sales".
5. For a detailed analysis of the nationwide development of the traditional transportation industry, see Matsumoto (2004b).
6. Needless to say, this assumption is made for convenience and because data restrictions prevent any other assumption. Because the estimation of (1) is the most difficult, the method of estimation of (1) is shown as follows: "Gainfully Occupied Workers in All Manufacturing Industries" $-(2) - (3) = (1)$.

   The sources for the "Gainfully Occupied Workers in All Manufacturing Industries", (2) and (3) are Tables 8, 9, 18 and 19 by Umemura (1988). However, because data (2) and (3) are missing between 1885 and 1905, figures have been extrapolated to allow estimation. On the characteristics of the data of "Gainfully Occupied Workers in All Manufacturing Industries" (2) and (3), see Umemura (1988: 164).
7. Needless to say, some of (2) transformed into (3) as the Japanese economy developed.
8. On the work opportunities that traditional manufacturing industry provided to gainfully occupied workers, especially to younger or female workers, see Ministry of Agriculture and Industry (1902: Ch. 1).
9. The Business Tax was a direct tax imposed on commercial and industrial businesses according to their capital, sales and the number of employees. It was carried out from 1897 to 1926. However, in using Business Tax statistics, one has to note that the standard of exemption was changed during this period and those who were exempted may not appear in the statistics. One must also note that inevitably there were people who evaded taxation.

References

Matsumoto, Takanori, "Meiji-Taishō-ki no nihon ni okeru buppin hanbaigyō no zenkoku tenkai" [The nationwide development of commerce in Meiji and Taishō periods], in Andō, Seiichi and Teiichirō Fujita (eds), *Shijō to Keiei no Rekishi IV: Keiei* (Tokyo, 1996).

———, "Senzenki nihon ni okeru zairai sābisu sangyō no zenkoku tenkai: Zairai unyugyō wo jirei toshite" [The nationwide development of traditional transportation industry in pre-war Japan], *Osakadaigaku Keizaigaku*, 54–33 (Osaka, 2004*a*).

———, "Kindai nihon no shōgyō tenkai" [The nationwide development of traditional commerce in modern Japan], in Matsumoto, Takanori (ed.), *Seisan to Ryūtsū no Keizai Zou* (Tokyo, 2004*b*).

———, and Miyako Okuda, "Senzen-ki nihon ni okeru zairai-sangyō no zenkokutenkai" [The nationwide development of traditional industries in pre-war Japan], in Nakamura, Takafusa (ed.), *Nihon no Keizai Hatten to Zairai Sangyō* (Tokyo, 1997).

Nakamura, Takafusa, *Senzen-ki Nihon Keizai Seichō no Bunseki* [Economic Growth in Prewar Japan] (Tokyo, 1971).

———, *Meiji-Taishō-ki no Keizai* [Economy of Meiji and Taishō Periods] (Tokyo, 1985).

Nōshōmushō [Ministry of Agriculture and Commerce], *Syokkō jijō* [The Situation of Workers] Vol. 1 (Tokyo, 1902).

Odaka, Kōnosuke, *Rōdō Shijō Bunseki: Nijū-kōzō no Nihonteki Tenkai* [The Analysis of the Labor Market: The Dual Structure in Japan] (Tokyo, 1984).

Ōhara Shakai Mondai Kenkyūjo, "Joshi shokugya mondai" [Women's Occupational Problems]", in *Nihon Rōdō Nenkan* 12, (Tokyo, 1922).

Umemura, Mataji *et al.*, *Chōki Keizai Tōkei*, Vol. 2 [Estimates of Long Term Economic Statistics] (Tokyo, 1988).

PART II

Tradition in Industrialization

3

The Role of "Early Factories" in Japanese Industrialization

JOHZEN TAKEUCHI

1. Preface

In the latter half of the nineteenth century the Meiji government, together with private entrepreneurs, strove to introduce the modern factory system of production in Japan. As a result of those efforts, a number of relatively large factories using modern equipment were established. However, in a number of industries, it was not long before those modern and large factories—what I have termed "early factories"—found themselves facing stiff competition from small- and medium-scale enterprises (SMEs). In a number of cases the early factories lost out in the competition with smaller rivals. This paper explores the conditions that gave rise to this industrial structure in which SMEs played a significant role.

In this paper I will explore three central concerns related to the rise of small- and medium-size enterprises. The first of these is the historical and economic conditions that gave rise to this industrial structure.

The second major concern is related to some common misconceptions about the process of the transfer of modern technology. Many newly industrializing economies seem to operate on the premise that all that is required for the development of modern industry is the purchase and efficient operation of the most up-to-date technology. However, as this study will show, there is more involved than simply the purchase and operation of cutting edge equipment. New industrial equipment and organizing forms give rise to various socio-economic problems, and the ways in which those problems are resolved will shape the industrial structure.

The third concern is to explore, in some detail, the process of technology transfer in the Japanese case and how Japan, as a late developing economy, was able to develop an unusual industrial structure that allowed it to attain comparative advantage. Many economists have assumed that the comparative advantage of late developing states lies in their high population density which gives rise to a large force and thus relatively low wages—in other words, a production cost advantage through lower wages. In my view, however, the key to Japan's success was not low wages, but rather the creation of an industrial framework that supported an industrial structure in which medium and small enterprises played a significant role.

2. The Development of Japanese SMEs

Kamekichi Takahashi, who was famous for both his empirical and policy-oriented analysis was one of the leading economists before the Second World War. Takahashi once tried to classify Japanese export goods and identified 27 items that he regarded as "critical goods" for Japanese industrial development. Takahashi carried out detailed investigations of these manufacturing sectors, and found that fourteen of the sectors had reached their peak of production in the Meiji era (1868–1911). He classified these fourteen sectors as "stagnating industries". The majority of these were agriculture-based manufacturing sectors such as tea, straw goods and so on. In contrast, the other thirteen sectors continued to develop into the Taishō era (1912–25), and he classified these sectors as "developing industries" (Takahashi 1925: 393–7). The thirteen developing industries included:

A. silk thread, cotton cloth, silk cloth;
B. knitted goods, headgear, glassware, toys, ironware;
C. camphor, sugar, coal, cement, beer.

Those industries included in the A group were textile-related industries that were Japan's leading industrial sectors before the Second World War. This category included both big businesses and numerous small and medium size firms. Firms involved in the B sector industries were primarily small businesses; this group was often referred to collectively as "miscellaneous industries". Production in the industries in group C was dominated by big business groups from the early stages of development. The camphor and sugar industries represented new forms of production that were created to fully utilize raw materials obtained from Taiwan after it became the first colony under Japanese imperialism.

Excluding the C sector group, most of the other eight sectors had been developed as a result of the aggressive business activities of small- and medium-scale firms. In the textile industries, big business groups, including those of the "zaibatsu", succeeded in expanding their activities. However, in spite of the rapid growth of the large firms, small- and medium-scale firms were able to maintain a significant market share, and in some sub-sectors they were able to increase their market shares. Furthermore, it can be safely said that it was, in fact, the development of industrial down-stream sectors like weaving, knitting and manufacture of specialty fabrics that played a decisive role in the rapid expansion of industrial up-stream sectors like cotton spinning and silk reeling. The development of the down-stream production activities that provided markets for the output of the up-stream sectors, creating the conditions that allowed them to obtain economies of scale. The links between the two up-stream and down-steam in the spinning sector were so effective that the spinning sector was able to develop rapidly without the support or control of any of the leading zaibatsu groups.

In some modern industries like iron and glass manufacturing, up-stream production came to be managed by big business groups or state enterprises, while intermediate and final goods were mostly supplied by small- and medium-scale firms. Among the products the smaller firms manufactured were tiny electrical lamps for Christmas decorations, imitation pearls, and small iron goods like enameled ironware, surgical instruments, cycle parts, industrial needles, wire nets and so forth. In almost all of these sectors, there were no big firms, and they were usually classified as "small- and medium-scale industries". Such manufacturers were quite common in export-oriented sectors, and the concept of "export-oriented small- and medium-scale industries" became popular among bureaucrats and economists in those days.

While large firms and small- and medium-scale firms co-existed during the late nineteenth and early twentieth centuries, the majority of Japanese economists believed that the smaller firms would eventually be integrated into or eliminated by large firms, and the important role played by such small- and medium-scale firms was regarded as one of the symbols of the backwardness of the Japanese economy. In official ceremonies and statements, such small- and medium-scale firms were highly—and sometimes exaggeratedly—praised, primarily because their owners represented a large and important social group, but in fact bureaucrats and experts did not really hold them in such high regard. Furthermore, they were sometimes severely criticized, irrespective of their international comparative advantage, for the simple reason that they utilized cheap labor and transferred technology without paying for it. Some leading Western economists like Thorstein Veblen disdainfully remarked that Japan had only a tentative advantage that should be called the "Japanese opportunity" (Veblen 1915). His basic idea still exercises influence on modern economists like Paul Krugman, who has made light of the potential for Asian industrial development after the 1980s (Krugman 1994).

One of the aims of this paper is to consider whether the Japanese economy followed the same economic development path as Europe or America. In considering this question, the important role of small- and medium-scale firms is a major question. The small- and medium-scale firm sector continued to play a significant role in Japan even after the country had achieved high levels of economic development. It is thus important to consider the features of this economic structure and to identify the specific conditions that contributed to this phenomenon. In the following sections this report will concentrate on clarifying these factors through case studies of Japanese factories during the early stages of industrialization. In this paper, I have labeled such organizations as "early factories".

3. Some Typical Cases of "Early Factories"

In Meiji Japan there were few big firms, and the industrial structure was not well developed. However, when Meiji-era Japanese started to transfer new industrial sectors, they successfully established new big businesses, which used cutting edge technology. Table 3.1 shows these typical industrial sectors and the leading companies at the early stages of technology transfer.

Such large-scale factories combined the use of new machinery imported from the industrialized countries with successful utilization of cheap domestic labor, just as Veblen and Krugman imagined. Some companies were founded with the intent of producing goods for export while others were organized to supply products to the domestic market. Among the products produced primarily for export were buttons and Western headgear, which were not popular among Japanese but could find a market outside Japan. Almost all the brushes were exported too, but soaps and knitwear were already becoming popular among the Japanese and bicycles were among the consumer goods sought after by the Japanese rich. Among these products, knitwear had been produced by traditional methods, but the traditional system of production was not sufficient to meet expanding demand, especially the demand for military use.

Table 3.1. Newly transferred industries and leading early factories

Year of Establishment	Industrial Sector	Name of Factory	Founders	Social Status
1870	Soap	Walsch	Walsch, Wagner	FE
1872	Knitting	Model Factory	N. Watanabe	Governor of Osaka
1873	Knitting	Hōraisha	Z. Konoike	Merchant
*	Match	Shinsuisha	S.	S. company
1899	Brush	Teikoku Burashi	J. Matsumoto	Merchant
1890	Headgear	Meijiseibo	E. Shibusawa	Bureaucrat
1890	Button	*	Winkler	G. merchant
1909	Bicycle	Premier	Premier Co.	B. company

Sources: Fujimoto (1910: 35, 76), Kobayashi (1918: 28–30), Ichikawa *et al.* (1960: 40), JSSK (1973: 218), Takeuchi (1975*a*: 92).

Notes: FE: Foreigners employed by Japanese Government at a high salary. S.: Swedish, B.: British, G.: German, *: not identified.

Unfortunately, the records of these early factories have not survived, so our only sources about the companies and their managerial practices come from scattered printed materials. For example, Winkler's button factory was established in Kobe, and an old hand-written draft preserved in the central library of Osaka City University introduces the factory as follows:

Mr. Winkler was an owner of Trading House No. 85 located within the compound of the Kobe foreigners' residential area. The number of the trading house was later changed to No. 100.

Winkler noticed that it was easy to get shell materials like abalone and pearl oysters, which were suitable for producing shell buttons. He decided to establish a factory secretly in order to keep the technological know-how secret, and started to employ workers and installed 200 turning machines which were supplied by Hyogo Miyanaga Machine Shop, in addition to 48 drill machines and 30 jigs which were imported. He also installed a power generator, and commenced to produce abalone and turbo shell buttons in 1890 . . . . He trained several hundreds of workers and . . . later tried to improve the production system, by inviting skilled workers from Germany . . . (Kobayashi 1918: 28–30).

In brush manufacturing, Teikoku Burashi (Imperial Brush) was by far the biggest company, and it was famous for its modern production system. The company was introduced in a booklet written by a well-known reporter. The writer, who was known as an anarchist, was fascinated with the scale and efficiency of the factory. At the end of the nineteenth century, Tokyo was the center of politics, but not of business. Osaka was by far the biggest center of the Japanese economy, and it was often referred to as the "Manchester of the East", since Osaka was becoming a new center of the global cotton spinning industry. The anarchist writer enthusiastically described Teikoku Burashi as one of the most advanced large factories in the city; all of the machines and equipment had been imported from the United States, and its huge steam engine was one of the great prides of Osaka. The company was founded by Jūtarō Matsumoto who was one of the leading merchants of the city and the president of the 130th National Bank. Three hundred workers were employed in 1891, and 500 by 1897 (Yokoyama 1950: 175–87). The success of the company stimulated the establishment of new factories in this field of industry. Most were located in the Osaka and Kyoto area. Table 3.2 provides data on the factories.

These factories adopted the integrated production system based on a division of labor, and workers had the right to move freely to take other opportunities of employment. Driving power engines were installed in almost all of the factories. Judging from these facts, it is possible to say that the modern factory system had taken root in Japan in those days.

Table 3.2. Early factories of brush industry

Year	Company name	Type of company
1888	Osaka Seigyo*	Joint-stock company
1896	Kansai Boeki	Joint-stock company
1897	Nihon Burashi	Joint-stock company
1898	Yamura Burashi	Private company
1898	Osaka Burashi	Joint-stock company
1902	The Royal Burashi	Limited partnership
1903	Nagato Burashi	Private company
1906	Sakabe Shokai	Private company

Source: Takeuchi (1975*a*: 91–2).

Note: * The company later changed its name to Teikoku Burashi.

However, such factories depended upon imported raw materials, imported machines, and the foreign export market. In some factories in other industrial sectors, managers were foreigners. This list of dependencies on foreign equipment and markets is very similar to those we would find among typical colonial factories and contemporary factories in numerous developing countries that use cheap domestic labor to manufacture products for export markets at cheap prices.

It is important to note that in each of these industrial sectors producers succeeded in maintaining an economic environment that contributed to the national economy. In the brush industry, raw materials like pig bristle and ox bone for handles were imported from China. Production machinery was also imported, and sales largely depended upon the American market, but all of the managers were Japanese. It was these Japanese managers who controlled the factories and who handled all of the dealings with foreigners.

In the button industry, production was primarily for export markets, and the managers were foreigners. At the beginning, raw materials were purchased in Japan, but later the button firms shifted to the use of imported raw materials. In the case of the button industry, some of the machinery was of Japanese manufacture, and as the industry developed domestic machinery came to play an increasingly important role (Takeuchi 1979*a*, 1979*b*).

In the knitwear and headgear sectors managers could acquire raw materials in the domestic market. Only when they were producing high quality goods for export was it necessary to import some basic materials. The major market for goods was domestic, and the importance of the domestic market increased over time (Takeuchi 1975*b*, 1979*a*).

Bicycles were another important consumer good. The Premier Bicycle Company was the first bicycle company to establish integrated production in Japan. Bicycle production was more complicated than many of the other industries we have discussed to this point. Bicycle manufacture required the use of numerous parts, and also various processing lines. The British company, which set up the first larger factory, imported almost all of its production facilities, and relied on the parent company to supply some of the more sophisticated parts like coaster brakes and gears. Tires were supplied by Dunlop Corporation, which had originally proposed the establishment of the Premier Bicycle Company in Japan (Jitensha Sangyō Shinkō Kyōkai 1973: 218). Before the establishment of the company, there were numerous bicycle manufacturers in Japan, and some of them were already big firms. However, they could only supply certain parts, and even large-scale companies had to concentrate on assembling completed bicycles made with imported parts. (Takeuchi 1980).

In the early stage of Japanese industrialization, both Japanese and foreign merchants managed to transfer the first modern integrated factories introduced in each industrial sector as cited on p. 78. They were genuinely distinguished in terms of the scale of employment, production capacity, integration, and the level of facilities. In most of these industries there was little competition for the leading firm, and the firms were able to draw on an abundant supply of cheap labor, especially from rural areas.

These factories played an important role in developing a new domestic market in Japan. New commodities like buttons, headgear or brushes became popular among Japanese living in urban areas by the end of the nineteenth century. Modern army and school education helped to create markets for such new commodities. Bicycle manufacturers also found a big market in the army, and at the beginning of the twentieth century, the market expanded quickly when people noticed that they could use bicycles for daily business.

Among the owners and managers of some of these companies were foreigners, who were also able to take advantage of Veblen's so-called "Japanese opportunity". German merchants already occupied the leading position in the global shell button market, and they succeeded in getting a new production base in Japan. However, Japanese were also rapidly moving into the manufacturing sector, as we can see from Table 3.1. Shibusawa Eiichi was the founder of the First National Bank and many other companies, which contributed to the development of new industrial sectors in Japan. He was one of the most prominent business figures in Tokyo, and Jūtarō Matsumoto who established the Teikoku Burashi (see Table 3.2 on p. 80) was a similar key person in Osaka, the largest business center of Japan (Ōe 1968, Shibusawa Eiichi Denkishiryō Kankōkai 1957, Tsuchiya 1989). Generally speaking, these early factories were able to utilize rich human resources in addition to adequate labor, technology, raw materials, and an expanding market. However, in spite of these favorable conditions, the early factories were not able to sustain their business activity.

Dimensions of industrialization

	Household production		Factory production
Manual operation	①	→	②
	↓		↓
Machine operation	③	→	④

Fig. 3.1. Dimensions of industrialization.

This was not because of mismanagement or market failures. European historical experience showed that household production shifted to factory production, and manual operation shifted to machine operation. In the diagram in Fig. 3.1, this is represented by the movement from ① to ② and then to ④. But, this was not the only path to modern industrialization. In nineteenth-century Japan there were many small producers of dimension ①, and they were going to take a different route from the Europeans, as we will see in the next section.

4. Decline of "Early Factories"

Early factories succeeded in introducing a modern manufacturing system to Japan during the latter half of the nineteenth century and the beginning of the twentieth century, but they could not sustain their own businesses and very soon began to decline. For example, the Osaka prefectural government tabulated statistics on shell button production that reveal an interesting trend. Table 3.3 shows that the total number of factories and workers increased rapidly from the first decade of the century to the time of the First World War. While the total numbers increased, the number of workers per factory decreased, a trend that did not change even after the war. The number of workers per factory shrank partly because of the general downturn in the business cycle after the war. In addition to that, changed business conditions led to a spatial shift in industry with labor-intensive sectors moving out of the urban centers to rural areas near Osaka. Nara and Wakayama became the new production base for the shell button industry. We should also note that the German-owned factory, which had once been the largest and most technologically sophisticated manufacturer, disappeared from the records. In the post-war records it is difficult to find even middle-scale factories; production in the shell button industry came to be concentrated in small-scale units.

We can see the same trend in numerous industrial sectors. Table 3.4 shows the statistics on brush producers in Osaka city, and here too we can see an increase in the total number of businesses and a simultaneous decline in the average number of workers employed in each. Teikoku Burashi, the

Table 3.3. Button factories in Osaka

			*; persons
Year	A) Factory	B) Employment*	B/A*
1902	5	315	63
1904	9	426	47
1908	48	985	20
1912	188	1,310	7
1915	257	2,273	9
1917	527	4,388	8
1919	512	3,391	6
1921	332	1,927	6
1923	345	1,534	4
1925	293	1,538	5
1927	278	1,557	5

Source: Osaka-fu Tokeisho [Statistics of Osaka Prefecture, annual edition].

Table 3.4. Brush producers in Osaka City

			*; persons
Year	Producers	Employment*	B/A*
1906	65	1,760	27.1
1907	80	1,767	22.1
1908	88	1,256	14.3
1909	104	1,297	12.5
1910	98	1,257	12.8
1911	167	1,969	11.8
1912	120	996	8.3
1913	163	1,291	7.9
1914	203	1,526	7.5
1915	218	1,634	7.5

Source: Osaka-shi Tōkeisho [Statistics of Osaka City, annual edition].

firm we considered earlier saw a decline in its employees from 341 persons in 1914 to 188 in 1915. This decline in workers occurred in spite of the fact that the general business climate was extremely bright at the time of the First World War (Takeuchi 1975*a*: 97).

   In addition to this trend, large-scale firms with modern facilities and fairly integrated production lines were obliged to shrink their businesses, and all of the early factories introduced in Table 3.2 went into bankruptcy between 1902 and 1927. During this same period, most of the factories shifted from using an integrated system of organization to an organizational system based on differentiation (Takeuchi 1991).

We can identify a similar trend in soap production. The company history of Kao Corporation notes that the pioneering Walsch factory, which was founded at the beginning of the Meiji era, ran into trouble shortly after its establishment (Kaōsekken 1940: 193). At that time the Japanese domestic market was still quite small, and it is certainly possible that market conditions dealt a fatal blow to this pioneering early factory in the soap industry. Later on, even after the market began to expand, the business scale continued to shrink. Table 3.5 shows this tendency, and the industry was also obliged to develop as a SMI (small and medium-scale industries) for several decades.

Among the industrial sectors introduced as SMIs in this paper, only the metal manufacturing and machine industry followed a different pattern of development. Let us turn to the bicycle industry as a way of exploring this pattern of development. When a British company set up a large-scale modern factory at Kobe in 1909, there were already many small-scale Japanese bicycle factories. The Japanese Ministry of Agriculture and Commerce (MAC, Nōshōmushō) published a special report on domestic factories, which noted that there were 35 factories supplying bicycles and their parts. Three of these factories employed more than 30 workers each, but only one of them employed more than 100 (Nōshōmushō 1910: 825–60). It is very hard to find detailed information about the biggest Japanese bicycle factory, but we do know that it was an assembler using imported parts from the United States. It did not have its own production line of parts (Miyata 1959: 36). Another factory later grew into one of Japan's major bicycle firms, the Miyata Corporation. According to the published report of the MAC, the factory employed 88 workers; however, since this factory produced a wide variety of industrial goods, it could supply only some limited metal parts for bicycles. It could only produce completed bicycles by purchasing the parts which were not manufactured in the domestic market (Takeuchi 1984: 49–50).

Table 3.5. Decline of soap factories in Tokyo

				(unit: persons)
	Year			
Name of Factory	1882	1883	1884	1887
Tokyosekkensha	82	50	25	10
Ushigomesha	*	20	8	2
Machidakojyo	7	6	2	*
Meishunsha	*	*	11	*

Source: Kaōsekken (1956: 247).

Note: * data unidentified.

It is evident that Premier, the factory with British investment, maintained an exceptionally sophisticated factory that was able to produce various parts within its own compound, and that finished bicycles were produced on its own assembly lines. In technological terms, this factory was the leading firm in Japan. However, it was not such large-scale firms but rather the small- and medium-scale firms that supplied small parts or assembled bicycles using parts made by other small and tiny firms that survived. Premier ran into financial troubles in 1920, and the business was transferred to Maruishi, which was one of the major distributors, and the production line disappeared in the 1930s (Takeuchi 1984: 61).

One of the features of early Japanese industrialization was the simultaneous presence of various production systems. For example, the cotton spinning industry adopted the same system of organization that was used in most other industrialized countries and tried to develop its comparative advantage on that basis. At the same time, firms operating in the numerous traditional sectors preferred to maintain their conventional systems and succeeded in expanding the traditional market. Not a few of them elected to join the arts and crafts sector as a survival strategy. Furthermore, there were numerous industries in which there was competition between firms that used modern managerial systems that had been transferred from abroad, and firms that were building on more traditional managerial practices utilized in small- and medium-scale firms.

Why did this phenomenon occur of modern factories failing while their less sophisticated rivals survived in such a wide range of industries in Japan? In answering this question we must begin by noting that the conventional answer to such questions—namely, cheap labor—is not always sufficient. To provide a better answer we need to turn to the kind of socio-economic factors suggested by the Institutionalists' school of economics.

In the Japanese textile industry there were sectors, like cotton spinning, where the modern factory system was very successful. There were other sectors like knitwear, street clothes, under clothes, socks, gloves and so on, where the small- and medium-scale model seemed to work better. When we examine these two large categories of industries, it should be noted that there were significant differences in the economic and managerial conditions that related to market stability, labor intensity, skill accumulation and so forth. In some of these industries that were producing consumer goods, market demand and product preferences changed easily. Especially, during the era of Japanese imperialism, the society was unable to expand its domestic market as smoothly as it could after the Second World War, and the overseas market was severely fluctuated through political reasons and economic conditions. The markets for small- and mediums-scale firms were characterized by a high level of differentiation in consumer demand and a large variety of goods. In down-stream sectors where firms were supplying products to small and specific foreign markets, small- and medium-scale firms had to cope with sharp fluctuations in demand and unpredictable changes in prices. They could meet such conditions by using strategies that played on flexibility, which allowed them to vary working hours, and the intensity of work.

Conditions were very similar in most of the sectors that were producing consumption goods for export markets. Such market conditions meant that for firms to survive they had to be able to adjust both prices and products. For example, price fluctuation directly impacted on the brush industry when the price of brushes decreased 40 percent within a few months in 1921 (Ōkurashō 1921: 322). The button industry was one in which flexibility of product was important. Button manufacturers were asked to supply 29 designs, 22 sizes, and 13 materials within a small production area of Osaka City. They had to supply a total of 8,294 kinds of buttons (Takeuchi 1979a: 75). In order to meet this kind of capricious market demand, small firms needed to have a highly skilled workforce, but one that at the same time would work for low wages and follow a frugal life style. One of the keys to the survival of such firms was their ability to draw on a large supply of labor that was willing to move from rural areas to work in such factories.

Shell button production expanded very rapidly. In 1914, the industry was 177 times larger than it had been in 1904, and in 1918 it was more than 3,000 times the level of 1904. While these figures have not been deflated to compensate for price increase, we can still see aggressive industrial expansion, an expansion that was sustained by the diffusion of small- and medium-scale firms and agricultural by-employment to rural areas near big cities (Takeuchi 1979b: 66). Stress should be laid on the fact that urban small- and medium-scale firms preferred to employ those from rural areas, and Japanese agriculture had its own tradition of labor intensity. This attitude was also one of the key factors in the rapid development of small- and medium-scale firms.

One of the factors we have noted is labor intensity. The idea of labor intensity does not always involve the use of cheap labor and long working hours; it can also refer to the intensification of the formation of skills within individuals and the accumulation of skills within industrial sectors. It should be stressed that this kind of "intensification of labor" played a decisive role in the success of small- and medium-scale firms and was one of the important reasons why they were able to supplant larger "early factories" in some industries. However, skill formation was only possible within a production system that promoted such factors. Small- and medium-scale firms were not in a position to use the most advanced models of machinery. To compensate for this they worked to accelerate adaptation of the machinery they did have, and tried to support their workers with a cheap but efficient production system, encouraging workers to spin off to start their own tiny businesses. This combination became one of the strengths of the Japanese economy, but also an element that had certain tragic implications. Japan succeeded in combining cheap labor with skill formation, and this became one of the characteristic features of Japanese socio-economic development. The result was production systems that were small and miserable when compared with large and well-integrated Western systems. Such systems were, however, a milestone in that they allowed Japan to gain certain comparative advantages in the world economy (Takeuchi 1991).

Such small- and medium-scale firms fully utilized the functions of adaptation, which allowed them to drastically reduce fixed capital costs. For example, in silk reeling they promoted the adaptation of French and Italian technology, and were able to supply simplified production systems whose initial cost was less than 5 percent of transferred European facilities (Wada 1969). They were also good at minimizing running costs; this stood in sharp contrast to modern factories that had to place special orders for machinery repair and spare parts, which had to be ordered from foreign suppliers.

In addition to these factors, it is noteworthy that Japanese society had accumulated certain skills that made it easier to achieve technological adaptation, and traditional manufacturers were able to produce similar goods to those supplied from industrialized countries (Takeuchi 1979: 55, 1980: 7). It should be noted that craftsmen and small masters were able to maintain freedom, and this allowed them to adapt production processes based on newly introduced production systems and to think of new ways to produce substitutive items. Their systems were often very compact and simple, but when they were combined with traditional skills, they gave birth to new SMEs that were sufficiently efficient to compete with the products of modern factories in the market. For these kinds of adaptation, small masters were also able to find any capital to support the trial production of their odd but effective items.

One of the factors that accelerated Japanese adaptation was the possibility of separating modern production processes into small sub-processes, which could then be sub-contracted to highly skilled workers who became independent self-employed workers or managers of small workshops. The possibilities for such independence is one of the explanations for why the Japanese workers remained as obedient and hard working rather than becoming aggressive unionists, in spite of their miserable working conditions. This is linked to another feature of Japanese society: high social, and vertical, mobility.

However, such factors did not always produce success if they were not well combined with other economic conditions, including suitability for the market or for technology. For example, in the decline of both the brush and button industries we can see challenges by new materials. Brush production had originally used pig bristle and ox bone, but there was a sharp decline in production when a new material (celluloid) was introduced (Takeuchi, 1975*a*). In the button industry, the shell button sector was brought to a standstill when plastic material was introduced after the Second World War (Takeuchi, 1979*b*).

In contrast to these small- and medium-scale industries, various machine industries were able to appropriately utilize the features of the adaptation-oriented and differentiation-oriented tradition of Japanese manufacturing sectors. For example, dies and moulding pattern production is a single production process in many industrialized countries, but it has been developed as an independent industrial sector in Japan. This is closely related to this historical background of manufacturing sector (Takeuchi, 1991).

The development of Japanese small- and medium-scale firms is also related to the rapid expansion of large firms. We can see this most clearly in the fact that the small- and medium-scale firms were often the most important customers for the products of the large scale firms. Among the sectors in which large scale firms thrived were cotton spinning, the modern steel manufacturing, cement and so on. While some of these industries tried to export their products, their chief markets were within Japan. For example, small- and medium-scale weaving firms were the chief customers for the cotton yarn produced by large spinning mills. If such small- and medium-scale manufacture had not developed, we can imagine that Japan would have been obliged to produce simple goods within a mono-cultural economic structure.

5. Related Questions

Finally, let us go back to Fig. 3.1. Western societies mostly adopted the process from dimension ① to ②, and then to ④ (Route 1). Japanese society tried to transfer the process, but developed another route (Route 2) simultaneously. In recent years, many developing countries have made a direct shift from ① to ④ (Route 3). However, on this new route, it became harder for manufacturers to develop new production systems and principles, because they depend entirely upon introducing new systems combined with cheap labor but which lack the conditions to accumulate skills. Furthermore, there are some interesting reports that impetuous adoption of modern technology will often bring about reversals. In China's well-known ceramics center of Jingdezhen in Jiangxi Province (China), numerous small masters returned to their traditional ways of production after the fatal decline of modern large scale state enterprise (Yu 2003). This suggests that it would also be possible to have a route from ④ to ①, if the market were able to appreciate human skills. These historical experiences show us that there are multiple paths and backward flows

that occur along the course of development of the modern factory systems and their concomitant technological development. For the Japanese
small manufacturers, it could be that this difference was one of the factors that helped to create modern comparative advantage. Also it means
that the early factories were unique not only in developing Route 2 but
also in shaping the Japanese industrial structure, within which the focus
was on developing some industrial sectors with their own particular combination of modern technology and traditional skills.

In considering these industrial experiences, we need also to consider
long-term historical processes from the feudalistic putting-out system to
the modern factory system. Stage I of Fig. 3.2 shows a typical case of a
traditional putting-out system. Under this system, merchants organized
small masters and artisans separately. As the market expanded, merchants
or masters needed to get higher productivity, and they began to promote
a social division of labor among small masters. This is represented in the
second stage of the figure. Both merchants and masters competed to gain
control over the reorganization of production. There is not time to consider this struggle in detail; what is important here is that the struggle for

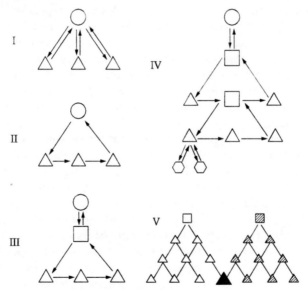

Fig. 3.2. Japanese transformation from putting out system.
Notes:
○ Wholesale merchant
△ Manufacturer, Small Master, Artisan
□ Organizing Agent
◯ House by-Employment

leadership led to a new style of factory management in Western society. In this system, the expanding market and successful introduction of new machines and power system, led easily to the modern factory system. However, Japanese society followed a different course, partly because there was neither an expanding market nor sufficient market stability, and partly because industrialization took place in a system characterized by insufficient capital formation. Under these restrictions, they hit upon a unique system to have a new subcontracting person to organize small masters (Stage III). These new subcontractors were mostly selected from among former small masters and assigned the task of concentrating on organizing numerous masters and intensifying the social division of labor among them. They were organizers of small masters, but at the same time, they were a kind of agent for traditional merchants. In Japan, merchants, especially nationwide wholesale merchants, could maintain strong and strict leadership against manufacturers, and their social status had been stable. They would not directly invest in the sectors where they could not have sufficient prospect of market expansion, but tried to fully utilize these agents. Because of these double-faced features, we can call these middlemen "organizing agents". Once Japanese SMIs started to employ such organizing agents, their production network expanded into multifarious tiers of small masters and tiny workshops (Stage IV). This process is closely related to the Japanese hierarchical social system, and it was one of the chief factors contributing to the elimination of early factories in many industrial sectors. However, the results were not always negative.

This system often intensified the authoritarian and hierarchical nature of human relations, but in accordance with the development of the social division of labor, new industrial relations were created. In other industrialized countries, small parts like screws and pins were easily produced in a small section of a modern factory. However, Japanese merchants and large-scale manufacturers traditionally utilized small manufacturers for the supply of such items, and this is one of the reasons why Japanese society has maintained so many SMEs for such a long time. The social status of their proprietors was not high and most of them did not have much bargaining power; however, in some cases they were able to produce high quality goods or develop efficient production capacity to meet multiple demands, and in those cases bargaining power might have increased. (Stage V). In this way, Japanese society created numerous SMEs with sufficient competitiveness. One example will suffice to illustrate the process. Needles for hand sewing are very small items at present. In Japan, they were produced by fairly typical SMIs. Some firms in this sector developed the capacity to supply dot pins for computers, and for a while these firms occupied the major share of the global market before new technologies like the bubble-jet printing system was introduced. Furthermore, a small company in Hiroshima became famous as it succeeded in supplying a special shield pin for automobile engines, and the latest model of engines are unable to get sufficient power without this small pin. The Japanese path for industrialization was unusually well-suited to developments of this type. While the firms were small and often struggling, they also adapted to certain kinds of innovation. Such small- and medium-scale innovative firms today are the descendants of similar types of management created in the early stages of Japanese industrialization, when such small firms were one of the factors leading to the decline of larger-scale factory production in some industries.

References

Fujimoto, Masayoshi, *Nihon Meriyasushi* [A History of Japanese Hosiery Industry] (Tokyo, 1910).

Ichikawa, Hirokatsu *et al.* (ed.), *Kōza Chūshōkigyō* [Lectures on Small- and Medium-scale Enterprises] Vol. 1 (Tokyo, 1960).

Jitensha Sangyō Shinkō Kyōkai (JSSK), *Jitensha no Isseiki* [One Century of Bicycles] (Tokyo, 1973).

Kaōsekken Gojyūnenshi Hensaniinkai, *Kaōsekken Gojyūnenshi* [A 50-year History of Kaō Soap Corporation] (Tokyo, 1940).

Kobayashi, Tsunetarō, *Nihon Kaibotangyō oyobi Genryō* [Japanese Shell Button Industry and its Material], hand draft (Osaka, 1918).

Krugman, P., "The myth of Asia's miracle", *Foreign Affairs* (November/December, 1994).

Miyata Seisakusho 70-nenshi Hensan Iinkai, *Miyata Seisakusho 70-nenshi* [A 70-year History of Miyata Seisakusho] (Tokyo, 1959).

Nōshōmushō [Ministry of Agriculture and Commerce (MAC)], *Kōjyō Tsūran* [General Information of Factories] (Tokyo, 1910).

Ōkurashō [Ministry of Finance (MOF)], *Gaikoku Bōeki Gairan* [General Report of Foreign Trade] (Tokyo, annual editions).

Ōe, Shinobu, *Nihon no Sangyō Kakumei* [Industrial Revolution of Japan] (Tokyo, 1968).

Osaka Shiyakusho Sangyō-Bu [Osaka City Hall, Dept. of Industry (OCDI)], *Osaka no Burashikōgyō* [Brush Industry in Osaka] (Osaka, 1931).

——, *Osaka no Meriyasukōgyō* [Hosiery Industry in Osaka] (Osaka, 1931).

Shibusawa Eiichi Denkishiryō Kankōkai (SEDK), *Shibusawa Eiichi Denki Shiryō* [Autobiographical Materials of Shibusawa Eiichi] Vol. 1–15 (Tokyo, 1957).

Takahashi, Kamekichi, *Meiji Taisho Sangyō Hattatsushi* [Industrial Development in the Meiji and Taishō Eras] (Tokyo, 1929).

Takeuchi, Johzen, "Wagakuni niokeru toiyasei kaitaino ichidanmen" [An aspect of the decline of Japanese putting-out system], *Shōgakuronshū* 43–4 (1975*a*), 80–153.

——, "Toshigata chūshōkōgyō no toiyaseiteki saihen ni tsuite" [On the re-organization of Japanese urban small and medium industries] I, II, III, *Seikeironsō*, 25–1, 25–2, 26–1 (1975*b*, 1975*c*, 1976), 43–71, 51–78, 63–91.

——, "Toshigata chūshōkōgyō no nōson kōgyōka jirei", [A case study on rural development of urban based small and medium industries] I, II, *Hiroshima Daigaku Keizaironsō* 2–3, 3–1 (1979*a*, 1979*b*), 47–78, 49–75.

Takeuchi, Johzen, *Keiseiki no Wagakuni Jitenshasangyō* [The Formation of the Japanese Bicycle Industry] (Tokyo, 1980).

——, "Kakuritsuki no wagakuni jitenshasangyō" [The development of the Japanese bicycle industry], *Nenpō-keizaigaku*, Vol. 5 (1984), 39–70.

——, *The Role of Labour-Intensive Sectors in Japanese Industrialization* (Tokyo, 1991).

Tsuchiya, Takao, *Shibusawa Eiichi* (Tokyo, 1989).

Veblen, T., "The opportunity of Japan", *Journal of Race Development*, Vol. VI (July 1915).

Wada, Hide, *Tomioka Nikki* [Diary at Tomioka] (Tokyo, 1969).

Yokoyama, Gennosuke, "Osaka kōjō meguri" [A Guide to Factories in Osaka], *Naichizakkyo go no Nihon* [Japan after the Cohabitation with Foreigners] (reprint, Tokyo 1950).

Yu, Zhonggan, "Dentōsangyō niokeru shukouseisan to kikaiseisan" [Hand production and machine production in traditional industry], in Sakurai, Tatsuhiko *et al.* (eds), *Kawaru Chūgoku Kawaranu Chūgoku* [Changing China and Unchanging China] (Tokyo, 2003).

4

Dualism in the Silk-reeling Industry in Suwa from the 1910s to the 1930s*

SATOSHI MATSUMURA

1. Introduction

Let me begin by explaining some of the concepts that will be used in this chapter. The term "machine filature" will be used to refer to mills in which reelers devote their energies to feeding the ends of silk into a reeling machine, the rotary power of which is supplied by outside equipment, for example, by a water wheel or a motor. Thus machine filature takes the form of factory industry. It was introduced to Japan from Europe at the beginning of the Meiji period and came into widespread use after the 1870s. Before the 1870s, silk had been produced in Japan using the hand-reeled (zaguri or tebiki) process, a production style that was usually part of the domestic economy. The silk industry began to develop rapidly at the end of the Edo period as a result of Japan's entrance into foreign silk markets. Japanese machine filature was successful as a result of both its high productivity levels and its ability to easily clear the quality and price constraints of the foreign silk market. The production volume of machine filature surpassed that of hand-reeled for the first time in 1894.

Previous studies in Japanese economic history have viewed the modernization of the Japanese silk-reeling industry as a story dominated by two themes: the first is the developmental limits of the hand-reeled production method and the second, the remarkable development of the machine filatures. The machine filatures in the Suwa district provide a representative example of the rapid development of such machine filatures. As for the hand-reeled (zaguri) production method, this form of production continued to spread as by-employment among peasant farmers and did not begin to decline until the 1900s. The experience of hand-reeling production in Gumma Prefecture is a fairly typical example of this style of production. It is important to note that a large quantity of the hand-reeled

* This chapter has been substantially revised from Matsumura 1992, Ch. 3, Sec. 2.

raw silk was also exported to America and Europe. Thus, from the 1870s until the 1900s, mass production in factories and production by traditional hand-reelers grew side by side in the Japanese silk-reeling industry. Among the many small-scale producers in the traditional sector there were attempts to reorganize the industry for mass production for the export market through such methods as gathering and standardization of each product. At that time there was not much difference in the level of productivity in the two sectors and so the traditional sector was able to compete with the factory sector as a result of its efforts at improvement. Therefore, in the districts where the hand-reelers were well developed as a form of domestic industry, merchants did not need to introduce machine filature techniques and to construct steam-reeling factories. Over time, however, the gap in productivity began to increase and the production for export of hand-reeled silk began to decline (Ishii 1972).

To turn to the evidence from silk reeling in Suwa, it is interesting to note that although machine filature was a form of mass production, many of the machine filatures were actually medium or small-scale production units. These medium and small filatures were also able to produce standardized raw silk for the export market. In other words, both large machine filatures and small ones were engaged in mass production. Thus we can say that before the second decade of the twentieth century economies of scale were not clearly evident in the machine filature industry. Beginning in the 1910s, however, the competition between reeling firms intensified, and as a result of technological development the scale of investment in reeling plants grew. American demand for higher grade raw silk increased and rayon (which was often referred to as artificial silk) began to make inroads into a part of the raw silk market. Smaller reeling firms could not compete under these conditions and large reeling firms like Katakura and Gunze came to lead the Japanese silk-reeling industry in the 1920s and the 1930s (Matsumura 1992).

Despite these developments, smaller machine-reeling firms and hand-reelers were still in operation and continued to play a historical role in the Japanese silk-reeling industry. As large reeling firms developed, smaller machine-reeling firms and hand-reelers came to life again in some districts during the 1910s. The reason is that these operators served the domestic market which demanded small quantities of differentiated goods but tolerated less uniform quality than that demanded by the export market. Moreover, the larger mills, which were producing for the export market, often discarded substandard cocoons that were unsuitable for the production of high-quality raw silk required by the export market. Smaller mills and hand-reelers could use such substandard cocoons.

At the same time the domestic raw silk market was also growing as a result of the increase in consumption of silk fabric. Thus, during the second decade growth spurt, the small reeling firms were no longer competing directly with their larger rivals in the export market. Even after the Second

World War, this small scale sector continued to survive as a result of changes in the demand structure. After the Second World War, the main demand was in the domestic raw silk market. Medium and small-scale firms producing for the domestic market continued to compete tenaciously with mass production until quite recently.

As this brief summary suggests, the reasons why the sectors of mass production and non-mass production in the Japanese silk-reeling industry developed side by side changed dramatically in the second decade of the twentieth century. The theme of this chapter is the relationship between the mass producers and the small producers in the silk-reeling industry in the Suwa district from the 1910s to the 1930s. This chapter will also analyse the state of the smaller machine-reeling firms and hand-reelers in Suwa. The conclusions which are drawn from the case study of the Suwa district can be applied to other leading silk-reeling districts like Maebashi in Gumma Prefecture.

This article will consider these patterns of production that are often referred to as "dualism" in the Japanese silk-reeling industry. "Dualism", as used in the title of this chapter, refers to the differentiation between the larger reeling mills that produced raw silk mainly for export and the smaller reeling units (small reeling mills and hand-reelers) that produced goods also mainly for the domestic silk market.

Japanese economists term the coexistence of the modern industrial sector with the pre-modern one, or the coexistence of large concerns with small firms within the economic structure of a country, a "dual structure". Many scholars have been engaged in studies on dualistic structures in Japan, focusing on the existence of wage differentials between the two sectors. It is commonly assumed that this dualism came to characterize the Japanese economic structure in the 1920s. It has also been noted that we can identify economic structures in which small firms became dependent on large firms. The reduction or disappearance of wage differentials after the 1960s also has been pointed out (for example, Nakamura 1993: 108–12). Some scholars have discussed "dualistic development" of this type as specific to later developing nations such as Japan. This dualism develops as traditional factors of the economy are combined with modern factors, that is, dualism is characterized by the coexistence of the pre-modern sector with the modern sector (Ohkawa and Kohama 1993: 32–5). While this chapter will take into account such considerations, I do not believe that the relationship between the modern industrial sector and the pre-modern one can be fully understood if one assumes that it is a relationship between an exploiting sector and an exploited one. After the 1920s, small firms, which still incorporated many traditional factors, served different markets from those served by the larger concerns and the smaller firms also played an important part in Japanese modern economic history.

M. Piore, C. Sabel and J. Zeitlin in writing about "industrial dualism" (and "flexible specialization") have argued that sectors of non-mass production have survived in fields where the sectors of mass production experienced difficulty and that they thus compensated for the latter (Piore and Sabel 1984, Sabel and Zeitlin 1985, 1997). In this case study I will argue that small firms supplemented the mass production sector, or divided roles with the latter. In general, however, I prefer to use the concept of dualism also for cases in which the small firms do not supplement the mass production sector and both sectors are competitively alive at the same time such as during the Meiji Period.

The major question then is how the non-mass production sector survived in the face of competition with the mass production sector and what the characteristics of the non-mass production sector were in such cases. Although small reeling mills did not disappear with the development of larger reeling firms, it would be inaccurate to assume that there was no change in the small reeling firms. One of our central concerns is how the management of small reelers was transformed under the influences of large factories.

In order to understand developments during this period we need to turn briefly to consider domestic raw silk demand. To start with, in the 1910s and the 1920s, 30 to 40 percent of raw silk production in Japan was consumed by the domestic market (Asahi Shinbunsha 1930). The greater part of domestic consumption was made up of hand-reeled raw silk or doupion silk; such hand-reeled or doupion silk was consumed mainly by the domestic market. Additionally, this market also consumed 10 to 20 per cent of machine-reeled silk. During these two decades domestic consumption grew (Table 4.1). Machine-reeled silk for the domestic market was produced both by larger factories, which worked mainly for export, and by smaller mills which were equipped with fewer than one hundred basins. The total number of such smaller mills increased in the period after the First World War. At that time, although there were small mills producing raw silk for the domestic market throughout the country, the major

Table 4.1. Raw silk production in Japan   (thousand kan)

Annual average	Machine-reeled raw silk			Hand-reeled raw silk & doupion silk
	Export	Domestic	Total	
1914–1916	3,005	199	3,204	901
1917–1919	4,163	565	4,728	1,094
1920–1922	4,140	1,068	5,208	948
1923–1925	5,693	858	6,551	987
1926–1928	8,042	735	8,777	1,076
1929–1931	8,537	1,714	10,251	1,194

Source: Yokohama-shi (1971), Figures 73, 74.

centers for such production were in Nagano and Aichi prefectures. In 1927 these two prefectures accounted for 37 percent of all silk production for the domestic market (Yokohama-shi 1971: 254, 266–71). In Nagano, production in the Suwa district was a major contributor to the prefecture's overall standing.

As we might guess from the above short description of the characteristics of silk production for the domestic market, the silk-reeling industry in Suwa in the 1910s and the 1920s can be divided into three groups according to the scale of production:

a) The first group included the large machine-reeling mills established before 1910; these mills produced for the export market.

b) The second group included the many small machine-reeling mills which were established mainly after 1910. This group included mills with fewer than 100 basins. Some of the mills were independent and some of them were subcontractors for large reeling mills. Such subcontracting, known as chinbiki, produced raw silk mainly for the domestic market.

c) The third group included hand-reelers or domestic production units operating under the putting-out system, the so-called dashigama. Reelers produced raw silk under contract to merchants, and this production was, of course, for the domestic market.

Earlier studies by Akira Ebato and Yasushi Hirano examined the differentiation of machine-reeling mills, subcontracting by small mills and the production of small reeling mills for the domestic market in Suwa (Ebato 1969, Hirano 1990). However, there are still many unanswered questions about the transformation after 1910. Further, although national statistics show that hand-reeling production had started to decline after about 1910, in Suwa there was an increase. While this increase seems to be due to similar factors that affected the development of small machine-reeling mills, Japanese economic historians have not paid attention at all to the resilience or durability of the traditional domestic industry. In effect, these second and third groups in the reeling industry were of a very different nature from the large firms. Moreover, it was these groups that supported the regional economy during the depression in silk exports in the 1930s. In spite of their importance for the regional economy these smaller firms have been neglected; first, because it was assumed that their demise should have been the natural result of economic progress and, second, small firms were much less likely to leave adequate records, hindering study of this sector of the reeling industry. In the statistics compiled by government offices there is very little data on the subcontractors who worked for large reeling firms, and no data at all on hand-reeled silk production units which operated as domestic units under the putting-out system. There is, however, some valuable data in the historical records of local governments. We will make use of such data in our search for answers to the questions about the differences between the small machine-reeling mills that produced for the domestic market and the large mills that worked for export. How did the small reeling mills survive in spite of a shortage of funds? Why did hand-reeled silk, a form of traditional domestic industry, revive and continue to develop? Finally, we will consider why small-scale industry with its relatively low levels of labor-intensive management is not generally included in the picture of the modern economic history of Japan.

2. Subcontracting Firms

This section will examine questions related to subcontracting firms: first it will consider how many subcontracting mills were operating in Suwa and then it will discuss the process by which the subcontracting mills gradually became independent from parent firms.

As we have already seen above, the growth of small, subcontracting mills took place along side the development of mechanized filatures. This pattern of development can be explained by the fact that the subcontracting mills—as well as hand-reelers—were able to make use of substandard cocoons that were unsuitable for processing by the larger mechanized mills. The smaller mills were able to use such cocoons which were either not sufficiently fine or which were uneven. In the period before the Second World War, the silk produced from such substandard cocoons was destined for the enlarging domestic market.

Let us begin with an overview of production in the various producing units in the towns of Suwa in 1924 (see Map 4.1). In looking at this data we want to pay particular attention to the proportion of firms that were producing for the domestic market. As we can see from Table 4.2, an overwhelming majority of the firms were producing silk only for the domestic market. We can also observe a direct connection between the scale of production and the target market. Most of the mills with more than 100 basins produced goods for export while most of the mills with less than 50 basins produced raw silk only for the domestic market. We can also identify a concentration of certain types of production in distinct regional areas. For example, the large mills producing for export markets were concentrated in Hirano village which was the center of the silk industry in Suwa. Many smaller mills were located in the surrounding towns and villages. Shimosuwa town had the largest number of mills producing only for the domestic market. Kawagishi village had the second largest number of such mills.

Kawagishi and Hirano villages were the villages that had given birth to such large firms as Katakura, which had grown to be a major silk-reeling firm with many mills both in Nagano and in other prefectures. The smaller machine-reeling mills in Kawagishi village which had been newly

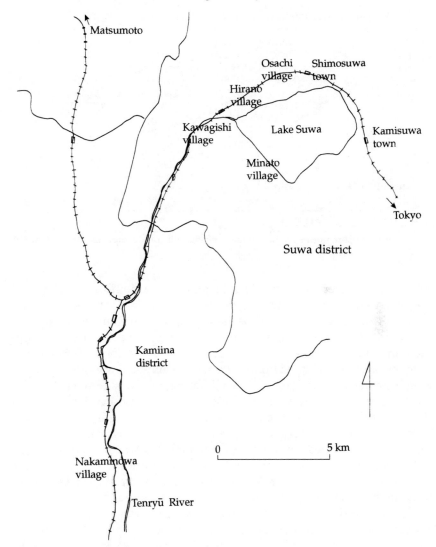

Map 4.1. Suwa district and nearby areas.

constructed after 1910 were managed by men who had originally worked in the larger village firms; many of the new firms had received support in the form of advances or subcontracts from the larger firms. There were more mills producing raw silk only for the domestic market in this village than in Shimosuwa town until the middle teens.

Shimosuwa town represented a different style of production. The machine-reeling industry had begun to develop in Shimosuwa in the latter half of the 1870s. In 1893 here were 29 mills with 1,100 basins, while in 1912 there were 9 mills with 2,880 basins. As we can clearly see,

Table 4.2. Machine-reeling mills in Suwa (1924)

Number of basins	Hirano village	Kawagishi village	Shimosuwa town	Minato village	Osachi village
10– 19	0(0)	5(5)	24(24)	5(5)	4(4)
20– 49	8(6)	34(25)	23(23)	14(13)	6(6)
50– 99	12(6)	5(3)	1(0)	7(5)	2(1)
100–199	19(0)	4(2)	3(0)	1(1)	1(0)
200–499	32(0)	6(0)	2(0)	2(0)	0(0)
500–	9(0)	3(0)	3(0)	0(0)	1(0)
Total	80(12)	57(35)	56(47)	29(24)	14(11)
Silk mills producing for domestic market	15%	61%	84%	83%	79%

Source: Nōshōmushō (1926).

Notes: Figures in parentheses are the numbers of silk mills producing only for the domestic market.

while the number of basins had increased, the number of mills had decreased since the 1890s. During this period some of the firms producing for export markets had grown while others had been unable to survive the competition and had gone out of business. The pattern of development in Shimosuwa changed as a result of a business innovation in 1907. In that year a merchant in Shimosuwa successfully sold raw silk produced by a hand-reeler to producers in neighboring Yamanashi Prefecture who used the raw silk as raw material for weaving traditional Japanese textiles. The realization that there was still a market for hand-reeled silk led many others in the village to get involved in producing hand-reeled silk. Out of this developed a new style of production in which hand-reeling as a domestic industry flourished within a putting-out system. Small-scale machine-reeling mills producing only for the domestic market also began to flourish in the village in 1915 and 1916 (Shimosuwa-chō 1985).

Previous studies showed that small mills producing silk only for the domestic market subcontracted using the methods described below (Ebato 1969, Hirano 1990).

(1) The parent mill furnished the small mill with old-type reeling machines and substandard cocoons as materials.
(2) The small mill produced silk using their own machines from cocoons provided by the parent mill.
(3) Reelers who were unskilled young female workers were provided by the parent mill.
(4) Re-reeling was done by the parent mill.

We need to reconsider some of these conclusions. For example, the evidence for the first assertion—that the parent firms supplied used equipment, is based only on hearsay evidence. There is also evidence, as we shall see later, that indicates that small mills sometimes recruited their own reelers independently from the parent mill.

From the point of view of the parent mill, subcontracting was necessary for three reasons: first, to train unskilled reelers; second, to reel substandard cocoons which had been rejected by the parent mill; and third, in cases where the small mills were able to produce high quality raw silk, to support the export-oriented drive of the parent mill. On the other hand, from the point of view of the small mill, subcontracting also was advantageous. Given the dominant position of the larger mills after 1900 it was difficult for small-scale newly established mills to enter the cocoon market and also difficult to compete in the labor market for reelers. But in the case of subcontracting, a new small mill did not need to prepare funds to buy cocoons and machines, and did not need to recruit reelers. Consequently, it was relatively easy to enter the subcontracting business (Fig. 4.1). Moreover, many of the subcontracting firms were started by individuals who shared family or native place ties with owners or managers of the parent firms.

The subcontracting mills were dependent on the parent mill in many ways. However, the level of dependency varied according to the contribution in equipment and personnel (reelers) that was made by the parent mill. Small mills often moved back and forth between greater and lesser conditions of dependency, adjusting their strategic decisions to conditions in the market. Extant records provide the following information about one small mill in Kawagishi village:

It was in 1914 that he started the management of a silk-reeling mill. He built a new mill on his rice field and operated 60 basins. Initially, he worked on a subcontract basis to Yamato-gumi (a large reeling concern). However, he personally recruited and trained his reeling workers. Because his mill was completely equipped, he was able to produce exportable raw silk from reelable cocoons. In 1918 and 1919, when the economic conditions were good, he financed his operations by himself and was able to show a profit. In 1920 when the economy entered a slump, he was, by chance, also taken ill. So he returned to subcontracting and stopped financing his operations by himself. As a result, he was able to avoid making a loss. After some time had passed, he began to finance his own operations once again. With this type of clever maneuvering, his mill was able to perform better than any others in his place of residence, Misawa-ku of Kawagishi village, despite the fact that it was operating on a small scale (Yamato 1972: 121–2).

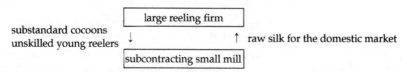

Fig. 4.1. Subcontracting of small reeling mills under large reeling firms.

Next we want to consider the position of subcontracting reeling mills within the whole sector of small-scale reeling mills that were producing for the domestic market. Did the relative weight of subcontracting change over time? One previous study asserted that, beginning from the time of the First World War, subcontracting reeling mills had become increasingly independent (Ebato 1969: 90–1). Another study, however, argued that as the number of small-scale reeling mills increased, the small mills also increased their dependency on the larger mills (Hirano 1990: 57). Therefore, it is necessary for us to more carefully examine the changes in the number of subcontracting mills.

Tables 4.3 and 4.4 provide data on what we know about the number of subcontracting basins under the control of large firms in Suwa. This data includes basins subcontracted outside the Suwa district and outside Nagano prefecture. It is quite likely, however, that most of the subcontracted basins under the large firms, which had their head offices in Suwa, were under large mills in the Suwa area. This can be supposed from the evidence we have on Katakura, the largest reeling concern in Japan, after 1927 (Table 4.4). According to the company history of Katakura, subcontracting mills under the Kawagishi Mill of Katakura were scattered in Suwa and the neighbouring Ina district (Katakura Bōseki Kabushiki Kaisha 1941: 349). To understand why this was so we must consider the conditions in the general region. Since Suwa was a region with a very high concentration of silk-reeling firms, it was also a region where there were many trained reelers, as well as individuals with managerial skills and knowledge of the silk industry who might be drawn into new industrial activities. As can be seen from Table 4.3, Katakura was the firm with the largest number of subcontracted basins. Generally, as a reeling firm developed, the number of subcontracted basins also increased. However, among the larger firms the ratio of subcontracted basins to basins operated by the parent firm varied. As will be seen further on, the large firms based in Kawagishi village such as Katakura, Yamato and Maruto had relatively high ratios of subcontracted basins. This suggests that it was in Kawagishi village that subcontracting relations between the large mills and the smaller ones—particularly during the early stage of development—were deliberately nurtured. In Shimosuwa, which later became a major center for the domestic reeling industry, there seem to have been very few subcontracting mills. As shown in Table 4.4, Katakura Company had many subcontracted reeling mills operating under its Kawagishi Mill even though the firm also had large branch mills in Hirano village and Shimosuwa town. In Kawagishi village, many of the small mills, which were constructed after 1910, started out as subcontracted mills receiving support from parent mills. In contrast, in Simosuwa town the small mills constructed at roughly the same time usually got their start as independent mills; the growth of these independent mills was aided by the steady enlargement of the domestic market for raw silk.

Table 4.3. Subcontracted basins under large reeling firms (1) (1914–1918)

Year	Katakura-gumi (11,225)	Yamajū-gumi (10,581)	Oguchi-gumi (6,520)	Okaya Seishi (4,254)	Hayashi-gumi (3,208)	Ozawa-gumi (2,664)	Kasahara-gumi (2,558)	Yamato-gumi (1,930)	Maruto-gumi (1,516)	Watanabe-gumi (1,402)	Komatsu-gumi (1,140)
1914	715	...	...	268	...	...	...	247	225	...	43
1915	839	281	314	268	...	143	...	291	165	...	32
1916	971	493	488	184	34	143	...	256	167	...	...
1917	1,093	607	601	113	34	157	...	218	108	...	...
1918	1,080	532	441	181	32	85	60	190	108	52	...

Source: Dai Jūku Ginkō (1914–19).

Notes: Figures in parentheses are the numbers of basins in 1918.

Table 4.4. Subcontracted basins under large reeling firms (2) (1919–1931)

Year	Katakura & Co.					Oguchi-gumi
	Total	Nagano prefecture	Suwa	Other prefectures	(Kawagishi Mill)	
1919	1,100	. . .	. . .	. . .	(. . .)	401
1920	872	. . .	. . .	. . .	(. . .)	447
1921	1,120	. . .	. . .	. . .	(. . .)	0
1922	1,120	. . .	. . .	. . .	(. . .)	236
1923	942	. . .	. . .	. . .	(. . .)	236
1924	992	. . .	. . .	. . .	(. . .)	236
1925	1,032	. . .	. . .	. . .	(. . .)	236
1926	1,062	. . .	. . .	. . .	(. . .)	(240)
1927	1,062	1,062	702	0	(625)	. . .
1928	685	625	417	60	(. . .)	. . .
1929	511	451	331	60	(288)	. . .
1930	614	554	389	60	(305)	. . .
1931	. . .	. . .	. . .	. . .	(182)	. . .

Source: Katakura Seishi Bōseki Kabushiki Kaisha (1927, 1929, 1930*a*, 1931); Dai Jūku Ginkō (1919–30).

Notes: The figure for Oguchi-gumi in 1926 is recorded as "rented basins are 240".

When we turn to examine changes in the practice of subcontracting, we are confronted with a complex picture. Not all of the large firms followed the same patterns of development. For example, very large firms such as Katakura, Yamajū and Oguchi increased the number of their subcontracted basins during the First World War at the same time that the number of basins in their own large mills also increased. In contrast, some other large firms had already started to reduce the number of basins operating under subcontract. As for the large firms cited above, the Oguchi began to reduce the number of its subcontracted basins in the early 1920s and Katakura rapidly reduced the number of their subcontracted basins after 1927. Such was the extent of reduction that Katakura's Kawagishi Mill cut the number of subcontracted mills from 18 with about 800 basins in 1913 to zero by 1936 at the latest (Katakura Seishi Bōseki Kabushiki Kaisha 1936). Among the large firms, the ratio of subcontracted basins to basins in their own mills was 21 percent for the Yamato and 40 percent for the Maruto according to statistics for 1914. For these two firms, subcontracting not only improved firm efficiency by providing a way to process substandard cocoons, the subcontracted firms also aided the parent mills by producing raw silk for the export market. This boom in subcontracting, however, was not to last and by 1918 the ratio of subcontracted basins had already started to decline.

To get a better picture of the overall developments, I would now like to look at the relationship between subcontracted reeling mills and other forms of production using data from 1918, the year for which the best data is available. If we assume that each subcontracted reeling mill attached to the large firms based in Suwa had less than 100 basins and that the sub-contracted mills were all located in Suwa, the computed ratio would then be 35 percent. On the basis of this calculation for 1918 we will then argue that at that time 30 to 40 percent of the small reeling mills in Suwa with less than 100 basins were subcontracted mills. Moreover, since many of the subcontracted mills would have had less than 50 basins, the ratio of subcontracted mills among this even small-scale group would probably have been still higher. This ratio is higher than our expectations. As the number of small mills continued to increase until the Great Depression of the 1930s, the ratio of subcontracted firms probably began to decrease gradually after 1918. Thus, the subcontracted reeling mills operating under the wings of large firms gradually decreased in number beginning in the latter half of the decade of the teens. This decrease was a decrease in absolute terms, as well as that in the relative proportion of subcontracted basins to those operated directly by the large firms. Moreover, the pro-portion of subcontracted small mills to all small mills also declined. After about 1927, the decline intensified as a result of the bankruptcy of some of the large firms during the Great Depression. Therefore, while it is true that small mills had come to specialize in the production of raw silk for the domestic market, we cannot directly conclude that this necessarily made the small mills more dependent on established large firms. Rather, it may safely be said that small mills had shown a tendency to become inde-pendent. It is necessary, therefore, to examine the reasons for this pattern of development. But before analysing the factors that led to this somewhat surprising result, we need to turn our attention to the significance of sub-contracting for the large firms. We will again examine data from Katakura.

In 1927 Katakura's Kawagishi Mill, as shown in Table 4.5, operated about one thousand basins in its own mill; in addition it had contracts with several small mills with a total of approximately 600 basins in Kawagishi village, and in April of that year, it added to its productive capacity by renting a small mill equipped with 127 basins. This rented mill was located in Nakaminowa village, Kamiina district which was 15 kilometers from Kawagishi. The company paid a rent of 1,100 yen for the period from April to December, and formally registered the contract at the registry office. The Kawagishi Mill was equipped with efficient five-end and six-end basins which produced high-quality raw silk for export. The subcontracting mills used old-fashioned three-end and four-end basins; four-end basins had already comprised more than half of all basins in the Suwa district in 1910. Since operation of three-end and four-end basins required less skill, we can assume that one of the tasks of the sub-contracted mills was the training of young, unskilled reelers. As for the rented mill, this unit produced equal amounts of silk for export and for the domestic market and also seems to have been engaged in the training

Table 4.5. Basins of Katakura's Kawagishi Mill (1927)

		Jan.–Mar.	Apr.–1st half of June	2nd half of June–Dec.
Directly	5 ends	605	605	605
managed mill	6 ends	410	410	410
	Total	1,015	1,015	1,015
Subcontracted	3 ends	479	479	443
mills	4 ends	182	182	182
	Total	661	661	625
Rented mill	4 ends	—	127	127

Source: Katakura Seishi Bōseki Kabushiki Kaisha (1927).

of young reelers. In the mills under the direct management, including the rented mill, production was 4.5 bales per basin and 4.7 bales per worker. In the subcontracting mills production was 2.4 bales per basin and 2.5 bales per worker. Thus, the productivity of the latter was about half of that of the directly managed units. This difference in output was a result of the difference in quality between reelable and substandard cocoons. Other factors contributing to the differences in productivity were the quality of the machinery and the skills of the reelers. New recruits received training for one year in subcontracting mills before moving on to work in the directly managed mill (Kagami 1997: 81). While the work of the reelers in the subcontracting mills was supervised by the owners of such mills, those owners were themselves controlled by the parent mill. We can see this relationship clearly expressed in an account of a meeting that took place in November of 1927. The owner of Katakura called together the owners of all the subcontracting mills for a discussion, during which he offered technical advice on reeling. From this account we can easily see that when a large firm rented a small mill, the staff of the large firm advised and directed the work of reelers in the smaller firm.

In summary, we can say that in the 1910s, 30 to 40 percent of the small reeling mills in Suwa were operating under contract to larger firms. Large reeling firms sought such relationships because they provided outlets for the processing of substandard cocoons and provided training for unskilled young reelers. Over time, however, many of the small reeling mills broke their business connections with the large reeling firms and went on to operate as independent firms.

3. The Independence of Subcontracting Small Mills from Large Firms

Why did small mills end their subcontracting relationships with large firms and become independent? This section will explore ways of answering this question.

The first question we need to consider is whether there was really development of the small mill after the First World War. To answer this question let us turn to two sets of data based on surveys of silk-reeling mills undertaken separately by the Ministry of Agriculture and Commerce and the Ministry of Agriculture and Forestry. The results of those surveys are displayed in Tables 4.6 and 4.7. All of the mills included in Table 4.7 had less than 100 basins except for one mill in Kawagishi village and 90 percent of the mills had less than 50 basins in 1927, the last year for the survey. The data show that while some of the small mills had grown in scale after the middle of the 1910s, many other small mills had disappeared from the records by the time of the last survey in 1927. On the other hand, many small mills producing raw silk only for the domestic market had been newly established, especially after 1921. Many of the managers of these new small mills had previously been associated with the silk-reeling industry as workers or in related occupations. A 1926 investigation into the backgrounds of managers of Shimosuwa reeling mills which were producing for the domestic market revealed that 56 percent of them had

Table 4.6. Operation status of small reeling mills (1914–1927)

	Hirano village	Kawagishi village	Shimosuwa town	Minato village	Osachi village
Operation status					
Grew to 100 basins or more	2	3	1	2	—
Grew to less than 100 basins	5	5	—	5	—
No change in basins	1	2	—	1	—
Decrease in basins	2	4	—	5	—
Unknown	3	6	—	3	—
Total	13	20	1	16	—
Disappeared	28	24	1	14	2

Source: Nōshōmushō (1916). Nōrinshō (1929).

Notes: On machine-reeling mills with less than 100 basins in 1914, which continued to operate until 1927, or disappeared before 1927.

Table 4.7. Data of establishment of reeling mills serving the domestic market

	Hirano village	Kawagishi village	Shimosuwa town	Minato village	Osachi village
Number of reeling mills in 1927	15	21	59	18	10
Established after 1915	12	9	56	8	10
Established after 1921	10	3	43	6	5

Source: Nōrinshō (1929).

formerly been workers in reeling firms or cocoon merchants or cocoon buyers. If we exclude from the totals those whose background was not known, the ratio of those with previous experience in the silk-reeling industry rises to 63 percent. Moreover, even those who had no previous experience in the silk-reeling industry received support and advice from persons associated with this industry when they started their firms (Shimosuwa-chō 1985: 175–6, Imai 1989: 315).

In summary, we can see that one of the characteristics of the small reeling mills—unchanged since the earlier part of the century—was the easy entry and easy exit from the business. Many new firms were created at the same time that many former firms were going out of business. And also at that time the larger firms with their headquarters and main mills in the Suwa area continued to establish their branch mills outside of Nagano Prefecture and did not reduce the number and the scale of their own mills in Suwa. Rather, it would seem that the larger firms' mills in this area also continued to grow in scale until 1930. Therefore, even though we know there was a tendency for formerly subcontracted firms to become independent after 1910, scholars have been unable to find a satisfactory explanation for this phenomenon.

In trying to unravel the complicated relationships in the Suwa region that were the background to this shift, let us begin with the question of training. One of the functions of the subcontracting system was to provide training for newly recruited workers who would first learn how to reel in the subcontracted mill where they were put to work reeling substandard cocoons. The output of such mills was targeted for the domestic market which is assumed to have been less quality sensitive than the export market. Beginning in the second decade of the twentieth century, large mills gradually began to train their own reelers. Although the evidence is not yet conclusive, it has been suggested that some larger Suwa mills began to set up systems to train reelers within their own mills (Tōjō 1990: 235–7). If we turn to look at the evidence for this within Katakura, however, we discover that the development of an internal training system progressed fairly slowly in their Suwa mills. For example, a training school for the women who were to serve as reeling teachers was not established at the Matsumoto branch mill until 1926. A branch mill in Kawagishi village which had originally been engaged in re-reeling was finally designated as a training mill with the mission of supplying trained reelers to four other Suwa mills in 1934 (Katakura Seishi Bōseki Kabushiki Kaisha 1941: 143, 421). As for why there was a shift to internal training, the records of Katakura show that managers within the company were convinced that training by subcontracting mills was not functioning satisfactorily. At a meeting of Katakura factory heads in 1926, the head of one branch mill which supervised the training of reelers at subcontracting firms made the following comments. He also proposed that each mill should undertake its own internal training and should be willing to designate 10 percent of its basins for training purposes:

As training has been entrusted to subcontracted mills there have been unceasing troubles, and the reelers themselves fail to develop any sense of affection for our firm. Since the regulations of the Nagano authorities do not allow the firm that has contracted-out its training to make any claims on the labor of the trainees, it is quite common for the workers, who we have struggled so hard to recruit and train, to seek employment with other firms after they have become skilled workers. Moreover, even if reelers continue to work for our firm they are difficult to handle since, thanks to inadequate basic training, they have become accustomed to producing raw silk roughly. These habits are very difficult to correct in the second year of employment. So, I think that we should quickly abandon the system of entrusting training to subcontracted mills and instead undertake the training in our own mills, setting aside 10 percent of the basins to be used for training of new recruits (Katakura Seishi Bōseki Kabushiki Kaisha 1928).

This proposal was in the end withdrawn. Although it was not realized, the speech quoted above does point to fundamental problems with a system that left training to the subcontracting mills. Not only were there problems with loyalty to the firm, as seen in the ease with which other firms raided skilled workers, but also problems with inadequate skills. The skills problem was undoubtedly aggravated by the fact that technological improvement in the larger mills had led to rising quality standards and the use of more sophisticated machinery. The problem became more acute when companies like Katakura began to introduce 'multi-ends reeling machines' (tajō-kuriitoki) in earnest during the latter half of the 1920s. It was said that even experienced workers who were accustomed to the older reeling machinery needed 3 to 6 months of retraining if they were to become skilled on the new multi-ends reeling machine. As the parent mills introduced the new technology, they also moved to end subcontracting arrangements, simply announcing the decisions to their former subcontractors. While the trend was against subcontracting, the practice was not totally abandoned during this period since the parent firms could still make some profit from subcontracting relationships. According to the Katakura company history, the original stimulus for subcontracting had come from the fact that it was more profitable to sell the raw silk manufactured from the substandard cocoons by the subcontracted firms than to simply sell the substandard cocoons (Katakura Seishi Bōseki Kabushiki Kaisha 1941: 349). That training was not the main motivation for subcontracting can also be seen in remarks the president of the company made at a meeting of factory heads in 1925. On that occasion, the president commented, "It is impossible to unify the training of recruits for all the Katakura mills. The object of subcontracting is not the training of recruits." (This can be interpreted to mean that the object of subcontracting was gaining profit.) After the discussion at the 1925 meeting, the factory heads decided to follow the president's proposal which was to continue subcontracting while at the same time establishing a school to train women to become reeling teachers. The school was eventually set up in Matsumoto Mill (Katakura Seishi Bōseki Kabushiki Kaisha 1928). This method of training recruits within the large mills spread very gradually in the Suwa area in the mid-1920s.

Let us now turn to examining the situation of small reeling mills that did not engage in subcontracting. In the period after the First World War, conditions were created which allowed small reeling mills to thrive even without subcontracting arrangements. For example, we can identify a growth in domestic market demand for better quality raw silk. There were also major shifts in the supply of cocoons. In order to produce such higher quality raw silk, small reelers needed to acquire 'lower grade reelable cocoons', which were different from the substandard cocoons sold off by the large mills. While in an earlier day the large mills had played a dominant role in the cocoon trade, in the period before the First World War Suwa cocoon wholesalers began to acquire cocoons from outside the region. As the supply of cocoons increased, smaller reelers became less dependent on the discards from the large mills. We can see this trend very clearly in reports on cocoon purchase by the small mills of Hirano village and its neighborhood in the first half of the 1910s. At that time, 60 to 70 percent of the cocoons acquired by small reelers were substandard cocoons which were bought directly from large firms, while 30 to 40 percent were substandard or lower grade cocoons which had been purchased through merchants in Suwa (Hirano 1990: 55). By the second half of the 1920s, the situation had reversed. At that time, 70 percent of the supply of cocoons used by the small reelers in Hirano village came from substandard and lower grade reelable cocoons purchased through the merchants from outside the region, and only 30 percent came from the large mills (Hirano-mura 1932: 526).

In line with these changes in production, a group of Suwa raw silk merchants specializing in trade for the domestic market began to develop. The domestic raw silk market had a number of special characteristics. First, the products were diversified and orders often were placed in small lots for different local markets. Moreover, demand for specific products varied over time. Second, on the supply side there were many producers marketing a wide variety of products in very small volumes. Given these characteristics of the market, the raw silk merchants played an important role as mediators between the suppliers of raw silk producers and the weavers who were the most important consumers. The silk merchants bought raw silk for domestic use not only from small mills but also from large firms. In order to assure their supply, the silk merchants of Suwa sometimes provided funds to finance the purchase of cocoons by small mills. This practice seems to have contributed to the independent operation of small mills, and allowed them to operate without establishing subcontract relations with large mills (Fig. 4.2). In Hirano village in 1930, there were seven or

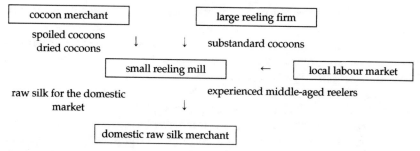

Fig. 4.2. Raw silk reeling by small independent mills.

eight silk merchants who financed small mills, and one leading merchant among them, had transactions with 14 mills (more than 600 basins) in Hirano village and four other nearby villages. Moreover, it is said that some silk merchants lent small mills cocoons or arranged for them to subcontract rather than financing them directly (Dai Jūku Ginkō 1930, Hirano-mura 1932: 547–8, Nippon Ginkō Matsumoto Shiten 1935: 129).

One of the characteristic methods of operation of the small, independent raw silk-reeling mills that distinguished their mode of operation from larger reelers was the practice of operation in small lots: small mills would lay in dried, substandard cocoons, reel and then sell the finished product before acquiring a new supply of cocoons. This practice was quite different from that of the large reelers which required significant sums of capital for purchase of large volumes of cocoons during the cocoon purchasing season. For example, in February 1930, the heads of the Katakura mill in Suwa made the following report about the domestic silk-reeling mills:

Head of Hirano Mill: "Domestic silk-reeling mills buy and reel materials on a day by day basis, and so some of them do kanbiki (reeling in the coldest season, that is, in January and February)."

Head of Shimosuwa Mill: "Shimosuwa town is a center of the domestic silk-reeling industry, and there are about 78 mills (2,000 basins) in this town. Their capital backing is very small, and they usually only buy the number of cocoons necessary for a single day's reeling. Because of this practice, the mills are operating successfully. The reason why such small businesses continue in this way without going bankrupt is the spirit of effort characteristic of Suwa" (Katakura Seishi Bōseki Kabushiki Kaisha 1930*b*).

In mills operating in this fashion, the ratio of interest to the cost of production was relatively low. According to a study of the costs of silk production per 100 kin (75 pounds) in the Suwa reeling industry in 1934, the costs of production for silk-reeling mills working for the domestic market was 30 percent less than those for raw silk-reeling firms producing for the export market. The most important factor explaining the lower costs was the lower payment for interest (Shimosuwa-chō 1990: 526). These same reasons explain why such small domestic raw silk-reeling mills sprang up and continued to operate without making subcontracting arrangements even during the depression after the 1920s.

Also, the spread of transactions in dried cocoons led to this practice of buying small amounts of cocoons on an almost daily basis. During the early 1910s, transactions of dried cocoons were not yet commonly a part of the general cocoon market, but, by the 1920s it had become much more common, partly as a result of policies that promoted the sale of dry cocoons as part of a policy program to protect the interests of small peasant operations. As a result of the spread of this trade form, it was quite easy for small silk-reeling mills to lay in dried cocoons produced in distant parts of the country from merchants daily all the year round. In Suwa, the Suwa Dried Cocoons Commission Co. was established in 1928, and this company went on to play a major role in spreading the practice (Hirano-mura 1932: 477–9).

Small mills used all means possible to reduce the cost of equipment and working capital. For example, they might use inferior lumber as building materials for a mill, even though mills were easily damaged by dampness, or use wide, ceramic earthen pipes as material for a chimney. One of the biggest expenses in setting up a mill was the cost of boilers: before 1910, boilers had to be purchased at very high cost from Yokohama, but after 1910, local producers in Suwa began to manufacture boilers at much lower prices. In large firms, the change of motive power from water or steam to electricity progressed rapidly in the decade after 1910. However, there were still many small silk mills in Shimosuwa and Kamisuwa in the 1920s that continued to use water power as a way to hold down the costs of production.

Entrepreneurs who wanted to use water power, however, were limited when they tried to find sites to locate new mills. Not only was suitable land beside water sources in short supply, the steady increase in small mills often meant that water was short during the summer months. As a result of these limitations, many of the small mills began to shift to the use of electric power in the 1920s when the supply of electric power was increased by the Suwa Electric Power Company and power rates declined. At the same time, new waterworks were completed and water rates for filatures were given preferential treatment in Shimosuwa, with rates standing at about one-fourth of the rate for home use. As a result of the increase in electric powered mills, small silk mills came to be located not only along the banks of rivers but also in town. These improvements in the infrastructure seem to have been an important factor contributing to the proliferation of small reeling mills. Indeed, before 1920, due to the inadequate supply of electric power from the Suwa Electric Power, many of the larger mills were equipped with steam engines as well as electrically powered motors, and also they had set up their own power generating units; others had invested funds in private waterworks as a way to overcome the water shortages that sometimes plagued the filatures.

As for fuel, while the large firms exclusively used coal after the second half of the 1900s, many smaller mills continued to use cheap firewood or pine needles. But, in the 1920s, the small silk mills also switched to coal. This shift required the construction of new, iron chimneys, the financing of which was made easier by a reduction in the price of iron.

In addition, the creation of a new silk-reeling firm did not always involve the construction of a new mill. When we look at the figures listing the number of firms going out of business and those just starting up, it is important to remember that this often only meant that the managers of existing small mills had been changed or that vacant mills were coming into operation again. Managers of small silk-reeling businesses could often buy outdated, small mills cheaply or they could arrange to rent dormant mills. When such facilities could be used, the start-up costs were even lower. Since less had been invested in starting a new mill, it may also have made it easier for managers to close a mill if it was not doing well. As a result of these conditions, we sometimes discover cases of a single individual repeatedly opening and closing businesses in this industry. These practices sharply distinguish patterns of management in the small silk-reeling sector from those used in the larger silk-reeling firms producing for the export market. Among the large firms, management continued for the long term (Shimosuwa-chō 1990, Imai 1989, Morisugi 1987).

As for the labor force, the pool of trained, but not currently working, reeling workers which consisted of retired, married and former machine-reeling workers began to form around 1910 at the latest, and it became a major source of workers for the small domestic silk-reeling mills. Let us take a look at the work force in 55 silk mills in Shimosuwa producing for the domestic market. The 55 mills employed about one thousand female workers in 1925. Among those workers, 53 percent reported that they had a husband. From this we can see that such silk mills were able to employ middle-aged housewives who had experience in reeling raw silk easily and cheaply. These female workers who had husbands were also the mothers of small children. In order to make it easier for such women to work in the silk mills, day nurseries were established after 1925, and it is said that this was the origin of the day nursery system in Nagano Prefecture (Shimosuwa-chō 1985: 117). Table 4.8 shows the occupations of the heads of workers' households; as we can see from this data, roughly half were day laborers. Some were also reported as unemployed. This data strongly suggests that these workers came from families that belonged mainly to the lower classes of the town. About 20 percent of them were peasants. But peasant women were also busy with farm labor, so they worked in reeling mills mainly during the slack seasons of winter and spring. Therefore, it may safely be said that although they paid low wages, the small domestic silk mills provided important supplements to the income of the lower class in the towns and supported the regional economy during the depression.

Table 4.8. Occupations of the heads of reeler's families

Occupations	Shimosuwa town	Hirano village
	Small reeling mills (1925.9)	Hand-reeling filature (1928.7)
Day laborers	272(49)	173(16)
Peasants	128(23)	109(10)
Various workers	48(9)	187(17)
Workers of reeling mill	40(7)	261(24)
Unemployed	34(6)	71(6)
Commerce	21(4)	129(12)
Fishery	7(1)	2(0)
Others & unknown	6(1)	175(16)
Total	556(100)	1,107(100)

Source: Shimosuwa-chō (1985: 178); Hirano-mura (1932: 535).

Notes: The data on for Shimosuwa only includes workers who had spouses. Figures in parentheses are as % of total.

The low wages in small silk-reeling mills also applied in Hirano village. By the 1920s we can identify a phenomenon in which wage differentials very closely parallel differences in the scale of the mill (Hirano-mura 1932: 419–21). The smaller the scale of a mill, the lower the wage. For example, the daily wages of reeling workers at the end of 1926 were 1 yen 50 sen in mills with more than 500 basins, 1 yen 2 sen in mills with 100–500 basins, and 95 sen in mills with less than 100 basins. The reason for the formation of this pattern of wage differentials was the separation of the labor market of small reeling mills from that of large ones. Another factor we need to consider is the ability of the firms to pay wages: as we have seen, larger mills were more capital intensive than smaller mills, and the output of the different scale production units was directed at different markets. Substantial differences in value-added productivity, then, were made up. The capital-intensity differential was the result of differences in equipment; the large firms, producing for the export market, were equipped with improved "sitting system reeling machines" (futsū-kuriitoki) and multi-ends reeling machines, which increased the number of reeling threads. Such factories divided reeling labor from cocoon cooking labor by the introduction of a cocoon cooking machine. While the larger firms were introducing improved equipment which improved productivity, the smaller firms continued to use the old-fashioned sitting system reeling machinery. However, during the early days of the Shōwa silk depression in 1930, when prices on the export market were spiraling downward, we can actually observe the paradoxical phenomenon in which the wages were higher in the small firms than in the large ones.

In the 1930s, as a result of the depression in the world silk market, many of the large reeling firms producing for the export market were bankrupted.

The skilled labor force came to be concentrated in the surviving firms such as Katakura. As that happened, the opportunities for young, unskilled workers to enter such firms were diminished, and many young people in the local area began to seek employment in the small mills. As a result of this, the small mills which had once employed almost exclusively older workers who had received their training in the larger mills but had stopped work after marriage, now found themselves employing young, unskilled workers who needed training.

Let us now turn briefly to consider working conditions in the small reeling mills. Many of the small mills employed fewer than 15 workers. Mills with fewer than 15 employees were not subject to the regulations by the Factory Act which was enacted in 1916. People often imagine that working conditions in small mills not covered by the law, which was designed to protect laborers, must have been miserable. In fact, it would seem that conditions were in some ways better than in large mills where workers were protected by the Factory Act. The intensity of work in small mills was less than in the large reeling firms. In these mills, since management had become accustomed to employing a labor force that included married female workers who did not live in the firm, they were also accustomed to allowing absences for family reasons. Moreover, production management and raw silk testing were not as strict as in the larger mills.

During this period of turmoil in the world silk markets, silk for export could still, in general, sell at higher prices than those for the domestic market. Some of the small mills in Suwa tried to shift to production for the export market, improving equipment and using higher grade reelable cocoons. Several of the firms organized associations, and they started to send raw silk to small silk export merchants in Yokohama.

In summary, it can be said that the reason why the subcontracting of small mills became independent of large reeling firms was not because of the development of small mills into large firms. Rather, the relationships that had integrated subcontracting firms in to the overall structure of training of workers became less necessary. Large firms came to train their own reelers. Other factors which influenced the shift to independent status were the enlargement of the domestic raw silk market, the building of a systematized infrastructure which improved the supply of water and power, and expansion in the supply of dried cocoons. Under these changing conditions, it became possible for small reeling mills to survive independently of large reeling firms.

4. The Evolution of Hand-reelers as Subcontractors

In this section we will examine a third style of production, the production of raw silk for the domestic market by hand-reelers. The object of this section is to explain how and why the hand-reeled style of production continued to develop in Suwa after 1910 in spite of the decline of this form of management in the rest of the country.

The hand-reeling machine used in Japan was operated by a reeler who moved the gears by hand. A more advanced form of hand reeling, the treadle reeling machine, was used in China before the modern period, but was not introduced to Japan until the end of the Tokugawa era. After the 1870s, the treadle style reeling-machine, which was more efficient since both the reeler's hands were free to feed the ends, gradually spread throughout Japan. In the Suwa area the improved treadle reeling machine came to displace the older types of hand-held reeling devices. The treadle reeling machine was used together with a simple apparatus for cooking the cocoons which simply used a pan or a pot on a portable clay cooking stove known as a shichirin. The bearings of bicycles were utilized in the moving parts of the reeling machine. As a result of these innovations the hand-reeling machine was much more efficient than those that had been used at the end of the Tokugawa era. After 1900, a former carpenter in Suwa began to produce large numbers of the machines and to market them throughout Nagano Prefecture; eventually he was selling the machines in a nationwide market. In Hirano and neighboring villages, there were ten firms producing the reeling machines in the early 1930s, and at the peak of production they marketed more than 1,000 machines a year. The machine was cheap, selling for 2 to 4 yen. The low cost of the reeling machine made it easy for rural households to purchase the equipment, and this led to a style of organization in which the reeler owned her own reeling equipment, while the merchants supplied the raw materials in the form of substandard cocoons that were not suitable for mechanized filatures. The reelers worked as subcontractors to the cocoon-supplying merchants (Fig. 4.3). The machines were placed in the homes of the workers, either in the dirt-floored entrance room or in a shed under the eaves of the house. Machines were put in these locations because of the smoke that was emitted by the fires used to cook the cocoons.

While most reelers owned their own machine, merchants did rent machines to reelers who did not own them and sometimes the merchants supplied wood for fuel. As for the labor supply, most of the hand-reelers were drawn from the pool of retired and former machine-reeling workers. This pattern of labor supply was similar to that we have seen above for the small reeling mills producing for the domestic market. Many of the reelers in this style of operation were women who had to be at home for family reasons. Needless to say, workers in this style of operation were not covered by the regulations of the Factory Act. Many of the reelers in these small home operations worked from early morning till late at night. Even though hand-reeling is often regarded as relatively light work, the long hours must have induced fatigue since the reeler had to do all parts of the reeling work, including adding wood to the fire, treading the reeling

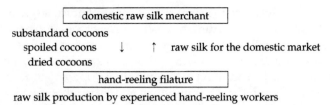

Fig. 4.3. Raw silk reeling by hand-reeling filature.

machine, cooking the cocoons, and reeling the silk. Statistics from Hirano village, which had been urbanized as a result of the development of the silk-reeling industry, suggest that most of the hand-reelers came from the lower classes of what could be considered a town population, rather than from farming families. As we can see from Table 4.8, on the occupation list of the heads of households which included the hand-reelers, are workers in reeling mills, various other kinds of workers, day laborers, and merchants. These data strongly indicate that the income from hand-reeling was an important part of the total income of lower-class families whose heads were apt to lose their jobs, especially during the depression of the 1920s and 1930s.

During the second half of the 1920s, the putting-out merchants organized trade associations in each local production area and made agreements among themselves which were designed to prevent wage competition and the raiding of skilled reelers. They also reached agreements on quality standards, and set up a system of awards for outstanding reelers. The putting-out merchants also tried to maintain stable arrangements with the better reelers by supplying cocoons even during the depression.

As a result of all these conditions, hand-reeled production continued to thrive in Suwa despite the long-term downward trend throughout the rest of Japan. For the whole of Japan, hand-reeled silk reached peak production in 1911, but in Suwa development really took off after 1910. For example, if we look at the case of Hirano village we find that in 1896 the village was reported to have 40 households engaged in hand-reeling, operating 40 basins (one basin per household). In contrast, in 1928 there were 1,107 hand-reelers. About 90 percent of hand-reelers in 1928 were married, and about 80 percent had previously worked in machine-reeling mills. If one assumes that one hand-reeler was engaged per reeling household, this means that one out of every nine households was engaged in the production of hand-reeled silk in Hirano village in that year. In 1930, the number of basins for hand-reeling amounted to one thousand and several hundreds, and the number of the putting-out merchants reached more than one hundred in the three villages of the western Suwa area, that is Hirano, Kawagishi and Minato villages. Using this data, we can see that an average putting-out merchant had about ten basins under contract. From this we can see that the putting-out merchants were generally very small operators. However, there are also accounts of much larger operations. For example, one leading putting-out merchant is reported to have had sub-contract arrangements with about two hundreds basins in 1930. This same merchant had established a branch office outside Suwa and operated a machine-reeling mill in addition to his putting-out operations. Records from the putting-out association of Shimosuwa and its neighborhood show that the number of the putting-out merchants and the number of basins for hand-reeling, far from decreasing, increased throughout the 1930s. This increase in hand-reeling, which continued into the war period paralleled the increase in demand for raw silk in the domestic market (Hirano-mura 1932: 528–37, Shimosuwa-chō 1990: 515–7, Okaya-shi 1971: 709–10).

As we have seen above, a multi-layered, stratified structure in the production of raw silk had emerged in the Suwa region following the development of mechanized filatures after 1910. While the large mechanized filatures produced raw silk for the export market, small reeling mills and hand-reelers also flourished, producing raw silk for the domestic market. Since the market fluctuations which brought depression to the larger silk-reeling mills in the 1930s did not necessarily effect the domestic market, the small mills and hand-reelers continued to prosper even during the depression of the 1930s. These lower strata of producers working for the domestic market also experienced a strong revival in the later 1940s, after the end of the war.

5. Conclusion

The high level of development of the silk-reeling industry in Suwa led to the proliferation of small machine-reeling mills and hand-reeled production creating a symbiotic relationship in which the latter supported the development of large reeling firms through the training of unskilled reelers and the processing of substandard cocoons which the large mills were unwilling to use. Furthermore, the development of the small reeling mills and hand-reeled production units contributed to the revival of the regional economy by offering employment opportunities to retired middle-aged reelers.

Management in these smaller scale units was based on a combination of traditional and modern practices. On the traditional side we can point to a number of elements. For example, middle-class entrepreneurs who wanted to start new businesses but were short of capital could easily take advantage of relationships based on regional and blood ties to raise money. If we turn to examine the technology used in such small scale units, we note that it was primarily improved forms of traditional machinery. Moreover, in the smallest units—the subcontracted hand-reeling sector, the labor force was made up of domestic workers who worked within their own households. As for more modern elements, we have seen how these seemingly traditional forms of managements actually developed and flourished only after the formation and development of large, modern firms and a new-style regional economy. Once this structure was formed, the small managerial units producing for the domestic market continued to prosper, regardless of what was happening to the large modern factories. We should also note that the spread of such modern infrastructure as electrification and waterworks played a role in supporting the development of the small managerial units.

The Suwa case may be just one illustration of the development of a "dual structure" in Japan which was formed against the background of stagnating employment opportunities in the pre-war period. The coexistence of large firms, small mills and domestic industry was possible because of the differences in labor intensity and working conditions between them. Such patterns of coexistence, however, had already appeared during the Meiji period in various sectors. In the silk-reeling industry, these patterns of coexistence were not limited to such famous silk-reeling industrial districts as Suwa, Maebashi and Kofu, but were found more generally in other areas. We can identify similar patterns in many other areas where young female workers were employed in large reeling firms away from home and local female workers were employed in small firms scattered in agricultural districts. This pattern was not restricted to the silk industry. For example, in the copper mining industry, large mines like those at Ashio which drew on a male labor force can be paired with small copper mines scattered throughout rural regions. At the large mines like Ashio wages were higher in exchange for hard labor throughout the year. In the latter, the wages were lower, and employment was often on a seasonal basis, with seasonal work serving as an income supplement for those who engaged in farming throughout the rest of the year. While many of our images of Japan's modern economic history are based on understandings of large firms, we are missing a major part of the story if we neglect these patterns of symbiosis which existed between the larger firms and smaller units including domestic industry.

References

Asahi Shinbunsha [Asahi Newspaper Company] (ed.), *Nippon Keizai Tōkei Sōran* [Handbook on Japanese Economic Statistics] (Tokyo, 1930).

Dai Jūku Ginkō [The Nineteenth Banking Co.], *Seishi Shikin Kashidashi Keikakusho* [The Loan Programmes for Silk-reeling Manufacturers, MSS] (1914–30).

Ebato, Akira, *Sanshigyō-chiiki no Keizaichirigaku-teki Kenkyū* [An Economic-Geographical Study on Sericultural Districts] (Tokyo, 1969).

Hirano, Yasushi, *Kindai Yōsangyō no Hatten to Kumiai Seishi* [The Development of Modern Sericulture and Cooperative Silk-reeling Manufacturing] (Tokyo, 1990).

Hirano-mura [Hirano Village Office], *Hirano-son Shi* [The History of Hirano Village] Vol. 2 (Hirano, 1932).

Imai, Hisao, *Mura no Saijiki* [An Essay on Village Life in the Four Seasons] Vol. 3 (Shimosuwa, 1989).

Ishii, Kanji, *Nihon Sanshigyō Shi Bunseki* [An Analytical History of the Japanese Silk Industry] (Tokyo, 1972).

Kagami, Yasuyuki, *Echigo Jokōshi Saihakken* [Rediscovery of the History of Factory Girls in Niigata Prefecture] (Tokyo, 1997).

Katakura Seishi Bōseki Kabushiki Kaisha [Katakura & Co], *Jūyō Jikō Kiroku* [The Record of Important Matters, MSS] (1927, 1929, 1930a, 1931).

——, *Shochō Kaigi Kankei Zasshorui* [The Documents Concerning the Meetings of Factory Heads, MSS] (1928).

——, *Shochō Kaigi Kiroku* [The Records of the Meeting of Factory Heads, MSS] (1930b).

——, *Son'eki Keisansho* [The Statement of Profit and Loss, MSS] (1936).

——, *Katakura Seishi Bōseki Kabushiki Kaisha 20-nen Shi* [A 20-year History of Katakura & Company] (Tokyo, 1941).

Matsumura, Satoshi, *Senkanki Nippon Sanshigyō Shi Kenkyū* [Katakura & Company and the Japanese Silk Industry in the Interwar Period] (Tokyo, 1992).

Morisugi, Yasutarō, *Seishi no Machi no Suidō Monogatari* [The Story of Waterworks in the Raw Silk Town] (Shimosuwa, 1987).

Nakamura, Takafusa, *Nihon Keizai* [The Japanese Economy] 3rd edn (Tokyo, 1993).

Nippon Ginkō Matsumoto Shiten [Bank of Japan, Matsumoto Branch Office], *Saikin no Seishi Kinyū* [Recent Finances of the Silk-reeling Industry] (Tokyo, 1935).

Nōrinshō [Ministry of Agriculture and Forestry], *Dai 11-ji Zenkoku Seishi Kōjō Chōsa* [The 11th Survey of Silk-reeling Factories] (Tokyo, 1929).

Nōshōmushō [Ministry of Agriculture and Commerce], *Dai 7-ji Zenkoku Seishi Kōjō Chōsahyō* [The 7th Survey of Silk-reeling Factories] (Tokyo, 1916).

——, *Dai 10-ji Zenkoku Seishi Kōjō Chōsa* [The 10th Survey of Silk-reeling Factories] (Tokyo, 1926).

Ohkawa, Kazushi and Hirohisa Kohama, *Keizai Hatten Ron* [The Theory of Economic Development] (Tokyo, 1993).

Okaya-shi [Okaya City Hall], *Okaya-shi Shi* [The History of Okaya City] Vol. 2 (Okaya, 1971).

Piore, M. J. and C. F. Sabel, *The Second Industrial Divide: Possibilities for Prosperity* (New York, 1984).

Sabel, C. and J. Zeitlin, "Historical alternatives to mass production", *Past and Present* 108 (1985), 133–76.

—— (eds), *World of Possibilities*, (Cambridge, 1997).

Shimosuwa-chō [Shimosuwa Town Hall], *Zōtei Shimosuwa-chō Shi* [The History of Shimosuwa Town, rev. edn] Vol. 1 (Shimosuwa, 1985).

——, *Zōtei Shimosuwa-chō Shi* [The History of Shimosuwa Town, rev. edn] Vol. 3 (Shimosuwa, 1990).

Tōjō, Yukihiko, *Seishi Dōmei no Jokō Tōroku Seido* [The Registration System of Female Workers in the Suwa Silk League] (Tokyo, 1990).

Yamato (Kabushiki Kaisha) [Yamato & Co.], *Yamato 100-nen Kaikoroku* [The 100-Year Memoirs of Yamato Company] (Okaya, 1972).

Yokohama-shi [Yokohama City Hall], *Yokohama-shi Shi* [The History of Yokohama City] Vol. 5 No.1 (Yokohama, 1971).

5

Factory Girls in an Agrarian Setting circa 1910

JUN SASAKI

1. Introduction

During the early twentieth century the Japanese local cotton weaving industry experienced remarkable progress: the gross value of annual output increased from 19 million yen in 1903 to 405 million yen in 1919 (Abe 1989: 36–7; Abe 1990: 192). This progress was led by a significant increase in the output of cotton cloth in advanced cotton weaving districts that had introduced power looms after the Russo–Japanese war of 1904–5. These districts included such well-known weaving areas as Sen'nan, Senboku, Chita, Banshū and Enshū. In such advanced cotton weaving districts the clothiers not only organized networks of subcontractors to whom they supplied cotton yarn and from whom they collected cloth, they also had begun to produce cotton cloth in their own power-loom weaving factories. Economic historians usually assume that the introduction of the mechanized factory system marks a major divide in the industrial development process. This shift marks the move from 'domestic industry' to "modern industry". At the same time it is usually assumed that this passage changes household workers into modern blue-collar workers. Do these assumptions apply in the case of the Japanese cotton-weaving districts that had introduced mechanized factory production methods in the 1910s?

This paper tries to answer this question through a case study of the Okada family, one of the clothiers in Banshū, an advanced weaving district in Hyōgo Prefecture during the second decade of the twentieth century. It will focus on the young women weavers, who came from farm households in the neighborhood and who worked in the Okada power loom weaving factory. The paper is based on a set of records kept by the Okada family firm that provide daily records on operations in the factory and on the work records of each of the young women employed in the factory. While we can assume that many small factories and workshops kept such records, very few collections seem to survive. The daily records allow us to examine, at the micro level, the nature of employment in a village weaving factory in the second decade of the twentieth century. While the records concern only one small weaving factory in one weaving district, the information they record allows us to grasp the nature of rural industry in this period and the patterns of work participation among rural workers.

2. Production System in the Banshū Cotton Weaving Industry in the 1910s

Let me begin by providing a sketch of the production system in the Banshū cotton weaving industry of the 1910s.

Banshū, a semi-urban area covering Taka-, Katō- and Kasai-gun in Hyōgo Prefecture (see Map 5.1) had developed as a weaving district specializing in the production of yarn-dyed, narrow-width striped cotton fabrics (shimamomen) during the latter half of the Edo period (1603–1868). Several leading clothiers including the Okada family began to establish their own power loom weaving factories in the 1900s. (For the leading clothiers' cotton weaving businesses including factory management, see Takamura 1974, Kasai 1982, Mori 1982, Abe 1987, and Abe 1989, ch. 5.) Under the leadership of the clothiers, the power looms were widely introduced into Banshū in the period following the end of the Russo–Japanese war.

The commonest form of cotton cloth production by the clothiers in Banshū during the 1910s is illustrated in Fig. 5.1. In the earliest stages, vertically striped cloth (tatejima) was usually produced by power looms while cross-striped cloth (kōshijima) was produced by handlooms or treadle looms. At that time the clothiers produced the vertically striped cloth in their own power loom weaving factories, supplemented by the agent-weavers power loom weaving factories. All cross-striped fabric was produced through the putting-out system.

The clothiers sold the finished goods to cotton cloth merchants in Kyoto and Osaka. As for the raw materials consumed in the weaving process,

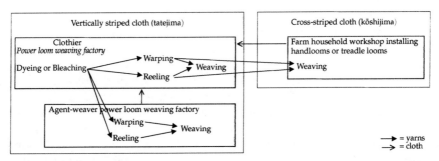

Fig. 5.1. Commonest forms of cotton cloth production by the clothiers in Banshū during the 1910s.

Map 5.1. Banshū, a semi-urban area covering Taka-, Katō- and Kasai-gun in Hyōgo Prefecture (Abe 1989: 208).

the clothiers bought machine-spun cotton yarn produced in domestic spinning mills; the main yarn suppliers were yarn merchants in the Semba area of Osaka. The clothiers dyed (or bleached) the yarn and did the reeling and warping in their own factories.

3. Weaving in the Factory as a Side Job— Residence, Employment Age and Employment Terms

In 1907, the Okada family started to operate its own power loom weaving factory at Hori in Hieshō village located in Taka-gun, which had forty-five workers, seven of whom were male workers (Nōshōmushō [Ministry of Agriculture and Commerce] 1909). (For the establishment of the Okada power loom weaving factory, see Kasai 1982: 133–5.) In this section, after

Table 5.1. Workers classified by their place of birth (residence), February 1914–January 1924

Place of birth (residence)	No. of females	No. of males	No. of total
Hori in Hieshō village located in Taka-gun	25	8	33
Hie in Hieshō village located in Taka-gun	11	0	11
Okuhata in Hieshō village located in Taka-gun	5	1	6
Shimohie in Hieshō village located in Taka-gun	2	0	2
Takashima in Hieshō village located in Taka-gun	2	0	2
Kamihie in Hieshō village located in Taka-gun	1	0	1
Nakahata in Hieshō village located in Taka-gun	1	0	1
Total	47	9	56
Shimotoda in Tsuma village[1] located in Taka-gun	7	0	7
Nishiwaki town in Taka-gun	1	1	2
Nomadani village in Taka-gun	3	0	3
Kurodanoshō village in Taka-gun	2	0	2
Katō-gun	4	1	5[2]
Kuge village in Hikami-gun	2	0	2
Grand Total	66	11	77

Source: Okada MSS; *Shokkō-meibo* (Worker List of Names); Gender, name, date of birth, place of birth (residence), history, and date of first employment & retirement were listed by 77 workers (eleven of whom were men) who had been taken into employment between February 1914 and January 1924.

Notes: [1] Tsuma village was renamed Nishiwaki town on 1 November 1917.
[2] The workers classified by village were as follows: Kishi village: two female workers; Fukuda village: one female worker; Kamifukuda village: one female worker; and unknown: one male worker.

examining the location of residence, employment age and employment terms for workers, including women, I would like to take a closer look at the production of vertically striped cloth by women weavers in the Okada power loom weaving factory from 21 January to 18 March in 1917.

Table 5.1 shows workers, including women, classified by their place of birth (residence). The data includes the place of birth (residence) for seventy-seven workers, of whom seventy were born and lived in Taka-gun. The remaining seven workers were natives of Katō or Hikami-gun, areas neighboring Taka-gun. The figures show that 80 percent of the weavers from Taka-gun came from the village of Hieshō. A breakdown of the data by the seven sub-villages in Hieshō shows that Hori, where the Okada power loom weaving factory was located, headed the list (see Map 5.2).

Of the total number of seventy-seven workers (eleven of whom were men), fifty-six workers (nine of whom were men) commuted to the Okada power loom weaving factory from farm households in the neighborhood, while the remaining twenty-one (two of whom were men) lived in the Okada house (Okada MSS; *Shokkō-meibo* [Worker List of Names]). The

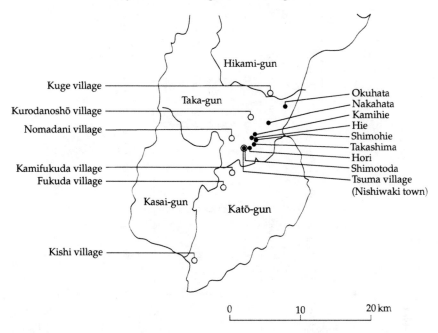

Map 5.2. Place of birth (residence) of workers, February 1914–January 1924.

workers who lived on the premises seem to have come from more distant residences. From this information we can see that most of the workers went back and forth to the factory from their own farm households which were in the neighborhood. A prefectural government survey, undertaken between May and October of 1917, on the side jobs held by members of farm families in the Banshū region suggests that this pattern of work was not peculiar to the Okada power loom weaving factory (Hyōgo-ken Naimu-bu 1919: 649).

Table 5.2 shows the distribution of workers by age at first employment and the number of years they had been employed. The Table shows that all of the workers, except for five female workers whose ages were unknown, fell in the range of nine to thirty-three years of age. Fifty-four workers (nine of whom were men), making up 75 percent of the total work force, were in their teens. Most of these were over twelve years old, the minimum age provided by the Factory Law that was in force in September 1916. The majority of them, twenty-three workers (four of whom were men) had been taken into employment immediately after leaving the ordinary elementary school.

Most of the women weavers, who had begun to work around the age of thirteen years, were engaged in the weaving process which took place after reeling. Since this work required some skill, women who had acquired the skills tended to stay in the factory longer as can be seen by

Table 5.2. Employment age and employment terms of workers, February 1914–January 1924

Employment ages	Age of 9–11		Age of 12–14		Age of 15–19		Age of 23–28		Age of 31–33		unknown		TOTAL	
Employment terms	No. of females	No. of males	No. of females	No. of males	No. of females	No. of males	No. of females	No. of males	No. of females	No. of males	No. of females	No. of males	No. of females	No. of males
Less than one year	0	0	2	1	1	0	1	0	1	0	5	0	10	1
Less than three years	2	0	4	4	3	1	2	0	0	0	0	0	11	5
Less than five years	1	1	7	0	3	0	1	0	0	0	0	0	12	1
Less than seven years	1	0	4	0	1	0	0	1	0	0	0	0	6	1
Less than eight years	1	0	0	0	0	0	0	0	0	0	0	0	1	0
Under employment[1]	2	0	10	1	10	2	1	0	3	0	0	0	26	3
Total	7	1	27	6	18	3	5	1	4	0	5	0	66	11

Source: Same as Table 5.1.

Note: [1] The term "under employment" means that a worker entered the Okada power-loom weaving factory after February 1914 and was employed as of January 1924.

the fact that their employment terms exceeded three years. In contrast, many of the male workers retired within three years, even if they had begun to work around the age of thirteen. There were, however, exceptions to this pattern. For example, one male worker included in the group between 23 and 28 years of age, had been engaged in the warping process for six years and seven months, having first entered the Okada power-loom weaving factory on 10 February 1914. It seems that male workers who had no chance to become weavers tended to work for relatively shorter terms except for those who worked in the warping process which required a longer period of training.

To sum up, during the decade of the 1910s, most of the women weavers who had been taken into employment immediately after leaving elementary school went to the factory from farm households in the neighborhood and specialized in the weaving process.

4. Production of Vertically Striped Cloth

I would now like to consider the production of vertically striped cloth by the women weavers working in the Okada power loom weaving factory from 21 January to 18 March 1917. A close examination of the patterns of work attendance, control of the power-loom operations, payment of wages and patterns of weaving should help us get a better idea of how this style of production should be classified.

4.1. Attendance patterns

Thirty-one women weavers were employed in the Okada power loom weaving factory during the period we will consider. The records from the factory provide information on how many, and which, looms were operating on each shift. Each loom was numbered and they will be referred to by number in this section. The records show which woman was operating which loom on each shift. Ten of the women workers are recorded as operating looms numbered 1–24. Another ten were reported as operating both looms numbered 1–24 and looms numbered 25–44. And a further eleven women were reported as operating looms numbered 25–44. Of these three groups of women workers, we can confirm the number of days worked for women in the first group.

Table 5.3 shows which power loom among those numbered between 1–24 each of the women weavers operated on each weaving day; the original data also makes distinctions between day and night shifts. Table 5.4 shows the number days each woman worked, making a distinction between day and night shifts, and the proportion of night shifts to the total number of weaving days as calculated from Table 5.3.

Table 5.3. Number of power looms each weaver operated from 21 January to 18 March 1917

Date of weaving	Matsu Kotani (18)		Haru Kotani		Koshima Kataoka (17)		Tomie Fujimoto		Tomi Tamada		Masae Toda (16)		Chika Kotani (18)		Fusa Konishi'ike (16)		Yukue Toda (16)		Mie Kobata (20)	
	Day	Night	Day	Night	Day	Night	Day	Night	Day	Night	Day	Night	Day	Night	Day	Night	Day	Night	Day	Night
22 Jan.					16				16							19				
28	13,14	14			16,18	16,18		16,18		7				20	11,12	10				4,6
29	13									8,9				19,21		11				4,5
30	13	13,14,15	13,14,15	15	17,18	17,18		17,18	8,9		8,9			20	11	10,12	3			5
31					16	16	16	16	7	7	7			19		10				4,6
1 Feb.	13,15	13,15	13,15			17	17	17	8,9			8,9		21						
2	14	14	14				18							20	12					4,5
3							18		7		7	7			11	11				
4	13	13	13	13	18	16	16	18	8	8	8	8		19,21	10	10				4,5
5	14,15	14,15	14	14,15	16			16	9	9	9	9	19	20	10	12				6
7									7	7	7	7	21	19	11	11				
8					17										12	10,12				4,5
9	13	13																		
10	14,15	14,15										20								
12														20						5
13	13	13	13	13	18	17,18		17,18		8,9	8,9		19	21	12	11,12	3			4,6
14		14	14	14						7	7		21				1,2	1		
15		15	15	15	16			16					19		11	11		3		
17		13	13	13										20	11	10				
18		14	14	14	18		18		8		8	8	19,21	19	10	12				5,6
19		15	15	15					7,9	7,9	19,21	19,21			12					
20		13,14	13,14	13,14	17	17	17	17	7,9		8		19,21	19			2	2		4
22					16		16			8			20	20,21			1	1		5,6
23		13,14,15	13,14,15	13,14,15		16,17			7,9		20,21			19		10,11,12	2	2		4,5
24										7	19			20			1	1		6
25						18		18			20		20	19,20,21	10,11,12					
1 Mar.	14,15	14,15	14,15	14,15	18	17	18	17	9	8	19,20,21	19,20	19,20,21	19,20,21			3	3		5
2	13	13	13	13	16,17		16,17		7,8		20	20	22	20	10,11,12		2	2		4,6
12	13,14,15	13,14,15	13,14,15	13,14,15	16,17,18	24	16,17,18	16,17,18	8,9	7,8,9	14,19,21	19,20	19,20,21	19,20,21			1,2,3	2,3		5
13	8								10		20		19	20	9	10	1	1		4,6
14	7				7		7			9	19			19			4			
15	13,15										13						1			
																	3			

Source: Okada MSS; *Chingin-uchiwake-chō* (Book of output statistics calculated per numbered power loom); Output statistics calculated between 1–25 power loom were recorded with the name of each of the women weavers assigned on each weaving day, making distinctions between day and night shifts, from 14 January to 18 March 1917.

Note: Figures in parentheses on the right side of the name of each weaver except Haru Kotani, Tomie Fujimoto, and Tomi Tamada are the age as of 1917; this has been calculated from the date of her birth.

Table 5.4. Number of weaving days, 21 January–18 March 1917

Weaver	No. of weaving days (A)	No. of day shifts	No. of night shifts (B)	(B)/(A) (%)
Chika Kotani	24	10	22	91.7
Matsu Kotani	23	21	5	21.7
Tomie Fujimoto	21	14	14	66.7
Haru Kotani	20	5	18	90.0
Tomi Tamada	19	11	12	63.2
Masae Toda	19	15	7	36.8
Mie Kobata	16	0	16	100.0
Fusa Konishi'ike	16	13	12	75.0
Koshima Kataoka	14	9	7	50.0
Yukue Toda	13	11	8	61.5
Average	19	11	12	65.7

Source: Same as Table 5.3.

As we can see from this data, the assignment of women weavers to power looms followed a somewhat regular pattern. Thus, Matsu Kotani and Haru Kotani were usually assigned to looms 13–15, Koshima Kataoka and Tomie Fujimoto to looms 16–18, Tomi Tamada and Masae Toda to looms 7–9, Masae Toda and Chika Kotani to looms 19–21, Fusa Konishi'ike to looms 10–12, Yukue Toda to looms 1–3, and Mie Kobata to looms 4–6 (see Table 5.3).

Four of the women, Chika Kotani, Matsu Kotani, Tomie Fujimoto and Haru Kotani, worked for more than twenty days during the period in question, while the remaining six women worked for less than twenty days (see Table 5.4). The woman who is recorded as working the most days, Chika Kotani, is reported to have worked only twenty-four days. Since the time period covered a total of two months, this seems like an unusually small number of days.

In addition to using the data on assignment to looms, we can also use output statistics to measure performance in the workshop. Output statistics can be calculated per numbered loom. The records show that the ten women who worked on power looms 1–24 produced 2,698 tan 4 shaku[1] of vertically striped cloth during the period, while the ten working on looms both 1–24 and 25–44 produced 2,686 tan 26 shaku, and the eleven who worked on looms 25–44 produced 1,924 tan 20 shaku (Okada MSS; *Orikōchin-meisai-chō* [Book of wages statistics calculated not only per weaver but also per worker engaged in the preparatory process]).[2] Since the output recorded for the two latter groups was less than that of the first, this would suggest that these power looms were in operation for fewer days than the first group. Calculations based on these figures suggest that the number of women weavers actually working each day would be less than the total of thirty-one. One of the questions we must answer then is why the young women were working for so few days. One additional piece of evidence we have about employment patterns is data on the reasons women workers gave for retiring from the factory.

Of the forty women workers who retired before January 1924, we can identify twenty-four whose reasons for leaving the factory were recorded. The list of reasons in the records are as follows: retiring because of family commitments, eleven, including Masae Toda, Mie Kobata and Haru Kotani; retiring in order to marry, six, including Chika Kotani and Koshima Kataoka; transfer to another factory in Taka-gun or Katō-gun, three;[3] voluntary retirement, two; and finally two left the factory as a result of death from diseases.[4] In the cases of the women who left the factory to marry, most had begun to work around the age of thirteen and left to marry around the age of twenty. This pattern is one that was often seen in the case of female by-employment, and the ages for start of work around thirteen and retirement to marry at twenty also follow the patterns that have been seen in other forms of by-employment.

I would like to stress the fact that half of the twenty-four women, who were compelled to retire, did so because of family commitments. First we look at the case of Haru Kotani. Her employment records show that she was dismissed because of family commitments on 13 January 1917, but that she was able to rejoin the Okada power-loom weaving factory and worked for an additional twenty days between that time and 18 March 1917. Absences like hers were most commonly due to the heavy burden of housework, as well as agricultural chores. It seems safe to assume that the "family commitments" that appear so often in the records are references to such household and farm chores, and that these same responsibilities were the main reason why women workers were not able to work more regularly.

4.2. *Control of the power-loom operations*

Given what can only be described as high rates of absenteeism, we need to examine the ways in which the factory was able to deal with the problem of not having operators for all of its looms during every shift. At the time we are considering, the Okada power-loom weaving factory had forty-four Toyoda power looms which were used in the production of vertically striped cottons. The looms were powered by a 12-horsepower gas motor which used coke as a fuel. The looms were all attached to the power source by a system of shaft-and-belt transmissions. Operation of individual power looms could be halted by detaching the power transmission belt which was hooked up to the power loom's crankshaft. Using this system, it was relatively easy to adjust the number of looms to the number of operatives who arrived to work.

4.3. Payment of wages

Weavers' wages for work in the Okada power loom weaving factory were paid on a piece-work basis. Piece wages were adjusted by certain other factors. For example, night shift workers received almost 15 percent more than those working on the day shift. Wages also varied by the type of cloth produced, since some weaves were technically more difficult than others. Records for the time provide the following record of piece wages: Aosujijima, 3.5 sen/tan (day shift) and 4.0 sen/tan (night shift); Mogusa, 2.8 sen/tan (day shift) and 3.2 sen/tan (night shift) (Okada MSS; *Orikōchin-meisai-chō* [Book of wages statistics calculated not only per weaver but also per worker engaged in the preparatory process]). As we will see later, the night shift system had been put into practice at this time in order to ensure the volume of production for vertically striped cloth, and the higher piece-wage rates paid for night shift work do seem to have played a role in encouraging women to work the night shift.

Table 5.5 shows the output, wages and earnings of each of the woman weavers who are mentioned in Tables 5.3 and 5.4. When we examine them together we can get a fuller picture of the working history of individual women weavers. For example, Chika Kotani wove 104 tan 18 shaku of vertically striped cloth during ten day shifts (wages ¥3.590) and 333 tan 20 shaku during twenty-two night shifts (wages ¥12.107), so that she received earnings of ¥15.697 yen which were equal to her total wages. All except Tomi Tamada, Mie Kobata and Fusa Konishi'ike received earnings which were equal to the total of their piece wage payments. In the cases of Tomi, Mie and Fusa it would seem that they had been paid some of their wages in advance,[5] so that they are recorded as having received earnings that were less than the total they had accumulated in piece-wage payments.

As is noted on p. 122, in the Banshū area during the 1910s clothiers like the Okada family also produced cross-striped cloth through the putting-out system. The subcontractors for the cross-striped cloth were workshops operated by farm households that had installed either hand-looms or treadle looms. Most of them were not able to do their own warping work. The Okada family provided the dyed or bleached weft and the pre-set warp ready for weaving, later collecting the finished cloth in exchange for a piece-wage payment (for details, see Sasaki 1991). Piece wages varied, as they did in the production of vertically striped fabrics, according to the difficulty of the weaving process. Thus the production of vertically striped fabric in the power-loom factory and the production of cross-striped fabric in the putting-out system both shared a wage system based on wages calculated according to piece wage rates.

Table 5.5. Output, wages and earnings of weavers, 21 January–18 March 1917

Weaver	Day shifts Output		Wages (¥)	Night shifts Output		Wages (¥)	Total of wages (¥)	Earnings (¥)
Chika Kotani	104 tan	18 shaku	3.590	333 tan	20 shaku	12.107	15.697	15.697
Matsu Kotani	341	26	11.404	74	22	2.387	13.791	13.791
Tomie Fujimoto	116	10	3.771	197	17	6.995	10.766	10.766
Haru Kotani	65	25	1.705	225	17	8.704	10.409	10.409
Tomi Tamada	111	25	3.527	122		4.447	7.974	4.974
Masae Toda	162	28	5.309	62	25	2.027	7.336	7.336
Mie Kobata		0	0	257	23	9.206	9.206	4.206
Fusa Konishi'ike	115	1	3.658	109	22	3.845	7.503	1.503
Koshima Kataoka	73	5	2.078	52	13	1.671	3.749	3.749
Yukue Toda	106	9	3.692	63	17	2.526	6.218	6.218

Source: Okada MSS; *Orikōchin-meisai-chō* (Book of wages statistics calculated not only per weaver but also per worker engaged in the preparatory process).

4.4. Weaving patterns in the Okada power-loom weaving factory

Standard pattern of operation

How did women weavers produce vertically striped cloth in the Okada power loom weaving factory? First, I will examine the standard pattern of operation, in which the woman weaver processed 20 tan of the pre-set warp as a single product unit during a daytime shift. Let us focus on the example of Fujie Kobata, the sixteen-year-old younger sister of Mie Kobata who has already been mentioned. Between 15 March and 25 March 1917, Fujie wove 40 tan of Aosujijima cloth on power loom No. 6. According to the records she received 20 tan of pre-set warp on 15 March. When she finished weaving that portion and turned over the finished cloth on 20 March, she received another 20 tan of pre-set warp. She finished weaving the second 20 tan on 25 March (Okada MSS; *Dai-roku-gō Chin'ori-chō* [Book of processing 20 tan of the pre-set warp on power loom No. 6 during a daytime shift]).[6] From this account we can see that she received pre-set warp in 20 tan lots, and was given the warp for the next loom only after finishing the raw materials she had received earlier. This pattern of operation, in which raw materials for the next production cycle were provided in exchange for the finished goods from the previous production cycle, was a common way of operating in the putting-out system.[7] Moreover, wage systems in the factory, in which women weavers were paid according to the amount of cloth they had finished weaving, also resembled practices in the putting-out industry. That is to say, the production of vertically striped cloth in the factory was organized in ways that were similar to those used in the production of cross-striped fabrics by weavers working in the putting-out industry. When we consider this together with what we have already learned about working days, that is that family commitments often prevented the young women workers from going to the factory every day, we can conclude that the factory functioned almost as a centralized workshop for household workers. The one major difference was the fact that machinery in the factory was powered.

Non-standard pattern of operation

The description given above depicts the usual patterns of work in the Okada power loom weaving factory. However, the records also show examples that do not fit this pattern. I would now like to consider some of these unusual patterns of production. First, I will consider the case where a pair of weavers processed 20 tan of pre-set warp during a double shift. In this case the work of the two women was calculated as a single unit. We can identify four pairs of women weavers who operated power looms between No. 1 and No. 24 between the 21 January and 18 March 1917. The four pairs included Matsu Kotani and Haru Kotani,

Koshima Kataoka and Tomie Fujimoto, Tomi Tamada and Masae Toda
and Masae Toda and Chika Kotani.

As we can see from Table 5.6, there were three different types of double shifts. Type 1 involved a pair of weavers processing 20 tan of pre-set
warp in two continuous shifts. For example, on 28 January, Matsu Kotani
and Haru Kotani worked on power loom No. 13. During the day shift
Matsu Kotani had finished 10 tan 27 shaku of vertically striped cloth,
before turning the loom over to Haru Kotani who finished the remaining
9 tan 2 shaku during the night shift. The cases of the other three pairs of
weavers follow the same pattern, with each pair processing 20 tan in two
successive shifts. The rest of type 1 cases included twenty-two examples
of this pattern. Matsu Kotani and Haru Kotani had followed this pattern
on nine occasions, Koshima Kataoka and Tomie Fujimoto on six occasions,
Tomi Tamada and Masae Toda on five occasions, and Masae Toda and
Chika Kotani on two occasions.

The second style of operation (type 2) involved a pair of weavers processing 20 tan of warp over four shifts (see Table 5.6). While the pattern
seems clear, it is impossible to identify which woman began each cycle.
The pairs of weavers involved in this type of production were Koshima
Kataoka and Tomie Fujimoto, and Tomi Tamada and Masae Toda.

The third type includes cases were a pair of weavers processed the
20 tan unit of cloth in three shifts (see Table 5.6). According to the company records on 28 January, the pair of Matsu Kotani and Haru Kotani
was engaged in this pattern of production. The two women worked on
the No. 14 power loom. Matsu Kotani wove 7 tan 8 shaku during the day
shift and then the two women worked together during the night shift to
finish the remaining 12 tan 21 shaku. The second example of this type
involved the two women Masae Toda and Chika Kotani working on the
No. 20 power loom. The two women, working together during the daytime shift, wove 9 tan 12 shaku, and then Chika Kotani finished off the
remaining 10 tan 17 shaku during the night shift. The remaining examples
in this type included two occasions on which Matsu Kotani and Haru
Kotani worked in this fashion.

We can see other exceptions if we look at the work of Matsu Kotani
and Haru Kotani on 28 January. On that day they wove 20 tan of vertically striped cloth working on power loom No. 13 (type 1) and they also
were weaving on power loom No. 14 (type 3). Matsu had woven 18 tan
6 shaku on power looms No. 13 and No. 14 during the day shift, and
then she continued to work on the night shift finishing off 6 tan 4 shaku
on loom No. 14. It would seem that this night work was to make up for
the shortage of cloth produced on loom No. 14. However, this was an
exception.[8]

Thus the double shift of type 1 was used in the Okada power loom
weaving factory between 21 January and 18 March 1917 as a way to

Table 5.6. Typology of the double shift, 21 January–18 March 1917

Name of girl weaver		Matsu Kotani	Haru Kotani	Koshima Kataoka	Tomie Fujimoto	Tomi Tamada	Masae Toda	Masae Toda	Chika Kotani
Type 1	Day	10 tan 27 shaku	—	9 tan 17 shaku	—	9 tan 23 shaku	—	6 tan 26 shaku	—
	Night	—	9 tan 2 shaku	—	10 tan 12 shaku	—	10 tan 6 shaku	—	13 tan 3 shaku
Date of weaving			28 Jan.		22 Jan.		1 Feb.		24 Feb.
Power Loom Number			No. 13		No.16		No.8		No.19
Type 2	Day			4 tan 2 shaku	1tan 27 shaku	5 tan 5 shaku	3 tan		
	Night			6 tan	8 tan	4 tan 16 shaku	7 tan 8 shaku		
Date of weaving				31 Jan.			8 Feb.		
Power Loom Number				No. 16			No. 7		
Type 3	Day	7 tan 8 shaku	—	10 tan 20 shaku	7 tan 22 shaku			4 tan18 shaku	4 tan 23 shaku
	Night	6 tan 4 shaku	6 tan 17 shaku		1 tan 16 shaku			—	10 tan 17 shaku
Date of weaving		28 Jan.		1 Feb.				23 Feb.	
Power Loom Number		No. 14		No. 17				No. 20	

Source: Same as Table 5.3.

Note: One tan of cloth is 29 shaku.

ensure the prompt completion of vertically striped cloth. Why was the Okada power loom weaving factory in such a rush to complete the weaving? In order to answer this question, we need to consider the data on patterns of sales. During the period under consideration (from 21 January to 18 March 1917), the Okada family sold 10,710 tan of Aosujijima and 4,758 tan of Mogusa to cotton cloth merchants in Kyoto and Osaka (Okada MSS; *Uriage-chō* [Cloth Sales Book]).[9] If we look at the dates on which sales are recorded we can see that the sales of Aosujijima were made on thirteen separate days (January 22, February 17, 22, 25, and 26, and March 5, 9, 11, 13, 15, 16, 17, and 18), and of Mogusa on seven days (January 21 and 30, February 3, 9, 15, and 24 and March 5). As these records make clear, there were frequent sales of cloth. If we compare these sales to the records on total annual sales, we can see that the sales during this period comprised 42.1 percent of the annual total sales of Aosujijima and 24.1 percent of the sales of Mogusa. In other words there was a concentration of sales, particularly of Aosujijima, during this period.

Let us now compare the records for cloth production with cloth sales. Total production figures for Aosujijima between 11 September 1916 and 18 March 1917 was 10,081 tan, while that for Mogusa was 5,223 tan (Okada MSS; *Orikōchin-meisai-chō* [Book of wages statistics calculated not only per weaver but also per worker engaged in the preparatory process]). While the output of Mogusa exceed recorded sales, the Aosujijima shows that sales exceeded production by 600 tan. In order to meet the rising demand for Aosujijima, the Okada family collected 2,766 tan of Aosujijima from one of its sub-contracted weavers, Kojirō Uchibashi, who ran a power loom weaving factory of his own.[10] The collection of cloth was made between 26 December 1916 and 15 March 1917 (Okada MSS; *Shōhin-shiire-chō* [Yarn, Cloth & Dyestuff Stocking Book]).

Under these conditions in which there was a high demand for the Aosujijima cloth, we can imagine that the Okada family was anxious to assure supplies and urged the women to weave as much as possible. However, as we noted above, family obligations often prevented the young women from going to work every day. Thus the Okada family tried to assure supplies by allowing women to work double shifts when they could get time to do so, and by making up shortages through purchases from agent-weavers who had their own small power loom weaving factories.

5. Concluding Remarks

During the decade of the 1910s clothiers in Banshū, a specialized weaving district, produced yarn-dyed, vertically striped cotton cloth. The cloth was produced in factories equipped with power looms. At the same time cross-striped cloth, which was more difficult to weave, was produced by weaving households which were working under the putting-out system for clothiers. As we have seen from the records of the Okada factory, control of production within the power-loom weaving factory was managed in ways very similar to those used in dealing with weaving households working in the putting-out system. Although the Okada factory was mechanized, it seemed to operate almost as if it were a centralized workshop for household weavers. In fact, the young women who worked in the factory had family commitments that prevented them from going to work every day. In other words, the days and hours actually worked by female workers in the factory were still influenced by the labor demand from agriculture and housework, as in the patterns of "domestic production" examined by Tanimoto in the introduction. This type of employment system which used the labor of young women in a rural setting was rational in the sense that by using these methods the factory was able to meet demand for vertically striped cloth, as long at it could be supplemented when there were shortages with cloth produced under the putting-out system. Thus, this evidence from Banshū suggests that the introduction of mechanization into rural factories in the early twentieth century did not mark the major divide that is commonly assumed by economic historians.

Notes

1. The tan is a unit of measure. One tan of cloth is 29 shaku long. The shaku used in this case is the measure known as the Kujira-shaku. One Kujira-shaku is 37.5 cm.
2. Wages statistics calculated not only per weaver but also worker engaged in the preparatory process [dyeing or bleaching, warping, and reeling] were recorded, making distinctions between day and night shifts, from September 1916 to December 1918. Because weavers' wages for work in the Okada power-loom weaving factory were paid on a piece-work basis, we can also get output statistics calculated per weaver.
3. These three female workers were transferred to the Yoshibei Murakami factory in Nishiwaki town in Taka-gun, the Fujimoto weaving factory in Kurodanoshō village in Taka-gun and the Taishō weaving factory in Kamo village in Katō-gun.
4. The names of the diseases responsible for their deaths are not recorded.
5. According to the Okada MSS; *Dai-ni-gō Sho-kanjyō-ruibetsu-bo* (Book of miscellaneous expenses, Vol. 2), women weavers were paid ¥2–5 in advance per month, on the average.
6. We can get output statistics calculated per vertically-striped cloth on power loom No. 6 with the name of each of the women weavers assigned on each weaving day between 3 March 1917 and 25 March 1918.

7. According to the Okada MSS; *Dai-ni-gō Nakamura-meguri-shikake-chō* (Book of *Chinbata* [wage weaver] in Naka Village in Katō-gun, Vol. 2), *Orimono-shikake-chō* (*Chinbata* Book) and *Dashibata-shikake-chō* (*Chinbata* Book), the number of tan of the pre-set warp was not uniform. Examples in which the warp was between 6 and 16 tan are found, but records suggest 20 tan was most common.

8. According to the Okada MSS; *Chingin-uchiwake-chō* (Book of output statistics calculated per numbered power loom), the only other case of this type involved the pair of Matsu Kotani and Haru Kotani on 5 February (type 1 on the No. 15 power loom and type 3 on the No. 14 power loom).

9. The sales of cloth, by type, were recorded as follows: Aosujijima: to Yahei Kaihatsu (Osaka) 4,730 tan, to Ibuki Gōmei Gaisha (Kyoto) 2,310 tan, to Kobayashi Gōmei Gaisha (Osaka) 1, 120 tan, to Genjirō Yai (Osaka) 960 tan, to Chūrobei Tsuji (Kyoto) 800 tan and to Amori Shōten (Kyoto) 790 tan. During the same period, the Okada family sold 4,758 tan of Mogusa to Amori Shōten (Kyoto).

10. Kojirō Uchibashi operated his own power loom weaving factory which had thirteen workers, one of whom was a male worker, at Ochikata in Yoshida village located in Kasai-gun at the end of 1917 (Nōshōmushō [Ministry of Agriculture and Commerce] 1919).

References

Abe, Takeshi, "Senzen-ki nihon ni okeru chihō jigyō-ka no shihon chikuseki" [Capital accumulation of a rural entrepreneur in prewar Japan], *Shakai-kagakukenkyū* (University of Tokyo), 39–4 (1987), 83–111.

——, *Nihon niokeru Sanchi Menorimono-gyō no Tenkai* [The Development of the Producing-center of the Cotton Textile Industry] (Tokyo, 1989).

——, "Men kōgyō" [The Cotton industry], in Nishikawa, Syunsaku and Abe Takeshi (eds), *Nihon Keizaishi 4, Sangyōka no Jidai* (Tokyo, 1990).

Hyōgo-ken Naimu-bu [Hyōgo Prefectural Office, Home Affairs Department], *Fukugyō ni kansuru Chōsa 1* [Survey on sideline work Vol. 1] (Hyōgo, 1919).

Kasai, Yamato, "Men orimono-gyō no hatten to nishiwaki men kōgyō chi'iki no keisei" [The development of the cotton weaving industry and the formation of the Nishiwaki cotton industrial area], *Okayamadaigaku Bungaku-bu Kiyō* 3 (1982), 95–146.

Mori, Yasuhiro, "Banshū ori no jiba sangyō to shite no seiritsu" [The formation of the Banshū cotton weaving industry as a local industry], in Kaneko, Seiji (ed.), *Jibasangyō no Kenkyū: Banshūori no Rekishi to Genjyō* (Kyoto, 1982).

Nōshōmushō [Ministry of Agriculture and Commerce], *Kōjyō Tsūran* [Directory of Japanese Factories] (Tokyo, 1909, 1919).

Ohzumi, Gohachi, *Rikishoku kikōgaku* [Study of the Mechanism of the Power Loom] (Tokyo, 1942).

Sasaki, Jun, "Sanchi men orimono-gyō ni okeru rikishokki dōnyū-go no tonya seido" [The putting-out system after the introduction of the power loom in the cotton weaving districts], *Keizaigaku Zasshi* 91–5 & 6, 92–1 (1991): 110–28: 53–68.

——, "Sanchi men orimono-gyō ni okeru rikishokki dōnyū-go no orimoto jika kōjō seisan" [The role of the power loom in cotton cloth production], *Shakaikeizaishigaku* 59–5 (1994), 32–57.

Takamura, Naosuke, "Banshū men orimono-gyō to kinyū" [The Banshū cotton weaving industry and finance], in Yamaguchi, Kazuo (ed.), *Nihon Sangyō Kinyūshi Kenkyū: Orimono Kinyū Hen* (Tokyo, 1974).

Yokoi, Torao, *Jitsuyō Hataori-hō* [Practical Weaving Method] (Tokyo, 1913).

6

The Humble Origins of Modern Japan's Machine Industry

JUN SUZUKI

1. Introduction

The Japanese machine industry at the end of the nineteenth century consisted of two distinct sectors: several large factories and many artisan workshops. The large factories had their origins in factories established by the early Meiji government, and found markets in such modern industries as ocean shipping, railway, cotton spinning, paper manufacture and electric power production. Most of these factories survive today, and are represented by corporations such as Mitsubishi, Kawasaki and Ishikawajima Harima. Artisan workshops were composed of various types of small scale enterprises, from traditional smith shops that made agricultural tools to workshops in which steam engines were built. However, while professionally trained engineers took the initiative in factories of the first sector, skilled artisans were solely responsible for technical matters in their own shops.

During the nineteenth century, the main machines used in modern industries were imported from Western countries. They were repaired in the large first-sector factories or in workshops belonging to the user industry and gradually the large factories attempted to construct copies. The artisan workshops produced tools and machines for the use of all traditional industries such as agriculture, fishery, silk reeling, weaving, and small collieries.

Japan's economic growth from the Meiji Restoration of 1868 to the First World War was a balanced growth of its modern and traditional industries (Nakamura 1983: 45–136). Because modern industries needed imports, notably iron and steel, raw cotton and machinery, they could not develop without the expansion of exports (Takamura 1975: 43–62). Until the First World War, silk was the number one export item, followed by coal. In this sense, the development of those industries that used machinery made in artisan workshops was essential for Japan's rapid economic expansion in the modern era. On examining China and India in the same period, one finds modern industries and factories of the first sector, but no development or improvement of artisan workshops comparable with Japan. This difference suggests that the broad development of artisan workshops may have been an important factor in the more rapid pace of Japanese economic development.

Despite their obvious importance, there was little research on Japan's artisan workshops until 1972, when Toshiaki Chokki published his study of the power-loom industry, from which the famous automobile manufactures Toyota and Suzuki developed. Only in recent years has the artisan sector of the machine industry attracted significant scholarly interest. For instance, Minoru Sawai published his first study of machine tools in 1981, while Hoshimi Uchida's study of the clock and watch industry appeared in 1985. The author of this essay examined machinery for coal mining in 1989. Together, these scholars have created a general view of the machine industry (Uchida 1989, Sawa 1990, Suzuki 1996). In addition, Kōnosuke Odaka has studied the artisans who appeared in published histories of shipbuilding and machine-making companies (Odaka 1993).

This chapter aims to introduce fruits of recent studies on artisan workshops in modern Japan and clarify the causes and effects of their development. After outlining the principal machines produced in artisan workshops in the late nineteenth and early twentieth centuries, it examines the historical emergence and development of the artisan machine workshops. Finally, it evaluates the role of artisan workshops in the subsequent development of the Japanese machine industry.

2. The Main Products of Artisan Workshops[1]

Artisan workshops provided machines to suit the wishes of the users. Since almost all of the users were small enterprises with low wage labors, they wanted the lower price machine; even though they were less efficient than Western ones. Some representative examples are given in the following.

2.1. *Boilers for silk filatures*

In order to expand exports in the 1880s, it was necessary for the Japanese silk-reeling industry to aim for quality and standardization, as well as simply increasing production. Heating was an important part of the silk-reeling process. The cocoons were first boiled to soften the natural gum that covered the fibre. Then, during the reeling, the cocoons had to be kept at a constant temperature in basins of warm water so that they would not re-coagulate. Since these processes had traditionally taken place over an open fire, the temperature of the water in the basin was unstable. To improve the quality of silk, it was necessary therefore to standardize both the degree of cocoon boiling and to keep the water in the basin at a uniform temperature during reeling. Boilers were developed for these purposes. Steam produced in the boiler was guided by pipes to the basins, where it could be used for boiling and reeling. Work-women operated controlling cocks to let in steam and water, easily maintaining the appropriate temperature in the basin.

In 1872, the government-run filature factory at Tomioka in Gunma Prefecture introduced a French cocoon reeling system that used boilers for engine power and heating (Tomioka Seishijōshi, 1977: 141-3). Soon afterwards, certain managers and entrepreneurs in local silk mills in Gunma and in neighbouring Nagano Prefecture realised the importance of using boilers for heating. Because of the high cost of importing foreign equipment, they asked Japanese casters and coppersmiths to construct similar boilers at lower cost. The Japanese craftsmen used traditional techniques for casting iron and riveting the copper sheets. The final product was not, of course, comparable in quality with the foreign boilers that were designed for high pressure steam engines. However, high-strength boilers were not required for silk reeling because high-pressure steam was not necessary for heating and because the fuel used in the Nagano area was wood rather than coal. Domestic boilers were therefore adequate (Dainihon Sanshikai 1937: 940-1, 966-70). Moreover, because domestic boilers cost less than one-twentieth the price of imported models,[2] they diffused rapidly: in 1879 more than 150 filatures in Nagano Prefecture used boilers. Since the largest boiler made by the craftsmen in this area could supply steam for no more than 30 reelers, large filatures purchased Western-style, mainly Cornish, boilers from ironworks in Tokyo and Yokohama (Nagano-ken 1879).

A new thin-plate boiler was invented in 1879 by Yasaburō Maruyama, a manufacturer of iron and brass goods who lived in the former castle town of Matsumoto, in Nagano Prefecture. Maruyama had made many cast iron boilers for local filatures but at the request of local filatures and with their financial support, he set about developing an improved model. After four years and five failed attempts, he successfully developed a thin plate boiler. It was structurally modeled after the Cornish boiler, but the iron plate was only 1/8 inch, thinner than that of Western boilers. Maruyama's thin-plate boiler proved to be more efficient than the cast-iron boiler and it could be used in larger filatures, despite the relatively low cost. Maruyama manufactured 165 thin-plate boilers from 1879 to 1882 (Maruyama 1875-84). In 1882, a total of 383 filatures in Nagano Prefecture used boilers.

Because the diameter of the thin-plate boiler was limited by the thinness of the outer plate, its capacity was restricted to about 60 reelers. Since the boiler was cylindrical, the capacity could be expanding by extending the length of the boiler. Nevertheless, because the diameter of the inner cylinder, in which the fuel burned and the heated air flowed to the funnel was limited, a long boiler could not transmit sufficient heat to boil the water inside. By 1886, Maruyama and his competitors had developed new thin-plate boilers to overcome this limitation. A combination of the Cornish boiler and the multi-tube boiler, the new model used fire tubes to increase the efficiency of heating water, making it possible to double the length of the boiler.

By the late 1880s, growth in the silk-reeling industry had accelerated, and some skilled craftsmen trained in Tokyo and Yokohama factories opened workshops in Suwa, the centre of silk reeling in Nagano Prefecture (Okaya-shi 1976: 317–19). In the 1890s, Maruyama and one of the new makers used 1/4 inch plate to construct the largest boiler demanded in the area, one that could service 220 reelers (Maruyama 1884–91, Kawagishi-mura, 1953: 186–290). At the same time, some filatures began to use steam engines instead of water wheels and coal instead of wood. These new filatures needed Western-style boilers, which were manufactured by Maruyama and by some other workshops in Nagano Prefecture.

The cast iron boiler, the thin-plate boiler and the combination Cornish and multi-tube boiler were unique to the Nagano region. From 1874 to the 1890s, filatures in Nagano Prefecture were able to obtain boilers at roughly one-fifth of the price asked to filatures in The Fukushima Prefecture, which was the other traditional producing center of raw silk (Fukushima-ken 1966: 335). The development of the boiler manufacturing industry was an important condition for the growth of silk reeling industry in Nagano Prefecture and its environs.

2.2. Machinery for coal mining

Machinery for coal mining was manufactured by the Ministry of Public Works from 1875 (Koubushō 1875). The Ministry's products were higher in cost and lower in quality than those made in Western countries or in the foreign-managed ironworks in the treaty ports of China and Japan, being used only in the collieries managed by that Ministry. The successive managers of those mines, Shōjirō Gotō at Takashima coal mine began to purchase machinery from foreign countries or the foreign-managed iron works in Nagasaki in 1874 (Mitsubishi-gōshi 1922: 1178–80), and the Ministry of Finance at Miike coal mine imported primary machines from 1886 onwards.

By the end of the nineteenth century, high-quality machines imported from the West were used at Miike, Japan's largest coal mine, and simple steam-powered machines were widely used in the Chikuhō coalfields of northern Kyūshū (Fukuoka Prefecture). At that time, more than half of the coal mined in Japan came from the Chikuhō coalfields. Because the subterranean coal seam at Chikuhō was distributed across a plain and near a river, the mechanization of drainage was essential to expand production. A donkey pump and boiler were introduced into Chikuhō in 1875, but the first successful steam machines were two Cameron Special pumps and a boiler, used from 1880 (Nōgata Tekkō 1981: 32–5). Thereafter, the Cameron Special, which was a direct acting pump located underground, and a winding machine became standard machinery for private collieries in Chikuhō. By 1897, as many as 672 Special pumps and 99 winding machines were in use (Takanoe 1898).

The machinery used in Chikuhō came from various makers. Most prominent at the end of the 1880s was Kamejirō Kawano, who was based in Kobe. When Takichi Asoh, a Chikuhō mine owner, gathered quotations for Cornish boilers in 1886, Kawano set his price at 828 yen, compared with the 1,895 yen level of the national shipyard in Kobe (Asō 1887). For the next several years, Kawano sold Asoh all sorts of mine-related machinery: boilers, winding machines, pumps, engines and a lathe.

But Kawano's monopoly did not last. In 1890, the Fukushima Ironworks, a rival workshop in Chikuhō, charged 300 yen for a Cameron Special with a 12-inch diameter steam cylinder, while Kawano charged 380 yen for the same item (Asō Kasamatsu-Kou Jimusho 1890). Lower prices were possible because of the emergence of local manufacturers who supplied simple, small machinery. Workshops in Chikuhō were so small that winding machines were not made there, but were supplied by workshops in Kobe and in the castle towns of northern Kyūshū. In 1888, a 12-inch pump imported from England was quoted at 615 yen by a trading company in Nagasaki (Asō Namazuda-Kou Jimusho 1888). Because of the relatively high cost, very little foreign-made machinery was imported into Chikuhō.

In the mid-1890s, some colliery owners in Chikuhō jointly invested in the establishment of a workshop named Kōbukuro Factory. The factory employed a full time engineer graduated from Tokyo Kōgyō Gakkō [Tokyo Technical College] and the engineer sometimes was helped by his schoolmates belonging nearby collieries (Nakano 1982: 103). They designed and produced winding machines, high-grade boilers, and improved pumps. Some Chikuhō owners continued to buy general machines such as boilers and tool machines from companies in big cities, and the largest winding machines were imported from England. However, almost all other necessary machinery was made and supplied locally. This system was unchanged until the introduction of electric machinery and steel in the twentieth century.

2.3. Power looms for traditional weavers

Japanese traditional cloth was narrower than the Western equivalent, measuring about 30–40 cm.[3] From 1885, Western power looms were imported into Japan, and were used mainly by the large companies integrating spinning and weaving. But the imported looms wove only the wider cloth, which had a limited market in Japan. As a result, most domestic-use cloth was woven on wooden hand looms. Many people tried to develop a narrow power loom in the style of the imported wide machines, and the first successful result was obtained in 1897 by Sakichi Toyoda. Since, however, Toyoda's power loom could weave only white cotton (*shiromomen*), efforts continued in traditional weaving areas to produce wooden narrow power looms suitable for local cotton stripes (*shimamomen*) and other cloth. At this time, cloth with a single weft was woven by power looms, while hand looms were used for cloth having several wefts. Following the Russo–Japanese war in 1904–5, Toyoda's improved looms were used in many cotton weaving areas, although cheaper imitations and locally-made looms more suited to local conditions were also used. Toyoda looms were made in Nagoya; other power looms for cotton cloth were made in Hiroshima, Osaka, Nagoya and Hamamatsu (Minami, Ishii, Makino, 1982: 334–59).

Habutae (plain silk cloth), was an important export item. The first power loom for silk cloth was invented in 1898 by Toichi Saito at Tsuruoka, an important silk-weaving area in Yamagata Prefecture, known as the Saito type loom. Different from the cities where power looms for cotton weaving were manufactured, there was no machine making shop in Tsuruoka until a blacksmith shop established in Tokugawa era purchased machine tools and provided iron parts of power looms in 1906. Yonekichi Hirata, the other loom maker of the town, hired skilled artisans from Tokyo and opened his machine shop in 1907 (Tsuruoka-shi 1975: 488–91). These loom inventors could provide funds for purchasing machine tools or even for establishing machine shops, as Saito was a big landowner meanwhile Hirata was a representative Habutae trader of this area.

Nationwide, a total of 20,000 power looms were in use by 1906, increasing rapidly to 120,000 in 1914. Most of the new looms were domestically made: 20,000 for Habutae, and almost all of the remainder for narrow cotton cloth (Nōshōmushō 1916: 218–259).

2.4. Internal combustion engines

Internal combustion engines were first made in Japan in 1895, when a petroleum engine was constructed at Tokyo Technical College and another was produced at a private ironworks located in Tokyo. Following the Russo–Japanese war, many artisan workshops and ironworks made internal combustion engines, which by 1907 were used at 2,629 sites, excluding mines and ships. More than half of the sites were rice and flour mills; in addition, there were 472 machine shops and 425 textile mills (Nanboku Sekiyu 1908). In the 1910s, the number of internal combustion engines used on land decreased because of the rapid spread of electric motors, whereas the number used on fishing boats increased to 2,073 by 1914 (Makino 1989). In most cases engines were made in artisan workshops located near users (Nōshōmushō 1913, Wada 1913). With the exception of Niigata Ironworks, which developed from a workshop attached to an oil driller, none of the big factories belonging to the first sector of the machine industry manufactured internal combustion engines (Yamashita 1934: 167–71). Reflecting the expansion of higher technical education, a few artisans produced large or higher-quality engines under the guidance of technical school graduates.

2.5. Machine tools

In 1903, a report issued by the Ministry of Finance stated that most machine tools used in the second sector of the Japanese machine industry were made domestically, by seven large manufacturers and many small ones based in Osaka (Ishii 1976: 178). For these Osaka workshops, China was an important market as well as Japan. Cotton gins were manufactured in Osaka from 1884 or 1885 and exported to China from 1887. In 1903, some machine tools made in Osaka were exported to Shanghai for use in repair shops that serviced cotton gins (Sawai 1999: 118). Machine tools were also produced in Tokyo. Artisan workshops in Osaka and Tokyo produced a variety of tools on demand, responding flexibly with the cooperation of fellow traders (Sawai 1990: 239–53).

From the 1910s, Nagaoka, too, became a production centre for machine tools. Nagaoka was a former castle town located near the oil fields of Niigata Prefecture, and from the late 1880s, some artisan workshops in the city began making machinery and instruments for oil mining. Some of the workshops also made machine tools in response to increased demand during the First World War (Sawai 1981: 53–4).

3. The Factors of Artisan Workshops' Development

Artisan workshops were not peculiar to the modern era. In the pre-modern era, artisans tried not only to succeed in their fathers' shops but also to open their own new shops, notwithstanding the restrictions imposed by the guilds or trade associations (Endō 1985, P4: 86–7). Thus, the number of shops increased rapidly and their technical level became higher from the end of pre-modern era.

3.1. Arms manufacture in the late Tokugawa period

The consumption of iron in Japan between 1886 and 1890 is estimated to have averaged 2.7 kg per person a year. This figure represented about one-fiftieth of British consumption in the same period and one-fifth of British consumption one hundred years earlier (Nōshōmushō 1918: 18). Japanese output of metal goods before the industrial revolution was clearly smaller than that of Britain. Before the first half of the nineteenth century, only a few cannon were cast in Japan and cast-iron stoves were not in use. Indeed the main products of pre-industrial Japanese foundries were pans. Some clocks and simple locks were made by hand without the use of machine tools. In that sense, Japanese people had little preparation for machine making because of their scant experience in casting large objects and their lack of experience in using machine tools.

In 1853, Commodore Matthew Perry arrived in Japan with four American warships and pressed the Tokugawa Bakufu to open the country. The Bakufu and some major daimyō (feudal lords) had in fact already started to expand their armaments. But the shock of Perry's arrival led to a full-scale arms reinforcement, especially using Western-style weapons. More than twenty daimyō established arsenals in their domains (Suzuki 1996: 15–34). In 1857, the Bakufu established the Nagasaki Ironworks with the assistance of the Dutch Navy; the first imported machine tools for metalwork were used in this factory. In 1864, the Bakufu started construction of the Yokosuka Dockyard with the help of the French Navy; work continued under the Meiji government and Japan's first dry dock opened in 1871.

Most of the arsenals established by the daimyō consisted of foundries for making cannon or factories where gunsmiths worked by division of labor to make guns. Some arsenals were equipped with machine tools. Skilled mechanics were hired from Bakufu factories and the domain's own craftsmen were sent to Bakufu factories to learn how to use machine tools. Most arsenals used somewhat advanced techniques because traditional methods were inadequate for making big cannon or large quantities of Western-style small arms. For example, the spring in a flintlock was stronger than that used in an old-style matchlock. While matchlock springs were made of brass, flintlock springs had to be made of steel; traditional gunsmiths were called in to hammer them out (Kōshaku Shimazuke 1927: 849–50).

The efforts of the Bakufu and daimyō to make advanced weapons in their domains were extraordinarily expensive, and became a major cause of their fiscal crises. Since, however, the Bakufu's mandate included the defence of the entire Japanese nation and daimyō had to support the Bakufu militarily, both Bakufu and daimyō were obliged to build up their armaments despite the financial burden. In 1871, the daimyō domains were abolished and regional armies were integrated under a centralized Meiji government. The Meiji government continued the arsenal, ironworks and dockyard projects of the Bakufu and established a new arsenal at Osaka (Koyama 1972: 64–70). However, it abolished most of the daimyō-established arsenals and discharged many workers, including skilled machine-tool operators as well as artisans who had acquired slightly more advanced skills than traditional artisans.

Some of the discharged workers got jobs in the ironworks run by foreigners in Yokohama, where they could improve their skills in using machine tools. In the following years, some of them moved to Tokyo to open their own workshops, forming the first generation of entrepreneurs in the machine industry (Odaka 1993: 64–6). Most of the discharged workers, however, returned to traditional jobs, waiting for an opportunity to use the skills they had learned in the arsenals.

3.2. The Ministry of Public Works

By the late 1870s the numbers of ironworks run by foreigners declined because those run by the Ministry of Public Works could meet most government needs. The Ministry tried to make all kinds of necessary machinery including pumps, agricultural machines, iron fences, wooden steamers and spinning machines. Despite efforts to keep costs at reasonable levels, the outlay for building large steamers and spinning machinery exceeded expectations. Losses incurred in making such machines were important factors in forcing the government to privatize its factories and in 1885 to abolish the Ministry of Public Works (Nakanishi 1983: 616–20).

However, the Ministry's efforts made it possible to train craftsmen in the new technologies. In 1888, Moriaki Yasunaga, a graduate of the Imperial College of Engineering, reported on the Ministry's Akabane factory of a few years before as follows: "Not a few of its artisans became sufficiently skilled to make a simple steam engine" (Yasunaga 1888: 787). While the munitions works at the end of the Tokugawa period trained artisans as mechanics on the eve of the industrial revolution, the enterprises of the Ministry of Public Works trained artisans as mechanics who could make steam engines and other simple machines necessary for Japan's industrial revolution. Many artisans were trained because the foreign ironworks, the Meiji government arsenals and a few privatized factories played similar roles in the same age. Afterwards, the Ministry's factories offered a comparatively various and large number of jobs to artisans. These artisans promoted the development of machine-making workshops. For example, Akabane factory manufactured the Cameron Special pump before 1881 (Akabane 1881: 13), which became standard product of artisan workshops few years later. Besides Yasaburō Maruyama, boiler maker in Matsumoto visited the factory in 1882 to study new technique (Maruyama 1882).

3.3. The emergence of artisan workshops

Artisan workshops in the machine industry were established wherever there was demand. Three types can be identified, according to location.

The first was workshops established in large cities where the government factories had operated. Beginning with 1873, when artisans formerly employed in a government shipyard founded their own workshop in Nagasaki (Nakanishi 1883: 378), other artisans experienced in government establishments set up shops in the 1870s. Some traditional workshops began to make machines with the assistance of highly trained artisans.

The second type of machinery workshop could be found in some former castle towns. During the 1870s and 1880s, some local entrepreneurs and government officials requested artisans who had experience in weapons factories and now owned traditional workshops to make or repair machinery for filatures and other new factories. Funds were usually made available so that artisans could travel to large cities to purchase machine tools and learn how to use them. For an example, at Yonezawa, a former castle town in Yamagata Prefecture, a filature, invested by the former daimyō, financed the traditional foundry of Seibei Suzuki to purchase a lathe. Afterwards, Suzuki's foundry became the first machine-making shop in that area and manufactured pumps for fire brigade and power looms (Yonezawashi 1987: 124).

The third type of machinery workshop was in other towns or villages, such as Suwa or Chikuhō, where machine experts were needed. From the latter half of the 1880s, local entrepreneurs in such towns requested skilled artisans to establish workshops that could service their factories and mines. Some of the artisans who responded were born locally; others were acquaintances of the town elite; and still others were journeymen who happened to settle in the town. After the establishment of the earliest workshops, information about the demand for skilled artisans was transmitted through the networks of artisans and journeymen. If profits seemed likely, artisans might move to a given area to open workshops (Okaya-shi 1976: 317–19, Nōgata Tekkō 1981: 34, 35, 67). Employed artisans tended to open their own workshops where possible.

Workers in artisan shops can be classified in three categories. The first category comprised family members of the owner. Almost all shop owners were skilled artisans, whose wives assisted them with incidental jobs and occasionally with shop management or customer dealings (Nishiyama 1997: 412–19, Kubotatekkō 1970: 15). In many cases, the brothers of the owners also had important roles. Since they were also skilled artisans, they customarily gained experience through apprenticeships as journeymen in different workshops or different of businesses. They supported the workshop owners with their different skills (Miyata Seisakusho 1959: 1–6, Ikegai Tekkōsho 1943: 3–5).

The second category of workers was skilled artisans. Most worked as journeymen. Large factories had a system of artisan probation, training unskilled young men on the job with virtually no pay for several years. But training was so inadequate because of the shortage of responsible trainers, that most probationers moved to other factories and workshops during or soon after their training (Naitō 1962: 57–63). At the same time, many ordinary artisans came to the factories from workshops. Most had carried out their apprenticeships in traditional smiths or foundries, and had to journey to other workshops, factories, and arsenals to learn higher-level techniques including the use of modern machine tools (Hata 1958: 40–54). Moreover highly skilled artisans of large factories might move to workshops to improve their skills in a different environment or learn workshop management. Sometimes they brought new techniques or exercised considerable influence on the products and management of the workshop (Nishiyama 1997: 228–62). Though the journeying of artisans was traditional practice from the Middle Ages in Japan (Endō 1985, P4: 60–2), it became more important in the Meijiera as learning techniques increased.

The third category of shop workers was resident apprentices. While large factories hired laborers for simple tasks, workshops used apprentices to clean up the work area and sometimes even the owner's house. Apprentices also operated the wheels that supplied power to machine tools, and gradually learned to assist in other work. From the owners' point of view, apprentices were more economical than ordinary laborers, because they received no compensation beyond what was necessary for daily living (Nishiyama 1997: 407–12).

In the countryside, apprentices came from nearby towns and villages (Asō 1897). In large cities, however, they were drawn not only from nearby locations but also from the birthplaces of the shop owner or customers. In fact, using connections to obtain an apprenticeship was a common way for young men to move from the countryside to the large cities.

3.4. War and Artisans

The Sino–Japanese war of 1894–5 and the Russo–Japanese war of 1904–5 caused an increase in the number of workers in the machine industry. Moreover, irregular employment encouraged the practice of journeying. During wartime, military authorities not only expanded the scale of arsenals but also increased demand for war supplies from the private sector. At first, war encouraged the movement of craftsmen, primarily from the private sector to the military sector. A secondary flow came from rural districts to large cities, since most orders for war supplies went to private factories operating there. According to the Statists Reports of prefectural government, workers in the machine and iron goods industries increased from 5,676 in Osaka at the end of 1901 to 9,825 in 1904. In Nogata, the largest machine-making town in the Chikuhō coalfields, the number decreased from 334 to 112 in the same period.

Since military authorities demanded advanced technology for quality control and offered guidance, wartime offered a golden opportunity to improve the techniques of artisan workshops (Ōe 1976: 408–11). After the Russo–Japanese war, when the number of workmen in military factories, which produced all of the homemade weapons and more than half of the warships in Meiji Japan, declined from 91, 922 at the end of 1905 to 65,068 in 1909 (Nōshōmushō 1907: 300–3; 1911: 336–7). Many unemployed artisans, who had amassed considerable capital from wages earned during the war, began looking for an opportunity to establish their own workshops. Moreover, the improved technology and the machine tools developed for military use were diverted to civil use. Factories were active in developing new products, including advanced internal combustion engines and strong iron parts for power looms (Suzuki 1996: 224–6, 268–9).

3.5. School education and emergence of new-type factories

In the first half of the Meiji era, artisan workshops depended entirely on the skill level of individual workers. Professionally trained engineers were hired by just a few large factories. The first schools to exert an influence through education on artisan training were the night schools, established since 1887, where some artisans learned how to draw machine plans and secured the basic knowledge for further self-education. Subsequently, some educated artisans began to make improved machinery in their own shops. For example, in 1905 the Ikegai Ironworks, managed by Shōtarō Ikegai who had studied at night school, made Japan's first accurately measured lathe under the guidance of an American engineer who had worked at Platt and Whitney Co. and was currently employed at the Tokyo Technical College (Ikegai Tekkōsho 1941: 70–3).

Accumulated graduates of engineering departments in imperial universities and technical colleges increased from about 100 in 1894 to over 1,000 in 1909. So many graduates were produced in this era that some sought employment at privately owned machine factories (Uchida 1978a, 1978b). Shōtarō Ikegai invited a Tokyo technical college graduate to his enterprise as son-in-law in 1907, and began to manufacture oil-engines and lathes with interchangeable parts (Ikegai Tekkōsho 1943: 97–9). Besides, Sakichi Toyoda hired two Imperial University graduates in 1905 and built a new factory in 1907 under the guidance of the above-mentioned American engineer W. C. A. Francis. In this factory, Toyoda succeeded in manufacturing the iron loom with interchangeable parts, the first in Japan. Some other graduates opened their own factories or were hired by the mining companies represented by Hitachi, which intended to extend machine repair section as machine-making factory (Uchida 1989: 252–70). Workshops like Toyoda, Ikegai and Hitachi and some other factories with professionally trained engineers in those days could be called medium-sized factories.

While artisan workshops made machinery for users who could not afford the cost of imported items or who had specific, out-of-the-ordinary demands, shops managed by professionally trained engineers were able to produce machines that could actually replace the imported models.

The emergence of medium-sized factories in the 1910s eliminated the gap between the two sectors of machine industry because both modern and traditional industries used machinery manufactured in these factories. While some medium-sized factories were newly established in the form of companies, such as Tobata Imono (the origins of Nissan) and Osaka Hatsudōki Seizō (Daihatsu), and arose from workshops belonging to mines, artisan workshops also developed into medium-sized factories. But most artisan workshops stayed small. After the First World War, some of these workshops became subcontractors of large factories, while others continued to manufacture tools and machines for traditional industries.

4. Conclusion

The broad development of artisan workshops was a result of rapid change in Japanese political and military conditions. In the mid-nineteenth century, the need for defence against Western countries stimulated the development of military manufacturing. After the Meiji Restoration, the new government managed Western-style factories in order to speed up commercial and industrial development, and to display the fruits of Japanese civilisation to the nation and the world. Two military campaigns, which allowed Japan to advance into, and protect profits, in Korea and China, encouraged the development of the machine industry. All these factors helped to increase artisan skills and numbers. However, it was short-lived and accordingly, artisans had to set out to seek work daily on their own. Under these circumstances, the traditional pattern of artisans, journeying and setting up their own businesses, expanded and supported the development of artisan workshops.

Meanwhile, the Meiji government guaranteed freedom of economic activity and promoted business by spreading new information on foreign trade and domestic industries and advancing compulsory education and a national banking system. Many rural elite families accepted the building of new structures, actively initiated new businesses and improved traditional industries. These activities produced a large demand for artisans while at the same time the existence of artisans all over the country made the activities possible. Some might emphasize the high level of skilled traditional artisans but there is no clear evidence that the skill of traditional artisans in Japan was higher than that of their Chinese counterparts. The social changes mentioned above were the main factor that produced the particular characteristics of Japan in this period.

Artisan workshops in the Meiji era contributed to the development of Japan's modern machine industry in two ways. The first contribution was in the training of mechanics. Many large factories were established during the First World War because it became difficult to import machinery. Ships became a principal export and other machines were produced domestically for the first time. A survey conducted in October 1917 showed a total of 52,000 workers employed in newly established factories that manufactured machinery and instruments. Of these, 46.7 percent had transferred from other shops in the same industry, more than double the 21.8 percent figure found in the chemical industry (Uchida 1989: 271). Artisan workshops were located all over Japan and trained apprentices who were a potential supply of skilled labor for the new factories. The broad national development of artisan workshops allowed rapid expansion of the machine industry.

The second contribution of artisan workshops was in the preparation of markets for advanced modern factories. In the 1910s, Toyoda and Ikegai began to manufacture broad power looms and marine internal combustion engines with interchangeable parts. The main markets for these machines were medium-sized weavers and fishermen who had accumulated their capital by making use of narrow power looms and simple fishing boats with humble engines. In both cases former machines were made in artisan workshops.

Notes

1. The following paragraphs on boilers for silk filatures, machinery for coal mining, power looms for traditional weavers, and internal combustion engines are summary of Suzuki (1996). This book is summarized in English as Suzuki (1999).
2. The model filature of Nagano Prefecture imported a boiler for 2,236 yen in 1877 (Dainihon Sanshi-kai Shinano-shikai 1937: 410). It was used for heating basins of 40 reelers. So it cost 56 yen for one reeler. In the same year a filature in Suwa purchased a boiler made by cast iron for 55 yen, included the pipings (Takagi 1969: 113). The filature had 20 reelers, then it cost one twentieth for a reeler.
3. The kinds of Japanese cloth of those days are explained in English by Uchida 1988.

References

Akabane Engineering Works, *Illustrated Catalogue of Engines, Boilers, Machinery Tools etc.* (Tokyo, 1881).

Asō, Takichi, "Namazuda kouzan shokikai ni kannsuru shorui-dome" [Documents on machinery of Namazuda Colliery from January 1887] file M21-19, Asō Archives, Research Center for Coal Mining Materials, Kyushu University.

Asō Namazuda-kou Jimusho, "Kikai ni kannsuru shorui-dome" [Documents on machiney from January 1888] file M21-23, Asō Archives, Research Center for Coal Mining Materials, Kyushu University.

Asō Kasamatsu-kou Jimusho, "Meiji 23 nen bun kikaikankei shorui-tome" [Documents on machinery in 1890] file Kasamatsu A-8, Asō Archives, Research Center for Coal Mining Materials, Kyushu University.

Asō Yoshio Seikōsho, "Yakuin shokuin koin meibo, Meiji 30 nen 12 gatsu sei" [A list of officials, staffs and workers from Dec. 1897] file M32B-15, Asō Archives, Research Center for Coal Mining Materials, Kyushu University.

Chokki, Toshiaki, "Meiji taishō-ki no sangyō-kikai—shokki" [Manufacturing of industrial machine during the Meiji and Taisho period: mainly on loom-building], *Keiei Shigaku 7–1* (1972): 44–61.

Dainihon Sanshikai Sinanoshikai, *Shinano Sanshigyōshi Seishihen* [A History of Silk Industry in Shinano—the volume on silk reeling] (Nagano 1937).

Endō, Motoo, *Nihon Shokuninshi no Kenkyū IV* [A study on Artisan History Japan Pt 4] (Tokyo, 1985).

Fukushima-ken, *Fukushimakenshi* 12 [The History of Fukushima Prefecture Pt 12] (Fukushima, 1966).

Hata, Kouichi, *Tōyōkōgyō to Matsuda Shigejirō* [Tōyō Industry Co. and Matsuda Shigejirō] (Hiroshima, 1958).

Ikegai Tekkōsho, *Ikegai Tekkōsho 50 nenshi* [A 50-year History of Ikegai Ironworks] (Tokyo, 1941).

——, *Ikegai Kishirō Tsuisōroku* [Reminiscences of Mr. Ikegai Kishirō] (Tokyo, 1943).

Ishii Kanji, *Nihon Keizaishi* [The Economic History of Japan] (Tokyo, 1976).

Kawagishi-mura, *Kawagishi-sonshi* [A History of Kawagishi Village] (Kawagishi, 1953).

Kōshaku Shimazuke Hensansho, *Sappan Kaigun Shi Chū* [The History of Satsuma Navy Pt 2] (Tokyo, 1927).

Kōbushō "Kōbushō Kōkajō 8" [The half year report of the Ministry of Public Works No. 8] 1875, National Archive of Japan.

Koyama, Hirotake, *Nihon Gunjikōgyō no Shiteki Bunseki* [A Historical Analysis on Japanese Munitions Industry] (Tokyo, 1972).

Kubotatekkō Kabusikikaisha [Co. Ltd.], *Kubota Tekkō 80 nen no Ayumi* [A 80-year History of Kubota Ironworks] (Osaka, 1970).

Makino, Fumio "Nihon gyogyō ni okeru gijutsu shinpo (1905–40 nen)—Gyosen douryokuka no keizai bunseki" [Technological progress in the Japanese fishing industry before the Second World War: an economical analysis of mechanization of fishing boats], *Gijutsu to Bunmei* 5–1 (1989), 47–64.

Maruyama, Yasaburō, "Chūmon seizō namae hikae" [The List of ordered manufacturing] 1875–1884, Maruyama House Archive, Shiojiri, Nagano Prefecture.

——, "Gobasho haiken negai" [An application for visiting Akabane factory] Jan.1882, ibid.

——, "Kanamono seizō Touzachō" [The temporary list of iron goods manufacturing] 1884–91, ibid.

Mitsubishi-gōshi, *Mitsubishi Shashi: Shodai shachō jidai* [The History of Mitsubishi-sha: the first President's era] 1922, Mitsubishi Archives.

Minami, Ryōshin, Ishii, Tadashi, and Makino, Fumio "Gijutsu fukyū no shojōken: Rikishokki no baai" [Conditions for Technological diffusion: Case study for power looms], *Keizai Kenkyū* 33–4 (1982), 334–59.

Miyata Seisakusho, *Miyata Seisakusho 70 nen-shi* [A 70-year History of the Miyata Factory] (Tokyo, 1959).

Nagano-ken, "Meiji 12-nen kiito mayu kyōsinkai ikken 3, 4" [Documents on the contest of raw silk and cocoons 1879 Part 3, 4] Documents of Nagano Prefecture, Nagano Prefectural Museum of History.

Naitō, Norikuni, "Sangyō shihon kakuritsuki ni okeru 'Tekkō' no keisei to touta ni tsuite" [On the formation and sift of 'Iron artisan' in the period of the establishment of the Japanese capitalism], *Rikkyou Keizaigaku Kenkyu* 16–2 (1962) 37–78.

Nakamura, Takafusa, (trans.) Feldman, R. A., *Economic Growth in Prewar Japan* (New Haven, 1983).

Nakanishi, Hirosi, *Nihon Kindaika no Kiso Katei, Chū* [The Basic Process of Japan's Modernization: Pt II] (Tokyo, 1883).

Nakano, Shiyō, *Itō Den'emonou den* [The Biography of Itō Den-emon] (Fukuoka, 1982).

Nanboku Sekyū, *Sekyū Hatsudōki oyobi Kikan Kiki Tōkei* [The Statistics on Petroleum engines, Boilers and Steam Engines] (Tokyo, 1908).

Nishiyama, Uzō, *Ajigawa Monogatari—Tekkō Shokunin Unosuke to Meiji no Osaka* [Ajigawa Story—Unosuke the Iron Craftsman and Osaka in the Meiji Era] (Tokyo, 1997).

Nōgata Tekkō 80 Nen-shi Hensan Iinkai, *Nōgata Tekkōkai no Ayumi* [A history of the Nōgata Ironworkers' World] (Nōgata, 1981).

Nōshōmushō, *Nōshōmu Tōkeihyō* [The Statistics of the Ministry of Agriculture and Commerce] (Tokyo, 22nd, 1907; 26th, 1911; 31st, 1917).

Nōshōmushō Kōzankyoku, *Seitetsugyō ni kansuru Sankoushiryō* [Reference Data for Iron Industry] (Tokyo, 1918).

Nōshōmushō Nōmu-kyoku, *Nōgyōyō Yōsuiki Chōsa dai-2-ji* [The Second Survey on the pumping engines for the agriculture] (Tokyo, 1913).

Odaka, Kōnosuke, *Shokunin no Sekai/Kōjō no Sekai* [The Craftsman's World/The Factory World] (Tokyo, 1993).

Ōe, Shinobu, *Nichiro Sensō no Gunjishiteki Kenkyū* [A Study on the Military History of the Russo–Japanese War] (Tokyo, 1976).

Okaya-shi, *Okaya-shi shi Chū* [The History of Okaya City, Pt 2] (Okaya, 1976).

Sawai, Minoru, "Dai-ichi-ji sekaitaisen zengo ni okeru Nihon kōsakukikai-kōgyō no honkakuteki tenkai" [The development of the Japanese machine tool industry around the First World War] *Shakai-keizai shigaku* 47–2 (1981): 33–58.

——, "Kikaikōgyō" [Machine Industry], in Nishikawa Shunsaku and Abe Takeshi (eds), *Nihon Keizaishi, IV: Sangyōka no Jidai* (Tokyo, 1990).

——, "Meiji chūkōki Osaka no kikai kōgyō" [The deveropment of machine industries in Osaka in the latter half of the Meiji era] *Osaka Daigaku Keizaigaku* 48–3.4 (1999)

Suzuki, Jun, "Meiji zenchūki no tankōyou kikaikōgyō" [The coal mining machine industry in the early and mid-Meiji era] *Shigaku Zasshi* 98–22 (1989): 1–37.

——, *Meiji no Kikai Kōgyō* [The Machine Industry in Meiji Japan] (Kyoto, 1996).

——, "The machine industry in the Meiji period", *Japanese Yearbook on Business History* 19 (1999), 113–133.

Takamura, Naosuke, "Sangyō-bōeki kōzō" [The structure of industry and foreign trading], in Ohishi Kaichiro (ed.), *Nihon Sangyō-Kakumei no Kenkyū* (Tokyo, 1975).

Takanoe, Mototarō, *Chikuhō Tankō-shi* [A Description of Chikuhō Coalfield] (Moji, 1898).

Takayama, Ryūzō, "Meiji 10 nendai ni okeru seishishihon no keisei to sonrakukōzō no henka III" [Development of silk manufacture and a change of a village structure in the early Meiji era III], *Mitagakkaizasshi* 62–6 (1969) 111–25.

Takeuchi, Jōzen, *Keiseiki no Wagakuni Jitensha Sangyō* [The Formation of Japanese Bicycle Industry] (Tokyo, 1980).

Tomioka Seishijōshi Hensan Iinkai, *Tomioka Seishijō-shi Jō* [The Historical Material on Tomioka Filature Pt I] (Tomioka, 1977).

Tsuruoka-shi, *Tsuruoka Shishi Ge* [The History of Tsuruoka City Pt 2] (Tsuruoka, 1975).

Uchida, Hoshimi, "Shoki kōkō sotsugyōsha no katsudōbunya shūkeikekka" [Statistical data for the employment of technical college graduates in industries, 1900–20] *Tokyokeidai Gakkaishi* 108 (1978*a*), 139–82.

——, "Kigyōnai gijutsusha soshiki no keiseiki" [The emergence of engineers' organization in Japanese corporations, 1900–10], *Tokyokeidai Gakkaishi* 109/110 (1978*b*), 53–74.

——, *Tokei Kōgyō no Hattatsu* [The Development of Clock and Watch Industry] (Tokyo, 1985).

——, "Narrow cotton stripes and their substitutes: Fashion change, technological progress, and manufacturing organizations in Japanese popular clothing, 1850–1920", *Textile History*, 19–2 (1988).

——, "Oushū taisen mae no kikai kōjō" [Machine shops of Japan before the First World War], *Tokyokeidai gakkaishi* 163 (1989): 233–72.

Wada, Sukekazu, *Nihon Kōgyō Yōkan Dai- 6-ji* [The Japan Engineering & Trade Directory 1914 & 1915] (Tokyo, 1913).

Yamashita, Yoshihiko, *Niigata Tekkōjo 40-nen-shi* [The 40-years' History of Niigata Iron Works] (Niigata, 1934).

Yasunaga, Yoshiaki, "Akabane kōsakubunkyoku bōseki kikai" [On cotton spinning machines made in Akabane Factory of Ministry of Public Works], *Kougakukaishi* 81 (1888), 782–95.

Yonezawa-Shi Hensan Iinkai, "Yonezawa seishijō kankei shiryō" [Historical documents on the Yonezawa filature], *Yonezawa-Shi Henshūshiryō* 20 (1987), 9–146.

7

How Local Trade Associations and Manufacturers' Associations Worked in Pre-war Japan

KAZUHIRO ŌMORI

1. Introduction

In the years prior to the Second World War, the Japanese government pursued a policy of organizing traditional industries through local associations regulated by acts and codes. Merchants and manufacturers supported such regulation as a means of advancing industry in their own regions, while the government's concern was to promote exports. Most significant for the organization of traditional industries were two acts: The Trade Association Act for Strategic Export Commodities [*Jūyō Yushutsuhin Dōgyō Kumiai Hō*], enacted in 1897, and the Trade Association Act for Strategic Commodities [*Jūyō Bussan Dōgyō Kumiai Hō*], which was passed in 1900 as a revision of the 1897 Act. These local trade association acts are said to be original to Japan, having no known counterparts in the West. Small and medium business owners who joined the associations were classified by business type and by geographic area; merchants and manufacturers were grouped together (Abe 1999: 229; Hirshmeier and Yui 1977: 274). The number of local trade associations [*Dōgyō Kumiai*] increased rapidly from the latter half of the Meiji Period to the beginning of the Shōwa Period: from 246 in 1901, to 770 in 1909, 1,262 in 1920, and 1,586 in 1929 (Nōshōmushō [Ministry of Agriculture and Commerce] annual edition; Shōkōshō [Ministry of Commerce and Industry] annual edition). In the first two decades of the twentieth century, associations were organized in virtually all types of business in the traditional sector.

In 1925 the government enacted the Manufacturers' Associations Act for Strategic Export Commodities [*Jūyō Yushutsuhn Kōgyō Kumiai Hō*] in order to strengthen the organization of export manufacturers and thereby reverse the unfavorable balance of trade that had developed after the First World War. This Act was revised in 1931 to become the Manufacturers' Associations Act [*Kōgyō Kumiai Hō*], applicable not just to those who manufactured important exports but to all small and medium manufacturing businesses (Yui 1964: 285–302). After these Acts were enacted, many members of the local trade associations also became members of a manufacturers' association. The number of manufacturers' associations likewise increased year by year: from 20 in 1925, to 111 in 1930, and 662 in 1935 (Shōkōshō 1937: 26–30).

The local trade associations and manufacturers' associations encompassed various types of businesses. Table 7.1 shows that the silk-reeling industry had the largest number of local trade associations, followed by weaving, and then rice and cereals, wood and charcoal, soybean paste [*miso*] and soy sauce, lumber, and paper. By contrast, Table 7.2 demonstrates that cotton textiles had the largest number of manufacturers' associations, followed by silk textiles, pottery, knitwear, hemp braid, and metal goods.

This paper investigates the functioning of local trade associations and manufacturers' associations by focusing on the pottery industry and the straw goods industry. Pottery was represented in both local trade associations and manufacturers' associations. The pottery industry was already well developed in the Tokugawa period, and the manufacturing process was further modernized in the late Meiji, Taishō and early Shōwa periods. Manufacturers and merchants were commonly

Table 7.1. Number of local trade associations by type of business (1920)

Business	Number
Silk reeling	295
Weaving	146
Rice or Cereals	69
Wood or Charcoal	67
Soybean paste and Soy sauce	38
Lumber	34
Paper	34
Metalworking	31
Fertilizer	29
Fruit and Vegetables	26
Pottery	24
Tatami facing, etc.	23
Straw	22
Paper-thin sheet of wood or Braid, etc.	22
Others	402
Total	1,262

Source: Nōshōmushō [Ministry of Agriculture and Commerce] (annual edn).

Table 7.2. Number of manufacturers' associations by type of manufacturing industry (1931)

Manufacturing industry	Number
Cotton textile	43
Silk textile	16
Pottery	15
Knitwear	11
Hemp braid	9
Metal goods	6
Celluloid goods	6
Brushes	6
Others	40
Total	152

Source: Shōkōshō [Ministry of Commerce and Industry] (1937).

concentrated in a relatively few, limited areas such as Seto, Tokoname, and Arita. In contrast to pottery, straw goods did not develop as a mechanized industry in the modern era. As in the Tokugawa period, farm families continued to produce straw items at home as a source of additional income; power tools were not used. For this reason, while local trade associations were formed in the straw goods industry, straw goods producers were not a policy target of the Manufacturers' Associations Act, which focused specifically on small and medium businesses rather than farm households. Accordingly, while this investigation of local trade associations focuses on both pottery and straw goods, the examination of manufacturers' associations will use only pottery as an example. The paper explains how the local trade associations and manufacturers' associations functioned from 1897 to the mid-1930s and examines their contribution to the development of traditional industry in the modern era. Moreover, by making comparisons between the pottery and straw goods industries, it attempts to evaluate the practical significance of the government's policy of organizing traditional industries in pre-war Japan.

2. The Pottery Industry[1]

2.1. The development of the pottery industry

Fig. 7.1 illustrates shifts in the production value and export value of pottery in Japan's modern era. Production value grew from 5M (million) yen in 1897 to 29M yen in 1917, reaching 100M yen in 1936. Export values dipped in 1908, 1921, 1926, 1930, and 1931, but were high in the years 1902–6, 1915–20, and 1932–7. It is worth noting particularly that in 1937

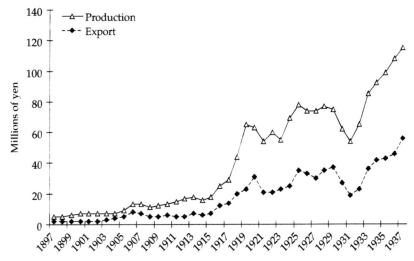

Fig. 7.1. Pottery production and export 1897–1937.
Source: Shinohara (1972:221), and Ōkurashō [Ministry of Finance] (annual edn).

the export value of pottery reached 50M yen. Calculations of the export ratio (export/production) show a high of 60.0 percent in 1905 and a low of 27.6 percent in 1915. In other words, the export market remained relatively important in the development of the pottery industry throughout the pre-war era. Regarding the destinations of pottery exports, Table 7.3 shows that the biggest importer was the United States. Also noteworthy, however, was the increasing export value of goods shipped to countries classified as "other". This trend suggests that the number of countries importing Japanese pottery was increasing. Furthermore, an examination of imports into the United States shows that Japanese pottery held a 12.3 percent share in 1912, ranking fourth behind German, British, and French pottery (Gaimushō [Ministry of Foreign Affairs] 1913: 12). By 1934, however, Japanese pottery accounted for 57.9 percent of imports into the United States, putting Japan in first place as the source of U.S. pottery imports (Nagoya Tōjiki Yushutsu Kumiai 1936).

Table 7.4 indicates the main pottery-producing districts throughout Japan by listing the top ten counties and cities by production value for the years 1909, 1919, and 1937. The largest producer by value of output for all three years was Nagoya City, followed by Seto City (Higashikasugai-gun [gun denotes county][2] and Toki-gun. Since biscuit-fired ready-for-glazing-pieces produced in Seto were often finished in Nagoya (Kuhara 1971: 118–20; Nōshōmushō 1912*a*: 59), it is possible that the production figures given in Table 7.4 may be inflated by double counting. Nevertheless, if Seto and Nagoya are considered as one region, characterized by division

Table 7.3. Destinations of exported pottery(1900–1937)

		(1,000 yen)
1900	1919	1937
United States 1,028 (41.6%)	United States 6,055 (26.8%)	United States 19,460 (36.0%)
Hong Kong 329 (13.3%)	China 2,854 (12.6%)	British India 4,240 (7.9%)
Great Britain 249 (10.1%)	British India 2,261 (10.0%)	Dutch India 3,109 (5.8%)
Korea 151 (6.1%)	Dutch India 1,797 (7.9%)	Australia 2,596 (4.8%)
British India 146 (5.9%)	Australia 1,486 (6.6%)	Kwantung province 2,353 (4.4%)
others 569 (23.0%)	others 8,176 (36.1%)	others 22,213 (41.2%)

Source: *Ōkurashō* [Ministry of Finance] (annual edn).

Table 7.4. Output value of main pottery-producing districts (1909–1937)

							(1,000 yen)
Ranking	Gun (County)·City (Prefecture)	1909	Gun (County)·City (Prefecture)	1919	Gun (County)·City (Prefecture)	1937	
1	Nagoya (Aichi)	2,878	Nagoya	14,588	Nagoya	37,147	
2	Kyoto (Kyoto)	1,205	Toki	10,397	Seto	16,446	
3	Toki (Gifu)	1,190	Aichi	7,377	Toki	12,326	
4	Seto (Aichi)	1,124	Seto	5,878	Kyoto	9,073	
5	Chita (Aichi)	681	Kyoto	4,429	Yokkaichi (Mie)	5,299	
6	Nishimatsura (Saga)	544	Nishimatsura	2,415	Chita	5,100	
7	Hekikai (Aichi)	282	Fujitsu	2,263	Sennan (Osaka)	3,543	
8	Ena (Gifu)	253	Chita	1,369	Nishimatsura	3,269	
9	Aichi (Aichi)	241	Kanazawa (Ishikawa)	1,274	Kokura (Fukuoka)	2,655	
10	Fujitsu (Saga)	232	Ena	1,256	Ena	1,820	

Source: Each prefectural government (annual edn).

Note: The output values of Seto in 1909 and 1919 were those of Higashikasugai-gun, and in 1937 the value of Seto was the total output value in Seto City and Higashikasugai-gun.

of labor and specialization, it can safely be said that it was by far the largest pottery-producing region in Japan. Other places that ranked in the top 10 in all three years were Kyōto, Nishimatsura-gun (Arita), Chita-gun (Tokoname),[3] and Ena-gun. All seven top-ranking locations were identified with well-known pottery styles and traced their history back at least to the Tokugawa period (Dai Nihon Yōgyō Kyōkai 1922).

Local trade associations were organized in the top-producing pottery districts as follows: Nagoya in 1909; Seto in 1899; Toki in 1902; Kyoto in 1900; Nishimatsura in 1900; Chita in 1900; and Ena in 1911. Manufacturers' associations were organized in the following years: Nagoya in 1930; Seto in 1926; Toki in 1930; Kyoto in 1934; Nishimatsura in 1929; Chita in 1926; and Ena in 1930 (Nōshōmushō annual edition; Isobe 1936: 486–90). In summary, then, it can be seen that by 1934 local trade associations and manufacturers' associations were organized in all major producing districts. Among them, this paper will investigate the functions of the local trade association and manufacturers' association in Seto. As mentioned earlier, Seto was the largest pottery-producing district, and its trade and manufacturers' associations were among the earliest in the country. In addition, it should be noted that a large quantity of tableware was produced in Seto by medium and small manufacturers using power equipment (Ōmori 1995a: 6–7; Nihon Ginkō Chōsa-kyoku 1931: 3–7). The percentage of pottery-for-export to total pottery output in Seto was 71.1 percent in 1902 (Aichi Kenchō Monjo, 1903)[4] and 60.0 percent in 1934 (Seto Tōjiki Kōgyō Kumiai 1934). Judging from these facts, it can be concluded that Seto was Japan's leading producer of pottery for export.

2.2 Seto Pottery Manufacturers and Merchants Local Trade Association

The Trade Association Act for Strategic Export Commodities stipulated that in order to organize a local trade association, it was necessary either to obtain the agreement of more than two-thirds of the business people active in the same industry in the same district, or to receive an order from the Ministry of Agriculture and Commerce. However, once an association was authorized, it was permitted by act to compel all business people of the same industry in the district to join. Moreover, the association was allowed to establish regulations concerning inspections and arbitration and to impose fines on those who did not follow the regulations. But it must be added that associations were prohibited from conducting joint enterprises or from setting up price or wage scales (Yui 1964: 40–1).

The Seto Pottery Manufacturers and Merchants Local Trade Association was set up and authorized in December 1899. Its membership included 559 manufacturers and 61 merchants in 1901 (Aichi Kenchō Monjo 1903), and 497 manufacturers and 46 merchants in 1909 (Aichi Kenchō Monjo 1910). Each year, the Association drew up a budget based primarily on dues that it imposed on members according to their financial standing and on prefectural, gun and town subsidies (Aichi Kenchō Monjo 1912*a*; Aichi Kenchō Monjo 1912*b*). The budget allowed the Association to carry out various activities, including the inspection of manufactured goods, the sponsoring of contests, and the extraction, preparation and distribution of clay.

Let us consider first the inspection of manufactured goods. Beginning in 1910, four inspectors employed by the Association inspected toilet bowls, Chinese pillows [*Shinamakura*], and "nested boxes" [*jūbako*]. They distinguished "approved goods" from "disqualified goods", ranking the approved goods from first class (best) to fifth class (worst). In 1911, the disqualification rate for inspected goods was 7 percent for toilet bowls, 5 percent for Chinese pillows, and 4 percent for nested boxes (Dai Nihon Yōgyō Kyōkai 1912: 70). After the inspection process had been set in motion, the Association recognized its validity and in 1914 went so far as to investigate the possibility of broadening the range of items to be inspected (Aichi Kenchō Monjo 1914*a*). We can safely say that the inspections carried out by the Association helped to raise the quality of goods produced.

It should be noted, however, the Association did not inspect that tableware for export, a significant part of Seto pottery production. The reasons are not clear, but it is possible that both the exporters in Nagoya and the Seto manufacturers who had special arrangements with them opposed inspection from the standpoint of maintaining trade secrets. As will be discussed later, it was not until the 1930s that Association inspections of tableware began in earnest. In 1930, pottery exporters in Nagoya organized the Nagoya Pottery Manufacturers' Association [*Nagoya Tōjiki Kōgyō Kumiai*], and in the next year, the Nagoya Association, together with the Seto Pottery Manufacturers' Associations [*Seto Tōjiki Kōgyō Kumiai*], joined the newly-formed Japan Pottery Manufacturers' Federation (JPMF) [*Nippon Tōjiki Kōgyō Kumiai Rengōkai*] (Isobe 1936: 486, 488). It was thus in the 1930s that the Nagoya and Seto associations established a cooperative framework.

A second activity of the Seto Pottery Manufacturers' and Merchants' Local Trade Association was sponsoring ceramics contests. From 1901, the Association, supported by gun and town subsidies, usually held contests twice a year for the purpose of fostering technical progress in the industry. Items were judged in various categories, as set by the Association. It was said that the contests did a great deal to raise the technical level of pottery in the area, and over time the proportion of "old-fashioned" items decreased (Kuroda 1908: 117–21). Members of the Association showed deep interest in these events, and in one 1912 contest, for instance, 318 exhibitors presented a total of 517 items. Moreover, the Association took an interest in competitive exhibitions held by other groups in other areas and encouraged its members to participate (Dai Nihon Yōgyō Kyōkai 1912: 71–2).

Another activity of the Association was the digging, refining and distribution of potter's clay (Aichi Kenchō Monjo 1910). It also budgeted funds for soil erosion control and road repairs in an effort to improve the conditions for clay extraction (Aichi Kenchō Monjo 1912*b*). Since we lack precise data on the quality, quantity, and price of the potter's clay prepared by the Association and on the methods of distribution, it is difficult to evaluate the impact of this enterprise. However, it is noteworthy that, even after the Second World War, clay preparation and distribution remained a core function of the Association (Seto Tōjiki Jigyō Kyōdō Kumiai 1976: 29). Conceivably it offered the Association a means of checking and controlling private clay dealers, with the aim of preventing them from setting prices too high or selling poor-quality clay.

Finally, the Association engaged in various other activities such as the protection of designers' rights (Kuroda 1908: 72–3, 95), the commissioning of testing and research at the Seto Pottery school [*Seto Tōki Gakkō*] and the Seto Pottery Experimental Station [*Seto Tōjiki Shikenjyō*] (*Aichi Kenchō Monjo* 1914*b*), and financial support for an exhibition hall, the Tōjiki Chinretsukan (*Aichi Kenchō Monjo* 1912*b*). To sum up, the Seto Pottery Manufacturers' and Merchants' Local Trade Association actively implemented various activities to promote the development of the pottery industry in Seto.

2.3. *The Seto Pottery Manufacturers' Association*

According to the Manufactures' Association Act for Strategic Export Commodities and its successor, the Manufacturers' Association Act, manufacturers' associations were permitted to carry out all functions conducted by the local trade associations as well as additional activities such as production and sales control, joint purchasing of materials, joint sales of products, joint financing, and joint production. A manufacturers' association could not compel manufacturers in the same business to become members, but those who did join were obliged to support the association financially (Abe 1999: 241–4, Yui 1964: Ch. 3).

The Seto Pottery Manufacturers' Association was authorized in 1926 in accordance with the Manufactures' Association Act for Strategic Export Commodities. The Association had 827 members in 1927, 1,026 members in 1932, and 1,095 members in 1934. It derived revenues from member shares issued at a rate of 20 yen per share, inspection fees paid by members, subsidies from the Ministry of Commerce and Industry and the Aichi prefectural government as well as a low interest loan obtained from the deposit bureau of the Ministry of Finance [*Ōkurashō*] (Ōmori 1996: 226–31).

In considering the activities of the Manufacturers' Association, one should note first that it placed highest priority on carrying out inspections.

It can be confirmed that in 1929 the Association inspected five types of articles, including toilets and coffee cups. Year by year the number of categories increased, totalling 10 in 1930, 22 in 1931, 45 in 1932, 61 in 1933, and 117 in 1934. From the beginning of the 1930s, inspections were carried out on a large scale on goods such as tableware-for-export. Moreover, from 1931, some of these inspections were conducted in cooperation with the above-mentioned JPMF. In 1934, for example, inspections in 47 of the 117 categories were handled by the JPMF (Seto Tōjiki Kōgyō Kumiai annual edition; Seto Tōjiki Kōgyō Kumiai 1934).

The inspections separated approved goods from disqualified goods and ranked them from first through fourth class. Disqualified goods accounted for 1.7 percent of all inspected goods in 1929, 0.1 percent in 1930, 0.3 percent from 1931 to 1933, and 0.7 percent in 1934. Among the approved goods, the percentages by rank in 1932 were: 94.9 percent for first class, 4.6 percent for second class, 0.5 percent for third class, and 0.0 percent for fourth class. In 1934, the comparable percentages were 92.0 percent, 5.7 percent, 2.3 percent, and 0.0 percent. Inspections were carried out either at joint sale locations or at the factories of Manufacturers' Association members. In 1934, there were 71 inspectors, 58 of them belonged to the Association; the rest were sent from JPMF (Seto Tōjiki Kōgyō Kumiai annual edition). As stated above, the Manufacturers' Association encouraged inspections as a means of guaranteeing product quality. Further, it seems likely that, by promoting stable, trusting relations with buyers, the inspections gave producers the opportunity to make long-term profits. In this sense it can be said that, by enforcing quality control and raising the reputation of pottery products, the inspections contributed to the increase in export demand.

A second focus of activity for the Seto Pottery Manufacturers' Association was the implementation of production quotas as a means of maintaining quality and preventing dumping. As far as can be confirmed, controls were imposed on 10 product groups in 1927, growing to 17 in 1928, 56 in 1932, 79 in 1933, and 83 in 1934. Like the inspections, controls were implemented in cooperation with the JPMF. For instance, 43 of the 83 production quotas imposed in 1934 were set by the JPMF for the Manufacturers' Association (Seto Tōjiki Kōgyō Kumiai annual edition). Ultimately, however, the controls were not sufficiently effective in supporting prices, and in 1935 the system was reformed (Shirakizawa 1999: ch. 8).

Another activity of the Association was the designation of certain wholesalers as approved merchants with whom the potters had executed previous dealing and the joint sale of products (Seto Tōjiki Jigyō Kyodō Kumiai 1976, 40). Because many goods were inspected on the spot at joint-sale locations and because, as a general rule, production quotas were also checked there (Seto Tōjiki Jigyō Kyodō Kumiai annual edition; Nihon

Tōjiki Jigyō Kyodō Kumiai Rengōkai 1931: 35), the effective implementation of inspections and production controls required the administration and expansion of joint sales. Accordingly, as the system of inspections and production controls developed, joint sales also expanded in scale. In 1929 there were just two joint-sale departments in the Manufacturers' Association, but the number increased to 18 in 1932 and 23 in 1934. Business volume was 486,000 yen in 1929, 3,055,000 yen in 1932, and 3,685,939 yen in 1935. In 1935 joint sales accounted for 25.4 percent of the total pottery production value of Manufacturers' Association members (Seto Tōjiki Kyodō Kumiai annual edition).

The third major activity of the Manufacturers' Association was the extraction and distribution to members of potters' clay. It assumed this task at its foundation from the Seto Pottery Manufacturers' and Merchants' Local Trade Association. The aim was to improve the quality of materials and reduce production costs (Seto Tōjiki Jigyō Kyodō Kumiai 1976: 28–35). The Manufacturers' Association bought potters' clay totalling 15,000 yen in 1930, 21,000 yen in 1932, and 40,000 yen in 1934. Sales proceeds were 26,000 yen, 34,000 yen, and 61,000 yen, respectively (Seto Tōjiki Kōgyo Kumiai annual edition; Seto Tōjiki Kōgyō Kumiai 1934). In 1934 clay handled by the Manufacturers' Association represented some 25 percent of total clay extractions in Seto (Aichi-ken Jitsugyō Kyōiku Shinkō kai 1941: 65).

Along with clay, fuel costs accounted for a considerable part of the total cost of pottery production. As a step toward reducing production costs, the Manufacturers' Association initiated joint purchases of coal and other fuel in 1932. With regard to coal, the Association first plan was to sell 40 million *kin* (1*kin* = 600 g) per year, equivalent to one-third of the total annual consumption of Association members. In practice, however, the Association bought only 9,162,000 *kin* in 1933, and 6,340,000 *kin* in 1934; the purchases came to 88,000 yen and 64,000 yen respectively. The Manufacturers' Association also carried out joint purchases of heavy oil and firewood, though the total outlay for these fuels was far smaller than that for coal (Seto Tōjiki Kōgyō Kumiai annual edition, Seto Tōjiki Kōgyō Kumiai 1934).

With the extraction and distribution of potters' clay and the joint purchases of fuels, the Manufacturers' Association aimed to hold down the prices of materials and fuel, and at the same time prevent a deterioration in the quality of goods produced by its members. In addition, in order to standardize products, in 1932 the Association began making plaster casts in one factory that it managed directly; it compelled members to use these casts (Seto Tōjiki Jigyō Kyōdō Kumiai 1976: 23–4). The Association also worked at protecting designers' rights, and it conducted research and development on new goods and techniques. Finally, it held exhibitions and encouraged its members to send their products to exhibitions held by other organizations (Seto Tōjiki Kōgyō Kumiai annual edition).

In short, Seto Pottery Manufacturers' Association was even more active than Seto Pottery Manufacturers' and Merchants' Local Trade Association in implementing various programs aimed at promoting regional industry and increasing Seto's competitive position in world markets. It is not too much to say that the Association played a significant role in the development of the pottery industry in Seto in the pre-war period.

3. The Straw Goods Industry[5]

3.1. The development of the straw goods industry

Fig. 7.2 illustrates that nominal production (current price) of straw goods suffered sharp fluctuations in the period 1897–1937. The range of fluctuation was 10M to 19M yen from 1897 to 1910, and 17M to 26M between 1911 and 1917. In 1918 nominal production jumped to 44M yen, and in 1919 it reached 69M yen. From 1920 until 1929 nominal production continued to fluctuate but did not drop below the level of 40M yen. However, in 1930 it fell suddenly, dropping to 26M yen in 1931. Thereafter, it recovered smoothly, reaching 54M yen in 1937.

Real production (1934–6 price) showed a somewhat different trend. It fluctuated between 22M and 34M yen between 1897 and 1905. From 1906

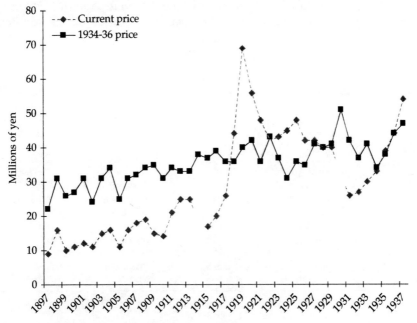

Fig. 7.2. Straw goods production 1897–1937.
Source: Umenura, et al. (1966: 146–147, 152–153).

to 1918 it moved between 31M and 39M yen. In 1919 it reached 40M yen, and thereafter fluctuated between 31M and 51M yen. It may safely be said that the real production showed a gradual tendency to increase.

The principal kinds of straw goods were rope, straw mats [*mushiro*], and straw bags [*kamasu*]. In 1917 rope accounted for 26.5 percent of all straw goods; mats accounted for another 19.9 percent, and bags accounted for 9.0 percent (Nōshōmushō [Ministry of Agriculture and Commerce] 1920: 13, 23). In 1931 the figures were 34.1 percent, 23.3 percent, and 24.1 percent, respectively (Nōrinshō [Ministry of Agriculture and Forestry] 1935: 8). It is noteworthy that in 1917 93.5 percent of all straw goods were produced by farm households as a side business (Nōshōmushō 1920: 13). The number of farm households making straw goods for the market numbered 850,000 in 1917, 940,000 in 1927, and 1,015,000 in 1933. Each of these figures accounted for 15–20 percent of all farmhouses in Japan at the time (Nōshōmushō 1920: 13; Nōrinshō 1935: 9).

Income from a side business in straw goods contributed greatly to farm household income (Nōrinshō 1935: 290, Osaka Asahi Shinbun-sha Keizai-bu 1931: 237). Therefore, households struck by natural disaster or crop failure tended to work at improving on the traditional techniques of straw goods production. By increasing production, they could become commercial producers of straw goods and thus expand household income.

Table 7.5 presents the output of straw goods by prefecture in 1916 and 1932. In 1916 the main producing prefectures were Aomori, Saitama, Toyama, Shizuoka, Hyōgo, and Kagawa. The output of the top ten

Table 7.5. Output of straw goods by prefecture (1,000 yen)

Ranking	Prefecture	Output (1916)	Prefecture	Output (1932)
1	*Hyōgo	1,799	Hyōgo	2,139
2	Shizuoka	970	Kagawa	1,709
3	Aomori	899	Toyama	1,499
4	Kagawa	815	Ishikawa	1,184
5	Toyama	780	Niigata	1,138
6	Saitama	735	Hokkaidō	1,128
7	Yamagata	698	Shizuoka	1,089
8	Saga	682	Aomori	1,067
9	Mie	679	Fukuoka	1,035
10	Niigata	669	Mie	886

Source: Nōshōmushō [Ministry of Agriculture and Commerce] (1920: 4–23), and *Nōrinshō* [Ministry of Agriculture and Forestry] (1935: 3–9).

Notes: (1) The output values are averaged over three years.
(2) The output value of *Hyōgo in 1916 includes the output for home consumption.

prefectures accounted for 51.5 percent of national output in yen terms. In 1932, production in Hokkaidō, Aomori, Niigata, Toyama, Ishikawa, Shizuoka, Hyōgo, Kagawa, and Fukuoka prefectures each exceeded 1M yen. The output of the top ten prefectures amounted to 46.5 percent of national output.

Moving to the gun (county) level, Table 7.6 shows the output of straw goods in yen terms of the top twenty counties in 1917 and 1931. Fourteen counties, including Minamitsugaru (Aomori), Nishimurayama (Yamagata), and Kitakatsushika (Saitama) are listed for both years. These 14 can be considered the main producing areas for straw goods in the interwar period. Among the large quantity of straw goods produced for market in each gun, tendencies to specialize were apparent. In 1931, for example, Japanese sandals (zōri) accounted for 98.1 percent of all straw goods made in Nishimurayama; rope accounted for 89.6 percent of straw goods output in Kitakatsushika; and straw bags accounted for 98.0 percent of output in Nakatado (Nōrinshō 1935: 158, 188, 484).

In order to identify the consumers of straw goods, consider the import values by prefecture listed in Table 7.7. We see that in 1931 Hokkaidō, Osaka, and Tokyo imported the largest volume of straw goods in yen terms. Hokkaidō imported especially from Aomori, Niigata, Toyama, and Ishikawa. Straw goods produced in Saitama, Chiba, Shizuoka, and Kagawa supplied much of the consumer market in Tokyo. Goods from Hyōgo, Kagawa, and Tokushima were shipped in large quantities to Osaka (Nōrinshō 1935: 119, 223, 263, 275, 393, 476, 485). It is safe to say that a large percentage of the straw goods made in the top producing areas were sold in Hokkaidō, Tokyo, and Osaka.

It is possible to identify some of the buyers who placed especially large orders for straw goods in Hokkaidō, Tokyo, and Osaka. First, in Hokkaidō (Nōrinshō 1927: 54–64), big companies such as Nichiro Fishery [Nichiro Gyogyō], Ōji Paper [Ōji Seishi] (Tomakomai factory), Fuji Paper [Fuji Seishi] (Ebetsu, Ikeda, and Kushiro factories), Mitsui Trading Company [Mitsui Bussan], and Nippon Steel [Nihon Seikō-jyo] (Muroran factory) bought a large amount of straw goods in 1924. The total assets of each of these companies were over 10M yen.[6] Small and medium firms such as Kadokura Shōten and Meiji Shōkai also dealt in straw goods on a large scale (Nōrinshō 1927: 1, 45–53, 71–2). In Hokkaidō, not only the big businesses, but also farmers, fishermen, civil engineering constructors, and mine operators demanded large quantities of straw goods.

Next are some examples from Tokyo. In 1930, Dai Nippon Fertilizer [Dai Nihon Jinzō Hiryō], Dai Nippon Tokkyo Fertilizer [Dai Nihon Tokkyo Hiryō], Nippon Oil [Nihon Sekiyu], Karafut Kōgyō, Mitsubishi Paper [Mitsubishi Seishi] (Nakagawa factory), Kanegafuchi Spinning [Kanegafuchi Bōseki],

Table 7.6. Output of straw goods by gun (county)

(1,000yen)

	Gun (Prefecture)	Output (1917)	Gun (Prefecture)	Output (1932)
1	Minamitsugaru (Aomori)	711	Minamitsugaru	552
2	Minamisaitama (Saitama)	677	Mitoyo	547
3	Kako (Hyōgo)	594	Kashima	471
4	Shimoshinkawa (Toyama)	524	Ogasa (Shizuoka)	396
5	*Iwata (Shizuoka)	446	Kanzaki	372
6	Kanzaki (Hyōgo)	444	Kako	368
7	Nishimurayama (Yamagata)	431	Nakatado	356
8	Kashima (Ishikawa)	408	Nishimurayama	291
9	Naka (Kagawa)	370	Ayauta	280
10	Mitoyo (Kagawa)	348	Himi (Toyama)	266
11	Chōsei (Chiba)	324	Nakashinkawa	262
12	Nakatado (Kagawa)	277	Shimoshinkawa	261
13	Mizuma (Fukuoka)	271	Naka	255
14	Nakashinkawa (Toyama)	245	Kishima (Saga)	250
15	Kitakatsushika (Saitama)	240	Yamato (Fukuoka)	235
16	Kasai (Hyōgo)	228	Mishima	215
17	Ayauta (Kagawa)	226	Kitakatsushika	209
18	Mishima (Osaka)	222	Sorachi (Hokkaidō)	197
19	Kamikawa (Hokkaidō)	218	Nakakanbara (Niigata)	193
20	Minamiakita (Akita)	203	Shimotsuga (Tochigi)	192

Source: Each prefectural government (annual edn), and Nōrinshō [Ministry of Agriculture and Forestry] (1935: 103–583).

Notes: (1) As the output value of *Iwata in 1917 is unknown, we have entered the value of Iwata in 1918 in its place.
(2) The underline means that the county had an association at that point of time.

Table 7.7. Demand, import and export values of straw goods by prefecture (1931)

(1,000 yen)

Ranking	Prefectural	demand	Prefectural	import	Prefectural	export
1	Hokkaidō	7,095	Hokkaidō	6,166	Kagawa	1,122
2	Osaka	2,929	Tokyo	2,558	Hyōgo	945
3	Tokyo	2,729	Osaka	2,340	Aomori	891
4	Niigata	933	Kumamoto	450	Ishikawa	744
5	Fukuoka	856	Yamaguchi	269	Niigata	701
6	Shizuoka	815	Iwate	194	Toyama	507
7	Hyōgo	800	Ōita	181	Chiba	500
8	Yamaguchi	757	Fukui	179	Fukui	438
9	Kumamoto	741	Okayama	150	Saitama	372
10	Toyama	665	Wakayama	148	Saga	343

Source: Nōrinshō [Ministry of Agriculture and Commerce] (1935: 16–28).

Tōyō Spinning [*Tōyō Bōseki*] (Ōji factory), Dai Nippon Salt Company [*Dai Nihon Engyō*], Tokyo Gas, and Dai Nippon Brewery (*Dai Nihon Biiru*) each purchased large quantities of straw goods (Nōrinshō 1931: 74–9). And in Osaka, Dai Nippon Fertilizer (Kitsugawa factory), Teikoku Fertilizer [*Teikoku Jinzō Hiryō*], Osaka Gōdō Spinning [*Osaka Gōdō Bōseki*], Tokunaga Glass Factory [*Tokunaga Garasu Kōjyō*], and Tōyō Spinning (a branch in Tenma) made big purchases of straw goods in 1931 (Nōrinshō 1935: 385). With the exception of Dai Nippon Tokkyo Fertilizer, Dai Nippon Salt Company, Teikoku Fertilizer, and Tokunaga Glass Factory, the total assets of each of these Tokyo and Osaka businesses were more than 10M yen. Total assets of Dai Nippon Salt Company amounted to 5,496,000 yen in 1931. As for Dai Nippon Tokkyo Fertilizer and the two other businesses, their total assets are unknown, but the paid-in capital of each was more than 1M yen. All of these examples underscore the fact that vast amounts of straw goods were consumed by big businesses in Japan's modern economy.

The main purchasers of straw goods nationwide appeared in *Wara Seihin ni Kansuru Chōsa* [Report on Straw Goods], which reported the results of an investigation carried out in 1931. The report indicates that 43 big businesses, each of them holding total assets valued at more than 10M yen, bought straw goods totalling 4,622,000 yen. The report identifies a further 25 medium-sized businesses, each of which had total assets valued at from 5M to 10M yen or paid-in capital of more than 1M yen. These businesses spent a total of 1,578,000 yen on straw goods in 1931.

Adding both categories of purchasers, one can conclude from the report that in 1931, big and medium-sized businesses purchased straw goods totalling 6,200,000 (4,622,000 + 1,578,000) yen. This figure accounts for 24 percent of the total output of straw goods, estimated at 26M yen in 1931.

However, it should be noted that not all of the big and medium-sized businesses that paid large sums of money for straw goods appeared in *Wara Seihin ni Kansuru Chōsa*. For example, the report does not mention Nichiro Fishery, Ōji Paper (Tomakomai factory), Fuji Paper (Ebetsu, Ikeda, Kushiro, Kanayama factories), Mitsui Trading Company, Nippon Steel (Muroran factory), Mitsubishi Paper, Tokyo Gas, and Dai Nippon Brewery, all of which bought large amount of straw goods in 1924 or 1930. Since it is hardly conceivable that these businesses stopped purchasing straw goods suddenly in 1931, one can conclude that the report lists only some of the main purchasers of straw goods in that year. In fact, therefore, the total spent on straw goods by big and medium-sized businesses in 1931 must have been a lot bigger than 6,200,000 yen. This evidence suggests first that big and medium-sized businesses were major consumers of straw goods and, further, that the development of big and medium-sized businesses in the modern era expanded the market demand for straw goods.

There was keen regional competition among straw goods producers. For instance, rope produced in Saitama, Chiba, and Shizuoka competed in the Tokyo market (Nōshōmushō 1920: 177; Nōrinshō 1931: 53, 55). Straw goods produced in Aomori, Akita, Toyama, and Ishikawa prefectures competed in the Hokkaidō market (Nōshōmushō 1920: 396). For each producing area, the important challenge was finding a way to make products that were cheaper and better than those of its competitors. To meet this challenge, local trade associations for straw goods producers and merchants were organized in one area after another: 1 in 1901; 6 in 1909; 22 in 1920; and 45 in 1935 (Nōshōmushō annual edition; Shōkōshō annual edition).

Table 7.6 shows (by underlining) the counties in which local trade associations had been organized by 1917 and 1932. Of 20 listed counties, 9 counties had associations in 1917; 15 had them in 1931. Note that the 13 top-producing counties had associations in 1931. Moreover, 8 of the 9 underlined counties in 1917 were listed again in 1931; all 8 still had associations. It can thus be seen that local trade associations had been organized in all the main straw goods producing districts by the beginning of the Shōwa era. Moreover, almost every top-producing district that had an association in 1917 remained in the top 20 in 1931. In short, there is a strong possibility that the local trade associations contributed to the development of the straw goods industry. Reports of the time substantiated this claim (Nōshōmushō 1912b: 95, 101,163; Nōshōmushō 1920: 514; Osaka Asahi Shinbun Keizai-bu 1931: 180). The following sections will clarify the functioning of the local trade associations with regard to straw goods manufacturing.

3.2. Local trade associations in the straw goods industry

Table 7.8 shows the names, districts, number of members, kinds of constituents, and year of establishment for local trade associations in the

Table 7.8. Local trade associations in the main producing districts (1931)

Name	District (Gun)	Number of members	Kind of constituents	Organization Year
Himi-gun Straw Mats Merchants L.T.A.	Himi	164	Merchants	1898
Nakashinkawa-gun Straw Mats Merchants L.T.A.	Nakashinkawa	146	Merchants	1906
Minamitsugaru-gun Straw Mats Merchants L.T.A.	Minamitsugaru	353	Merchants	1907
Shimoshinkawa-gun Straw Mats Merchants L.T.A.	Shimoshinkawa	406	Merchants	1907
Ayauta-gun Straw Bags L.T.A.	Ayauta	6,632	Manufacturers Merchants	1912
Kanzaki-gun Straw Mats and Straw Bags L.T.A.	Kanzaki	n.a	Manufacturers Merchants	1912
Mitoyo-gun Straw Goods L.T.A.	Mitoyo	11,526	Manufacturers Merchants	1912
Naka-gun Straw Mats and Straw Bags L.T.A.	Naka	5,765	Manufacturers Merchants	1912
Kasai-gun Straw Mats and Straw Bags L.T.A.	Kasai	1,660	Manufacturers Merchants	1914
Nakatado-gun Straw Bags L.T.A.	Nakatado and Marugame City	6,555	Manufacturers	1915
Uzen Sandal Facing L.T.A.	Nishimurayama	n.a	Manufacturers Merchants	1917
Noto Straw Goods L.T.A.	Kashima and Uzaku	11,940	Manufacturers Merchants	1919
Nakakanbara-gun Straw Goods L.T.A.	Nakakanbara	n.a	Manufacturers Merchants	1924
Saitama Straw Goods L.T.A	Kitakatsushika and a part of Minamikatsushika	9,481	Manufacturers Merchants	1925
Enshu Ogasa Straw Goods L.T.A.	Ogasa	10,955	Manufacturers Merchants	1926
Kako-gun Straw Mats and Bags L.T.A.	Kako	5,082	Manufacturers Merchants	1926

Source: Shōkōshō [Ministry of Commerce and Industry] (annual edn).

Note: L.T.A. = Local Trade Association.

main straw goods producing districts. Note that, with the exception of Nakatado-gun Straw Bag Local Trade Association (*Nakatado-gun Kamasu Dōgyō Kumiai*), every association included merchants in its membership. The following examination of the functioning of the local trade associations focuses especially on those listed in Table 7.8.

Most of the local trade associations carried out inspections. Since, as mentioned above, the buyers of straw goods were often big and medium-sized businesses from the modern sector, there was a need for uniformity and high quality. However, as the straw goods were usually made by farm households as side businesses, the quality of them tended to be uneven and the prices inclined to be low. Confronting this problem, local trade associations carried out inspections to improve the quality and standardize the size of straw goods (Nōrinshō 1931: 106–107).

The following examples may help to illustrate inspection procedures. The Saitama Straw Goods Local Trade Association [*Saitama Wara Kōhin Dōgyō Kumiai*], conducted inspections in response to requests by producers at the rate of about once every five days. Upon receiving a request, inspectors would travel to the site and inspect all the goods at once, separating them into "approved" and "disqualified" categories. In some cases, such as rope for wrapping soy sauce containers and wicker straw mats, the approved items were ranked from "special grade" to "third grade". The Saitama Association had 32 of its own inspectors. To help them improve their testing techniques, the Association offered short training courses for inspectors and held inspection study groups once every two months. Moreover, in order to achieve uniform standards, three or four inspectors would be placed in a group; every other month they would check each other's testing techniques in a process called "witnessed inspection" [*tachiai kensa*]. Furthermore, there was a need to consider the requirements of straw goods buyers in establishing inspection standards. The Saitama Association set up a committee for establishing inspection standards and dispatched its directors and inspectors to various districts with a view to studying the demands of buyers (Saitama-ken Gyōsei Monjyo 1936).[7]

The Kagawa Prefecture Mitoyo-gun Straw Bag Local Trade Association [*Kagawa Ken Mitoyo-gun Kamasu Dōgyō Kumiai*] conducted two types of inspections: individual inspections [*kakuko kensa*] were carried out by inspectors who travelled around the district; group inspections [*shūgō kensa*] were conducted at an office. The Association had 22 inspectors, all of whom were expected to judge straw goods according to a uniform standard. To ensure uniformity, the president and secretaries of the Kagawa Association sometimes supervised the inspectors directly, and from time to time they conducted double checks on already inspected goods. Like the Saitama Association, the Kagawa Association also maintained the practice of witnessed inspection (Nōshōmushō 1920: 490, 505–6, Nōrinshō 1931: 133).

In addition to the usual inspections, some local trade associations conducted the practice of export inspection [*ishutsu kensa*] on goods meant for export outside the gun. For example, in the Enshū Ogasa Straw Goods Local Trade Association [*Enshū Ogasa Wara Kōhin Dōgyō Kumiai*] based in Shizuoka Prefecture, export inspections were carried out on 53 percent of all rope inspected. In the Hyōgo Prefecture Kanzaki-gun Straw Mat and Straw Bag Local Trade Association [*Hyōgo Ken Kanzaki-gun Mushiro Kamasu Dōgyō Kumiai*], export inspections were conducted on 96 percent of straw bags produced (Nōrinshō 1939: 55, 65, 79, 85).

Table 7.9. Results of inspections (1937)

Name of Associations	Kind of goods	First class	Second class	Third class	Total (Approved)	Disqualified %
Enshu Ogasa Straw	Rope	65.8	33.8		99.6	0.4
Goods L.T.A.	Rope (*ishutsu*)	75.4	24.6		100.0	—
	Straw Mats	83	17		100.0	0
	Straw (*ishutsu*)	98.4	1.6		100.0	—
	Straw Bags	48.7	51.2		99.9	0.1
	Straw (*ishutsu*)	75.4	24.6		100.0	0
Kako-gun Straw Mats	Straw Mats	94.9	5	0.1	100.0	—
and Straw Bags L.T.A.	Straw (*ishutsu*)				100.0	—
Kanzaki-gun Straw Mats	Straw Mats				80.0	20
and Straw Bags L.T.A.	Straw (*ishutsu*)				76.9	23.1
	Straw Bags				72.9	27.1
	Straw (*ishutsu*)				74.8	25.2
Kasai-gun Straw Mats	Straw Mats	58.5	19.6	21.9	100.0	—
and Straw Bags L.T.A.	Straw (*ishutsu*)	81.1	16	2.9	100.0	—
	Straw Bags	57.3	35.4	7.3	100.0	—
	Straw (*ishutsu*)	58.8	39.1	2.1	100.0	—
Ayauta-gun Straw Bags L.T.A.	Straw Bags				99.3	0.7
Mitoyo-gun Straw Goods L.T.A.	Straw Bags				99.1	0.9
Naka-gun Straw Mats	Straw Mats				99.7	0.3
and Straw Bags L.T.A.	Straw Bags				99.8	0.2
Nakatado-gun Straw	Straw Mats				95.9	4.1
Goods L.T.A.	Straw Bags				96.4	3.6
Saitama Straw Goods	Rope				53.7	46.3
L.T.A.	Straw Mats				94.1	5.9
	Straw Bags				80.3	19.7

Source: Nōrinshō [Ministry of Agriculture and Forestry] (1939: 5–88).

Note: See Note at Table 7.8.

Table 7.9 shows the results of straw goods inspections by various local trade associations. According to the table, the percentage of disqualified goods and the distribution of grades for approved goods varied significantly by association and by type of goods. It is not possible to clarify the reasons for the differences, but one possible explanation is that the policies of the associations, the intentions of producers and merchants, and customer demand of the customers all had an effect on the inspection standards established by the associations.

It should also be noted that inspection results had a strong influence on price. For instance, goods disqualified by the Ayauta-gun Straw Bag Local Trade Association [*Ayauta-gun Kamasu Dōgyō Kumiai*] were sold at prices that were roughly 40 percent of the prices of approved goods (Osak Asahi Shinbun Keizai-bu 1931: 216). And in Enshū Iwata Shūchi Straw Goods Local Trade Association [*Enshū Iwata Shūchi Wara Kōhin Dōgyō Kumiai*], the price of a straw bag fell by more than 5 *rin* (1 *rin* = 0.001 yen) for each step down in inspection rank (Nōrinshō 1939: 414–15). Some producers intentionally made goods that would be disqualified in order to meet the specific demand for cheap and low-quality goods (Nōrinshō 1939: 507, 512). In any case, producers and merchants showed a lively interest in the inspection procedures and cooperated with the association in carrying them out.

Having grasped the inspection procedures, let us now consider the significance of the inspections. Through the inspections, the local trade associations fulfilled the important function of bridging the information gap between big and medium-sized businesses on the one hand and farm households producers on the other. On the one hand, the fixed standard established by the associations provided farm households with information on customers' requirements. On the other hand, the inspection results provided information about the goods to the customers. The exchange of useful information made possible smooth transactions between big- and medium-sized businesses and individual farm households. We can safely say that such inspections were the basic activity of the associations.

Of course, the activities of the associations were not limited to inspections (Nōrinshō 1931: 127–45). For example, it can be confirmed that in 1917, the Kagawa Prefecture Mitoyo-gun Straw Bag Local Trade Association gave financial support to four exhibitions, held lecture meetings on production methods in 23 places, and dispatched inspectors to carry out marketing research in Kyoto, Osaka, Hyōgo, Okayama, Tottori, Shimane, and Tokushima Prefectures (Nōshōmushō 1920: 508–9). Again, records show that in 1935 the Saitama Straw Goods Local Trade Association sponsored exhibitions and contests, held 22 lecture meetings on improving and standardizing straw goods, dispatched inspectors and directors to the Keihin, Shikoku, and Kyūshū regions for observation and research, and recruited technical experts to teach production techniques on a volunteer basis (Saitama-ken Gyōsei Monjyo 1936). In such ways the associations worked to promote straw goods production in their areas.

Finally, two important association leaders merit a mention. Ichirōemon Kawaguchi, head of the Saitama Straw Goods Local Trade Association, was a man of property and a wholesale dealer of straw goods who lived in Kitakatsushika-gun (Saitama-ken Gyōsei Monjyo 1927). Chisaburō Taga headed the Himi-gun Straw Mat Merchants Local Trade Association [*Himi-gun Wara Mushiro Shō Dōgyō Kumiai*] and at the same time worked as sub-leader of the Federation of Toyama Prefecture Straw Goods Local Trade Association [*Toyama-ken Wara Kōhin Dōgyō Kumiai Rengōkai*]. Taga managed the straw goods shop that he had inherited in Himi-gun and exported straw mats to Hokkaidō and Osaka (Toyama-ken Naimu-bu Sangyō-ka 1922: 69). As merchants in the producing areas of Saitama and

Toyama, Kawaguchi and Taga took an active part in their respective straw goods local trade associations.

It is quite probable that, in other areas as well, local merchants took active leadership roles in the trade associations. Merchants had the specialized know-how and experience necessary to lead the associations in their work of inspection and grading, market research, and the teaching of production techniques. Local trade associations were not the only means of organizing straw goods producers in pre-war Japan: Industrial Cooperatives [*Sangyō Kumiai*], which were authorized in accordance with the Industrial Cooperative Act [*Sangyō Kumiai Hō*] enacted in 1900, were another effective channel for organizing agricultural labor. But industrial cooperative differed from local trade associations in that they consisted of agricultural labor alone. It seems likely, therefore, that in putting the local trade association system into operation, the government recognized the necessity of using merchants to promote the straw goods industry. This point is underscored by the fact that all of the areas that emerged as leaders in the straw goods industry had strong merchant leadership in their local trade associations. In the development of the straw goods industry, agricultural workers, who characteristically had little experience in marketing, were organized in merchant-led local trade associations that worked at opening up new markets. In this sense, the local trade associations provided a means for merchants and agricultural workers to join together in expanding the commercial possibilities of straw goods production.

4. Concluding Remarks

In pre-war Japan, local trade associations and manufacturers' associations conducted inspections and other activities aimed at encouraging regional industry. In the pottery industry, by guaranteeing quality, improving techniques, and cutting the costs of raw materials and fuel, both types of associations contributed to an increase in the productivity and sales of medium and small traders and manufacturers. As a result, Japanese pottery for export became highly competitive on the world market.

In the straw goods manufacturing industry, local trade associations fulfilled the function of promoting communication between traditional farm households and medium and large businesses of the modern sector. In this way, the associations played some part in alleviating the problem of poverty in rural communities. The examples of both pottery industry and straw goods point strongly to the conclusion that local trade associations and the manufacturers' association made significant contributions to the preservation and development of traditional industry in pre-war Japan.

Notes

1. This section is a summary of Ōmori 1995a and Ōmori 1996.
2. Seto town in Higashikasugai-gun became Seto city in 1929.
3. Arita and Tokoname are the local-government name in Nishimatsura-gun, and Chita-gun, respectively. On this point, see Kadokawa Shoten 1991.
4. Aichi Kenchō Manjo is owned by Kokuritsu Shiryō-kan [Department of Historical Documents, National Institute of Japanese Literature].
5. This section is a summary of Ōmori 1997.
6. On the total assets and paid-in capital of businesses in this period, see Nakamura 1976, Ōsakaya Shōten Chōsa-bu 1931, Tokyo Kōshin-jyo 1931, and Tōyō Keizai Shinpōsha 1931.
7. Saitama-ken Gyōsei Monjyo is owned by Saitama Kenritsu Shiryō-kan [Saitama Prefectural Archives].

References

Abe, Takeshi, "The development of the putting-out system in modern Japan: The Case of the cotton-weaving industry", in Odaka, Kōnosuke and Minoru Sawai (eds), *Small Firms, Large Concerns* (Oxford, 1999).

Aichi Kenchō Monjo [Aichi Prefectural Office Document], *Seto Tōji Kōshō Dōgyō Kumiai Gyōmu Seiseki Hōkokusho* [Annual Report on the Activities of Seto Pottery Manufacturers and Merchants Local Trade Association] in *Dōgyō Kumiai Bo 398* [Local Trade Association Bo 398] (Aichi, 1903).

——, *Seto Tōji Kōshō Dōgyō Kumiai Gyōmu Seiseki Hōkokusho* [Annual Report on the Activities of Seto Pottery Manufacturers and Merchants Local Trade Association] in *Dōgyō Kumiai Bo 399* [Local Trade Association Bo 399] (Aichi, 1910).

——, "Meiji Yonjūgonendo Keihi Fuka Chōshū Hōhō" [Report on the way of collecting association dues in 1912] in *Dōgyō Kumiai Hei 395* [Local Trade Association Hei 395] (Aichi, 1912a).

——, "Meiji yonjūgonendo Seto Tōji Kōshō Dōgyō Kumiai sainyushutsu Yosanhyō" [Budget report on Seto Pottery Manufacturers and Merchants Local Trade Association in 1912], in *Dōgyō Kumiai Hei 395* [Local Trade Association Hei 395] (Aichi, 1912b).

——, "Hojyokin kafu shinseisho" [Application for subsidy], in *Zassho Tsuzuri 575* [Miscellaneous Documents File 575] (Aichi, 1914a).

——, "Jigyō Hōhōsho"[Report on the way of implementing activities], in *Zassho Tsuzuri 575* [Miscellaneous Documents File 575] (Aichi, 1914b).

Aichi-ken Jitsugyō Kyōiku Shinkō-kai [Aichi Prefecture Promotion of Vocational Education Society], *Aichi-ken Tokushu Sangyō no Yurai Jō* [The History of Special Industry in Aichi Prefecture 1] (Aichi, 1941).

Aichi Prefectural Government, *Aichi-ken Tōkeisho* [Statistics of Aichi Prefecture] (Aichi, annual edn).

Dai Nihon Yōgyō Kyōkai [Ceramics Society of Japan], *Dai Nihon Yōgyō Kyōkai Zasshi* [Journal of Ceramic Society of Japan], 242 (Tokyo, 1912).

——, *Nihon Kinsei Yōgyōshi Dai San-hen Tōjiki Kogyo (Jō, Kan) (Ge Kan)* [Modern History of Ceramics in Japan No. 3, Pottery Industry 1, 2] (Tokyo, 1922).

Gaimushō [Ministry of Foreign Affairs], *Tsushō Isan* [Bulletin on Trade] 3 (Tokyo, 1913).

Hirshmeier, J. and Tsunehiko Yui, *Nihon no Keiei Hatten* [The Development of Japanese Business] (Tokyo, 1977).

Isobe, Ki'ichi, *Kōgyō Kumiai Ron* [Study of a Manufacturers' Association] (Tokyo/Osaka, 1936).

Kadokawa Shoten, *Kadokawa Nihon chimei daijiten* [Kadokawa's Encyclopedia of Japanese place names] Vol. 23, 41 (Tokyo, 1991).

Kuhara, Tsuneo, *Seto = Tsuchi to Hi no Machi* [Seto = Town of Clay and Flame] (Tokyo, 1971).

Kuroda, Masanori, *Seto no Tōgyō* [The Pottery Industry in Seto] (Tokyo, 1908).

Nagoya Tōjiki Yushutsu Kumiai [Nagoya Pottery Export Association], *Junpō Yushutsu Tōjiki* [Ten-day Report on Pottery for Export], 4/13 (Aichi, 1936).

Nakamura, Seiji, *Waga Kuni Dai-kigyō no Keisei Hatten Katei* [The Process of Formation and Development of Big Business in Japan] (Tokyo, 1976).

Nihon Ginkō Chōsa-kyoku [Research Bureau of Bank of Japan], *Seto Chihō ni okeru Tōjikigyō* [The Pottery Industry in Seto District] (Tokyo, 1931).

Nihon Tōjiki Kōgyō Kumiai Rengōkai [Japan Pottery Manufacturers' Federation], *Dai Ni-kai Jigyō Hōkokusho* [Annual Report of Activities of the Association No. 2] (Aichi, 1931).

Nōrinshō [Ministry of Agriculture and Forestry], *Hokkaido ni okeru Wara Kōhin no Torihiki narabi Seisan Jyōkyō Chōsa* [Report on Production and Transaction of Straw Goods in Hokkaido] (Tokyo, 1927).

——, *Tokyo ni okeru Wara Kohin Torihiki Jyōkyō Chōsa* [Report on Transaction of Straw Goods in Tokyo] (Tokyo, 1931).

——, *Wara Seihin ni kansuru Chōsa* [Report on Straw Goods] (Tokyo, 1935).

——,*Wara Seihin Kensa Seiseki Yōran No. 3* [Survey of the Results of Inspection on Straw Goods 3] (Tokyo, 1939).

Nōshōmushō [Ministry of Agriculture and Commerce], *Juyō Bussan Dōgyō Kumiai Ichiran* [List of Local Trade Associations] (Tokyo, annual edn).

——, *Juyō Yushutsuhin Kinyu oyobi Unchin ni kansuru Chōsa* [Report on Finance and Transportation Rates of Important Export Goods] (Tokyo, 1912*a*).

——, *Nōmu Isan Dai Sanjūn Nōka Fukugyō ni kansuru Chōsa* [Bulletin on Agriculture No. 32, Report on Side Work of Farm Houses] (Tokyo, 1912*b*).

——, *Wara Kōhin ni kansuru Chōsa* [Report on Straw Products] (Tokyo, 1920).

Ōkurashō [Ministry of Finance], *Dai Nihon Gaikoku Bōeki Nenpyō* [Annual Return of the Foreign Trade of Japan] (Tokyo, annual edn).

Ōmori, Kazuhiro, "Meiji kōki ni okeru tōjikigyō no hatten to dōgyō kumiai katsudō" [The development of pottery industry and the local trade associations in the latter half of the Meiji period], *Keiei Shigaku* 30–2 (Tokyo, 1995*a*), 1–30.

——, "Ryōtaisenkanki ni okeru kōgyō kumiai katsudō to tōjiki yushutsu no hatten" [The manufacturers' association and the development of pottery industry for export between the two world wars], in Matsumoto, Takanori (ed.), *Senzenki Nihon no Bōeki to Soshiki-kan Kankei* (Tokyo, 1996).

——, "Zairai sangyō to soshikika" [The organization of the traditional industry], in Takafusa, Nakamura (ed.), *Nihon no Keizai Hatten to Zairaisangyō* (Tokyo, 1997).

Osaka Asahi Shinbun-sha Keizai-bu [Economic Department of Osaka Asahi Newspaper], *Warera no Ikita Fukugyō wo Kataru* [Record of Verbal Evidence of Side- Work] (Osaka, 1931).

Ōsakaya Shōten Chōsa-bu [Research Department of Osakaya Shoten], *Kabushiki Nenkan* [*Year Book on Stocks*] (Osaka, 1931).

Prefectural Government, *Fuken Tōkeisho* [Statistics on each prefecture] (each prefecture, annual edn).

Saitama-ken Gyōsei Monjyo [Saitama Prefectural Office Document], "Fukugyō no nōson shinkō ni kiyoshital jirei ni kansuru chōsa no ken" [Report on cases of side-work which contributed to alleviating the problem of impoverishment in rural communities] in *Sho 1951* (Saitama, 1927).

——, "Shōwa jū nendo Saitama wara kōhin dōgyō kumiai gyōmu seiseki hōkoku" [Report on activities of Saitama straw goods local trade association in 1935], in *Sho 3393* (Saitama, 1936).

Seto Tōjiki Jigyō Kyōdō Kumiai [Seto Ceramic Industry Cooperative Society], *Gojūnenshi* [A 50-year History] (Aichi, 1976).

Seto Tōjiki Kōgyō Kumiai [Seto Pottery Manufacturers' Association], *Jigyō Hōkokusho* [Annual Report on Activities of Seto Pottery Manufacturers' Association] (Aichi, annual edn).

——, *Teiri Shikin Kariire Kankei Shorui* [Documents on Borrowing of Low Interest Loan] (Aichi, 1934).

Shinohara, Miyohei, *Chōki Keizai Tōkei 10 Kōkōgyō* [Estimates of Long-term Economic Statistics of Japan since 1868, 10 Mining and Manufacturing] (Tokyo, 1972).

Shirakizawa, Asahiko, *Dai Kyōkōki Nihon no Tsūshō Mondai* [Japanese Trade Problems in the Great Depression Period] (Tokyo, 1999).

Shōkōshō [Ministry of Commerce and Industry], *Jūyō Bussan Dōgyō Kumiai Ichiran* [List of Local Trade Associations] (Tokyo, annual edn).

Shōkōshō [Ministry of Commerce and Industry], *Kōgyō Kumiai Gaikyō* [General Situation of Manufacturers' Associations] (Tokyo, 1937).

Tokyo Kōshin-jyo [Tokyo Credit Bureau], *Ginkō Kaisha Yōroku* [Survey of Banks and Companies] (Tokyo, 1931).

Toyama-ken Naimu-bu Sangyō-ka [Toyama Prefecture Department of Internal Affairs, Industrial Section], *Fukugyō Shiryō Sono Ichi Wara Kōgyō ni kansuru Chōsa* [Record of Side-business No. 1, Report on Straw Goods Industry] (Toyama, 1922).

Tōyō Keizai Shinpōsha, *Tōyō Keizai Kabushiki Nenkan* [Tōyō Keizai Year Book on Joint Stock Companies] (Tokyo, 1931).

Umemura, Mataji et al., *Chōki Keizai Tōkei 9 Nōringyō* [Estimates of Long-Term Economic Statistics of Japan since 1868, 9 Agriculture and Forestry] (Tokyo, 1966).

Yui, Tsunehiko, *Chūshō Kigyō Seisaku no Shiteki Kenkyū* [Historical Study of Governmental Policies for Small- and Medium-sized Enterprise] (Tokyo, 1964).

PART III

The Modernization of Traditional Industries

8

The Rise of a Factory Industry: Silk Reeling in Suwa District

MASAKI NAKABAYASHI

1. Introduction

After Japan embarked on a new era of international trade in 1859, raw silk became the most important export shipped from the Yokohama treaty port to European markets. Traditional silk-reeling industry, which had developed in the preceding Tokugawa era, had the potential for comparative advantage (Huber 1971: 616–19).[1] However, Japanese hand-reeled silk attracted demand only as a low-grade product, especially in the French market; it could not dominate the international market. With the shift to modern silk reeling in the 1880s, Japanese filature (machine-reeled silk) displaced Italian and Chinese raw silk in the U.S. market. Then, the Japanese modern silk-reeling industry began to grow dramatically by export to the U.S., and had kept about 30 percent of the total export of Japan before the Second World War. By the 1920s, Japanese filature accounted for 80 percent of the U.S. market and 60 percent of the world market. (Sugiyama 1988: 77–139, Crawcour 1988: 423–4, Federico 1997: 200, 204). Not only was silk reeling Japan's first successful modern factory industry, but its development was the first example of a pattern that was to be repeated in modern Japan, that of a competitive export industry augmenting economic growth.

It was the silk-reeling industry in the Suwa district of Nagano Prefecture that took the initiative in this development. This chapter will examine the development of modern silk reeling in Suwa with the aim of elucidating the conditions that were important in the rise of factory industry. Previous studies have pointed to factors such as Japan's low wages relative to Italy and the assimilation of appropriate Western technologies. While such factors should not be overlooked, they do not explain why a silk-reeling industry capable of capturing the lucrative U.S. market developed in Japan but not in China, and in Suwa but not in other districts of Japan. In addition, the wage level in the Suwa district was almost same as that in Italy.[2] In order to discover conditions specific to Suwa, this study focuses on institutional efficiency as a crucial factor and one that was relatively independent of production technology (Williamson 1985: 15–42, Greif 1997: 84). Section 1 outlines the shift from traditional silk reeling to modern silk reeling as a strategy for keeping up with structural changes in the international market. The second section analyses the rise and development of modern silk-reeling industry in the Suwa district. Section 3 focuses on the financial institutions that supported the development of silk-reeling industry in Suwa.

2. The Reorganization of Sericulture

2.1. *Structural change in the international market*

From the late 1850s, the price of raw silk entered a rising trend, reflecting an upswing in world economic conditions. In response to this initial external stimulus, output in Japan's traditional raw silk industry increased to some extent. In the highly developed Lyons silk industry of the mid-nineteenth century, luxury silk fabrics were produced mainly by hand-looms, and there was demand for raw silk of various qualities, from traditional raw silk to high-grade machine-reeled thread (Cottereau 1997, Federico 1997: 61–78). Japanese traditional raw silk was shipped to France directly or by way of the U.K. or Italy. From the early 1870s, however, there was a downturn in the European market, and prices for raw silk tended downwards until the mid-1890s. On these falling prices, Japanese traditional raw silk was losing its comparative advantage over Chinese one (Nakabayashi 2003: 63–70). Although some machine-reeling factories were established in various parts of Nagano and Gunma prefectures in the early 1870s, machine production accounted for only a small proportion of Japan's total raw silk output.

In France, the recession in 1882 was followed by a serious depression: the output of silk fabrics declined and the French market declined in volume until 1885. The stagnant French market and the harsh competition with Chinese traditional raw silk damaged traditional silk reeling in Japan. The U.S. market, by contrast, had been expanding rapidly since the late 1870s. The modern silk-reeling industry of Japan developed in response to this second external stimulus.[3]

2.2. *Characteristics of the U.S. market for raw silk*

The simultaneous contraction of the French market and expansion of the US market prompted a surge of raw silk exports from Japan to the U.S. From 1884, when exports to the U.S. overtook exports to France, the U.S. became the primary market for Japanese raw silk (Table 8.1). By contrast, Chinese "Tsatlee" [*re-reeled*], a traditional raw silk, which was first hand-reeled and then re-reeled, lost out in the competition with Japanese raw

Table 8.1. Japanese production and export of raw silk

Year	Production of Raw Silk Total	Filature: Machine-reeled	Export of Raw Silk Total	To the U.S.	To France	To the U.K.	To others
	a	b	c = d + e + f + g	d	e	f	g
	ton	ton	ton	ton	ton	ton	ton
1873			721	4	232	340	145
1874			587	45	240	234	68
1875			709	3	383	256	68
1876	1,229		1,118	21	510	489	100
1877	1,294		1,106	74	508	460	63
1878	1,360		987	172	539	241	35
1879	1,669		931	278	395	248	11
1880	1,999		877	330	385	151	12
1881	1,729		1,081	261	611	205	4
1882	1,856		1,730	603	844	260	24
1883	1,712		1,873	622	959	284	8
1884	2,138		1,259	636	565	56	2
1885	1,905		1,474	793	629	37	15
1886	2,696		1,581	853	651	67	10
1887	3,019		1,862	1,040	653	93	76
1888	2,794		2,807	1,419	1,101	218	69
1889	3,307	1,338	2,476	1,363	1,022	33	59
1890	3,255	1,382	1,266	836	405	6	19
1891	4,187	1,690	3,195	1,869	1,171	83	72
1892	4,203	1,941	3,244	1,982	1,128	43	91
1893	4,626	2,206	2,227	919	1,136	88	85
1894	4,863	2,754	3,290	1,874	1,162	17	237
1895	6,012	3,389	3,486	2,009	1,231	19	227
1896	5,410	3,045	2,351	1,117	997	20	218
1897	5,766	3,132	4,152	2,367	1,539	16	229
1898	5,549	2,955	2,902	1,747	978	22	155
1899	6,578	3,503	3,568	2,292	1,082	17	177
1900	6,584	3,716	2,779	1,586	720	27	445
1901	6,564	3,890	5,219	3,085	1,221	10	902
1902	6,723	4,002	4,847	2,927	945	28	947
1903	6,916	4,362	4,389	2,751	992	2	644
1904	6,978	4,486	5,795	3,938	1,138	15	704
1905	6,897	4,527	4,345	3,243	676	0	426
1906	7,739	5,282	6,230	4,407	1,261	2	561
1907	8,735	6,137	5,613	3,805	1,220	0	588
1908	9,535	6,666	6,913	5,114	1,147	0	652
1909	10,277	7,595	8,082	5,529	1,641	9	903
1910	11,230	8,384	8,908	6,251	1,482	20	1,155
1911	12,085	8,994	8,674	5,970	1,439	24	1,241
1912	12,846	10,102	10,262	7,784	1,271	8	1,199
1913	13,080	10,693	12,137	8,004	2,120	42	1,971
1914	13,162	10,845	10,289	8,561	985	67	676

Table 8.1. (*Continued*)

	Production of Raw Silk		Export of Raw Silk				
	Total		Total		To the U.S.	To France	To the U.K.	To others
		Filature: Machine reeled						
Year	a	b	$c = d + e + f + g$	d	e	f	g
	ton	ton	ton	ton	ton	ton	ton
1915	14,088	11,934	10,688	8,918	1,447	58	265
1916	15,658	13,271	13,045	10,909	1,559	100	477
1917	18,321	16,047	15,497	13,238	1,606	312	341
1918	19,982	17,769	14,607	12,515	1,614	298	180
1919	21,495	19,382	17,173	16,518	500	95	61
1920	20,214	18,260	10,481	8,822	1,489	115	55

Source: Nakabayashi (2003, Appendix: 461–3, 470–2).

Notes: 'Raw Silk' does not include 'Waste' and, 'Dupion'. Original sources are Department of Agriculture, Ministry of Agriculture and Commerce, *Zenkoku nōsan hyō* [Statistics of agricultural products in the nation], (Tokyo, 1878), and Department of General Affairs, Ministry of Agriculture and Commerce, *Noshomu tōkei hyō* [Statistics of agriculture and commerce] (Tokyo, 1886–1922).

silk.[4] From the mid-1880s China's share of the U.S. market declined and it became more dependent on the post-Depression French market. The paired sets of Japan supplying the U.S. and China supplying France (Ma 1996: 335–43, Federico 1997: 61, Nakabayashi 2003: 63–86) emerged in the international silk market during the 1880s.

What kinds of changes occurred in the Japanese silk-reeling industry as it worked to secure its position in the promising American market? It was not easy for suppliers to France to switch suddenly to the U.S. because the demands of silk weavers differed in each market. In the Lyons market, since hand-woven goods remained dominant and production was characterized by low volume and much variety, the demand for various raw silk types continued until the turn of the twentieth century (Rawlley 1919: 66–73, Duran 1913: 72–7, Schober 1930: 242, Federico, 1994: 474, Federico 1997: 77). In the U.S., on the other hand, the mechanization of throwing and weaving progressed rapidly from the late 1870s, especially in the production of middle-and lower-grade fabrics for mass consumption. Above all, with the introduction of power looms, the work of weaving was transformed from the careful handling of a single handloom to the management of several looms. Moreover, there was strong dependence on female and child labor.[5] Mechanization in the U.S. created a demand for raw silk of uniform quality and even *denier*[6] that was shipped in large lots—in other words, raw silk produced by modern industrial processes. Only those who could produce thread of such specifications could hope to secure a foothold in the American market. Led by the machine-reeling manufacturers of Suwa district, the Japanese silk-reeling industry succeeded in producing the required raw silk.

2.3. *Change of the industrial organization*

The French depression of the early-and middle-1880s directly affected sericulture farmers who made traditional hand-reeled raw silk, or hanks. Because prices for Japanese hanks had collapsed in Lyons and Yokohama, the impact was especially severe on Japanese silk-producing farmers whose main cash income came from sericulture and hand reeling.[7] The Japanese government exacerbated the problem between 1882 and 1885 by introducing austerity policies that aimed to strengthen the monetary system and transfer income from farmers to the government through deflationary measures and tax increases (Patrick 1965: 199–202, Teranishi 1983, Minami 1994: 11, 16). As a result of these blows, traditional raw silk output decreased significantly in some districts in the mid-1880s.

By contrast with the expansion of the American market, the price of machine-reeled silk in New York rose relative to that of hanks in Lyons during the mid-1880s (Fig. 8.1). Responding to the price shift, Japanese machine-reeling businesses began to switch their exports to the U.S. from about 1882. A further reflection of the favorable conditions in the American market could be seen in Yokohama, where the price of filature rose relative to that of hanks (Fig. 8.2, Nakabayashi 2003: 90–1).

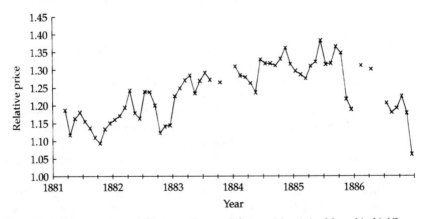

Fig. 8.1. Relative price of filature: (Japan Filature No. 1 in New York)/(Japan Hanks in Lyon).

Source: Nakabayashi (2003: 90).

Notes: Original sources are *Chūgai bukka shinpō* [Japan and international daily price indices], *Yūbin hōchi shinbun* [Daily mail], *Sanshigyō kumiai chūoubu geppō* [Monthly report of the head office of the Association of sericulture], and *Seishi danketsu dōshin kaisha itokata hōkoku* [Second annual report of Dōhisn Kaisha on raw silk], 1883.

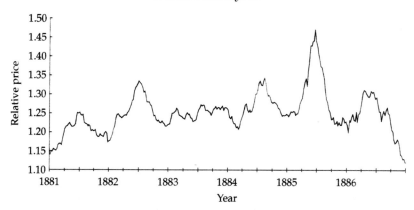

Fig. 8.2. Relative price of filature: (Filature in Yokohama)/(Hanks in Yokohama).
Source: Nakabayashi (2003: 91).
Notes: Original source is *Tokyo keizai zasshi* [Tokyo Economic Journal]. Weekly data.

Change in the international market thus had a negative impact on traditional raw silk producers, while on the other hand it created incentives for those engaged in machine reeling to export to the U.S. In particular, machine reeling manufacturers in Suwa who had shown themselves to be competitive in the American market increased their output sharply (Table 8.2). One immediate problem for Suwa reeling businesses was a shortage of cocoons. Since the local suppliers on whom they had relied could not meet the increased demand, from about 1886 Suwa reeling businesses started to purchase large quantities of cocoons from neighboring Saitama and Gunma Prefectures, the original suppliers of cocoons for hanks production. As a result, reliance on Nagano Prefecture cocoons by the silk-reeling manufacturers in Suwa dropped from over 80 percent in the early 1880s to lower than 50 percent at the end of the decade. At the same time, and responding to the new trends, many sericulture farmers gave up hand reeling and concentrated on supplying cocoons to machine-reeling businesses. The traditional link between sericulture and silk reeling was soon severed.[8]

The reorganization of the Japanese raw silk industry along capitalist lines was brought about by the expansion of demand for filature in the U.S. market, and it determined the structure of raw silk production in Japan until the 1920s. There is no doubt that the reorganization was driven initially by the rising price of filature relative to hanks that was caused in turn by the French depression. However, once a modern industrial organization had taken shape, the process was not reversed, even after the relative price of filature edged down. Supplying cocoons rather than hand-reeling had become attractive for silk farmers. In fact, even in 1886, when a small recovery of the French market caused the relative price of

Table 8.2. Production and equipment of silk-reeling industries in Nagano Prefecture, 1876–1930

Year	Nagano Prefecture, Production of Raw Silk — Total *a* (ton)	Filature *b* (ton)	Equipment Basins — Total *c*	Filature *d*	Factories — Filature *e*	Suwa county, Nagano Prefecture, Production of Raw Silk — Total *f* (kg)	Filature *g* (kg)	Equipment Basins — Filature *h*	Factories — Filature *i*	Productivity of Basins $j = g/h$ (kg)	Hirano village, Suwa county, Production of Raw Silk — Filature *i* (kg)	Equipment Basins — Filature *j*	Factories, ivity — Filatures *k*	Productivity of Basins $l = i/j$ (kg)
1876	143										6,750			
1877	82										6,548	445		14.7
1878	144										6,345	940	30	6.8
1879	211										6,143	655	57	9.4
1880	243										7,058	941	28	7.5
1881	297							1,369			11,925	1,046	60	11.4
1882	280							1,290			17,670	1,008	60	17.5
1883	306			13,560				1,301			18,105	912	51	19.9
1884	295					24,521		1,624			24,990	1,234	44	20.3
1885	285					57,083		2,242			32,040	1,399	50	22.9
1886	479					126,653		2,572			52,017	1,386	53	37.5
1887	489					135,788		3,159			71,994	1,755	50	41.0
1888	489					129,634		4,234			91,972	2,192	65	42.0
1889	642	547				217,391		5,352			111,949	2,594	70	43.2
1890	688	600				241,616		7,337			143,336	3,362	72	42.6
1891	803	671	40,167			297,724		7,452			174,900	3,461	84	50.5
1892	931	837	43,189			385,406		8,420			215,966	3,977	87	54.3
1893	1,060	955	53,881	31,847	868	412,999		10,883			227,160	4,764	89	47.7
1894	1,160	1,055	57,350	34,140	849	541,958		13,426			333,893	6,176	86	54.1
1895	1,480	1,331	59,293	34,762	890	577,496		13,499			307,226	5,772	106	53.2
1896	1,211	1,134	56,687	31,503	744	474,769		12,212			264,799	5,332	109	49.7
1897	1,108	1,019	54,323	30,081	732	323,325	323,335	9,909	158	32.5	200,989	4,889	89	41.1
1898	1,069	1,000			741	385,631	385,103	9,969	17	38.6	219,934	4,821	58	45.6
1899	1,280	1,215			664	509,918	509,265	10,653	161	47.8	293,344	5,411	57	54.2
1900	1,349	1,249			837	552,701	548,543	10,963	142	50.0	405,934	5,773	53	70.3
1901	1,470	1,368			743	563,359	562,834	10,634	157	52.9	362,314	5,539	50	65.4
1902	1,437	1,365			556	580,470	579,926	13,383	126	43.3	353,921	5,826	49	60.7
1903	1,653	1,575	65,216	33,925	562	654,671	654,323	12,030	129	54.4	404,063	6,537	52	61.8
1904	1,669	1,566	68,749	35,484	636	682,819	680,621	13,196	133	51.6	399,484	7,397	53	54.0
1905	1,694	1,559	70,461	37,487	778	690,896	686,220	14,415	157	47.6	379,196	7,981	52	47.5
1906	1,960	1,866	71,424	40,364	656	866,438	865,406	16,164	161	53.5	480,113	8,434	52	56.9
1907	2,176	2,074	71,343	12,832	664	956,119	955,181	16,962	140	56.3	501,859	8,599	51	58.4
1908	2,485	2,318	76,933	45,495	768	1,147,823	1,072,560	17,876	143	60.0	589,031	9,578	53	61.5
1909	2,829	2,728	75,164	49,786	829	1,324,110	1,323,638	20,202	159	65.5	862,646	10,293	59	83.8
1910	3,085	3,005	80,309	55,189	860	1,407,559	1,407,465	19,885	155	70.8	840,364	10,488	57	80.1
1911	3,230	3,146	88,543	63,066	621	1,410,743	1,410,743	22,563	184	62.5	843,514	11,868	63	71.1
1912	3,886	3,808	90,080	63,438	643	1,908,750	1,908,623	29,246	208	65.3	900,030	14,550	83	61.9
1913	4,214	4,102	89,381	63,776	603	1,914,214	1,914,071	29,001	205	66.0	1,126,961	15,394	81	73.2
1914	4,439	4,208	84,767	65,238	627	2,129,726	2,129,591	29,869	209	71.3	1,158,240	15,919	81	72.8
1915	4,713	4,597	100,524	70,335	689	2,443,121	2,443,016	30,550	216	80.0	969,420	16,419	85	59.0
1916	4,959	4,874	114,218	79,272	753	2,501,149	2,500,639	33,767	248	74.1	1,193,828	17,906	96	66.7
1917	5,677	5,582	119,852	84,475	757	2,471,333	2,470,684	37,231	276	66.4	1,377,671	19,904	102	69.2
1918	6,062	5,654	120,991	85,616	803	2,769,656	2,768,963	39,917	281	69.4	1,571,179	21,135	104	74.3
1919	6,188	6,079	120,309	83,026	770	2,887,410	2,886,694	40,515	322	71.3	1,550,085	20,884	104	74.2
1920	6,005	5,900				2,780,299	2,776,886	34,629	284	80.2	1,656,938	22,053	106	75.1

Source: Nakabayashi (2003, Appendix: 464–9).

Notes: Filature refers to modern silk reeling, its factory and its product. Hirano village belongs to Suwa district and Suwa district belongs to Nagano Prefecture. Original sources are *Naganoken tokei sho* [Annual statistics of Nagano Prefecture], Nagano, and *Hiranoson shi* [History of Hirano village]. 2. Each basin was operated by one worker.

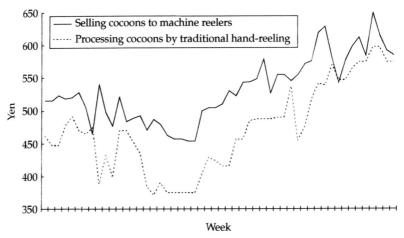

Fig. 8.3. Gross margins of peasants per 1 picul of silk in 1886.

Source: Nakabayashi (2003: 100).

Notes: Weekly data. See note (9).

filature to fall below its 1881 level, selling cocoons to machine-reeling businesses was almost always more profitable for sericulture farmers than hand-reeling (Fig. 8.3).[9] By the late 1880s, filature accounted for more than 50 percent of total raw silk exports (Table 8.3).

Furthermore, while hand-reeling by sericulture farmers was limited by the amount of family labor available,[10] narrowing the business focus to cocoon supply eased the demand for additional labor and allowed all available resources to be put into sericulture itself. The rapid growth of sericulture has already been identified as an important factor in the overall development of the silk industry. More specifically, however, the causes of sericulture growth can be classified as, first, the spread of summer-fall cocoon raising and, second, the geographical diffusion of sericulture.[11] Producing cocoons in summer or fall functioned as a type of double cropping. Although spring cocoons dominated until the 1890s, accounting for as much as 70 percent of all cocoons produced, summer–fall production spread rapidly after about 1900 with the development of the modern silk-reeling industry. By the second decade of the twentieth century, summer and fall cocoons represented more than 40 percent of total cocoon production. Use of the relatively slack months of August and September allowed farmers to expand the supply of cheap cocoons and became an important factor in raising the competitiveness of the Japanese silk-reeling industry (Nghiep and Hayami 1979, Federico 1997, 13, 80, 98–9, 220, Ikawa 1998: 51–151).

Geographic diffusion was the second factor in boosting sericulture. Since the main railway lines were laid in the 1890s and early 1900s, by the opening years of the twentieth century it was possible for the silk-reeling

Table 8.3. Raw silk sold to Yokohama trading companies in the Oct.–Dec. period, 1880–89

Year	Filatures	Re-reels	Kakedas	Hanks	Total
1880	124,723	3,561	49,697	219,088	397,069
1881	22,883	304	3,814	61,864	88,864
1882	281,509	4,185	91,159	243,641	620,494
1883	188,258	10,429	72,158	307,564	578,408
1884	209,942	15,626	41,175	75,870	342,613
1885	307,294	131,186	129,364	154,356	722,199
1886	245,599	207,293	23,861	216,371	693,124
1887	348,030	252,956	133,448	165,274	899,708
1888	630,653	493,425	164,093	330,126	1,618,296
1889	559,069	286,234	105,199	161,089	1,111,590

Source: Nakabayashi (2003: 95–8).

Notes: In 1881, silk trading was almost completely suspended because of a dispute between Western trading companies and Japanese silk wholesale merchants. *Kakedas* is a kind of *Re-reels* produced in Fukushima Prefecture. *Hanks* includes other kinds of traditional hand-reeled silk. Original sources are *Tokyo Yokohama mainichi shinbun* [Yokohama and Tokyo daily], *Chōya shinbun* [Government and public daily], *Jiyū shinbun* [liberty daily], *Jiji shinpō* [Daily News], and Ikawa [1991].

manufacturers in Suwa to purchase cocoons from all over eastern Japan. Responding to the demand, national and private railways scheduled trains or cars exclusively for the transport of cocoons. The use of railways significantly diminished the cost of cocoon transportation, and therefore strongly prompted fractional local markets converge.[12] Not only were long-time silk farmers in distant traditional silk districts encouraged to specialize in supplying cocoons, but also new farms oriented to cocoon production emerged in areas served by the railways. Both new and traditional sericulture districts supplied large numbers of cocoons for modern silk-reeling districts led by Suwa (Nakabayashi 2003). The network of trunk lines led to the convergence of the cocoon market, and then it caused the geographical concentration of silk reeling and the diffusion of sericulture. The development of the modern silk-reeling industry and the expansion of sericulture districts advanced together in Japan.

3. The Rise and Development of a Modern Silk-reeling Industry in Suwa District

3.1. The 1880s: the rise of a modern silk-reeling industry

Machine-reeling firms in the early 1880s

From the late 1870s Suwa had machine-reeling factories. They were equipped with reeling machines, which were cheap wooden imitations of Italian ones. They used the *Kennel* (*tavelle*) system, and they had boilers that generated steam for boiling cocoons.[13] Until the mid-1880s, however, silk-reeling factories in Suwa were small in scale, averaging only 20–30 basins (Table 8.2). The owners formed associations for cooperative shipments to wholesale merchants in Yokohama because joint liability made them creditworthy for the wholesalers and because large lots brought advantages in Yokohama. Kaimeisha, established in 1879, was one such association (Nakabayashi 2003: 163–70).

Neither individual factories nor cooperative shipment associations controlled quality systematically until the early 1880s. The associations packed raw silk of varying quality produced by member silk-reeling manufacturers and consigned it to wholesale merchants. During the packing, cards that recorded the producer's name were inserted in each 3.75-gram lot of raw silk. The wholesale merchants sold the consignments to Western trading companies in the concession. Before purchasing, the trading companies inspected the raw silk, assigning each 3.75-gram lot a grade, from 1 through 3; the purchase price reflected the assigned grades. The wholesalers forwarded the proceeds of the sale, together with a record of the grades, to the associations. The associations then paid each member according to the number and grades of raw silk lots submitted. The trading companies qualified raw silk and baled it again according to the quality, put their "private chops" [trademarks] on the shipments, and exported them to Europe and France.[14]

Silk-reeling manufacturers thus depended on Western trading companies for inspecting the quality of raw silk until the early 1880s. The price of raw silk, such as that of all other commodities, was determined by multidimensional factors of characteristic—composing the quality— especially by the evenness and luster of the threads.[15] If they relied on the trading companies for the inspection, the silk-reeling manufacturers could not find the evaluation in the market of the multidimensional quality vector of their own silk. They could know just the amount of money paid for their raw silk, but not the quality vector corresponding to the price vector of their raw silk. As they could not know the direction of quality which they were to pursue, it was costly and risky that the silk-reeling manufacturers decided the quality of raw silk. A further problem was "private chops" of the trading companies. Quality premium, which was generated by inspection and guarantee of quality, belonged to the Western trading companies.

After the French panic of 1882, many Japanese silk-reeling manufacturers switched production from the 10-to-12 or 11-to-13 denier raw silk intended for France, to the 13-to-15 denier raw silk demanded in the U.S. Suwa reeling manufacturers, in particular, increased their exports to the U.S. rapidly. Japanese filature, however, was inferior to the Italian until the early 1880s, especially in denier evenness.[16] If Japanese silk-reeling manufacturers had continued to produce and ship uneven raw silk, ignoring the need for innovation in the production process, they would not have secured such an overwhelming advantage in the American market.[17] They did, however, introduce innovation in the form of cooperative re-reeling.

Cooperative re-reeling and the "incentive compatible" organization
The reeling process is one of drawing silk threads from boiled cocoons and winding them. While in Italy, for instance, wound silk could simply be taken off the reel and shipped immediately, Japan's high humidity levels raised the possibility that once-reeled threads would stick to each other. Accordingly, Japanese raw silk had to be wound again on a second, larger reel for drying and conditioning.

Cooperative re-reeling was the use of group resources to install facilities for, and carry out, re-reeling. It was introduced into Japan in the late 1870s by traditional silk-reeling farmers in Gunma Prefecture who were attempting to enter the U.S. market.[18] Once it became clear that cooperative re-reeling was useful in producing the kind of uniform raw silk demanded in the U.S., machine-reeling manufacturers hastened to adopt the practice. In the 1880s, hand-powered reeling machines were still in use in a number of factories and it was difficult to maintain the constant speed that was necessary for producing uniform thread. To offset this problem to some extent, re-reeling wheels were generally operated by waterpower, which was helpful for the production of standardized raw silk (Nakabayashi 2003: 171).

In Suwa, the cooperative shipment association Kaimeisha established a re-reeling factory powered by a water wheel in 1884 and started cooperative re-reeling. Use of the water wheel was important technologically, because not a few members of Kaimeisha operated factories that depended on human power (Nakabayashi 2003: 191). Even more significant than the technological advance, however, were the accompanying changes in the organization of production that opened up advantages for Kaimeisha members in the U.S. export market. Not only did Kaimeisha work to standardize the product and reduce re-reeling costs by integrating the re-reeling process, but it also established a systematic inspection system aimed at controlling the quality of raw silk produced by all member factories. This organizational change set the direction of the Japanese silk-reeling industry (Nakabayashi 2003: 170–82).

Kaimeisha increased the number of administrative staff and other workers in its re-reeling factory. Moreover, it issued its stringent *Rules of Kaimeisha* to standardize office organization and inspection procedures. In the reeling process carried out in each member factory, raw silk was wound on to small reels. Attached to each reel was a card on which were entered the reeling factory name, the identification number of the female employee who had worked on the reeling, the date, and the cocoon type. A porter carried the reels to a registrar who checked the attached cards and registered the reels. Then the raw silk could be wound off the small reel on to a larger one that matched the standard skein used in the re-reeling process.

At this point, the silk thread was sampled to measure the denier. The weight of each bundle and the denier of thread were measured and entered in the record card. The bundle of raw silk then underwent the final quality inspection, receiving a grade of 1, 2, 3, or substandard, according to denier evenness, luster and consistency. It was then baled, imprinted with the chop of its grade and shipped to a wholesale merchant in Yokohama. After taking receipt of the bale, the wholesale merchant sent market information by telegram to Kaimeisha and received Kameisha's selling order in reply.

The record cards, on the other hand, were sent to the Kaimeisha accountant, who entered the date, denier, quality, and quantity under the name of the appropriate female employee in a section of the Quality and Quantity Book known as the "Raw Silk Detailed Record". The "Detailed Record" was passed to a travelling inspector, who transferred the information into each female employee's section in the "Denier Book" (Fig. 8.4).

"Detailed Record" and the "Denier Book," which logged the daily performance of individual female workers at their respective factories, were used as a means of controlling incentives mainly for factory owners and managers and partly for the female workers. Raw silk was sold according to grade, and proceeds of the sales were distributed according to grade. Moreover, female workers who met the requirement of quality on a continuing basis were rewarded. The travelling inspectors guided the factories by passing on the information about quality that accumulated in the "Detailed Record". Member silk-reeling manufacturers were thus given financial incentives to control quality and concrete information about quality. The "incentive compatible" organization, where thorough-going quality control meant the maximization of profit for each member factory, made high-quality production self-enforced by the members.

High-quality production costs more than low-quality production and the amount of cost increase is determined by the producer's level of efficiency. Therefore, high-quality production might not mean maximization of profit for a less efficient producer. In other words, Kaimeisha organization provided little incentive for less efficient factories. In fact, it prohibited as members, factories that could not achieve the Kaimeisha average in quality with 80 percent of the Kameisha average in productivity (*Article 7* of *Rules, 1884*). Continuity of membership was also important for quality control: most of the original members remained in

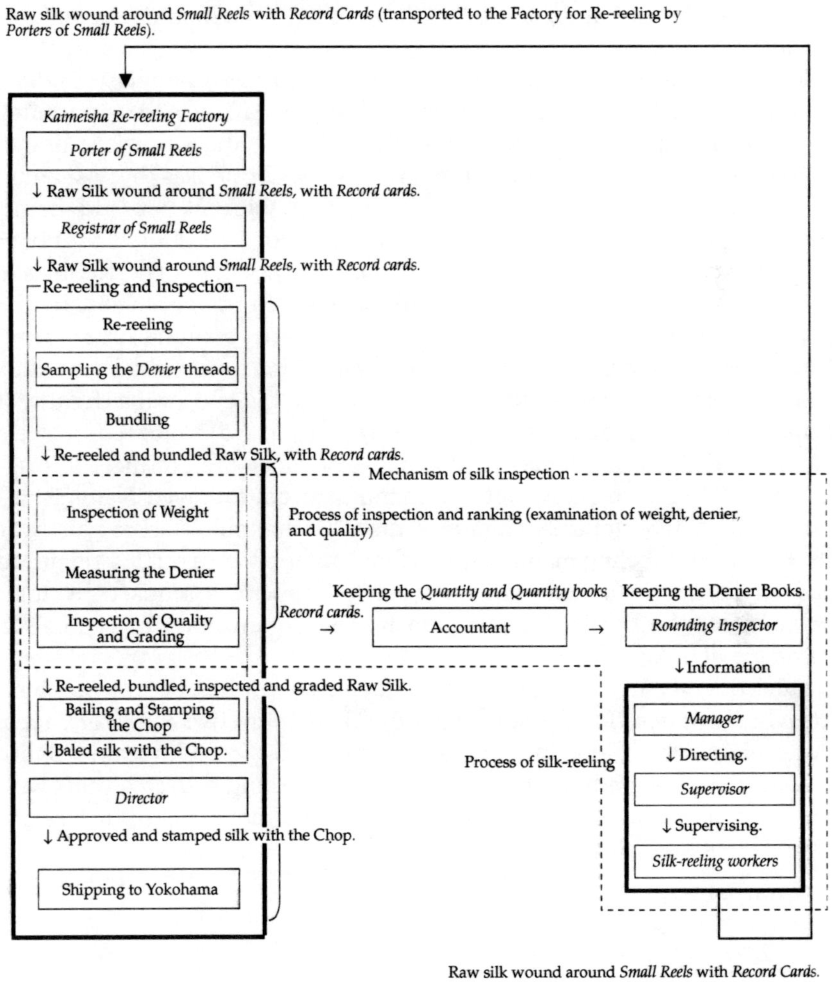

Raw silk wound around *Small Reels* with *Record Cards* (transported to the Factory for Re-reeling by *Porters* of *Small Reels*).

Kaimeisha Re-reeling Factory

Porter of Small Reels

↓ Raw Silk wound around *Small Reels*, with *Record cards.*

Registrar of Small Reels

↓ Raw Silk wound around *Small Reels*, with *Record cards.*

┌─ Re-reeling and Inspection ─┐

Re-reeling

Sampling the *Denier* threads

Bundling

↓ Re-reeled and bundled Raw Silk, with *Record cards.*

········· Mechanism of silk inspection ·········

Inspection of Weight

Process of inspection and ranking (examination of weight, denier, and quality)

Measuring the Denier

Keeping the *Quantity and Quantity books*   Keeping the Denier Books.

Record cards.

Inspection of Quality and Grading   → Accountant →   *Rounding Inspector*

↓ Information

↓ Re-reeled, bundled, inspected and graded Raw Silk.

Bailing and Stamping the Chop

↓ Baled silk with the Chop.

Process of silk-reeling

Manager

↓ Directing.

Director

Supervisor

↓ Approved and stamped silk with the Chop.

↓ Supervising.

Silk-reeling workers

Shipping to Yokohama

Raw silk wound around *Small Reels* with *Record Cards.*

Fig. 8.4 Silk re-reeling and inspection system of Kaimeisha from 1884.

Kaimeisha until at least the late 1890s. By contrast, associations, which had fluid members, could not sufficiently control quality even by introducing cooperative re-reeling (Nakabayashi 2003: 175–7, 186).

Brand establishment
If high quality production based on technological and organizational innovation was to generate profit, it was important that the product should be evaluated accurately and purchased at an appropriately high price. It was also important that the quality premium should belong not to a trading company or a wholesale merchant but to the producer. Accordingly, silk-reeling manufacturers had to supply a quality product

Masaki Nakabayashi

as indicated by the chop, and buyers had to trust the manufacturers' certification of quality.

Kaimeisha set the design for its chop in its *1884 Rules*, and its *1888 Rules* prescribed strict control of the brand quality. Raw silk was to be classified into three groups. Group 1 would be recognized as the Kaimeisha brand, within which there were three numbered ranks, Group 2 as the Soseigumi brand, and Group 3 in the domestic market without a brand name. According to the 1888 agreement, Kaimeisha No. 1 accounted for about 70 percent of total production (Nakabayashi 2003: 178). The Kaimeisha brand was recognized in the Yokohama market from about 1882. By the late 1880s, trading companies in Yokohama were receiving orders from New York that specified the Kaimeisha brand. The Kaimeisha brand thus seems to have become trusted in New York by the end of the decade. It gained quality premium clearly after 1884 (Fig. 8.5), and Kaimeisha's member factories developed rapidly.[19] It established the producer's "original chop". Other machine-reeling manufacturers followed Kaimeisha's lead, and in 1887 Japanese share of the U.S. raw silk market was over 50 percent. Silk-reeling manufacturers that had obtained a quality premium had an incentive to maintain the quality implicitly promised by their brand name, and they did maintain it. The organization of Kaimeisha became a standard.[20]

Subsequently, many of the chops in Japanese raw silk became jumbled (*Broad-silk manufacture and the tariff*, 50). There were two kinds of chops; those of major silk-reeling manufacturers who aimed to gain quality premium permanently, and those of small silk-reeling manufacturers who tried to make short-term profits by cheating buyers. Overall, it was the

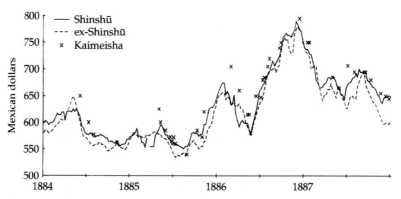

Fig. 8.5. Price of *Shinshū Filatures* and *Kaimeisha Filatures* in the Yokohama market 1884–1887: weekly data.

Source: Nakabayashi (2003: 100).

Notes: *Shinsū* is the old name of Nagano Prefecture. Original source is *Tokyo keizai zasshi* [Tokyo Economic journal].

major silk-reeling manufacturers, led by the Suwa-based businesses, which led the development of the Japanese silk-reeling industry. Several studies have emphasized that some Japanese filature brands were not trusted and that trading companies or wholesale merchants had to participate in quality control (Ishii 1972: 70–1, 208–9, Federico 1997, 162–4). Although this observation describes the conditions of the early 1880s, it does not apply to the leading silk-reeling manufacturers after the middle years of that decade.

Among Kaimeisha's member firms were Katakura, which later became the largest silk-reeling manufacturer in the world, and the silk-reeling manufacturer which later established Okaya Silk Reeling Co. The development of these two companies originated in the establishment of the Kaimeisha brand.

3.2. The development of modern silk reeling from the 1890s

Change in the U.S. market and the challenge of Shanghai filature
The Japanese share of the U.S. raw silk market declined somewhat in the 1890s. In particular, during the stagnation in the American weaving industry caused by the recession of 1893 to 1896 (Scranton 1989: 112–227), many weaving companies that produced middle- and lower-grade fabrics for mass consumption changed their organzine (a kind of twisted thread for warp) from Japanese to Shanghai filature.[21] Use of silk fabrics became more popular in the 1890s. The reason lay in the productivity gains caused by the increased speed of throwing machines and power looms in the 1890s. Yearly production of broad silk per loom increased from 197,471 yards in 1890 to 251,001 yards in 1899 (*Twelfth census*, 206). At the same time, and especially in the stagnation years from 1893, male workers were replaced by unskilled female workers in the production of middle- and lower-grade cloth. The raw silk demanded under such conditions was, above all, move even in denier, because it was suited to the high speed operation of power looms and made high productivity possible.[22] Raw silk of even denier was thus needed as the warp of middle- and lower-grade fabrics as well as high-grade ones.[23] Shanghai filature met that demand. Machine-reeling factories in Shanghai grew out of Western investment in the 1880s and developed rapidly in the 1890s. They were equipped with an average of 150–500 basins and the reeling machines were driven by steam power. Accordingly, they could produce filature that was superior to the Japanese product in terms of consistency in quality and evenness in denier.[24]

Large-scale factories and the resumption of development
In order to re-capture the markets they had lost, Suwa silk-reeling manufacturers had to restructure the raw silk industry. First, it was necessary

to move to a production process in which reeling and re-reeling were conducted continuously in one large factory. In other words, the system of quality control that had been established in the cooperative re-reeling associations (Fig. 8.4) had to be replaced by control procedures that were wholly integrated into the production system of each individual firm. As early as 1894, Katakura and Ozawa, who were members of Kaimeisha, established independent large factories that were equipped with 200–300 basins. In 1897, three small silk-reeling manufacturers, also members of Kaimeisha, took the lead with others in establishing Okaya Silk Reeling Co. The three Kaimeisha-affiliated manufacturers operated small-scale factories: each had between 30 and 60 basins; two relied on hand power. Their example reflects both the problems that the Suwa silk-reeling industry faced and the solutions attempted.

The Okaya Co. factory was driven by steam and water power. It began with 440 basins in 1897, expanding to 794 basins in its second year of operation. In 1903 Otojirō Oguchi, president of Okaya Co., stated the company's founding objectives and successes:

In the past, we silk-reeling manufacturers took the raw silk produced in our individual factories and gathered it together at the cooperative re-reeling location. We inspected it, put the same chop on it, and cooperatively sold it. . . . However, the raw silk threads were similar in appearance only; they could not be the same in essence. . . . Accordingly, foreign weavers always complained. In 1897, we established a large factory, standardized all raw materials, the water for boiling and the supervision. . . . Since we always produced high-grade raw silk of consistent quality, our products received increasingly high evaluations from foreign buyers. American weavers often place orders . . . that specify the name of Okaya Co. (Hiramoto 1985a: 46–7).

Okaya Co. achieved a uniform, high-level product at its large-scale factory, and its brand "Chicken" was recognized as the standard brand for the classification of "Shinshū No. 1" in the Yokohama market and that for "Japan No. 1" also in New York in the 1900s (Chittick 1913: 15, Duran 1913: 93, Hirano-son 1932: 275; Nakabayashi 2003: 204–5).[25] Moreover, in the early 1900s, silk-reeling factories in Suwa, including Okaya Co., raised labor productivity rapidly and overwhelmed the average of that in Italy, and thus the relative share of labor in the value added could be lowered, while keeping the same level of wages as those in Italy.[26]

Following the example of Katakura and the founders of Okaya Co., silk-reeling manufacturers in Suwa withdrew one after another from the cooperative re-reeling associations, establishing their own large-scale factories that included equipment for re-reeling. As a result, by around 1900, Suwa reeling factories averaged more than 100 basins (Table 8.2). Though many silk-reeling manufacturers collapsed during the late 1890s, those that survived produced uniform raw silk and established independent brands by establishing a continuous operation from reeling to re-reeling in their own large factories (Hiramoto 1985*b*: 20; Takamura 1995: 136–7; Nakabayashi 2003: 189–218).

By contrast, the modern silk-reeling industry of Shanghai became stagnant in the 1900s. Factors cited as causes for the stagnation include overly expensive French facilities as well as an increase in production costs caused by the inefficient labor and financial markets (Sota 1994: 170–83). In addition, however, one should probably consider the problem of organization. In general, the managers and owners of Shanghai silk-reeling companies were different people. Managers regularly contracted with owners to rent a factory and its chop for one year. Managers typically did not have a long-term commitment to a particular factory; nor were they interested in the improvement of equipment. Therefore, the chop of that factory could not guarantee a given quality (Li 1981: 171–3; Lieu 1933: 39–47; Lieu 1940: 96–102; Eng 1986: 70–9; Furuta 1988: 95–7).[27] Few Shanghai factories had an incentive structure for obtaining a quality premium by establishing an identifiable brand. Although Federico has criticized this argument on the grounds that some Shanghai filature was of high quality (Federico 1997: 24), the important issue is whether a management oriented to brand consolidation was predominant or not. It should be noted as a point of fact that the Japanese silk-reeling industry, in which a management orientation to maintaining brand name and quality premium was predominant, boosted its share of the U.S. market again after 1900 (Federico 1997: 214; Nakabayashi 2003: 212–13).

Complementary development
The "Japan No. 1" filature produced by large-scale factories in Suwa was inferior in luster and resilience both to the "Japan Extra" produced in other districts of Japan and to "Italian Extra". It was not high-grade filature in those terms (Ishii 1972: 57–92; Federico 1997: 136–8); it was uniform and cheap, suitable for the middle- and low-grade fabrics being made for mass consumption in the U.S. This was, however, the most profitable market in the world for the 50 years from the fourth quarter of the nineteenth century through the first quarter of the twentieth century. The Suwa silk-reeling industry adapted itself to the U.S. market and expanded it:

it is doubtful whether the silk-manufacturing industry could have established itself in this country on the scale to which it had grown by, say, 1880, not to speak of its growth since that time, without the equally phenomenal expansion of the raw-silk industry in Japan. In fact, the beginning of this expansion approximately coincided with the development of the broad-silk and ribbon industries in this country, and has continued to parallel it (*Broad-silk manufacture and the tariff* (1936): 36).

3.3. *The wage system and the labor market*

The wage system and the incentive structure

It should be noted, if the technological aspect were to be put aside, why couldn't the continuous system which contained both the reeling process and re-reeling process with the inspection process be more efficient than the cooperative re-reeling system? The most important reason was the control of workers by the incentive structure. Under the cooperative re-reeling system, it was the cooperative re-reeling factories, not respective reeling factories, that held all the information about the performance of female workers operating on the line of each reeling factory. In order to match the quality of raw silk with demand from the market more correctly, however, the silk-reeling manufacturers had to control workers more carefully and for this reason, they needed to obtain information about their performance. Sophisticating the incentive system for workers by getting the information about the performance of their workers was the most important reason for incorporating the re-reeling process with inspection process into their own factories. The change in the production organization came together with that of the organization of labor, especially, with that of the wage system.

One notable feature of the silk-reeling industry in Suwa was the wage system. Primarily, was a relative wage system, based on an after-the-fact estimate of each worker's productivity. In the Suwa silk industry, the term of an employment contract was usually one year or less; in no way did the contract specify the wage rate. The output of each female worker was calculated twice a month and totalled at the end of the year (or at the end of the contract period). The absolute value of the worker's annual performance minus the average of all female workers in the factory equalled the relative value of her performance. That relative value determined her basic wage, which was paid in one lump sum at the end of year.

The quality control system established by Kaimeisha relied on a daily calculation of each worker's productivity, allowing use of a relative wage system based on an after-the-fact estimation. By the end of the 1880s, a wage system that applied a relative evaluation to labor productivity and material productivity (output of raw silk/input of cocoons) was common throughout the Suwa silk-reeling industry (Nakabayashi 2003: 250–5). The relative wage system was able to give an incentive to workers by reducing the possibility that an evaluation error might be passed on. It could also give a powerful incentive to a particularly outstanding worker by expanding the skewness of the wage distribution, that allocates the relatively high wage to her (Rosen 1988: 60–2, Holmstrom 1982: 334–8). While Italian and Chinese factories maintained discipline by severe supervision and fines, female workers in Suwa exhibited a self-imposed concentration that derived from the relative wage system (Federico 1997: 28).

The second characteristic of the Suwa wage system was its use of multidimensional evaluation criteria, including labor and materials productivity, denier evenness and the luster of the thread produced by each worker. The profitability of silk reeling depended not only on labor productivity but also on materials productivity. At the same time, the price of raw silk was determined by a multidimensional quality vector, whose factors were evenness in denier and luster, as a multidimensional price function. The trade-off for increasing labor productivity usually resulted in a decline in those factors that required careful attention: materials productivity, denier evenness, and luster. Thus Suwa silk-reeling manufacturers constructed an incentive system that controlled multidimensional tasks simultaneously (Holmstrom and Milgrom 1991: 24–35, Nakabayashi 2003: 256–68). Although the relative wage system up to the mid-1890s monitored only labor materials productivity, it became more elaborate after the late 1890s. By the early 1900s, an incentive system that also controlled quality and materials productivity had been established.

Table 8.4 illustrates the various components of the basic wage for female workers in the Kasahara factory from 1905 to 1908. In producing these results, the following wage determinants are assumed to have been used in the factory:

W. Basic wage. d. *Penalty* deduction.

t_1: Labor Productivity. t_2: Material productivity. t_3: Evenness of threads. t_4: Luster of threads.

(1) $W = \alpha_{11}t_1 + \alpha_{12}d.$ $0 < \alpha_{11}, \alpha_{12}$
(2) $d = \alpha_{21}t_2 + \alpha_{22}t_3 + \alpha_{23}t_4.$ $0 > \alpha_{21}, \alpha_{22}, \alpha_{23}$

Table 8.4. Basic wage and performance of female workers in *Kasahara*'s factory (OLS)

W: Basic wage, t_1: Labor productivity, t_2: Materials productivity, t_3: Evenness in denier, t_4: Luster.
Equation: $W = \alpha_1 t_1 + \alpha_2 t_2 + \alpha_3 t_3 + \alpha_4 t_4.$

Years	Samples	α_1	α_2	α_3	α_4	se	R^2	F-value
1905	199	0.838	0.094	0.116	0.142	0.404	0.841	256.529**
t-value		(28.090)**	(3.072)**	(3.733)**	(4.772)**			
1906	150	0.798	0.152	0.050	0.164	0.451	0.804	148.425**
t-value		(20.108)**	(3.673)**	(1.314)*	(4.401)**			
1907	228	0.852	0.016	0.011	0.155	0.490	0.765	181.892**
t-value		(23.679)**	(0.404)	(0.278)	(4.688)**			

Source: Nakabayashi (2003: 262).

Notes: Since data are standardized, intercept are estimated as 0. Original source is "Chingin keisan bo" [Book for calculation of wage], in "Kasaharagumi shiryō" [Documents of Kasahara Co.], Okaya Sanshi Hakubutsukan [The Okaya Museum of Silk], Okaya. **: significant at 1%. *: significant at 5%.

First, using equation (2), *Penalty* deduction was determined on the basis of materials productivity, denier evenness, and luster. Then, using equation (1), an amount equivalent to labor productivity minus *Penalty* deduction was used to determine the basic wage. This wage model was estimated using 2SLS and the results are shown in Tables 8.5 *(a)* and 8.5 *(b)*. The performance factors that acted as a trade-off with labor productivity were demonstrated to the workers using the impressive *Penalty* method.

In the case of the Kasahara factory, during the period up to the early 1900s, when the wage system had measured only labor productivity and materials productivity, a number of workers displayed opportunistic behavior by lowering quality to raise productivity. After about the middle of the first decade of the twentieth century, however, workers came to allot appropriate effort to labor productivity, materials productivity, denier evenness, and luster. Using this "high powered incentive"

Table 8.5(a) Fine equation (2SLS)

d: *Penalty* deduction, t_2: Material productivity, t_3: Evenness in denier, t_4: Luster.
Equation: (2) $d = \alpha_{21}t_2 + \alpha_{22}t_3 + \alpha_{23}t_4$.

Year	α_{21}	α_{22}	α_{23}	se	R^2	F-value
1905	−0.162	−0.656	−0.257	0.606	0.640	115.721**
t-value	(−3.591)**	(−14.317)**	(−5.765)**			
1906	−0.233	−0.388	−0.408	0.780	0.408	33.508**
t-value	(−3.501)**	(−5.839)**	(−6.382)**			
1907	0.104	−0.410	−0.343	0.845	0.298	31.674**
t-value	(1.616)†	(−6.261)**	(−6.032)**			

Source: Nakabayashi (2003: 265).

Notes: Since data are standardized, intercepts are estimated as 0. **: significant at 1%.
†: significant at 10%.

Table 8.5(b) Wage equation (2SLS)

W: Basic wage, t_1: Labor productivity, d: *Penalty* deduction estimated by Equation (2)
Equation: (1) $W = \alpha_{11}t_1 + \alpha_{12}d$.

year	α_{11}	α_{12}	se	R^2	F-value
1905	0.840	−0.264	0.411	0.834	491.273**
t-value	(28.009)**	(−7.043)**			
1906	0.823	−0.318	0.457	0.796	286.043**
t-value	(21.498)**	(−5.307)**			
1907	0.840	−0.236	0.497	0.756	349.218**
t-value	(25.215)**	(−3.867)**			

Source: Nakabayashi (2003: 265).

Notes: Since data are standardized, intercepts are estimated as 0. **: significant at 1%.

(Williamson 1985: 131–62), silk-reeling manufacturers in Suwa had succeeded in optimizing the labor of their workers (Nakabayashi 2003: 256–74).

Negotiating labor transfers in the silk-reeling industry
In addition, for the incentive scheme to function well, it was necessary that workers unsuitable to one factory could move to another one at a reasonable transaction cost, because the mismatch of workers resulted in the reduced effectiveness of the incentive scheme in the factory (Milgrom [1988]: 42–4).

The rapid development of the Suwa silk-reeling industry led to a shortage of labor, but the problem was resolved with the absorption of workers from the surrounding region. Higher wages and a considerably higher living standard in the dormitories drew workers from agricultural villages into the silk-reeling factories (Saito 1998: 121–30, Hunter 2003: 50–88). However, as the rapid growth of the silk-reeling industry in Suwa continued, the labor market remained tight. Moreover, major silk-reeling manufacturers needed liquidity in the labor market. While the civil law enacted in 1898 allowed employers to make five-year contracts with employees, silk-reeling manufacturers in Suwa commonly offered no more than a one-year contract. Major manufacturers enticed especially able workers from their competitors and encouraged less valuable workers to leave. Such a fluid labor market needed institutions that would help manufacturers to transfer workers smoothly.

The League of Silk Reeling Manufacturers in Suwa (*Suwa seishi dōmei*) was organized in 1900 to realize this objective; the League, in turn, implemented a worker registration system from 1903. Specifically, the League obliged its member silk-reeling manufacturers to register all employees with the League secretariat while allowing each the exclusive right to employ the registered workers. Most scholarship to date, from the traditional one to the game theory one, has assumed that the purpose and effect of this registration system was to restrict the movement of workers from factory to factory (Iwamoto 1970, Ishii 1972: 277–90, Tsurumi 1990: 74–5, Kambayashi 2000, 2001). Major silk-reeling manu-facturers, however, had little need to restrain the movement of workers since they could entice them with the promise of high wages. In fact, most labor movement was the result of enticement by the same major silk-reeling manufacturers who dominated the League and, in principle, the League did not punish them. Consequently, it is estimated that, even after the establishment of the Institution for the Registration of Workers, as many as 50 percent of workers changed employers in any given year (Ishii 1972: 271).

The registration of workers functioned not to restrict worker movement but rather to minimize the transaction costs generated when workers moved. Employment contracts drawn up by silk-reeling manufacturers typically included a clause that obliged a given worker to pay damages equivalent to one year's income if she broke the contract. Therefore, a silk-reeling manufacturer who sought to entice a worker to move had to absorb this high cost. If a worker could be registered and the right to employ her protected as a kind of "real right", the movement of that worker could be handled by having the prospective employer lay claim to the right of the existing employer. In such a system, damages and legal costs might be reduced throughout the labor market by having rights cleared, ceded or held. But in fact, such a practice could not be introduced into the judicial system, because modern civil law does not allow "real rights" to be established over human beings (Nakabayashi 2003: 304–6).

This does not mean the judicial system did not work at all. The court could govern the transaction between a silk-reeling manufacturer and a worker. For instance, when a silk manufacturer sued a worker who moved from his factory to another factory thus breaching the contract for damages, the judgement required the worker to pay the damages. At the same time, however, the silk-reeling manufacturer *from* whom the worker moved was bargaining with the manufacturer *to* whom the worker moved. The damages were too great to be paid by the worker. So a deal was struck in favor of the manufacturer *from* whom the worker moved. The court appeared to govern the transaction between the manufacturer and the worker, but in fact it governed that between the manufacturers. This governance of trade was costly because it was made indirectly through the court. Therefore, a private institution was needed to govern the trade directly between manufacturers (Nakabayashi 2003: 291–306).[28]

Worker registration was therefore established as a private system for registering each worker, protecting the employer's real and exclusive right to employ her, and overseeing the negotiation of this right among member silk-reeling manufacturers. The League prohibited its members from filing legal compensation suits against workers who moved from one member employer to another. In this way, it made possible the efficient exchange of workers within the League (Nakabayashi 2003: 306–18).

Working conditions

The working day in a Suwa silk-reeling factory was ordinarily 13–15 hours, occasionally extending to 18 hours during boom periods.[29] Generally, workers were required to live in dormitories and were provided with meals. At the turn of the century, workers in large factories were offered three or four meals a day. They ate rapidly, taking barely five minutes for the meal, not because supervisors forced them but because the "relative wage" system gave them an incentive to return to work as soon as possible. Bathing was regulated: in the autumn months, for instance, workers were allowed a bath every four days. Some factories contracted with doctors to offer health care; some employed nurses. The most common illnesses were stomach-related (Nakabayashi 2003: 42, 416–17).

Most scholars have regarded conditions in the Suwa silk-reeling industry as a type of sweatshop labor (Ishii 1972: 253–315, Tsurumi 1990: 59–91). This assessment should, however, be re-examined in view of the complex system of incentives available to workers and their ensuing self-imposed concentration. For instance, if silk-reeling labor was really sweatshop labor, one might expect high tuberculosis rates among workers. On the other hand, one might expect a high incidence of stress-related stomach or intestinal conditions for workers operating under modern rational supervision. In fact, it was found that compared with workers in cotton spinning and weaving, those in silk reeling had a relatively low incidence of tuberculosis and a relatively high incidence of stomach and intestinal conditions. In particular, female workers of the silk-reeling factories in Suwa bought stomach medicines to support their productivity, thus showing evidence of their commitment and concentration (Hunter 1993: 77–9). It could be said that their working conditions marked the origin of a modern labor model with greater similarity to that of contemporary business people than to the old-fashioned sweatshop laborers.

High wages and competition among workers helped to transform workers into independent individuals. Most of them were women in their late teens or early twenties (Tsurumi 1990: 87) who had experienced working and living independently for the several years that they were employed in the silk-reeling factories. It is said that after marriage these women tended to look down on their husbands and to divorce more easily, because she experienced "the relaxation of working and living by herself" and felt "the stress of having a husband". Through their experience in the silk-reeling factories, country girls were changed into modern individuals who opposed the feudal social system. That is they became valuable human capital, motivated by the relative wage system to maximize their own payoff, though workers of low rank had hard times (Tsurumi 1990: 84–8, Nakabayashi 2003: 408–20).

4. The Development of the Silk-reeling Industry and the Financial System

4.1. Financing the purchase of material cocoons

The development of an efficient financial system was of central importance for the development of the silk-reeling industry (Federico 1997: 164–7). Financing purchases of raw materials is especially important in the textile industry (Hudson 1986: 17). In silk reeling, the cost of a cocoon accounted for some 80 percent of total costs. Given Japan's status as a developing country, however, financial restrictions were chronically tight from the late 1880s to the early 1900s.

Silk-reeling manufacturers in Suwa typically received financing for cocoon purchases from wholesale merchants in May, which marked the beginning of the purchasing season. Though the loans were granted without collateral, each silk-reeling manufacturer would contract with a wholesale merchant lender to ship him the entire output for that year. Wholesale merchants were familiar with the valuations of the various brands in the Yokohama market; they also monitored management conditions among the various silk-reeling manufacturers when determining how much they could lend and at what rate of interest. The loans offered by the wholesalers were known as the "original principal". Although silk-reeling manufacturers also obtained loans from local Nagano banks, the financial policies of the local banks were influenced by the policies of the wholesalers. The silk-reeling manufactures repaid local bank loans by relying on the "advances on documentary bills" granted by wholesale merchants, which will be explained below.

Silk-reeling manufacturers had great difficulty getting credit, especially in the 1880s and 1890s, when credit needs were growing rapidly but financial institutions were insufficiently developed. The problem was solved with credit grants by the Bank of Japan. From about 1890, the Bank of Japan offered credit to the Yokohama Specie Bank to be distributed as loans to wholesalers for funding cocoon purchases. In the late 1890s, the Bank of Japan expanded its credit supplies to include other city banks, in many cases by rediscounting promissory notes. The Yokohama Specie Bank, which was a foreign exchange bank established according to the financial policy of the government (Ishii 1994), and the city banks, used the credit for loans to wholesale merchants, who in turn made loans to the silk-reeling manufacturers. When credit from the Bank of Japan tightened in the 1900s, the mature city banks were able to take over the function of providing funds for cocoon purchases. However, it was important that in the late 1890s, when large-scale factories were being established in Suwa, the Bank of Japan was able to commit credit to the silk-reeling industry (Yamaguchi 1966, Ishii 1972: 163–215, Ishii 1991, Tsurumi 1991: 215–20, 263–7, Nakabayashi 2003: 333–60).

4.2. "Advances on documentary bills"

When a silk-reeling manufacturer shipped raw silk to a wholesale merchant in Yokohama, he was able to draw a domestic documentary bill on the wholesaler at a local Suwa bank up to a limit of about 80 percent of the current price of the shipment. The local bank charged the wholesaler through a correspondent bank located in Yokohama or Tokyo. The whole-saler had to make the payment before he sold the raw silk. Since the wholesale merchant was a commission agent, this payment represented an advance on the completed sale.

This kind of financing—a loan secured with raw silk—was called an "advance on a documentary bill". It served an important function in supplying operating funds to silk-reeling businesses, especially from the 1880s to the early 1900s. While it was necessary for silk-reeling manufac-turers to purchase cocoons continuously throughout the season, until the early 1900s even big businesses were short of operating funds for cocoon purchases. Credit granted by the Bank of Japan had an important role here, too. The Bank of Japan offered credit directly or through city banks to prominent wholesale merchants which dealt with prominent silk-reeling manufacturers by the discount or rediscount of promissory notes secured with raw silk. After about 1905, big silk-reeling manufacturers in Suwa gave up drawing domestic documentary bills as their supplies of operating funds had expanded. However, the existence of financial institutions that allowed advances on documentary bills was essential in the 1880s and 1890s, when the silk reeling-industry was developing in Suwa (Nakabayashi 2003: 361–80).

4.3. *The financial system and development of silk reeling*

Financing for the silk-reeling industry in Japan was secured by the commitment of the Bank of Japan to expanding credit. Some problems could have emerged from this system. First, if government funds had been made available without relevant monitoring, moral hazard may have ensued. In other words, inefficient silk-reeling manufacturers could have received credit by taking advantage of the asymmetry of information. Second, credit supplied by the Bank of Japan during boom periods could intensify the contraction of credit during periods of depression. The pre-war U.S. economy grew rapidly but it was volatile. Although the price of raw silk in Yokohama dropped whenever recession occurred in the U.S. market, the U.S. economy returned to a growth trend after its short reces-sions. If even prominent silk-reeling manufacturers had been forced to collapse, the impact on the development of the silk-reeling industry would have been severe.

The first problem was solved by monitoring under the long-term relationship between the city banks or the Yokohama Specie Bank and the wholesalers, and between the wholesalers and the silk-reeling manufac-turers. The Bank of Japan distributed credit only to a few major whole-salers who had accumulated information about the Yokohama market through the discount of notes endorsed by the banks in long-term relations with them, and the wholesalers were keeping long-term relations with silk-reeling manufactures. In this way, moral hazard from asymmetrical information could be avoided. Banks, wholesalers and silk-reeling manufacturers could capture a kind of rents by preventing opportunistic behavior on the part of wholesalers and silk-reeling manu-facturers, and the low rate credit from the Bank of Japan was able to increase those rents. Such rents could be earned endogenously even without the low rate credit from the Bank of Japan once that efficient mon-itoring system through the long-term relationship was established. Indeed, while the credit from the Bank of Japan decreased in the 1900s, this monitoring system worked well and the city banks continued to increase the financing of cocoon purchasing. The second problem was solved by offering relief inventory finance for prominent wholesale merchants during periods of panic. Although many silk-reeling manu-facturers collapsed in the mid-1890s (Table 8.2), those who had passed screening by wholesale merchants survived and established large-scale factories (Nakabayashi 2003: 381–404).

Modern financial institutions supplied sufficient money to the silk-reeling industry under the control of the Bank of Japan. In addition, the Bank of Japan adopted a mild inflationary policy (Patrick 1965, 1967) and during periods of depression provided selective financing to protect the inventories of silk-reeling manufacturers. The establishment of a modern financial system under the effective control of the Bank of Japan was of central importance. It offered a contrast with China, where the develop-ment of modern financial institutions failed, and with Italy, which lacked a financial system to protect silk-reeling manufacturers during periods of panic (Li 1981: 178–83, Federico 1997: 166–7).

5. Conclusion

Structural change in the international market forced Japan's silk-reeling industry to shift its direction toward exports to the U.S. Such a shift required the development of a modern silk-reeling industry that could produce uniform-quality raw silk. Silk-reeling manufacturers in Suwa led the way, forming associations to introduce cooperative re-reeling and establishing a system of quality control in which raw silk could be inspected and graded. In addition, silk-reeling businesses established brands that guaranteed a certain, consistent quality. Through the price of its brand, the silk-reeling manufacturer could get information about the multidimensional quality vector in the market. The quality of raw silk thus improved in an industrial structure that was incentive-compatible for member businesses. Quality premium came to belong not to trading companies or wholesale merchants but to silk-reeling businesses that had established their own brands. The Suwa silk-reeling industry expanded rapidly through its ability to supply middle- and lower-grade fabrics for mass consumption in the U.S.

In the 1890s, large factories established in Shanghai were able to produce uniform raw silk, causing a temporary decline in Japan's share of the U.S. market. However, with the emergence in Suwa of large-scale factories that integrated a system of quality control into their own operations, the Japanese silk-reeling industry was able to regain and expand Japan's share of the U.S. market in the 1900s. Moreover, in the early 1900s, Suwa silk-reeling factories established a multidimensional relative wage system that efficiently controlled incentives for workers. Under this wage system, information about the multidimensional price vector was effectively used for profit maximization. In the labor market, institutions for negotiating worker transfers minimized the transaction costs entailed by the movement of workers among factories. Finally, the development of the silk-reeling industry in Suwa was supported by a financial structure that included the Bank of Japan, the Yokohama Specie Bank, city banks, and major wholesale merchants. Money in the Yokohama financial market, which was supplied to prominent silk-reeling manufacturers selectively, mitigated financial restrictions and accelerated the efficient development of the silk-reeling industry.

The development of a modern silk-reeling industry in Suwa prompted the reorganization of sericulture from the mid-1880s. Sericulture farmers gave up traditional hand-reeling and switched to supplying cocoons to machine-reeling businesses. The subsequent rapid growth of sericulture was an important factor in the development of the silk-reeling industry.

Previous scholarship has argued that Italian silk-reeling businesses, as well as the few Japanese businesses that could compete in quality with the Italians, were superior to Suwa silk-reeling manufacturers in technology (Ishii 1972: 19–92, Federico 1997: 133–9). However, the European silk industry, which produced high-grade fabrics flexibly (Sable and Zeitlin 1985), and the U.S. silk industry, which developed mass production, should be considered separately. While the Italian and Chinese industries were forced to adapt themselves to the European market, the Japanese silk-reeling industry represented by Suwa was able to establish a production system suitable for the promising U.S. mass market from the 1880s to 1920s. Only a factory industry was suitable for mass production and efficient institutions were of central importance.

Notes

1. An epidemic (pebrine) in European sericulture was favorable to Japanese raw silk. See Federico (1997: 36–41).
2. In 1904, the average of wage per workday for female worker operating silk-reeling was 12.6 cents, and meals served by firms cost 4–7.5 cents per workday,

then total amount paid by firms amounted to 16.5–20.1 cents. The wage for skilled workers was 19.0 cents and thus 23.0–26.5 cents including meals. In addition, other living expenses than meals were also paid by firms under the dormitory system. In Milan and Lombardy, Italy, where "Italian No. 1" that was the counterpart of "Japan No. 1" was produced, the wage for skilled workers was 19.3–21.2 cents, or in Messina, Sicily, where the best raw silk in the world "Messina" was produced, the wage for skilled workers was 16.4–20.3 cents and there was not a dormitory system in Italy. The level of wages in Suwa were not only higher than those in other parts of Japan, but they were the same as, or higher than, those in Italy. See Nakabayashi (2003: 203), on Suwa in 1904 and, on the index from 1881–1919, Appendix: 487–90. On Italy, see "Tabulation of bottom facts regarding sericulture in Italy, China, and Japan", *The American silk journal*, Vol. 24, Apr., 1905, 38–9.

3. About the recession, see *The Economist*, London, 2,002, Jan. 7, 1882, 10–12, 2,004, Jan. 21, 1882, 65–6, 74–5; "Commercial history & review of 1882", *The Economist*, 2,061, Feb. 24, 1883, 26; Bouvier 1960: 140–87, 235–48. On the amount and share of import by the U.S., and of import and export of France, see Nakabayashi (2003, Appendix: 473–86). See also Federico (1997: 195–200, 213–16).

4. "Commercial history and review of 1883", *The Economist*, London, No. 2113, Feb. 23, 1884, 23; "Commercial history and review of 1885", *The Economist*, 2,217, Feb. 20, 1886, 24; "Commercial history and review of 1886", *The Economist*, 2,269, Feb. 19, 1887, 26.

5. This tendency was compatible with the introduction of power looms. "In 1870 and for a number of years after, hand looms which could be operated by men only were largely in use for weaving broad silk. They have practically ceased to exist and with their disappearance there has been a great increase in the number of looms which are operated largely by women" (The Senate of the United States, *Report on condition of woman and child wage-earners in the United States, Vol. 4: The silk industry*, Washington, Government Printing Office, 1911, 34). United States Tariff Commission, *Broad-silk manufacture and the tariff*, Washington, Government Printing Office (1926: 7, 38). See also Clark (1929a: 449–58); Matsui (1930: 131–53); Taussig (1931: 217–48); Golin (1988: 16–36); Federico (1997: 140–3). Though skilled workers were not unnecessary (Golin 1988: 31), they were no longer artisans. In the U.S., the number of power looms was 1,251 in 1870, 2,688 in 1875, 5,321 in 1880, 20,822 in 1890, 44,257 in 1900, and 59,775 in 1905; the number of hand looms was 188 in 1870, 1,814 in 1875, 3,153 in 1880, 1,747 in 1890, 173 in 1900, and 283 in 1905; Department of the Interior, Census Office, *Report on the Manufactures of the United States at the tenth census (June 1, 1880)*, Washington (1883: 928–9); Brocket (1875: 159); *Twelfth census of the United States, taken in the year 1900, manufacturers part 3, special reports on selected industries* (1902: 206); *Report on condition of woman and child wage-earners in the United States, Vol. 4: 34*. See also Federico (1994: 471). The proportion of female workers in the American silk industry was over 50 percent from the 1870s until the 1920s.

6. Denier is a unit of weight used to measure raw silk. The Lyonese denier was 476 meters divided by 0.05311 grams. (See Posselt 1919: 23.)

7. "[T]he Season 1882–1883 will long be remembered as probably the most disastrous in the history of the trade", Annual meeting of the Yokohama

General Chamber of Commerce, *The Japan Weekly Mail*, Yokohama, Feb. 17, 1883, 107. The silk trade had been suspended in autumn 1881 because of a dispute over raw silk between trading companies and Japanese wholesale merchants. As a result, large inventories were held in the Yokohama market at the beginning of 1882 (Unno 1967), increasing the losses of producers.

8. In the recovery of the late 1880s, raw-silk production increased significantly and cocoon production remained low in Nagano, while cocoon production increased significantly and raw-silk production increased only slightly in Saitama and Gunma, near Nagano. These trends suggest that raw-silk production in Suwa increased on the basis of material cocoons purchased from the neighboring sericulture areas. (See Nakabayashi 2003: 92–102.)

9. According to a survey by the *Sanshigya kumiai chboubu* [head office of the Association of Sericulture], the cost of material cocoons accounted for 78.6 percent of the price of filature); production cost was 75.2 yen per picul (60 kg) (*Sanshigyō kumiai chūoubu geppo* [Monthly report of the head office of the Association of Sericulture], 11, 1887: 39). Accordingly, gross margins of hand reeling and selling cocoons in Fig. 8.3 are estimated here as follows:
(Gross margin of cocoon sales) = 0.786 (price of filature) [Yen].
(Gross margin of hand reeling) = (price of hanks) − 75.2 [Yen].
It is estimated that hand reeling became more even unprofitable relative to machine reeling thereafter. (See Minami 1987: 186–92; Minami and Makino 1995: 37–44.)

10. Both sericulture and hand-reeling were secondary occupations for farmers, being conducted by residual labor after rice cultivation. Hand-reeling required family labor from June to July, a busy season for rice growing.

11. Poton, G. P., "Report on the raw silk industry", The Foreign Office and the Board of Trade of the U.K., (eds), *Diplomatic and consular reports. Japan. Reports on the raw silk industry of Japan and on Habutae* [Japanese manufactured silk], (London, 1909: 6–22).

12. Variation (standard deviation over average) of cocoon prices in East Japan decreased from 0.22 in 1888 to 0.05 in 1906. (See Nakabayashi 2003: 134–44.)

13. In the *Kennel* method, a number of threads drawn from the boiled cocoons was passed through a porcelain ring and twisted once after passing through the rollers (Honda 1909: 155). Silk-reeling factories in Suwa continued to adopt machines of the *Kennel* type.

14. Trademarks of trading companies were called "private chops" and those of silk-reeling manufacturers were called "original chops" in the New York market. (See Duran 1913: 105–6, Chittick 1913: 14, 28–9.)

15. When a commodity is priced in the market, the multidimensional quality vector of that commodity is mapped to the amount of money. That is, a price can be interpreted as a multidimensional price function, or a price vector. This price function was called "hedonic price" by Sherwin Rosen. (See Rosen 1974: 34–6.)

16. "The competition of Italian silk with Japan's was severely felt; the cost of the former to spinners and producers was low", in "The silk trade of the half year ending 31st December, 1881", *The Japan Weekly Mail*, Feb. 4, 1882, 138. The cost of spinning [throwing] increased when *denier* was not even.

17. As early as in the second half of 1882, U.S. weavers claimed that much Japanese raw silk was not uniform in *denier*. (See *Seishi-danketsu-Dōshin-Kaisha-dai-niji-itokata-hōkoku* (Annual report of Dōshin Kaisha Co., No. 2), 1883. Information about the New York market was sent to Japan by Ryōichirō Arai, the New York branch of Dōshin Kaisha (Reischauer 1986: 207–42), and the Consulate in New York and then it was presented in reports of Dōshin Kaisha and the official gazette.

18. See Kato, T. *et al.*, *Nichibei-kiito-bōeki shiryō* [Historical materials on the silk trade between Japan and the United States] 1, shiryō-hen [documents] 1, (Tokyo, 1987: 145–99); Federico (1997: 120).

19. *Shinshū* (the old name of Nagano) filature was appreciated especially after 1884. "*July* [1884] . . . About the middle of the month *Shinshū* Silks came in to some extent, and gave evidence of excellent quality . . . the good quality apparently making them prime favorites for the American Market" in "The silk trade of Japan", taken from Messrs. Griffin & Co.'s (a trading company in Yokohama) half-yearly Silk Report, *The Japan Weekly Mail*, Apr. 18, 1885, 373. There were 1,624 basins in Suwa in 1884, 691 of which were affiliated to Kaimeisha.

20. "In filature and *Re-reels*, some of producers who have a reputation to maintain have turned out good, worthy silk; while other chops especially in the Medium Grades, have been uneven and unreliable as of old" in "The silk trade of Japan", taken from Messrs. Griffin & Co.'s half-yearly Silk Report, *The Japan Weekly Mail*, Jan. 19, 1884, 68. (On quality premium, see Klein and Leffler 1981.)

21. See Federico (1997: 214) A report from B. Richardson, president of the American silk association, *Dai Nihon sanshi kaihō* [Journal of the Sericultural Association of Japan], No. 19, Jan. 1894, 27–34; reports from the New York branch of Yokohama Kiito Gōmei Kaisha, *Dai-Nihon-sanshi- kaihō*, 29, Nov. 1894, 34–5; 32, Feb. 1895, 42–3; No. 44, Feb. 1896, 45, 46, Apr. 1896, 24–5. Raw silk should be evener for the organzine than for tram.

22. "[T]he high-speed looms introduced between 1890 and 1900 are said to have caused a substitution of women for men, because the ease in manipulation made the work suitable for women" in The Senate of the United States, *Report on condition of woman and child wage-earners in the United States, Vol. 9: history of women in industry in the United States*, (Washington, 1910: 61). (See also Clark 1929*b*: 210–15; Scranton 1989: 195–7). On the wage difference between male and female workers, see Aldrich and Albelda (1980: 329–40). Replacement of male workers occurred in the mid-1890s. In Paterson, New Jersey, Italian immigrants also increased to become the main labor source of the industry after the recession of 1893–4, surpassing better-paid British and French immigrants in number. (See Brockett 1876: 119; The Senate of the United States, *Reports of the Immigration Commission: immigrants in industries*, Vol. 11, (Washington, 1911: 17–20)).

23. See the report of Iwajirō Honda, *Dai Nihon sanshi kaihō*, No. 52, Oct. 1896, 34–8. If the warp was uneven, it got entangled in the loom and the worker had to stop the loom to remove it. In addition, looms needed to be adjusted by skilled male workers. See Chittick (1913: 16–17) *Broad-silk manufacture and the tariff*, 51; *Report on condition of woman and child wage-earners in the United States, Vol. 4: the silk industry*, 34; Matsui (1930: 138).

24. See Umon Nishikido, *Shinkoku kenshi jijō* [Sericulture and silk reeling in China], 1897, 39–44; Li 1981: 163–8. Member factories of Kaimeisha in 1892 were 22, 15 of which were equipped with fewer than 100 basins.
25. That is, raw silks with the same quality as "Okaya Chicken" were recognized as "No. 1" both in Yokohama and in New York. The Silk Association of America officially recognized "Okaya Chicken" as the standard for the classification in 1908. (See "Classifications of raw silks", *The American silk journal*, 27–7, 1919, 147–50.) "No. 1" was in greatest demand for middle-lower grade fabrics in the U.S. market.
26. Increasing labor productivity mainly came from switching from two-end reeling machines to three-end machines. In Suwa district, the average yearly product per basin (per worker) was 70.8 kg in 1910. In Hirano village where there were large factories, it was 80 kg. Yearly product per worker of Okaya Co. was 58 kg in 1900 and 73 kg in 1906. Value added was 20.3 percent in 1900 and 19.0 percent in 1906. Labor share was 70.1 percent in 1900 and 47.4 percent in 1906. (See Nakabayashi 2003: 199, Appendix: 468–9.) In Italy, yearly product per worker was 65 kg in 1910. (See Federico 1997: 130.)
27. Many kinds of defect came from improperly reeling, while some came from poor cocoons. (See Seem 1922: 42–55.)
28. The governance of trade is to avoid the most inefficient equilibrium, stoppage of the trade, through enforcement by the official court, or through the self-enforcing strategy in the long-term relationship, the repeated transaction, the norm of community and so on, under asymmetry information where a player can cheat its partner. (See Aoki 2001: 60–1.)
29. "Kiito-shokkō-jijō" [The conditions of silk-reeling workers], Nōshōmushō Shōkōkyoku Kōjōchōsa-kakari, *Kiito-orimono-shokkō-jijō* [The conditions of silk reeling and weaving workers], 1903 (reprinted in 1976), 166–74.

References

Aldrich, M. and R. Aldelda, "Determinants of working women's wage during the progressive era", *Explorations in economic history*, 17–4 (1980): 323–41.
Aoki, Masahiko, *Toward a Comparative Institutional Analysis* (Cambridge, Mass., 2001).
Bouvier, J., *Le Krach de L'union Générale 1878–1885* (Paris, 1930).
Brockett, L. P., *The Silk Industry in America: A History* (New York, 1876).
Chittick, J., *Silk Manufacturing and its Problems* (New York, 1913).
Clark, V. S., *History of Manufactures in the U. S., volume 2, 1860–1893* (New York, 1929a).
——, *History of Manufactures in the Unites States, volume 3, 1893–1928* (New York, 1929b).
Cottereau, A., "The fate of collective manufactures in the industrial world: the silk industries of Lyons and London, 1800–1850", in Sable, C. F. and J. Zeitlin., *World of Possibilities: Flexibility and Mass Production in Western Industrialization* (Cambridge, 1997).
Crawcour, S. E., "Industrialization and technological change, 1885–1920", Duus, Peter (ed.), *The Cambridge History of Japan volume 6: The Twentieth Century* (New York, 1988).

Duran, L., *Raw Silk: A Practical Hand-book for the Buyer* (New York, 1913).

Eng, R. Y., *Economic Imperialism in China: Silk Production and Exports 1861–1932* (Berkeley, 1986).

Federico, G., *An Economic History of the Silk Industry, 1830–1930* (Cambridge, 1997).

——, *Il filo d'oro: L'industria Mondiale della Seta dalla Restaurazione alla Grande Crisi* (Venezia, 1994).

Furuta, Kazuko, "Technology transfer and local adaptation: the case of silk reeling in modern east Asia", unpublished Ph. D. dissertation (Princeton University, 1988).

Golin, S., *The Fragile Bridge: Paterson Silk Strike, 1913*, (Philadelphia, 1988).

Greif, A., "Microtheory and recent developments in the study of economic institutions through economic history", Krepes, D. M., and K. F. Wallis (eds), *Advances in Economics and Econometrics: Theory and Applications, Seventh World Congress*, 2 (Cambridge, 1997).

Hiramoto, Atsushi, "Gōshi Okaya Seishi Kaisha no seiritsu" [The establishment of Okaya Silk Reeling Co.], *Kenkyū Nenpō Keizaigaku*, Tōhoku University, 47–2 (1985a): 41–5.

——, "Gōshi Okaya Seishi Kaisha no shihon chikuseki" [Capital accumulation of Okaya Silk Reeling Co.], *Kenkyū Nenpō Keizaigaku*, Tōhoku University, 47–3 (1985b): 1–21.

Hirano-son, *Hirano Son Shi* [History of Hirano Village], 2, 1932.

Holstrom, B., "Moral hazard in teams", *The Bell Journal of Economics*, 13–2 (1982): 324–40.

—— and Milgrom, P., "Multitask principal–agent analysis: incentive contracts, asset ownership, and job design", *The Journal of Law, Economics and Organization*, 7-sp (1991): 24–52.

Honda, Iwajirō, *The Silk Industry of Japan* (Yokohama, 1909).

Huber, J. R., "Effect on prices of Japan's entry into world commerce after 1858", *Journal of Political Economy* 79–3 (1971): 614–28.

Hudson, P., *The Genesis of Industrial Capital: a Study of the West Riding Wool Textile Industry c. 1750–1850* (Cambridge, 1986).

Hunter, J. R., "Textile factories, tuberculosis and the quality of life in industrializing Japan", Hunter, J. (ed.), *Japanese Women Working* (London, 1993).

——, *Women and the Labour Market in Japan's Industrializing Economy: the Textile Industry before the Pacific War* (London, 2003).

Ikawa, Katsuhiko, "1880 nendai no kiito urikomi sho: kiito urikomi kiji shūkei kekka kara" (Japanese exporters at Yokohama in the 1880s: record of sales of raw silk), *Yokohama Kaikō Shiryōkan Kiyō*, 9, 1991.

——, *Kindai-Nihon-Seshigyō to Mayu-seisan* [The Japanese modern silk-reeling industry and sericulture] (Tokyo, 1998).

Ishii, Kanji, *Nihon-Sanshigyō-Shi-Bunseki* [An analysis of the history of sericulture and silk-reeling industry in Japan] (Tokyo, 1972).

——, "Japan", Cameron, R., and V. I. Bovykin. (eds), *International Banking 1870–1914* (New York, 1991).

——, "Japanese trade and the Yokohama Specie Bank", in Checkland, O., Nishimura, S., Tamaki, N. (eds), *Pacific Banking, 1859–1959* (London, 1994).

Iwamoto, Yoshiteru, "Suwa seishigyo chitai ni okeru rodosha-toroku-seido" [The institution of worker registration in Suwa silk-reeling district], *Kenkyū-nepō-Keizaigaku*, Tōhoku University, 31–4 (1970): 97–116.

Kambayashi, Ryō, "Chingin seido to rishokukōdō: Meiji kōki no Suwachihō no seishi no rei" [Wage system and activity of leaving jobs: a case in silk reeling in Suwa district in thelate Meiji era], *Keizai Kenkyū*, Hitotsubashi University, 51–2 (2000): 124–135.

——, "Tōkyū chingin seido to kōjō tōroku seido" ["Relative wage system and the registration system of female workers"], in Okazaki, Tetsuji, (ed.), *Torihiki Seido no Keizaishi* [Governing business transactions: a historical perspective] (Tokyo, 2001).

Klein, B., and Leffler, K. B., "The role of market forces in assuring contractual performance", *Journal of Political Economy* 89–4 (1981): 615–41.

Li, L. M., *China's Silk Trade: Traditional Industry in the Modern World 1842–1937* (Cambridge, Mass., 1981).

Lieu, D. K., *The Silk Reeling Industry in Shanghai* (Shanghai, 1933).

——, *The Silk Industry of China* (Shanghai, 1940).

Ma, D., "The modern silk road: the global raw-silk market, 1850–1930", *The Journal of Economic History* 56–2 (1996).

Matsui, S., *The History of the Silk Industry in the United States* (New York, 1930).

Milgrom, P., "Employment contracts, influence activities, and efficient organization", *The Journal of Political Economy* 96–1 (1988).

Minami, Ryōshin, *The economic development of Japan: a quantitative study* (Basing stoke, 1994).

—— and Fumio Makino, "The development of appropriate technologies for export promotion in the silk-reeling industry", in Ryoshin, M. K. S. Kim, F. Makino, and J. Seo, *Acquiring, Adapting and Developing Technologies: Lessons from the Japanese Experience* (New York, 1995).

Nakabayahi, Masaki, *Kindai-Shihonshugi no Soshiki: Seishigyō no Hatten ni okeru Torihiki no Tōchi to Seisan no Kōzō* [An Organization of Modern Capitalism: the Governance of Trade and the System of Organization in the Development of the Silk Reeling Industry] (Tokyo, 2003).

Nghiep, L. T., and Hayami, Y., "Mobilizing Slack Resources for Economic Development: the Summer–fall Rearing Technology of Sericulture in Japan", *Explorations in Economic History* 16–2 (1979): 163–181.

Nishikido, U., *Shinkoku Kenshi Jijō* [Sericulture and Silk Reeling in China] (Tokyo, 1897).

Patrick, H. T., "External equilibrium and internal convertibility: financial policy in Meiji Japan", *The Journal of Economic History* 25–2 (1965): 187–213.

——, "Japan, 1868–1914", Cameron, R., O. Crisp, H. T. Patrick, and R. Tilly (eds), *Banking in the Early Stages of Industrialization* (New York, 1967).

Posselt, E. A., *Hand Books of the Textile Industry volume 3: Silk Throwing* (Philadelphia, c. 1919).

Rawlley, R. C., *The Silk Industry and Trade* (London, 1919).

Reischauer, H. M., *Samurai and Silk: a Japanese and American Heritage* (Cambridge, Mass., 1986).

Rosen, S., "Hedonic prices and implicit markets: product differentiation in pure competition", *Journal of Political Economy* 82–1 (1974): 34–55.

——, "Transaction costs and internal labour market", *Journal of Law, Economics and Organization* 4–1, 1988.

Sable, C. F., and Zeitlin, J., "Historical alternatives to mass production: politics, markets and technology in nineteenth-century industrialization", *Past and Present* 108, 1985.

Saito, Osamu, *Chingin to Rōdō to Seikatsu-suijun* [Wage, Labour and the Standard of Living] (Tokyo, 1998).

Shober, J., *Silk and the Silk Industry* (London, 1930).

Scranton, P., *Figured Tapestry: Production, Markets, and Power in Philadelphia Textiles, 1885–1941* (Cambridge, 1989).

Seem, W. P., *Raw Silk Properties, Classifications of Raw Silk and Silk Throwing* (New York, 1922).

Sota, Saburō, *Chūgoku-Kindai-Seishigyō-Shi no Kenkyū* [Historical Study on the Modern Silk Reeling Industry in China] (Tokyo, 1994).

Sugiyama, Shinya, *Japan's Industrialization in the World Economy 1859–1899: Export Trade and Overseas Competition* (London, 1988).

Takamura, Naosuke, *Saihakken Meiji no Keizai* [The Economy in the Meiji Era: a Rivision] (Tokyo, 1995).

Taussig, F. W., *Some Aspects of the Tariff Question*, 3rd edn (Cambridge, Mass., 1931).

Teranishi, Jūrō, "Matsukata-defure no makuro-kezaigakteki-bunseki (kaitei-ban)" [Macroeconomic analysis of Matsukata-deflation: revised version], in Umemura, Mataji., and Takafusa Nakamura (eds), *Matsukata-Zaisei to Shokusan-Kōgyō-Seisaku* [Matsukata's Fiscal and Monetary Policy and the Promotion of Industry] (Tokyo, 1983).

Tsurumi, P. E., *Factory Girls: Women in the Thread Mills of Meiji Japan* (Princeton, 1990).

Tsurumi, Masayoshi, *Nihon-Shin-yō-Kikō no Kakuritsu: Nihon-Ginkō to Kin-yū-shijō* [The Establishment of Japanese Financial System: the Bank of Japan and the Financial Market] (Tokyo, 1991).

Unno, Fukuju, *Meiji no Bōeki* [Trade during the Meiji Era] (Tokyo, 1967).

Williamson, O. E., *The Economic Institutions of Capitalism* (New York, 1985).

Yamaguchi, Kazuo, "Kiito-urikomi-ton-ya no seishi-kin-yū" [Financing for silk-reeling industry by wholesale merchants], in Yamaguchi, Kazuo (ed.), *Nihon-Sangyō-kin-yū-shi-Kenkyū: Seishi-Kin-yū Hen* [A History of Industrial Finance in Japan: Financing of the Silk-Reeling Industry] (Tokyo, 1966).

9

The Export-oriented Industrialization of Japanese Pottery: The Adoption and Adaptation of Overseas Technology and Market Information

TAKEHISA YAMADA

1. Introduction

This paper examines the Japanese pottery industry as a means of exploring some of the ways in which a traditional Japanese industry adopted and then adapted modern technology to achieve significant export-oriented industrialization from the Meiji period onwards. Even before the modern era, pottery was one of Japan's most important industries. During the Tokugawa period, the Hizen-Arita region of Kyushu introduced porcelain manufacturing technology from China and Korea, and advanced the export of ceramic products to European and Asian countries (Ōhashi 1993). By the end of the Tokugawa period, porcelain manufacturing technology had spread beyond Hizen, and other Japanese regions were beginning to develop export-oriented products that matched the quality of those made in China. This expansion made possible a dramatic increase in Japanese ceramic exports. Initially the ceramics made for export were of Chinese design. But Japanese manufacturers gradually increased their use of Japanese designs, and further expanded production to include ceramics of European design. To elucidate the development process of an export-oriented pottery industry in Japanese traditional pottery districts, this chapter first examines the export figures for Japanese pottery in the late-nineteenth century, paying special attention to the parallel growth of ceramics manufacturing companies in the same period. It also examines the roles played by technical schools and trade associations in the build-up of basic industrial infrastructure.

Among the recent studies that touch on the industrialization of the Japanese pottery industry during the Meiji period, those by Kazuhiro Ōmori and the author focus on the growth of ceramics manufacturing companies (Ōmori 1995, 1997, Yamada 1996a). Kazuo Motomiya has analysed contemporary official reports prepared by consular representatives stationed overseas (Motomiya 1997). This chapter illustrates the ways in which the latest technology and market information was obtained overseas and utilized to advance the industrialization of an export-oriented pottery industry in Japan. It draws special attention to the roles played by technical schools and trade associations, hubs of technology and market information that served to disseminate the information to local industrial districts.

Section 2 provides an overview of local industrial districts in Japan, and clarifies how ceramic products made in those regions were received in overseas markets. It examines export figures for the years 1880–1900, supplementing the analysis with information contained in consular reports of the same period. Special emphasis is placed on the correlation between the overall increase in pottery exports and an increase in the volume of daily-use, as opposed to artistic, ceramic products of traditional design. This section thus attempts to clarify the characteristics of the export-oriented industrialization of Japanese pottery, centering on quality and the development of hard porcelain products.

Section 3 deals with the growth of pottery-manufacturing companies. By examining the historical development of production in the Arita and Nagoya regions, it illustrates the process by which companies absorbed and modified European manufacturing technology to improve the design and strength of their products. In particular, it demonstrates that, in order to develop hard porcelain products, Japanese companies studied manufacturing technology, first in Limoges, France, and then in Germany and Austria.

Section 4 attempts to shed light on the vital roles of two sets of players in the process of export-oriented industrialization: one, the graduates of Tokyo Technical School and, two, the trade associations that encouraged these graduates to improve their technological skills. Particularly noteworthy is a shift of focus in the research and training programs of local industrial districts from new product design to the development of high-strength porcelain. The coordination between Tokyo Technical School graduates and the trade associations advanced the export-oriented industrialization of ceramics in the 1890s. Using industrial fairs as a means of disseminating both technology and market information, the Technical School graduates and the trade associations stimulated technical innovation in the pottery districts and the development of new sales channels for their products.

2. The Expansion of Ceramic Exports and the Development of Daily-Use Products

2.1. *The shift in export structure: from artistic to daily-use ceramics*

The sales volume of Japanese ceramics increased significantly at the end of the Tokugawa period, owing especially to the activities of pottery traders who sold their products to foreign merchants in Nagasaki and Yokohama. Pottery traders who opened branches in Nagasaki and Yokohama performed the function of communicating overseas market trends, such as a preference for Chinese motifs, to local industrial districts. They encouraged the production of artistic ceramic ware that reflected a distinctively Japanese taste and they encouraged the development of sales channels overseas (Yamada 1995a). Japanese pottery at this time was strongly influenced by the traditions developed during the Tokugawa period. It was appreciated by foreign buyers primarily for its underglazes, for the cobalt blue paintings of Chinese landscapes and for the multicolored overglaze paintings. The foreign traders who gathered from around the world in Nagasaki, Yokohama and Kobe bought large quantities of artistic Japanese pottery products.

Responding to the high reputation of Japanese pottery, some European manufacturers had begun to imitate Japanese pottery by the 1880s. This trend reinforced the reputation of Japanese pottery in the European market, especially for its fine decoration and rich color (MOFA 1881, 1885). Market demand for Japanese pottery, however, shifted gradually from objects in Chinese style to those decorated with motifs in the Japanese *kachō-fūgetsu* style that portrayed nature manifested in such forms as birds, flowers, wind and moon. In response to the shifting demand, Japanese pottery manufacturers started to develop new products made with traditional technology and decorated with Japanese-style motifs.

Table 9.1 shows figures for Japanese pottery exports from 1887 to 1912. Exports increased significantly from the latter half of the 1880s, sustained by expanded shipments of inexpensive artistic products to Europe and the United States (MOAC 1887, MOFA 1887, 1888). In contrast with the sluggish condition of exports to China, there was a sharp increase in shipments to the United States of products designed with traditional Japanese motifs. In the 1890s, Japanese pottery exports expanded to Hong Kong and British India. At the same time, an increasing volume of daily-use ceramic products, such as bowls, dishes and pots, was exported to Korea. Reflecting the enhancement of product quality, beautiful and inexpensive Japanese pottery thus found its way into Asian markets outside China (MOF 1891, MOFA 1989, 1902).

Table 9.1. The amount of Japanese pottery exports in the Meiji period

(thousand yen)

Year	America	England	France	Germany	China	Hong Kong	Korea	India	Australia	Total Exports
1887	296	259	181	53	385		15		7	1,312
	(%) 23	20	14	4	29		1		1	100
1892	605	243	89	67	58	238	28	61	16	1,480
	(%) 41	16	6	5	4	16	2	4	1	100
1897	620	237	51	45	74	374	87	108	77	1,819
	(%) 34	13	3	2	4	21	5	6	4	100
1902	913	263	45	64	221	248	220	64	84	2,462
	(%) 37	11	2	3	9	10	9	3	3	100
1907	3,816	475	107	271	443	263	522	24	136	7,216
	(%) 53	7	1	4	6	4	7	0	2	100
1912	2,586	376	149	271	295	245		243	185	5,452
	(%) 47	7	3	5	5	4		4	3	100

Source: Gaimushō [Ministry of Foreign Affairs] (1887–1912).

In Europe and the United States, the closing years of the nineteenth century saw a growing appreciation for new Japanese products—not only those that retained the reputed traditional motifs but also those that incorporated the latest designs. This shift in demand was reflected, for example, in the product development activities initiated by the Japanese trading house, Morimura-gumi. Based in New York, Morimura-gumi spurred the development of new pottery products by conveying the latest design information to industrial districts in Japan and by giving detailed instructions concerning pottery design and shape to manufacturers in Japan (MOF 1891).

By the early 1900s, the United States had become the largest importer of Japanese pottery. During the same years, it was also importing a huge quantity of hard porcelain products from Europe. Responding to this trend, Japanese manufacturers started to produce hard porcelain products by adopting Art Nouveau design and European manufacturing technology. Japanese pottery decorated with the latest European design was evaluated highly in Europe, leading to the successful expansion of Japanese inexpensive and decorative daily ceramic products in the European market (MOFA 1900, 1901). The export of hard porcelain products was extended to Hong Kong and East India. Moreover, the declining export trend to China was reversed in the early twentieth century. Exports to Korea increased significantly as result of the tightening political relationship between Japan and Korea.

2.2. The activities of pottery districts in Japan

Pottery districts in Japan pursued export oriented industrialization by using traditional manufacturing technology while at the same time pursuing new product development. During the Meiji period, two methods of pottery preparation were available. In the first method, the clay was refined, shaped and underglazed with cobalt blue coloring (*sometsuke*). A large amount of clay was then fired at high temperature within a wood-burning *noborigama* or "climbing kiln", a series of linked kiln chambers that stretched over a vertical incline. In a variation of this method, a small amount of the clay was fired in a *tangama*, or single kiln chamber, using firewood or charcoal. The second method used a *nishikigama*, or decorating kiln. The refined and shaped clay was overglazed, mainly in red but often combined with many other colors. The clay was then fired in the kiln, at low temperature and using firewood. Although there were some large-scale pottery factories, most pottery manufacturers in the Meiji period operated medium- or small-scale factories that relied heavily on hand production by potters and painters. The typical production flow for pottery was therefore based on the division of labor between two parties. Medium- and small-scale factories first prepared the pottery body in jointly-owned *noborigama* or privately-owned *tangama*. Later, overglaze specialists turned the fired pot into a finished product.

Because of differences in clay-firing conditions and overglaze methods, the pottery of each industrial district gradually took on distinctive features. Accordingly, pottery manufacturers pursued the manufacturing technology and design scheme characteristic of their own industrial district and attempted to improve their wares accordingly. Map 9.1 lists the

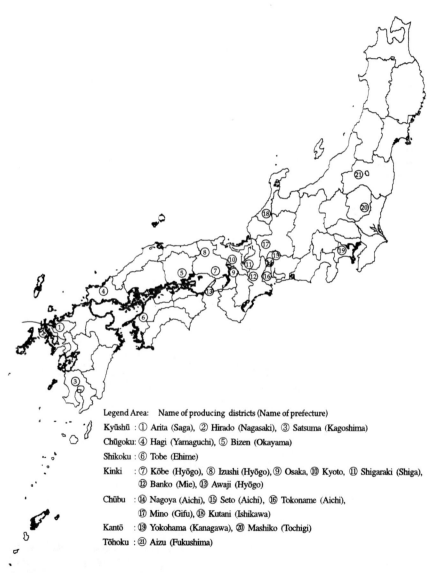

Legend Area: Name of producing districts (Name of prefecture)

Kyūshū : ① Arita (Saga), ② Hirado (Nagasaki), ③ Satsuma (Kagoshima)

Chūgoku: ④ Hagi (Yamaguchi), ⑤ Bizen (Okayama)

Shikoku : ⑥ Tobe (Ehime)

Kinki   : ⑦ Kōbe (Hyōgo), ⑧ Izushi (Hyōgo), ⑨ Osaka, ⑩ Kyoto, ⑪ Shigaraki (Shiga),
              ⑫ Banko (Mie), ⑬ Awaji (Hyōgo)

Chūbu   : ⑭ Nagoya (Aichi), ⑮ Seto (Aichi), ⑯ Tokoname (Aichi),
              ⑰ Mino (Gifu), ⑱ Kutani (Ishikawa)

Kantō   : ⑲ Yokohama (Kanagawa), ⑳ Mashiko (Tochigi)

Tōhoku : ㉑ Aizu (Fukushima)

Map 9.1. Location of pottery-producing districts in Meiji, Japan.

major industrial districts during the Meiji period. Hizen-Arita (in Saga and Nagasaki Prefectures) was a reputed center that had produced export-oriented pottery products since the Tokugawa period. Seto (in Aichi Prefecture) and Mino (in Gifu Prefecture) expanded their porcelain production by introducing manufacturing technology from Hizen at the end of Tokugawa period. Kyoto and Kutani (in Ishikawa Prefecture) increased their porcelain production during the same period. Nagoya, a major industrial district in Aichi Prefecture, specialized in overglaze work, purchasing fired pots from the Seto and Mino regions. Toward the end of the Tokugawa era, the Hizen-Arita and Kutani centers had started to export brilliantly colored, Chinese-style pottery. During the Meiji period, they shifted their focus to high-quality, artistic pottery designed with Japanese motifs. A marked contrast can be seen in Kyoto, where manufacturers began in the 1890s to concentrate on their unique line of high quality, artistic pottery with Western designs. In Nagoya, on the other hand, the pottery body procured from Seto and Mino regions became the basis of a new line of Western tableware; the production of hard porcelain expanded dramatically in the early 1900s.

Table 9.2 shows the production volume of the major pottery industrial districts in 1891. The distinctive production patterns for each center are also indicated. In terms of production volume, the largest center was Gifu Prefecture (Mino), followed by Saga Prefecture (Hizen) and Aichi Prefecture (Nagoya, Seto and Tokoname). A glimpse at sales volume, however, reveals that Saga Prefecture is ranked at the top, followed by Kyoto, Gifu and Aichi Prefectures. The relatively low ranking of Aichi Prefecture indicates that the biggest demand during the 1890s was for high-quality, artistic pottery, like the expensive and decorative items made in Kyoto and Ishikawa (Kutani) Prefectures. Table 9.3 lists the numbers and types of producers in each center in 1891. Hizen has the largest number of glaze painters, followed by Nagoya, Seto, Tokoname and Kutani.

While the numbers of manufacturers and craftsmen in Mino and Seto show only gradual increases from the 1890s onward, the numbers of *noborigama* and *nishikigama* increased significantly. The figures suggest that these regions successfully expanded their output of inexpensive, daily-use items through increased productivity.[1] Indeed, on the outset of the 1890s, one can detect a sharp contrast between the mild output increases in Saga and Nagasaki (Hizen-Arita) and Kyoto Prefectures and the drastic increases in Aichi (Seto) and Gifu (Mino) Prefectures (Table 9.4). The drastic increases reflect expanded exports, especially of porcelain products overglazed in Nagoya. This analysis is confirmed by the fact that many overglaze factories were set up in Nagoya by export traders. Similarly, production increases in Seto and Mino were probably triggered by the growing demand for pottery bodies by the overglazers based in Nagoya (Mishima 1955: 41). While production increases relied

Table 9.2. Demand for Japanese pottery in 1891

(quantity: thousand pieces; amount: thousand yen)

District	(Practical) Quantity Domestic	(Practical) Quantity Export	(Practical) Amount Domestic	(Practical) Amount Export	(Ornamental) Quantity Domestic	(Ornamental) Quantity Export	(Ornamental) Amount Domestic	(Ornamental) Amount Export
Kyoto	2,920	1,200	60.0	19.1	57	595	25.0	243.9
	(%)71	29 unit price (sen)	2.1	1.6	(%)9	91 unit price (sen)	44.3	41.0
Hyōgo	4,420	340	43.4	10.7	25	162	1.9	9.4
	(%)93	7 unit price (sen)	1.0	3.2	(%)13	87 unit price (sen)	7.6	5.8
Nagasaki	3,195	1,625	43.8	9.7	25	57	1.1	7.3
	(%)66	34 unit price (sen)	1.0	0.6	(%)30	70 unit price (sen)	4.6	12.7
Mie	1,193	435	17.8	6.5	73	290	1.1	0.4
	(%)73	27 unit price (sen)	1.5	15.0	(%)20	80 unit price (sen)	1.5	0.2
Aichi	7,232	2,653	151.5	102.4	327	70	9.1	7.5
	(%)73	27 unit price (sen)	2.1	3.9	(%)82	18 unit price (sen)	2.8	10.8
Gifu	17,370	29,756	80.3	227.2	1	29	1.2	0.6
	(%)37	63 unit price (sen)	0.5	0.8	(%)4	96 unit price (sen)	88.9	2.0
Fukushima	1,666	470	28.1	13.6	9	0	0.3	0
	(%)78	22 unit price (sen)	1.7	2.9	(%)100	0 unit price (sen)	3.7	0
Ishikawa	189	171	31.1	59.8	28	249	12.8	123.5
	(%)53	47 unit price (sen)	16.4	35.0	(%)10	90 unit price (sen)	45.4	49.7
Ehime	6,330	1,304	44.6	15.0	1	0	0.4	0
	(%)83	17 unit price (sen)	7.0	1.1	(%)100	0 Unit price (sen)	40.4	0
Saga	6,671	3,273	328.9	121.8	255	127	21.9	37.1
	(%)67	33 unit price (sen)	4.9	3.7	(%)67	33 unit price (sen)	8.6	29.1
Nation	61,454	41,935	1,086.2	612.3	1,151	1,650	89.6	441.9
	(%)59	41 unit price (sen)	1.8	1.5	(%)41	59 unit price (sen)	7.8	26.8

Source: Gaimushō [Ministry of Foreign Affairs] (1892).

Note: * Sen is equivalent to 0.01 yen.

Table 9.3. Employers and employees in pottery-producing districts in 1891

(person)

District	Manufacturer	Merchant	Painter	Jigger	Workman	Workers total
Kyoto	111	107	470	345	270	1,085
Hyōgo	143	159	69	368	311	748
Nagasaki	155	271	148	205	478	831
Mie	21	17	118	639	20	777
Aichi	761	212	1,902	3,617	3,644	9,163
Gifu	785	385	899	2,193	1,485	4,577
Fukushima	146	125	68	82	227	377
Ishikawa	90	50	1,743	241	649	2,633
Ehime	22	251	12	165	158	335
Saga	235	169	2,220	1,255	1,243	4,718
Nation	3,409	7,043	8,390	17,689	16,576	42,655

Source: Nōshōmushō [Ministry of Agriculture and Commerce] (1892).

on skilled workers such as jigger men and hand painters, it should not be overlooked that the mass production of inexpensive, daily-use ceramic products was sustained by a number of technological innovations. For example, the use of charcoal, instead of firewood, significantly reduced fuel costs; the introduction of copperplate printing made the printing process more efficient.

2.3. The issue of quality improvement for pottery exports

Given the gradual emergence of distinctive features among the pottery districts, what obstacles did they encounter in their efforts to expand Japanese pottery exports? And how did they cope with them? Consular representatives pointed out in the 1880s that the major sources of profit for European pottery manufacturers were products that featured the latest designs. Such market information made Japanese manufacturers realize the importance of new styles, and they began incorporating Western pottery designs and shapes in their products. In a speech delivered by the MOAC staff in 1891 to pottery manufacturers in Nagoya, it was stressed that shape and design, rather than painting, was the crucial element in determining the value of pottery products (Aichi Prefecture 1891: 35). Indeed, market demand in Europe was already shifting from Japanese-style pottery to the emerging, Art Nouveau ware. That trend was reflected in the sluggishness of exports from Kutani or Hizen (MOFA 1895, 1900). By contrast, flower vases and coffee mugs made in Kyoto, Seto and Mino that featured the latest European and American designs gained high popularity, especially in the United States (MOF 1892). As a result of the rising demand for relatively inexpensive pottery—artistic items made in Kyoto and daily-use ceramic products made in Seto and Mino—in overseas markets, the center of Japan's pottery trade gradually shifted

Table 9.4. Amount of pottery production in the Meiji period

(thousand yen)

Year	Aichi	Gifu	Kyoto	Saga	Ishikawa	Fukushima	Hyōgo	Ehime	Shiga	Nagasaki	Nation
1887	304	318	180	381	188	58	47	33	56	8	1,885
(%)	16	17	10	20	10	3	2	2	3	0	100
1892	867	1,273	200	462	188	69	63	87	25	43	3,762
(%)	23	34	5	12	5	2	2	2	1	1	100
1897	1,572	1,156	360	529	176	136	135	109	112	103	5,163
(%)	30	22	7	10	3	3	3	2	2	2	100
1902	2,300	936	648	565	222	146	209	181	127	95	6,911
(%)	33	14	9	8	3	2	3	3	2	1	100
1907	4,797	2,197	1,223	1,024	271	251	289	398	226	337	12,941
(%)	37	17	9	8	2	2	2	3	2	3	100
1912	6,206	2,181	2,017	1,649	614	283	278	218	245	342	16,546
(%)	38	13	12	10	4	2	2	1	1	2	100

Source: Nōshōmushō [Ministry of Agriculture and Commerce] (1887–1912).

from Nagasaki and Yokohama to Kobe, which was located nearer to industrial districts in Kyoto and Nagoya.

In addition to the issue of product design, it was gradually recognized that export levels were also affected by product quality. While the substantial decline in exports to China after 1889 could be explained in part by the failure of Japanese manufacturers to use Chinese motifs (MOAC 1886), quality was also an important factor. Since Japanese pottery was fired in wood-burning kilns, it was more fragile than European pottery and more prone to temperature cracks than Chinese ware. Consular representative reports warned against the overproduction of inferior goods, and recommended that Japanese manufacturers pay more attention to strength than to appearance when imitating Chinese pottery. Responding to the plea, producers in Hizen-Arita experimented with longer firing times to develop hard and robust products. Eventually, they achieved product quality higher than that found in Germany and Britain (MOF 1890, MOFA 1897, 1902). Moreover, in Seto and Mino, pottery manufacturers introduced charcoal kilns that enhanced the mechanical strength of their products (MOFA 1898, 1902).

The period after 1900 marked a new phase of Japanese pottery in that a growing number of factories, led by independent manufacturing companies such as Morimura-gumi, introduced Western technology. The next section focuses on companies that played a pioneering role in introducing and implementing the manufacturing technology of hard porcelain products.

3. Pottery Manufacturing Companies and the Development of Hard Porcelain Products

3.1. The emergence of pottery manufacturing companies

Before the start of hard porcelain production in Japan, manufacturers endured many rounds of trial and error. From its earliest years, the Meiji government seized upon the good reception that pottery products made in Hizen and Satsuma domains had gained at the 1867 international exposition held in Paris and encouraged Hizen and Satsuma craftsmen to develop new products. Gottfried Wagner, who was conducting chemical engineering research in Nagasaki, visited Arita and Kyoto in the early Meiji period and instructed manufacturers in modern pottery technology, including topics such as the firing conditions for charcoal kilns and the blaze blending method.

It was, however, much later that modern technology took firm root in the Japanese pottery industry. The abstract information received from Wagner had to be combined with on-site experience obtained at European pottery factories (Ide 1992). Japanese government officials who attended the 1873 international exposition in Vienna investigated the manufacturing processes and design development of Western pottery and purchased some sample products. Later, as it prepared for the 1876 international exposition held in Philadelphia, the Japanese government completed design illustrations for the pottery products and distributed them to the leading pottery manufacturers (Maeyama 1983, Ide 1976).

Responding to these governmental efforts, some of the leading manufacturers in Arita jointly established Kōransha, which became a pioneering pottery manufacturing company (Nakayama 1980). Financed by export traders and pottery manufacturers, Kōransha employed many shopworkers and installed a mechanized production line. Originally established as a Western-style incorporated company, Kōransha developed into a general partnership company. When some of the founding members of Kōransha set up their own independent company, they also established an integrated manufacturing factory equipped with machinery imported from Limoges, France (Yamada 1995*b*).

The entrepreneurial spirit of Kōransha can be seen in other areas. It did not limit itself to high-quality products but was ready to expand into industrial-use items. After installing its own kiln on its premises, it raised productivity by successfully shortening the firing cycle. As a result, it could mass produce ceramic products that were shaped and designed according to Western style but retained traditional Japanese motifs. In 1878, the company was awarded a gold medal at the international exposition in Paris. Kōransha delegates to the exposition used the occasion to visit pottery factories in Limoges, where they obtained samples of raw materials and finished products and a steam-powered clay mill. The Paris international exposition of 1889 offered an opportunity for Kōransha to obtain a Faure-style machine and samples of Limoges pottery. These provided a basis for the company's later attempts to produce a line of tableware shaped and designed according to Western taste (Yamada 1996*b*).

During the 1880s, a number of companies in Kutani and Kyoto introduced Western manufacturing technology; later they began to mass produce high-quality, artistic products (Tsukatani 1967, Fujioka 1962: 51–62). Kyoto Porcelain Company, established in 1887 by a Kyoto entrepreneur in cooperation with others in the region, started the production of Western-style, high-quality tableware. The company not only installed manufacturing equipment from Limoges but also constructed a charcoal kiln, an indispensable facility for hard porcelain production (Naramoto 1942: 60–6, 1943). Such companies, established in Arita and Kyoto, ended up producing high-quality Western-style tableware. One can conclude that the companies were aware of the need to develop high-quality Western-style tableware in order to compete squarely with Western manufacturers. The strategic move also suggests an awareness of the vital importance of hard porcelain technology. The activities of Morimura-gumi, a Japanese pottery trading house based in New York, well represent such awareness.

3.2. *The emergence of a hard porcelain manufacturer*

Morimura-gumi, a leading Japanese trader of pottery products in the early Meiji period, came to realize the need to develop hard porcelain products through its export activities to the United States. It constructed a charcoal kiln on its Nagoya branch premises in an attempt to produce the pure whiteness of porcelain; it also conducted experiments into firing conditions and the mixture ratio for materials. Acting with other pottery manufacturers in Seto, Morimura-gumi established a materials processing factory in 1901 and carried out basic research in the blending conditions for the raw materials used in a charcoal kiln (Nippon Tōki 1974: 193, NGK 1995: 11–12). In 1903, Morimura-gumi representatives visited an Austrian pottery factory to gather the latest technological information on hard porcelain production. At the same time, the company asked a laboratory in Berlin to conduct tests on material clay. Through such efforts, Morimura-gumi finally settled on a type of clay that would produce white porcelain. In 1904 Morimura-gumi established a general partnership company named Nippon Tōki, which in turn constructed a hard porcelain factory in Nagoya (NGK 1995: 12–13). The new company eagerly absorbed the advanced porcelain technology of Germany, procuring charcoal kilns and many different types of clay processing equipment. As a result, the company achieved preliminary success in establishing the stable production of hard porcelain.

Further technological advance was necessary, however, before Nippon Tōki could produce a full line of Western-style dinner sets. Meanwhile, the newly established company also started to develop high-voltage insulators. After much experimentation, Nippon Tōki eventually developed high-voltage insulators for transmission lines. Profits obtained from the insulator sales helped to compensate for the losses incurred in the company's start-up period. Moreover, insulator production helped raise the level of the company's hard porcelain technology. In 1912, Nippon Tōki representatives paid another visit to the Austrian pottery factory to study manufacturing technology and to eliminate potential problems in their production line. Based on the advice from the Berlin laboratory, the company was able to enhance the quality of its hard porcelain products. Eventually, it was able to produce an entire line of Western dinner set products (Ōmori 1997). Backed by its continuous efforts to improve product quality, Nippon Tōki brought on the market many new lines of world-class tableware under its brand name of Noritake. The company thus expanded its product line from artistic pottery to daily-use ceramic tableware, and secured its position as a reputed manufacturer of Western-style tableware.

Although initial attempts by Kyoto manufacturers to produce hard porcelain products ended in failure, they were able to develop special high-voltage insulators as good as those produced by Nippon Tōki. They were soon dealing with the utility companies that had been established in the hydraulic plant construction boom (Shōfū 1911: 5, 12). In Nagoya, also, newly emerging porcelain manufacturers built up high reputations. In the Kutani district of Kanazawa, one hard porcelain manufacturer put its management on track during this period and was able to expand exports of Western-style tableware to Asian countries (Ide 1908: 55). Expanded production of hard porcelain tableware boosted Japanese pottery exports during the early 1900s.

Through the application of charcoal kiln technology, former member of the Kōransha company in Arita developed decorative tiles; he started mass production of porcelain tiles during the 1910s (Tsuji 1920s: 7). Pottery manufacturers in Arita continued to produce high-quality items for the domestic market. With the development of hard porcelain products, these manufacturers produced Western-style tableware for delivery to the Imperial Household Agency and the Ministry of Navy. Moreover, Nippon Tōki in Nagoya commenced research and development into sanitary ceramics (ceramic toilet bowls) during the 1910s, eventually establishing in 1917 a new company with its own factory in Kokura (Fukuoka Prefecture).[2] Two years later, the manufacturing division responsible for special high voltage insulators also became independent from Nippon Tōki (NGK 1995). Efforts in various parts of Japan thus resulted in the mass production of toilet items and high-voltage insulators, thereby expanding the range of ceramics that reached international standards. Such technical advances in turn accelerated the export-oriented industrialization of Japanese pottery.

4. Research and Training Institutions and Trade associations

4.1. *Tokyo Technical School and the Pottery and Porcelain Institute*

Through the adoption and adaptation of Western technology, Gottfried Wagner and his students at Tokyo Technical School (Tokyo Kōgyō Gakkō) studied the traditional production in pottery districts and played a pivotal role in the development of pottery manufacture in modern Japan. After graduating from Tokyo Technical School, many of Wagner's students took research and teaching positions at institutes in the pottery districts, where they offered technical guidance to local pottery manufacturers. Local trade associations also took the initiative in inviting Technical School graduates. They could thus organize product improvement projects that involved themselves, the pottery manufacturers, and the research and training institutions. An examination of the role of the research and training institutions should therefore start with the activities of Wagner and his students at Tokyo Technical School.

Wagner carried out his research on pottery technology at an experimental factory that he established within the grounds of Tokyo Technical School. It was at this factory that he imparted his knowledge of the latest technology to ceramics engineers and to his students from Kutani and Arita (Tokyo Institute of Technology 1941: 365). In 1892, a group of Tokyo Technical School graduates who had been taught by Wagner, together with others engaged in the pottery business, established the Ceramic Society of Japan (Dainippon Yōgyō Kyōkai). Their aim was to disseminate the latest pottery and porcelain technology to manufacturers in various parts of Japan (Hirano 1940: 49–50). Touring industrial districts, the Technical School graduates gave presentations on the latest trends in pottery, including explanations of Western technology. The mutual information exchange encouraged by such activities gradually made pottery manufacturers aware of technological developments in Europe. Many Tokyo Technical School graduates took teaching positions at local technical or apprentice schools, where they enthusiastically pursued their experimental research on topics such as glaze blending and the firing conditions for charcoal kilns. Some published research papers on ceramic engineering technology (Kuroda 1909, Aichi High School 1995).

After unsuccessful attempts by manufacturers in Arita and Kyoto to develop hard porcelain products such as Western tableware, Tokyo Technical School continued experiments on the firing conditions of charcoal kilns. In 1898, it constructed a large charcoal kiln using funds received from the Ministry of Agriculture and Commerce (MOAC 1897, 1899, 1901). The school's efforts extended beyond its premises. Some of its graduates, who had joined pottery manufacturing companies mainly in the Nagoya region, took responsibility for the development of hard porcelain. They continued the experimental research on charcoal firing and on material mixtures, and had preliminary success in producing hard porcelain products. The successful launch of the products was, however, not easy. Since Japanese hard porcelain fired in charcoal kilns was inferior in quality to that produced in Europe, further development efforts were needed to achieve full-scale production of the hard white product. Some Tokyo Technical School graduates visited Europe during the early 1900s, either as overseas trainees of the Ministry of Agriculture and Commerce or as delegates to international expositions. They absorbed the latest pottery technology and market information through factory visits to major manufacturers in Europe and the United States. Through these activities they were also able to accumulate knowledge about other related products, such as high voltage insulators, decorative tiles and ceramics for sanitary use (Ikeda 1939: 37, 42). Once they had mastered the charcoal firing method, they successfully developed a comprehensive range of manufacturing technologies for hard porcelain products. Since they also found a way to reduce fuel costs substantially using charcoal, they promoted the new technology through the construction of charcoal-burning kilns in the pottery districts. By advancing hard porcelain production and disseminating Western technology and market information to the industrial districts, graduates of Tokyo Technical School played a pivotal role in the export-oriented industrialization of the Japanese pottery industry.

Another important agent of export-oriented industrialization was the Pottery and Porcelain Institute (Tōjiki Shikenjo). Proposed by the Ceramic Society of Japan and backed by various trade associations, the Institute was established by the Kyoto municipal government in 1896. Its first head was Nagataka Fujie, a graduate of Tokyo Technical School. As an overseas trainee, Fujie had visited major pottery districts in Germany and Austria, and he aimed to bring the latest Western pottery technology to Kyoto (Fujioka 1932). The Institute quickly became a regional center for the development of new products. Not only did it conduct experiments at the request of pottery manufacturers and traders, but it also developed an internship program. By these means, the Institute was able to produce workers skilled in the latest Western technology and support the product development activities of pottery manufacturing companies.

As an increasing number of Japanese pottery manufacturers introduced Western technology and developed Western tableware products, they urged the establishment of a national ceramics institute on the European model. Accordingly, in 1919 the National Pottery and Porcelain Institute was established with facilities and personnel transferred from the Kyoto Pottery and Porcelain Institute (NIRIN 1998: 3). The National Pottery and Porcelain Institute aggressively introduced Western technology and design, applying them to produce a uniquely Japanese style of pottery for export. The Institute also expanded its internship program to accelerate the dissemination of Western technology among pottery workers and engineers in Japan.

4.2. Training institutions in pottery districts

How did local pottery districts participate in activities conducted at the national level to improve technology and skills? During the 1890s, many pottery districts established local apprentice schools, originating from apprentice training institutions that had been established in the 1880s as seen in Fig. 9.1. For instance, in Arita, a center from which many products made their way to international expositions, the primary school was utilized as a facility for training shopworkers' children in glaze painting;

in 1881, a Pottery Craftwork School (Tōki Kōgei Gakkō) was established (Ide 1992).

The need for similar training institutions was felt in other districts. At a round-table discussion organized by the Ministry of Agriculture and Commerce in 1885, a pottery manufacturer stated that each district should have a training institute at which skilled workers could exchange information and improve their skills. Another opinion stressed the need for the institutionalization of apprentice schools throughout Japan, along the lines of the system that had developed in Limoges.[3] From the late 1880s, many of the higher elementary schools at local industrial districts started to offer apprenticeship training. A technical school was established in Kutani district of Kanazawa in 1887 to provide training in artistic handcrafts. Although the Kutani school was primarily concerned with the aesthetics of handcraft production, it also made a strong effort to instruct students in ceramics engineering technology (Ishikawa Prefecture 1887, Ishikawa High School 1957).

During the 1890s, as the Goni-kai (Five-two association),[4] a nationwide alliance of local trade associations, spread in the districts, trade associations called for the establishment of apprentice schools and industrial schools in local areas. At the same time, graduates from Tokyo Technical School and Tokyo School of Art who had taken up teaching positions at the local industrial districts, promoted the development of new products. Particularly active were the apprentice schools in Arita and Seto, where trade associations were established jointly by pottery manufacturers and traders. The trade associations organized annual pottery fairs and appointed apprentice school teachers as judges of new products (Terauchi 1933, Miyata 1985). In cooperation with the technical schools and apprentice schools, local trade associations also played a leading role in organizing exhibitions of pottery products meant for international and domestic industrial expositions.

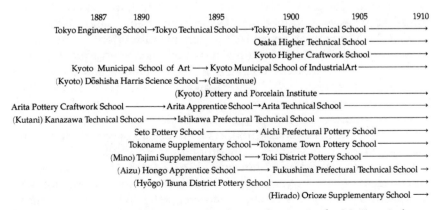

Fig. 9.1. Technical schools in pottery-producing districts in the Meiji period.

Graduates of Tokyo Technical School (Tokyo Higher Technical School) became headmasters and teachers at these apprentice and industrial schools. They established charcoal kilns at the schools and promoted research and development in the manufacturing technology of hard porcelain (Saga High School 2000). Some school graduates in the industrial districts went on to Tokyo Higher Technical School, acquired more advanced and updated knowledge of ceramics engineering technology, and then returned to their home towns. The feedback in technology and market information that linked the Tokyo Higher Technical School and the industrial districts spurred the development of Japanese ceramics technology through the early 1900s. Although Kyoto was relatively slow in introducing innovations to its traditional design training, faculty members of the Imperial University and other volunteers jointly established the Kyoto Higher Craftwork School in 1902 to provide a comprehensive educational program in artistic handicrafts. Similarly, the Osaka Higher Technical School set up a ceramics engineering department (Kawabe 1900, Kamoi 1935, Nakazawa 1912) and in the 1920s Kyoto Higher Craftwork School set up a pottery and porcelain department in addition to the department of design. Tokyo and Kyoto thus became the two major training and research centers for hard porcelain products and accelerated the dissemination of technology to pottery districts throughout Japan (Tsurumaki 1920).

4.3. *Trade associations*

The prototypical form of the modern pottery trade association dates back to the Tokugawa period, when those engaged in the pottery industry formed licensed commercial associations, or *kabu-nakama*, in major industrial districts. In the early Meiji era, domain (*han*) control of production and circulation control was abolished and *dōgyō-nakama*, or trade associations, were formed. The associations aimed, on one hand, to regulate business transactions between pottery manufacturers and traders, and, on the other, to train skilled shopworkers. In 1876 pottery manufacturers in Arita agreed on a set of rules that governed business transactions. In Kutani, pottery traders and manufacturers separately made agreements and set up trade associations (Terauchi 1933: 94–113, Ishikawa Prefecture 1883). After pottery exports from Seto and Tokoname substantially expanded, manufacturers there formed a trade association. In Seto, an exhibition hall was established to display pottery products with the aim of enhancing product quality and jointly developing new products (Katō 1910).

These various associations, however, were organized basically in a form reminiscent of the Tokugawa-era *kabu-nakama*. They were not well equipped to promote the product improvement activities by disseminating overseas technology and market information. At the roundtable discussion organized by the Ministry of Agriculture and Commerce in 1885, pottery manufacturers called for measures to enhance the technological level of the industrial districts, including the establishment of trade associations, exhibition spaces for pottery products and technical schools. The manufacturers claimed that both manufacturers and traders should pursue product improvement. In 1884, based on the statutes for trade associations stipulated by the Ministry of Agriculture and Commerce, pottery traders and manufacturers in Kyoto jointly established four pottery trade associations (MOAC 1885: 21). These associations were expected to promote mutual information exchange between traders and manufacturers with the aim of facilitating the development of new products that would meet the needs of overseas markets. The Kyoto move was followed by similar efforts in Arita and Mino, where trade associations were set up under the guidance of the industrial development section of the respective prefectural governments.

Responding to the demands for product improvement, Masana Maeda[5] took the position of chief judge at a domestic industrial exposition held in 1890. He gave instructions to Japanese pottery manufacturers that emphasized the importance of product development focusing on new designs. In 1893, Maeda organized the Goni-kai as a nationwide alliance of local associations and held a national industrial fair to encourage the participation of Japanese manufacturers and traders. At the general assembly of the Kyoto Goni-kai held in 1894, leading pottery manufacturers such as the Morimura-gumi and graduates of Tokyo Technical School acted as judges and advised participants on the latest pottery technology (Goni-kai 1894, 1897). With the product improvement movement gaining nationwide momentum, a pottery trade paper published by a Mino pottery manufacturer based in Tokyo functioned as a primary information provider. The trade paper promoted the local product improvement movements by covering topics such as the efforts of pottery districts and by introducing stories of pottery entrepreneurs.

In Kyoto, the center of the Goni-kai movement, pottery associations merged to promote shopworker training and the development of new products and sales channels. The merged associations took measures to protect monopoly sales of inventions, on the one hand, and to establish an exhibition hall on the other (Fujioka 1962: 39–41). Expanded to incorporate pottery districts throughout Japan, the Goni-kai organization pushed through a variety of product development schemes in local areas. Under its influence, trade associations incorporated pottery manufacturers. Traders were set up in Arita, Seto and Tokoname regions, based on The Trade Association Act for Strategic Export Commodities (Ōmori 1995). The formation process of trade associations in these regions suggests that joint development of new products and sales channels grew out of the activities of traders who promoted pottery exports by developing new products and new sales channels. Responding to the shifting need for export-oriented industrialization, the trade associations pushed product development by establishing the training and research institutes in the pottery districts.

5. Conclusion

During the Meiji and Taisho periods Japan's pottery industry took the path of export-oriented industrialization by shifting from Japanese-style products to Western-style tableware. Export-oriented industrialization was also spurred by the addition of daily-use ceramic products to the traditional line of artistic pottery. During the early 1900s, the reputation of Japanese pottery rose overseas after manufacturers successfully produced hard porcelain products and developed solid base material. Further progress was made in the 1910s, when Nagoya, Seto and Mino regions started to produce inexpensive daily-use ceramic products fired in charcoal kilns. This development dramatically increased the export, and hence the total production volume, of Japanese pottery products.

A pivotal role was played by a number of pioneering pottery companies. Kōransha in Arita exhibited their products at international expositions, and increased pottery exports through the production of high-quality artistic pottery. Morimura-gumi developed artistic pottery products during the 1890s and mass produced Western tableware products for export to the United States. In expanding its production base, Morimura-gumi subcontracted manufacturing tasks to producers in the Seto region and glaze painting to painters in Tokyo and Kyoto. During the 1900s, as Morimura-gumi worked to develop hard porcelain products based on the accumulation of conventional technologies, it overcame technical obstacles by aggressively recruiting Tokyo Technical School graduates and dispatching them to European pottery factories to learn the latest manufacturing technology. The line of products exported by Morimura-gumi and other manufacturers in Nagoya used traditional Japanese technology with a flavor of artistic handcraft. These products were eventually seen to reflect "Japan". Pottery manufacturers thus adopted Western manufacturing technology and developed it into something recognized as distinctively Japanese.

Also important in the export-oriented industrialization of Japanese pottery were the trade associations that established apprentice schools in local industrial districts and invited Tokyo Technical School graduates to work as teachers. The trade associations organized fairs to promote the development of new products and new sales channels. They disseminated among local pottery manufacturers the technology needed to produce hard porcelain of the kind made in charcoal kilns. Local apprentice schools and technical schools were organized not to train apprentices but to help ceramic engineers acquire Western manufacturing technology. In the early 1900s, some outstanding apprentice school graduates went on to Tokyo Higher Technical School or the Tokyo School of Art and later joined pottery manufacturing companies in various parts of Japan as engineers. The industrial policies of the Ministry of Agriculture and Commerce and the industrial development section of the local government supported the activities of pottery manufacturers. However, the primary energy for the export-oriented industrialization of Japanese pottery came from three other groups: innovative pottery manufacturing companies, technical schools that backed up the activities of these companies, and trade associations.

Notes

1. The survey carried out in Aichi Prefecture (1894—1902) shows that the number of pottery manufacturers in Aichi Prefecture increased from 681 in 1894 to 843 in 1899. The number of shopworkers decreased from 4,480 to 4,271 during the same period. By 1900, both figures had increased sharply to 1,132 and 8,700 respectively.
2. Tōyō Tōki, Co., Ltd. equipped the mass production line not only for sanitary ceramics, but also for hard porcelain products.
3. In 1883, art laboratories were established in Seto and Tokoname (Aichi Prefecture 1997).
4. The Goni-kai was organized by Maeda Masana in Kyoto in 1894 for the promotion of seven strategic export items (textiles, pottery, copperware, lacquer ware, papermaking, sculpture and carpets).
5. Maeda Masana was born in Satsuma domain, and went abroad to study in France in his youth. He worked as an administrative assistant at the Paris International Exposition in 1878 and later became a bureaucrat in the Ministry of Agriculture and Commerce. He compiled the publication, "*Kōgyō Iken*" [Opinions on industrial development] in 1884 (Soda 1975).

References

Aichi-Ken (Prefecture), *Aichi-ken Kangyō Zasshi* [The Journal of Industrial Promotion in Aichi Prefecture] 19 (Nagoya, 1891).
——, *Aichi kenchi Ippan* [The General View of Aichi Prefecture] 1–6 (Nagoya, 1894–1902).
Aichi-Ken Seto Yōgyō High School, *Seto Yōgyō Kōtō Gakkō Hyakunenshi* [A Hundred-Year History of Seto Yōgyō High School] (Seto, 1995).
Aichi-Ken Tokoname High School, *Hyakunen no Ayumi* [A Hundred-Year History of Tokoname High School] (Tokoname, 1997).
Fujioka, Kōji, *Fujie Nagataka Den* [The Biography of Fujie Nagataka] (Kyoto, 1932).

Fujioka, *Kyōyaki Hyakunen no Ayumi* [A Hundred-Year History of Kyoto Pottery] (Kyoto, 1962).

Gaimushō [Ministry of Foreign Affairs (MOFA)], *Tsūshō Ihen* [The Report on Foreign Trade] (Tokyo, 1881–85).

——, *Tsūshō Hōkoku* [The Report on Foreign Trade] (Tokyo, 1887–88).

——, *Tsūshō Ihen* [The Report on Foreign Trade] (Tokyo, 1895–1908).

Goni-kai, *Kyoto Goni-kai Taikai Hōkoku* [The Reports of Goni-kai General Meetings] (Kyoto, 1894).

Goni-kai, *Goni-kai Zenkoku Hinpyōkai Jimu Hōkoku* [The Business Report of the Goni-kai Competitive Exhibition in Japan] (Kyoto, 1897).

Hirano, Kōsuke, *Hoteiso Shōshi* [The Biography of Hirano Kōsuke] (Tokyo, 1940).

Ide, Seijirō, *Sangyō Kōgei no Senkaku: Noutomi Kaijirō Den* [The Leader of Industrial Arts: The Biography of Noutomi Kaijirō] (Tokyo, 1976).

——, "Tōjigyō Kindaika to Arita Sarayama no Dōkō" [The Modernization of the Porcelain Industry and Trends in the Arita Porcelain Industry], *Arita Machi Rekishi Minzoku Shiryōkan, Aritayaki Sankōkan Kenkyū Kiyō* (Saga, 1992).

Ide, Tetsuzō, *Kutani Tōjikigyō Gaikan* [The General View of Kutani Porcelain Industry], Kutani Genseki Hasai Company (Ishikawa, 1908).

Ikeda, Bunji, *Matsutō: Matsumura Hachijirō Den* [The Biography of Matsumura Hachijirō], The Memorial Association of Matsumura Hachijirō (Nagoya, 1939).

Ishikawa-ken (Prefecture), *Ishikawa-ken Kangyō Dai-5-kai Nenpō* [The Fifth Annual Report of Industrial Promotion in Ishikawa Prefecture] (Kanazawa, 1883).

——, *Ishikawa-ken Gakuji Hōkoku* [The Educational Report of Ishikawa Prefecture] (Kanazawa, 1887).

Ishikawa-ken Kōtō Kōgei Gakkō [Craftwork High School], *Nanajyūnenshi* [A Seventy-Year History] (Kanazawa, 1957).

Kamoi, Takeshi, *Nakazawa Iwata Hakase Kijyu Shukuga Kinenchō* [The Memorial Book of 77-year-old Dr. Nakazawa Iwata] (Tokyo, 1935).

Katō Kuniji, *Aichi-ken Tōjikigyō narabi ni Gaikoku Bōeki Chōsa Hōkoku* [The Report of the Porcelain Industry in Aichi Prefecture and Foreign Trade], Yamaguchi Higher Commercial School (Yamaguchi, 1910).

Kawabe, Masao, *Fukumeisho (Tokyo Kōgyō Gakkō)* [The Report (Tokyo Technical School)] (Tokyo, 1900).

Kokuritsu, Nagoya Sangyō Kenkyūjyo [National Industrial Research Institute of Nagoya], *Meikoken Tōjiki Bumon 75 nen no Ayumi* [A Seventy-five-year History of the Porcelain Department in the Nagoya Institute of Industrial Technology] (Nagoya, 1998).

Kuroda, Masanori: *Jitsuyō Seitōgaku* [Practical Methods of Porcelain Production] (Tokyo, 1909).

Kyoto Shiritsu Bijyutsu Kōgei Gakkō [Municipal Craftwork School], *Kyoto Shiritsu Bijyutsu Kōgei Gakkō Enkaku Ryaku* [The General History of Kyoto Municipal Industrial Arts School] (Kyoto, 1910).

Kyoto Shiritsu Geijyutsu Daigaku [Municipal University of Art], *Hyakunenshi* [Centennial History] (Kyoto, 1981).

Maeyama, Hiroshi, "Meiji zenki naigai hakurankai shuppin no tōjiki ni tsuite" [Porcelain in international and domestic exhibitions in the first half of the Meiji era], in *Kindai no Kyūshū Tōji Ten* [The Exhibition of Kyūshū Porcelain in the Modern Era] (Saga, 1983).

Mishima, Yasuo, "Tōjiki no sangyō kakumei: Seto to Nagoya" [The industrial revolution in the porcelain industry: Seto and Nagoya], in Keizai Ronsō 75–1, Kyoto University (1955): 39–60.

Miyata, Kotarō, *Arita Chōshi: Tōgyōhen II* [The History of Arita City: Pottery Industry], Arita City (Saga, 1985).

Motomiya, Kazuo, "Kaigai jyōhō to tōjiki yushutsu" [Foreign information and the export of porcelain], in Takamura, Naosuke (ed.), *Meiji no Sangyō Hatten to Shakai Shihon* (Kyoto, 1997).

Nagoya Kogyō, *Kenkyūjyo* [National Industrial Research Institute of Nagoya (NIRIN)], Meikōken Tōjikibumon 75-nen no Ayumi [A Seventy-five-year History of Pottery Branches] (Nagoya, 1998).

Nakayama, Seiki, *Arita Yōgyō no Nagare to sono Ashioto: Kōransha Hyakunen no Ayumi* [The Development of Arita Porcelain and its Effects: A Hundred-year History of Kōransha] (Saga, 1980).

Nakazawa Iwata (ed.), *Kyoto Kōtō Kōgei Gakkō Hajime Jyūnen Seiseki Hōkoku* [Report on the Ten Years of the Kyoto Higher Industrial Arts School] (Kyoto, 1912).

Naramoto Tatsuya, "Kaigai shijyō no keisei to Kyoko Tōki Kaisha" [The development of foreign markets and Kyoto Tōki Kaisha], *Rekishi-gaku Kenkyū* 95 (1942): 51–66.

——, *Kindai Tōjikigyō no Seiritsu* [The Establishment of a Modern Porcelain Industry] (Tokyo, 1943).

Nippon Gaishi Kaisha [NGK], *Nippon Gaishi 75 Nenshi* [A Seventy-five-year History of Nippon Gaishi Kaisha] (Nagoya, 1995).

Nippon Tōki Kaisha, *Nippon Tōki 70 Nenshi* [A Seventy-year History of Nippon Tōki Kaisha] (Nagoya, 1974).

Nōshōmushō, [Ministry of Agriculture and Commerce (MOAC)] *Tōki Shūdankai Kiji* [The Report of the Pottery Industry Meeting] (Tokyo, 1885).

——, *Tōjiki Chōsasho* [Reports on the Porcelain Industry] (Tokyo, 1892).

——, *Nōshōkō Kōhō* [Public Reports on Agriculture, Commerce and Industry] (Tokyo, 1885–7).

——, *Nōshōmu Tōkeihyō* [The Statistics of the Ministry of Agriculture and Commerce] (Tokyo, 1887–1912).

——, *Nōshōmushō Kōmukyoku Rinji Hōkoku* [The Special Report of the Industry Bureau, the Ministry of Agriculture and Commerce] (Tokyo, 1897–1901).

Ōhashi, Kōji, *Hizen Tōji* [Hizen Porcelain] (Tokyo, 1993).

Ōkurashō, [Ministry of Financial Affairs (MOF)], *Kanpō* [The Official Gazette] (Tokyo, 1890–2).

——, *Dainippon Gaikoku Bōeki Nenpyō* [The Statistics of Foreign Trade in Japan] (Tokyo, 1887–1912).

——, *Meiji Nijyūgonen Gaikoku Bōeki Gairan* [The General Outline of Foreign Trade in Twenty-five Years of Meiji] (Tokyo, 1892).

Ōmori, Kazuhiro, "Meiji kōki ni okeru tōjikigyō no hatten to dōgyō-kumiai katsudō" [The development of the porcelain industry and the activity of business associations in the second half of the Meiji era], in Keieishigaku 30–2 (1995: 1–30).

——, "Kaigai gijyutsu no dōnyū to jyōhō kōdō: Nippon Tōki Gōmei Kaisha" [The introduction of foreign technologies and information–gathering activities: Nippon Tōki Kaisha, Unlimited Partnership], in Sasaki, Satoru and Nobuyuki Fujii (eds), *Jyōhō to Keiei Kakushin* [Information and Management Innovation] (Tokyo, 1997).

Saga-ken Arita Kōtō Kōgyō Gakkō [Technical High School], *Hyakunenshi* [Centennial History] (Saga, 2000).

Shōfū Tōki Kaisha, Limited Partnership: *Shōfū Geppō* [Monthly Report of Shōfū Tōki Kaisha] 6 (1911).

Soda, Osamu, *Maeda Masana* [The Biography of Maeda Masana] (Tokyo, 1975).

Terauchi, Shinichi, *Arita Jigyōshi* [The History of the Arita Porcelain Industry] (Arita, 1933).

Tokyo Kōgyō Daigaku [Institute of Technology], *Tokyo Kōgyō Daigaku Rokujyūnenshi* [A Sixty-year History of Tokyo University of Technology] (Tokyo, 1941).

Tsuji Seitō Kaisha, *Tsuji no Shirube* [Guidebook of Tsuji Seitō Kaisha] (Saga, 1920s).

Tsukatani, Akihiro, "Kutaniyaki Tōjikigyōshi Jyosetsu" [Introduction to the Kutani Porcelain Industry], *Kokugakuin Keizaigaku* 15–1, Kokugakuin University, (Tokyo, 1966: 32–85).

Tsurumaki, Tsuruichi, *Tōjiki-ka Setchi Riyū Setsumeisho* [Explanation of the establishment of the Department of Porcelain Technology] (Kyoto, 1920).

Yamada Takehisa, "Tokugawa kōki ni okeru hizen tōjikigyō no tenkai" [The development of the hizen porcelain industry in the second half of the Tokugawa era], in *Shakaikeizaishigaku* 61–1 (1995a): 30–56.

——, "Meiji zenki tōjiki sanchi ni okeru kikai dōnyū" [The introduction of machinery technologies in porcelain production areas in the first half of the Meiji era], in *Osakadaigaku-keizaigaku* 45–1 (Osaka, 1995b): 33–47.

——, "Meiji zenki ni okeru hizen tōjikigyō no yushutsu senryaku" [Export strategies of the hizen porcelain industry in the first half of the Meiji era], in *Keieishigaku* 30–4 (Tokyo, 1996a): 32–58.

——, "Meiji zenki tōjiki sanchi ni okeru yushutsu senryaku" [Export strategies in porcelain production areas in the first half of the Meiji era], in *Sangyō to Keizai* 11–2,3, Nara Sangyō University (Nara, 1996b): 49–62.

PART IV

Industry and Regional Community

10

The Development of a Rural Weaving Industry and its Social Capital

HISAMI MATSUZAKI

1. Introduction

Communitarian characteristics have been identified as important features of the Japanese economy. If a society has such characteristics, the implication is that the society has substantial social capital. The term "social capital" includes cooperative activities, networks, mutual trust and general social morale. In this article, the development of one rural weaving industry will be examined to clarify the function of social capital in the development of regional industry.

The essay will begin with a discussion of the process through which social capital was strengthened or weakened. Some scholars assume that the production of social capital or social bonds is the result of cooperative activity, while others would see social capital as a prerequisite for the creation of cooperative activities. Piore and Sabel, who examined industrial districts in which small entrepreneurs were the chief actors, found them to be bound in a complex web of competition and cooperation. They argued, "The cohesion of the industry rests on a more fundamental sense of community, of which the various institutional forms of cooperation are more the result than the cause." They emphasized "ethnic ties" and "shared politics and religion" as characteristic features of the industrial district (Piore and Sabel 1984: 265–6). If we assume that entrepreneurs tried to maximize profits of their firms, cooperation among them must be seen as an exogenous factor affecting their economic activity. In other words, competitive entrepreneurs should be inherently opposed to cooperative activities that will also aid their competitors.[1] In this article, the relation between social capital and economic activity will be examined as a way of exploring the complex mix of cooperation and competition that we find in industrial districts, and I will examine how those factors affected each other.

The second question we will consider is how social capital affects the decision-making of entrepreneurs. When comparing the French, German and Japanese cultures with those of the Americans and the British, Hampden-Turner and Trompenaars argued that the French, Germans and Japanese "would say that if the needs of the group are considered first, then the invisible hand will . . . automatically take care of the desires of the individual" (Hampden-Turner and Trompenaars 1993: 14). This article, however, will argue that the main motivation for entrepreneurs was the pursuit of private benefit even in a traditional rural society like that of Japan. Our question then is how entrepreneurs, who were seeking private gain, got involved in decision-making that involved communitarian principles.

The third question we will consider is whether social capital negatively affects economic activity. Some historical studies assume mutuality as normal and consequently overlook the theoretical possibility that strong social bonds could have a negative impact on economic activity. (Turner and Trompenaars 1994: 14) In the conclusion to a study on historical comparison in Italian society, Putnam asserted: "stocks of social capital . . . tend to be self-reinforcing and cumulative. Virtuous circles resulted in social equilibria with high-levels of cooperation, trust, reciprocity, civic engagement and collective well-being" (Putnam 1993: 179). We will describe "reinforcing and cumulative" as it applies to the process of social capital in a Japanese weaving district.

To this point, we have only mentioned positive influences of cooperation; it is, of course, also possible to argue that strong social bonds can have a negative effect. In cases where cooperation between entrepreneurs reaches very high levels, the mechanisms of competition may not work well. It is the aim of this paper to clarify these complicated questions with regard to social capital and to seek a clearer understanding of the conditions in which social capital plays a positive or negative role.

In this article, the Isezaki weaving industry has been chosen as the subject for our empirical study (Matsuzaki 2001). The Isezaki weaving district was one of many weaving districts that made up the rural weaving industry in Japan during the period from 1880 to 1930. Each of the weaving districts included many small- and medium-sized companies, which were organized into trade associations. Isezaki is typical of the large number of weaving districts in which cooperation among entrepreneurs played an important role and it has enriched stock of corporate archives.[2]

2. Social Capital in the Development of the Isezaki Weaving District, 1890–1925

2.1. *Overall development of the Isezaki weaving industry*

The demand for textiles increased in the period from 1890 to 1926, as we can see from Table 10.1 Contents of Expenditures, which shows the

Table 10.1. Content of expenditure

(million yen, %)

Year	Food	Cloth	Dwelling	Total
1890	2,591(63)	170(4)	459(11)	4,123(100)
1900	3,254(60)	364(7)	558(10)	5,444(100)
1910	3,907(60)	445(7)	798(12)	6,513(100)
1920	5,296(60)	780(9)	921(10)	8,848(100)
1926	6,089(57)	918(9)	1,309(12)	10,760(100)

Source: Shinohara (1969: 138–9).

proportion of household expenditures devoted to different categories of goods. According to that table, the average expenditure for clothes doubled in the 1890s. The westernization of Japan had already begun at the time of the Meiji Restoration, but most Japanese people still wore traditional clothing at that time. Although clothing styles had not yet seen a major change, the expansion of the textile market allowed the traditional weaving industry to develop, making use of both imported and domestic raw materials, which were supplied from a modernized production system.

During the last decade of the nineteenth century and the first decade of the twentieth century, the proportion of income spent on clothes stabilized. This period included two wars, the Sino–Japanese war of 1894–95 and the Russo–Japanese war of 1904–1905, and the recession periods that followed each. No major increases in textile consumption would be seen until the period of the First World War, in the late teens. It was during this period that the Japanese economy grew very rapidly, as a result of the decline in the European presence and the boom in the American economy.

Table 10.2 provides data on the relative weight of different fabrics in overall textile consumption. Silk, which had slightly trailed cotton in 1910, moved into first place in 1920. At the same time the share of wool textiles, a newcomer that had entered Japan only after the Meiji Restoration, rose as high as 20 percent.

The first few years of the 1900s had already seen major changes in public taste in clothing, manifested in consumption patterns that turned to higher quality and more diversified fabrics. These changes became apparent in the 1910s and continued until the late 1920s. Owing to the boom which took place during the First World War the trend continued into the 1920s. Many people of the middle-class became affluent enough to buy more expensive clothes. The westernization of clothing also started to affect the daily lives and the consumption of middle- and lower-class people.

The Isezaki weaving industry, which developed as an industry producing for the domestic market, developed within the context of this

Table 10.2. Content of textile consumption in Japan

(million yen, %)

Year	Cotton	Silk	Ramie	Wool	Rayon	Total
1910	159(44)	148(41)	7(2)	45(13)	0(0)	359(100)
1920	543(37)	625(43)	21(1)	277(19)	2(0)	1,468(100)
1926	412(32)	507(40)	31(2)	311(24)	13(1)	1,274(100)

Source: Same as previous table.

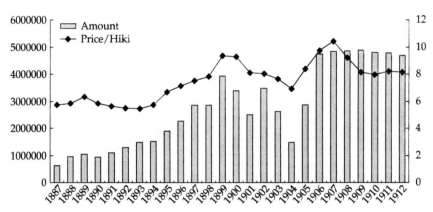

Fig. 10.1. Development of Isezaki weaving industry (Unit: yen).
Source: *Isezaki Orimono Dōgyō Kumiaishi* [The History of the Association of the Isesaki Weaving Industry] (Isezaki, 1931).
Note: *Hiki* is an unit of the fabric.

overall expansion of demand. Fig. 10.1 shows the development of the Isezaki weaving industry during this period. As we can see, there was a three-fold increase in output during the decade of the 1890s. During the following fifteen years, production stagnated in response to the financial panic after the Sino–Japanese war and the recession after the Russo–Japanese war. We can next see an increase in production during the First World War boom. During this period there was not only an increase in volume of output, but also in the price of goods, making this period a true boom period for the Isezaki industry. However, during the decade of the 1920s Japan entered a period of recession and this brought a sharp drop in the price of textile products. Volume reached a peak in 1921, and then continued to hold to the levels reached at that time for some years.

2.2. Structure of production in the Isezaki weaving industry

Let us begin this section with an examination of the structure of production and distribution in the Isezaki weaving industry.[3] The term "Isezaki

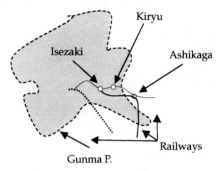

Fig. 10.2. Map around Isezaki.

weaving district" refers to an area in Sawa-gun [Sawa County], centered on the town of Isezaki. As we can see from Fig. 10.2, there were two other well-known weaving districts nearby, Kiryū and Ashikaga. Sawa County was an administrative sub-division of Gumma Prefecture which was one of Japan's main centers for the production of silk yarn. Isezaki was one of the regions that produced traditional textiles. During the Meiji era, Isezaki gained fame as a producer of silk yarn and spun silk goods. Among the best-known fabrics produced in the Isezaki weaving district were silk ikat textiles and silk stripes. Most Isezaki fabrics were plain weaves, and local weavers did not use the jacquard looms that were used for weaving the complicated patterns that were common on Kyoto's fine *kimono* [costumes].

During the Edo era, farm households in Isezaki wove silk cloth using home-made materials and simple looms. By the 1890s, Isezaki had begun to develop as a specialized weaving district, with output levels increasing three times over what they had been at the time of the Meiji restoration. The growth in volume was one indication of the shift toward market-oriented production that had led to Isezaki establishing a place in the national market. It was also in the 1890s that the social division of production that was to characterize Isezaki throughout its lifetime as a weaving district took shape. Fig. 10.3 provides an outline of the systems of production and distribution.

The social division of production in Isezaki was based on cooperation between many kinds of out-workers and subcontractors. Clothiers played a central role in the production system. A clothier first gained yarn material and then farmed out the preparatory process of weaving to out-house bleachers, warpers, dyers and so on. Prepared threads of warp and weft were then distributed to the weavers. When weaving was finished, the clothier gathered the cloth and brought it to an arranger house.

A clothier was not only an organizer of the production system but also a risk-taker in this economic activity. Isezaki's clothiers enlarged the

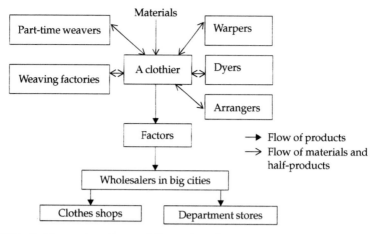

Fig. 10.3. Putting-out system and flow of products.

market for traditional Japanese clothing by supplying relatively cheap commodities. Although Isezaki textiles were relatively cheap compared to high-grade expensive textiles, such as Nishijin textiles made in Kyoto, silk textiles themselves were not necessities but luxuries. As in the case of other luxury goods, marketing depended on pleasing the customers' taste. The clothiers who managed the trade had to take risks when they decided what kind of materials to use, what kind of textiles to weave, and what patterns to apply to the textiles.

Since the cost of silk yarn accounted for 60 to 70 percent of the production cost, the silk weaving industry was vulnerable to the fluctuation of silk prices. This also made the management of a clothier very risky. If a clothier could acquire and process silk yarn at a low price and could sell his products on the upward trend of prices, he could gain huge profits. If his calculations or luck were off, then he might make great losses.

The clothiers could quite easily adapt their production capacity. When demand increased, they needed only to increase the number of weavers and other out-workers. Given the volatility of the market, clothiers could not assure their outworkers of constant orders, but their employees did try to maintain good relationships with the weavers.

Most of the weavers came from farming families. Weaving was dovetailed to fit into the rhythm of the agricultural year with its fluctuating demand for agricultural labor. Sometimes demand for cloth was high at the same times that the demand for agricultural labor was high. At those times, the clothiers who had worked hardest to maintain good relations with the weavers were in the best position to find weavers who were willing to work.

Although the work of these employees who acted as the intermediaries between the clothiers and the weavers was of crucial importance, such employees worked for very low wages. Many of them regarded themselves as apprentices or pupils of their clothier master, and looked on their work as an opportunity to learn the trade, which might eventually lead a former employee to set up his own business as a clothier.

As we saw from our brief consideration of Fig. 10.1 earlier, there was a great expansion of the silk weaving industry from the latter half of the teens through the first half of the 1920s. The rapid growth was attributable to the invention of a new product woven with power-looms and the expansion of putting out production. Table 10.3 shows that the number of power-looms increased rapidly during this period, and there was a corresponding decline in the use of hand-looms.

Many clothiers in Kiryū and Ashikaga, weaving districts near Isezaki, started to adopt power-looms during this boom period. However, following this increase in production capacity, the boom period abruptly came to an end. The Great Kantō Earthquake of 1923 was one of the factors that caused a decline in the demand for silk fabrics. Clothiers in the weaving districts found there was not a big enough market to absorb their products. The policy of producing middle- or low-graded silk textiles turned out to be effective. Entrepreneurs in Isezaki weaving district began to place orders with weavers belonging to associations outside the immediate Isezaki weaving area. Approximately half of the power-loom textiles bearing the Isezaki brand name were produced outside Isezaki around 1925.[4] This shift represented a significant change in the structure of production that had been in place since the 1890s.

2.3. Social capital and the development of the weaving industry

Social capital functioned to support the development of the weaving industry. In this section we will examine the functioning of social capital in the development of new products, and the roles played by the trade association, the purchasing agents, the clothiers and financial interests.

Table 10.3. Clothiers and looms in Isezaki region

	1912	1916	1920	1925
Clothiers and weavers (persons)	6,873	6,807	8,323	6,787
Number of power looms	1	41	288	992
Number of hand looms	7,224	7,494	8,898	7,586

Source: *Gunma Ken Tōkeisho* [Statistics of Gunma Prefecture].

Development of new products and quality control

It is important to note the crucial role played by the trade association in the development of new products and the improvement of quality. After the Meiji Restoration, various restrictions on economic activity had been lifted, and the rural economy was stimulated. The economic activity of manufacturers accelerated in response to the inflationary monetary policy taken by the Meiji government during the latter half of the 1870s. At that time the Meiji government issued huge amounts of notes to fund the suppression of a revolt by the old samurai class. Under these conditions, clothiers were enticed to produce larger volumes of low-quality products. While inflation was one factor in this lowering of quality, inexperience was another. Producers were just beginning to experiment with the use of imported synthetic dyes, and had not yet fully mastered the appropriate technologies.

Entrepreneurs operating in the Isezaki region formed a producers' association in a bid to maintain product quality in the 1880s.[5] The famous entrepreneur Yaichirō Shimojyō I,[6] who was then a clothier, became the leader of the organization. The association chose what it believed to be an appropriate method of dyeing and adopted strict rules to enforce quality standards. Special threads were to be woven into textiles as a mark that the goods were produced in Isezaki. Two years later, another device was introduced to assure quality: a tag showing the width and length of each textile and the producer's name had to be put at the end of each bolt. These efforts helped to raise quality standards and the Isezaki weaving district received a prize in a domestic industrial exhibition.[7]

In the 1890s, some manufacturers experimented with the use of spun silk yarn instead of low-grade pure silk yarn. Spun silk yarn was produced from inferior cocoons with much shorter silk fibers. The hint for the use of such shorter-fiber raw materials came from technology created for use in the cotton spinning industry, where manufacturers were developing techniques to deal with short-staple raw cotton. The experimentation with such new raw materials can be viewed as a type of innovation, in the Schumpeterian sense (Schumpeter 1983), even though the production system was still organized along traditional patterns. The introduction of spun silk yarn was not always easy. Spun silk yarn was considerably cheaper than the lowest grades of silk yarn produced with better cocoons. While the great advantage of using spun silk was the lower cost, this new raw material also presented certain problems to the weavers. Spun silk was not as lustrous as silk yarn, and moreover its fluffy nature made it harder to weave on a handloom.

The trade association played an important role in the development of new products using spun silk. In dealing with this issue, the association had to meet the criticisms that came from the agents of purchasing firms. For example, an influential group of merchants in Kyoto made the criticism that clothes made of spun silk were even worse than those made of silk and cotton blends, and the clothes made with spun silk easily lost their shape. As a result of such criticisms, the leader of the trade association, Shimojyō, tried to prohibit the introduction of spun silk as a raw material. Not all members of the association agreed with their leader. Another leader of the association, Morimura, asserted that the criticism of Kyoto merchants was the result of their own interests. When the lower cost Isezaki fabrics entered the market, it was difficult for Kyoto producers to compete with them. Morimura believed that Isezaki manufacturers should be cautious in accepting the criticism of the Kyoto dealers. This difference of opinions split the Isezaki association into two groups, and a new association was founded by Morimura's group.

It is very difficult to judge which opinion was correct and what the long-term effects of the introduction of the new raw materials were. There is no question, however, that the split in the trade association had negative effects. Mr Take, a politician who was once a member of the liberal movement in the region, and other people made efforts to mediate the dispute between the conflicting groups of clothiers. The leaders of the two groups were persuaded to simultaneously step aside, and a factor took the post of chairman of the reunited association. The new association adopted spun silk as an officially-recognized material.

As a result of this introduction of the new, lower-cost, raw materials, the Isezaki region emerged as one of the most important weaving districts where medium- and small-sized manufacturers produced traditional silk fabrics. Isezaki featured well-designed and low-priced products that could meet the demand of the working class, whose standard of living was improved as the Japanese economy rapidly expanded. The lowering of costs through the introduction of the new raw materials was an important factor in this development.

During the decade of the teens, when power-looms were introduced, the development of new products also played an important role. Yaichirō Shimojyō III and one of his subordinates invented a new kind of fabric that was based on the use of warp ikats. The surface of spun silk yarn was fluffy for weaving. They took advantage of this feature of the raw materials. If fluffy yarn is dyed and ikat patterns are designed on the warp threads, the yarn's non-smooth surface spreads the effect of coloring in narrow spaces. This processing creates a warp ikat that resembles that of double ikat[8] on which complicated patterns can be woven. Owing to this technology, the clothiers could use power looms to produce low-cost silk ikat textiles. These new designs played an important role in widening the market to suit the demands of the lower classes. Yaichirō Shimojyō III and his group had already started to produce warp ikat textiles with power looms during the period of the First World War, despite the bad reputation of spun silk textiles. Many clothiers followed suit in the first half of the 1920s.

While the association got off to a good start in the 1880s, it was forced to deal with several crises in later times. A long stagnation hit the Japanese economy after the rapid expansion caused by the Russo–Japanese war. Since many manufacturers in other weaving regions had adopted power-looms around 1910, the problem of over-production became serious. The financial situation of entrepreneurs in the weaving industry became worse, and some companies went bankrupt.

The Isezaki weaving industry, too, faced a severe recession around 1910. At that time Isezaki weavers had started to produce silk-cotton blends, which had been expected to widen the demand for Isezaki's products. Despite those predictions, the price of the blends fell, while the price for similar fabrics produced in the neighboring Ashikaga region remained relatively high. The association was forced to introduce aggressive poli-cies to cope with this crisis. It started a competition for silk products, in which clothiers competed with each other, and they invited officials of wholesalers and department stores to this competition as judges. The con-test aided entrepreneurs by raising their awareness of what kind of prod-ucts had higher market appeal. Due to the strengthened influence of the fashion, clothiers had to respond to the market demand as quickly as possible.

The competition prompted the clothiers to give greater attention to changing market demand. While such awareness of the links between fashion and market demand were to become commonplace in later times, the Isezaki entrepreneurs were among the first of Japan's regional silk associations to realize the connection and take steps to encourage mem-bers to adopt this new market awareness.

Factors and clothiers

The market for Isezaki fabrics was made up of many clothiers, a smaller number of factors, and agents of wholesalers who came to the region to buy up fabrics. All of the trade was managed through the market, which was held several times a month, with products or samples displayed in each factor's section of the market. One of the features of the Isezaki mar-keting system was the important role of factors who handled most sales.[9] In most cases the clothiers consigned finished goods for sale to the whole-salers' agents at the market, while in some cases the clothiers sold their products to the factors. After closing a bargain with wholesalers, the fac-tors then shipped them to the wholesalers. Thus, the most important rela-tionships that formed the market were the relationship between the clothiers and the factors, and the relationship between the factors and the agents of wholesalers.

What did the factors do? We can identify several important functions in addition to their work as intermediaries in the sale of goods.[10] The first of those functions was the supply of capital, in the form of loans, to clothiers to support production. These loans were an important way for the factors to financially control the clothiers, and assured advantageous conditions in their dealings with the clothiers. Certainly the practice of supplying loans to clothiers was an expensive business. The minutes of a management meeting held at the central office of the major factor Kakiage indicate that at least the Kakiage brokerage firm tried to stop offering loans in the early teens. The same documents also suggest that the factor still found it difficult to end the practice of loaning money to clothiers twenty years later.

Let us consider for a minute how loans would facilitate the work of a brokerage firm. There were only a few brokerage houses serving the Isezaki weaving district. As a result, it is possible to see the Isezaki market as one characterized by an oligopolistic market structure in which factors held a dominant position because of the funds they provided and the function they served. We might thus expect that the factors were able to make huge oligopolistic profits (Koshō 1980). However, records from the Kakiage brokerage firm, which show how much a dealer of the factor gained or lost on each deal, indicate that even when high-ranking officers of the firm dealt with a transaction, they could not always return a profit. The outcome of the contract depended on market conditions, and it was very difficult to always predict correctly changes in fashion and which patterns would be most welcomed in the market. Because of the very changeable nature of fashion choices, factors needed clothiers' cooperation in supplying fabrics with designs that would give them a strong competitive position. While documents from the brokerage house suggest that factors worried about becoming overly committed to relations with individual clothiers, factors also knew that they could not gain a profit without good relations with clothiers. Seen in this context, it seems clear that the use of loans was designed to build closer relationships with clothiers.

One of the major accomplishments of the Isezaki weaving district was its successful construction of an Isezaki brand name. Factors played an important role in the construction of the brand, often mediating competition between clothiers. Raising the reputation of Isezaki for good fashion and good quality was a common goal shared by factors and clothiers. For clothiers, there was a direct connection between their personal desires to become famous clothiers, and the success of the weaving district in establishing a distinctive brand. On the one hand, clothiers had to think about the success of their own individual firms, and on the other hand, they needed to promote the common interests of the regional brand. Their activities were thus characterized by a complex mix of competition with rival clothiers, and the need for cooperation in the pursuit of common goals. The difficulties of this mix were illustrated by the conflict in the 1890s over the introduction of spun silk yarn.

For the factors, development of a strong regional brand was an important goal since the factors' profits depended upon the appeal of the products they sold. As the agents who marketed almost all Isezaki fabrics, the factors had access to information on textile markets, and this made them more market-oriented and sensitive to the development of a regional brand. Since there were only a small number of factors, the oligopolistic structure of the Isezaki market made cooperation among the brokerage houses easier. Owners of brokerage houses were often chosen as chairmen of the association in this period, and they played an important role in promoting strategies to establish the regional brand.

One of the major problems during periods of recession was the attempt by wholesalers and retailers to return unsold goods. According to some reports, when prices dropped, some wholesalers would return commodities, asserting that they were defective. When fashion trends started to change, retailers also used the same tactics, returning unsold goods that they still held in stock. This practice of returning unsold goods raised the level of conflict between the factors in Isezaki and the wholesalers and retailers who came from urban consuming regions. Theoretically, a factor should not have been in a position to accept later claims about defects, since all commodities had been inspected by employees of the factor at the time of shipment. A strong policy toward wholesalers and retailers was also desirable from the clothiers' perspective. However, if wholesalers held superior bargaining power, they might be able to return goods, causing a big loss to clothiers. Records from the archives of brokerage firms indicate that factors could not always block the attempts of wholesalers to return already consigned goods.

Factors and clothiers often debated the question of how to deal with returned goods—and the responses of clothiers and factors to this problem were different. When factors were forced to take back consigned goods, there was always a temptation to push the loss off on the original producers. According to minutes from the archives of the factor Kakiage, on one occasion a top manager of the firm argued that a brokerage house should take responsibility for returned commodities and should not return them to the clothier. In fact, one of Kakiage's documents reveals that in the case of the Isezaki branch the percentage of returned commodities was 3.2 percent, lower than the rates for its Kiryū and Ashikaga branches, which had return rates of 5.8 percent and 5.1 percent respectively. Another document shows how the dealer managed returned commodities (see Table 10.4). The Isezaki branch of Kakiage sent back a substantial amount of "returned" commodities to the wholesalers; the rate of "returned" goods that were in turn sent back to the wholesalers was higher for the Isezaki branch, than for other branches of Kakiage. This situation suggests that factors in Isezaki played an important role in representing the clothiers' interests. The Isezaki brand was sufficiently strong

Table 10.4. Disposal of returned commodities in September 1917

(yen, %)

	Isesaki branch		Ashikaga branch	
	Amount	Proportion	Amount	Proportion
Selling to others	831	17.6	2,740	11.6
Return to a clothier	700	14.8	11,385	48.3
Inventory	1,836	38.8	9,439	40.1
re-shipping	1,365	28.8	0	0.0
Total	4,732	100.0	23,564	100.0

Source: "Kakiage Archive".

for wholesalers to fear losing business connections with the Isezaki factors if they insisted on returning goods.

We can see further the ways in which factors and clothiers acted together to protect their common interests by looking at what happened with regard to the proposed entrance into the Isezaki market of factors with their base in Ashikaga. In the early 1920s, an Ashikaga factor by the name of Kanetani, who had retreated from the Isezaki market during the severe 1910 recession, tried to reopen his branch in Isezaki.[11] During this period, Isezaki was experiencing an expansion as a result of the various measures that the entrepreneurs had taken to improve quality and raise the reputation of their goods. The members of the Isezaki association regarded this attempt as that of a "free rider" who had withdrawn from the Isezaki market during a time of crisis, and wanted to re-enter the market now that the brand had been established and the risks diminished. Most entrepreneurs, it can be supposed, were hostile toward this factor. At the time, the association had a factors' division, a clothiers' division and other divisions. The factors' and clothiers' divisions passed a joint resolution against Kanetani's re-entry. Additionally, one of the clothiers' groups resolved not to sell its products to his firm. In most cases we can assume that clothiers would have welcomed the entrance of new brokerage firms, since this would have increased the channels for sales and strengthened clothiers' bargaining power toward factors. The fact that the clothiers were not willing to welcome the re-entry of the Kanetani firm is one indication of the strength of the relationship between the brokerage firms and the clothiers and the fact that the clothiers saw their relationship with factors as more than simply short-term trading partners.

After the end of the First World War, a severe recession hit the textile market. Many wholesalers went bankrupt, and factors suffered huge losses due to soured drafts. In addition, the severest earthquake in modern

Japanese history hit Tokyo and its vicinity in 1923, and a large number of houses and buildings were destroyed. Many textile wholesalers in Tokyo lost their inventories and stopped their businesses. Factors in Isezaki had already paid clothiers for commodities with drafts, and clothiers had asked financial facilities to discount them. Consequently, factors suffered huge losses.

At this time of crisis for the factors, clothiers in Isezaki agreed to raise commission fees to cover factors' losses in Isezaki as well as those in Kiryū and Ashikaga, and factors compromised to deposit part of the fees for two years as a fund to cover the drafts. After this, Isezaki entrepreneurs established the Mutual Aid Association, a fund for supporting factors which had head offices in Isezaki and which were joint stock companies. Members of the association were prohibited from dealing with outsiders, and under the agreement each clothier and factor had to deposit 0.1 percent of their total business turnover for ten years. The association used the deposit to fund the loan to factors who suffered financial losses due to soured loans.

Some of the brokerage firms also turned to a change in their organizational style, registering their firms as limited liability corporations, as a way to overcome the crisis. In the early 1920s, the factor Shimojyō, the founder of which we have already encountered as the head of the Isezaki trade association, was bailed out by reorganizing the private company as a joint stock company. Many clothiers in Isezaki bought Shimojyō stock. By 1927, four major factors finished transforming their companies to joint stock companies in an attempt to stabilize their firms and ensure a flow of capital. Many clothiers invested in stocks at this time, too.[12]

Financial concerns
For the medium- and small-scale clothiers of Isezaki, assuring a steady flow of capital to support production was a major concern. In this section we will examine the methods they used to solve their financial problems.

Let us begin with a consideration of the demand for capital in the weaving industry. Clothiers were involved in managing production all year round, preparing warps and other materials, putting out the work to weavers, and collecting and delivering it to arrangers who prepared the finished goods for sale. To cover their running expenses, entrepreneurs issued promissory notes as a means of payment. Large numbers of notes were issued to pay for transactions between clothiers and yarn merchants, between factors and clothiers, and between wholesalers and factors. Most sales to wholesalers were contracted in just a few months, due to the fact that wholesalers conventionally prepared seasonal clothes in a few months preceding sales. There was, in turn, a long interval between the input of running capital such as materials and wages, and the collection of capital as promissory notes after the sale of finished goods. Most clothiers did not have enough capital to wait for this interval of capital circulation and had to depend upon loans supplied by banks and factors.[13]

The fact that the factors at the Isezaki market dealt mostly with regional products meant that a huge amount of capital had to be supplied by the entrepreneurs themselves and by financial institutions. Additionally, the geographical drawback of Isezaki—that it was located far away from the major marketing cities, Tokyo, Kyoto and Osaka—strengthened dependence upon regional banks. Most regional banks were willing to pay—at a discounted rate—on promissory notes, thus supplying capital for production expenses to the clothiers. Local banks later collected cash from wholesalers far from Isezaki. It was reported that the notes issued by wholesalers could not be discounted without the endorsement of major factors. Since not only clothiers' but also wholesalers' financial conditions were precarious, there was always a possibility that loans would not be recoverable.

In Isezaki there were several local banks that played a major role in supplying funds to textile entrepreneurs. One of these was a new bank that had been established in 1900 by the efforts of a group of entrepreneurs. This bank was the Gunma Shogyo Ginkō (the Gunma Commercial Bank). One of the leaders was Shimojyō, the prominent leader of the textile industry. Although most of the paid-up capital was supplied by Isezaki people, the bank was under the control of one of the Yasuda zaibatsu family members. The Yasuda zaibatsu was the fourth largest zaibatsu in Japan at the time, coming after the Mitsui, Mitsubishi and Sumitomo family organizations, and had its headquarter in Tokyo. Yasuda sent a manager to the bank and the leader of the zaibatsu was appointed as an advisor with the right to veto decisions of the bank's board. We can assume that the founders of the bank understood the seasonal fluctuation of capital demand, and realized that huge amounts of money had to be put into the regional industry by borrowing from other financial institutions.

We can see something of how the bank operated from an account related to the Shimojyō firm.[14] During the recession after the end of the Russo–Japanese war, Shimojyō I ran a manufacturing division and a brokerage division. His brokerage division seems to have suffered a huge loss due to bad loans made to clothiers. The advisor of the bank asserted that a principle of banking should be carried out: the bank should let Shimojyō become delinquent and should not bail out his management. Local members of the board took a different attitude. The top priority should be put on the development of the regional economy, and bailing out Shimojyō was an important step in this effort for them. They resisted the bank's strict policy toward Shimojyō. Eventually, the bank allowed a long-term repayment plan and promised to continue financing his brokerage division on the condition of endorsement by a local member of the board,

Mr Tokue. Consequently, the bank adopted a lenient policy toward other clothiers.

The Mr Tokue who appears in the above account was one of the leaders of a local political movement in the first half of the Meiji era. The movement put emphasis on regional economic development. As we can see from this anecdote, political factors—as well as economic concerns—played a role in determining the fate of both individual entrepreneurs and the regional industry as a whole.

Another controversy was provoked among bank board members when Shimojyō died a few years later. His two divisions of clothier and factor were separated and two of his sons took responsibility for the two new firms. The bank asked Mr Tokue for a stronger commitment in endorsing promissory notes issued by the Shimojyō factor house. On this occasion too, local members, including a politician-turned businessman cooperated to ease the condition of endorsement.

Gunma Commercial Bank played an indispensable role as a financial institution along with another old local bank, the Isezaki Bank. The Isezaki Bank had been established in 1888, drawing on regional savings, and the board consisted of textile factors, merchants and a banker. The board members were all residents of Isezaki town or neighboring villages. The first head of the bank was a man of wealth in the region who had once won election as a member of the upper house of the national parliament. Later he started managing a brokerage house. As we can see from this account, there were close links between politics and economic development in the minds of many local citizens, and this was reflected in the easy movement and interaction of individuals in the political and business worlds.

In 1915, Gunma Commercial Bank was taken over by the Meiji Commercial Bank, which belonged to Yasuda zaibatsu, and the latter bank was once again merged with Yasuda Bank in 1922. The Isezaki headquarter of Gunma Commercial Bank thus became a branch of the Yasuda Bank. Although the management and organization changed, the local branch continued to play a major role in financing the Isezaki weaving industry.

Meanwhile, the Isezaki Bank, the other local bank that was important in financing the textile industry, saw a four-fold increase in its capital in 1920 and it merged with a small local bank in 1922. It also continued to supply necessary capital to entrepreneurs of the textile industry.

Table 10.5 illustrates the content of mortgages in the loans of the Isezaki branch of Meiji Commercial Bank. Many stock companies were set up in this period and clothiers, factors and yarn merchants invested in these companies. This led to an increase in the practice of using the stocks as collateral for loans. Textiles and materials had already been used as collateral in the Meiji era. As we can see from Table 10.5, this type of loan became the leading style of loans for the Isezaki branch of the bank.

Table 10.5. Content of mortgage

(yen, %)

	Stock			Commodity			Land	
	Amount	Share	Ratio	Amount	Share	Ratio	Share	Ratio
1918	108,554	41.7	69.5	96,055	36.9	85.2	13.1	33.0
1919	211,781	50.7	54.9	159.225	38.1	70.9	8.2	36.3
1920	503,100	47.4	82.7	369,587	34.8	80.5	3.3	26.9

Source: Fuji Bank Archive, *Isezaki Shiten Eigyō Hōkokusho* [The Management Report of Isezaki Branch].

Note: "Ratio" is the ratio of loan amount to mortgage value.

Fundamentals of social capital

In reflecting on the various accounts that relate to the development of the Isezaki weaving industry, we can see a common thread of human connections that linked individual actors. The network of human connections that made possible the development of the Isezaki industry was based on the heritage of social capital and political action in the Meiji era.

The Isezaki region had a tradition of citizens' social movements. After the Meiji Restoration, people in many parts of the country joined together to petition the Imperial government to establish a national parliament. From a nationwide perspective, the movement appeared to focus on political goals; however, in Isezaki those who joined the movement emphasized economic development as a condition for popular participation in politics. They combined various economic activities with the political campaign. This emphasis on economic development was one of the characteristics of the local movement.

Social bonds between individuals were strengthened through participation in movement activities. Among those who had participated in the people's rights movement, some became businessmen, one a bureaucrat of the local government and another a mayor of Isezaki. Informal bonds continued to link those who had joined together in the movement, even as they pursued very different careers as entrepreneurs, politicians and intellectuals. We see how these ties influenced later solidarity in the local community. For example, on one occasion, during a period when the national government was trying to block development of a socialist opposition, a prominent member of the national socialist party was invited by a local socialist to the trade association's office building to make a speech. In spite of the national political environment, the speaker was welcomed; this act exemplifies how very tolerant Isezaki citizens were to different opinions.[15]

This kind of cooperation between men who were following very different careers continued in the establishment of both the trade association and the Meiji Commercial Bank. Through cooperative activities entrepreneurs recognized the importance of a trade association, which acted in an aggressive manner to promote the interests of local industry. In other words, they knew the cost and benefit of cooperative activities and the merit of participation in the association. The spirit of cooperation that characterized the Isezaki industry was not repeated any where else in Japan's weaving districts. For example, leaders in the Nara weaving region, who tried to establish a strict inspection system, were forced to flee from a general meeting of a trade association, when they failed to gain support from their members and feared a violent attack.[16]

As we have seen above, clothiers disagreed over the introduction of new materials in the 1890s. Once that disagreement was resolved and a unified association created, clothiers worked in a cooperative manner down to the beginning of the First World War. Clothiers, rather than traders, played the leading roles in the association during this period. The patterns we see in the Isezaki trade association are different from those that have been commonly cited as a characteristic of trade associations of this period. Earlier scholarship has often noted the important role taken by members of the upper class in the development of regional economies (Tanimoto and Abe 1995). As we can see from the Isezaki case, participants came from a wide range of classes and occupations. The top leader of the political movement himself was from the lower class.[17]

Another important characteristic of the Isezaki industry was the fact that apprentices trained within the region came to play an important role in the development of the industry, and became an important part of the human network within the region. The prosperity of the industry induced many local people to become clothiers. Table 10.6 shows how newcomers became clothiers in each period. Because this survey was completed around 1942, some clothiers had already withdrawn from the industry. The earlier the period at which clothiers began their businesses, the greater the number of clothiers who pulled out of the business. The limitation notwithstanding, the data indicate that on average, more newcomers entered the industry during this pre-First World War period than at any other time. More than 60 percent of clothiers whose earlier careers were known were classified as apprentices. Thus we can see that many of the newcomers were supplied through the training system of the putting-out system.

The prosperity of the region and the social capital
Mutual trust and cooperation among entrepreneurs in the Isezaki weaving industry were two main factors that worked to block decline in the regional industry. If a regional economy or an industry were considered to be strong, they would continue to attract capital investment. However, if an industry began to decline, what elements could change the trajectory

Table 10.6. Types of newcomers

						(person)
Type	1911–14	1915–19	1920–25	1926–30	1931–35	Total
A founder	0	4	2	1	1	8
A successor	5	5	7	0	3	20
An apprentice	3	9	20	8	24	64
A weaver	0	0	1	1	0	2
A dyer	1	1	1	0	0	3
Unknown	7	12	16	3	9	47
Total	16	31	47	13	37	144
Average / year	4.0	6.2	7.8	2.6	7.4	

Source: *Isezaki Kigyōka Meikan* [The List of Isezaki's Clothiers] (Isezaki,1942).

Note: A founder was a clothier who started his business without a career in this business; a successor was a clothier who succeeded a relative when starting his business.

of decline? Taub's research into regional economies suggests that objective economic elements themselves could not change this trend and that active participation of residents was needed (Taub 1988).

Entrepreneurs cooperated to make the industry competitive in the market. The development of new products and the establishment of the Isezaki brand name were two examples of these activities. Moreover, the factors in the region tried to protect the interests of the clothiers, and the clothiers cooperated to help factors' companies, by investing in factors' stocks and by rejecting the re-entry factor.

The strong regional economy made the interest of factors and clothiers reciprocal. When the factors' management brought good results, it made it easier for the clothiers to use their stocks as collateral for loans, and this ensured a stable supply of capital for continued production.

3. Crisis in the Weaving Industry and the Weakening of Social Capital

As we have seen above, the increase in output in the first half of the 1920s was based on cooperative activities. While we have discussed these developments as "successes", it is also important to note that the "success" also harbored the seeds of decline. For example, during this period of prosperity, the problem of oversupply was not given due attention. This problem deepened during the recession of the late 1920s and the worldwide depression of 1930, bringing great difficulties to the regional economy. This section will examine the measures taken by the entrepreneurs in

Isezaki to cope with the situation, considering the deterioration of the financial condition of individual firms and the impact on the patterns of cooperation that had been developed in an earlier era.

3.1. *Deterioration of the market and the problem of oversupply*

The Japanese economy underwent serious economic crises beginning in the latter half of the 1920s. In 1927, as a result of a major financial crisis, many local banks were forced to merge. The economic crisis deepened when the Great Depression hit the Japanese economy in 1930, greatly reducing rural incomes.

In response to these economic crises, the consumption of textiles—particularly cotton textiles—decreased dramatically in the latter half of the 1920s Table 10.7. This decline in consumption suggests that the recessions hit the middle- and lower-classes, and one of the consequences was a decline in the demand for less expensive silk textiles. This category of goods had played a central role in the development of the Isezaki weaving industry, and so it, too, was hard hit by the economic crises.

While the demand for certain textile goods saw a dramatic decline, the beginning of the 1930s also witnessed an increase of consumption of both silk and rayon. Traditional style textiles could be produced at lower cost with the use of rayon, in place of natural silk fiber. If we consider rayon as a substitute for, and thus in the same category as silk, then the overall demand for silk and rayon textiles increased. These new trends compelled Isezaki's entrepreneurs to adjust to the changes in market demand.

If we look only at total output figures, we might think that the Isezaki weaving industry flourished during this period since it registered the highest volume ever during this crisis period. However, financially speaking, clothiers encountered serious difficulties. For example, local newspapers reported that an electric company suspended its supply of power to some factories that had failed to pay their electricity bills, a sign that producers were experiencing difficulties in raising capital to support their activities.

Table 10.7. Content of textile consumption in Japan

(million yen, %)

Year	Cotton	Silk	Ramie	Wool	Rayon	Total
1926	412(32)	507(40)	31(2)	311(24)	13(1)	1274
1930	274(26)	519(49)	18(2)	237(22)	9(1)	1058
1934	420(26)	772(48)	23(1)	333(21)	49(3)	1597

Source: Shinohara (Tokyo, 1969: 138–9).

Table 10.8. Amount of silk textile production in Sawa-gun (county)

Year	1926	1928	1930	1932	1934
Amount (1000 yen)	21,827	34,880	27,621	12,542	10,443
Volume (1000 tan)	2,784	4,786	5,393	3,151	2,378
Price/Tan (yen)	7.6	6.9	5.0	3.8	4.0

Source: *Gunma Ken Tōkeisho* [Statistics of Gunma Prefecture].

Note: The amount includes the non-traditional silk textiles.
The volume and the price are for traditional silk textiles.

At the beginning of the depression period, output increased as we can see from Table 10.8. This boost in output, however, only illustrates how desperate the clothiers were. Per unit prices had dropped sharply in the late 1920s. The number of newcomers starting firms as clothiers decreased sharply in this period, as shown in Table 10.6 on p. 261. On the other hand, the number of medium-size out-house factories increased. Overall production capacity rose in the area of the association.

One of the chief retail outlets, the department stores, continued to place large orders, but the contract conditions were poor. One of the department stores advertisements read: "The Lowest Price in These Ten Years", with the Isezaki textile brand used to attract customers. So while volume rose, profits were squeezed. One of the clothiers argued that there was a vicious cycle in place: clothiers without enough running capital desperately sold goods for low prices; department stores, in turn, demanded textiles at increasingly lower prices; and factors adopted an obedient attitude.

Because of the growing capacity of factories, clothiers and factors in the industry gave up their strong policy toward wholesalers. They were forced to produce low-grade products at low prices.

3.2. Worsening conditions for clothiers and factors

Records from a clothier who was still producing on hand-looms shows a dramatic decline in business profitability. Records from the Shimojyō archive also prove that power-loom clothiers were also experiencing difficulties. Both the price and cost of products dropped, narrowing the margin. In the case of Shimojyō, the value of the stocks he held also declined, worsening the state of his firm. As we saw earlier, during the heydays in the first half of 1920s, some firms had transformed themselves into joint-stock companies, and people within the region had supported the industry by investing in shares. But activities that had been positive in the period of expansion, brought different results during the depression. As stock prices nose-dived, local firms and individuals not only faced pressure from the market, but also the declining value of their capital held in the stocks of their own and other firms.

One of the ways clothiers tried to deal with the situation was to increase production, thus contributing to the problem of oversupply that had led to the decline in prices. If a clothier increased in-house production, he had to train workers or try to hire skilled workers at an attractive wage. Under these conditions, the difficulties of finding sufficient labor played an important role in blocking excessive expansion. However, when Isezaki firms placed orders with factories outside the region, these natural adjustment mechanisms were no longer effective. As a result, some clothiers sharply increased supply by increasing orders to out-lying factories. Fig. 10.4 shows that the two clothiers who were the top suppliers of 1929 and 1931 increased their production during this period. Neither of these clothiers had production facilities under their direct control. The activities of clothiers like these two firms played a central role in destroying the mutual interests of those in the Isezaki weaving industry. Moreover, the patterns of textiles of a famous clothier were pirated in this period. This suggests that the mechanisms that had been developed to limit supply had ceased to function. We can also see this as the beginning of the collapse of the mutual trust among clothiers that had supported the Isezaki weaving industry.

The factors played the same role in this period as in the previous periods. They gathered commodities contracted by wholesalers, shipped them and paid clothiers with drafts. The volume of cloth traded increased in the second half of the 1920s, but since the unit price declined, overall value of the output did not increase. Since the various fees charged during the marketing process were linked to unit price, the factor's income

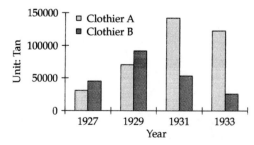

Fig. 10.4. Fluctuation of amounts.
Source: "Shimojyō Archive".

Table 10.9. Financial situation of Kakiage brokerage firm

								(1000 yen)
	1928	1929	1930	1931	1932	1933	1934	1935
Commission	156	142	107	91	78	61	97	102
Total Revenue	215	191	143	123	109	87	97	102
Cost	175	149	121	120	113	96	105	98
Profit/Loss	40	42	23	4	−4	−9	−8	4

Source: "Kakiage Archive".
Note: Figures are rounded from the original data and a disagreement among figures occurs.

Table 10.10. Stock prices of brokerage firm

						(Unit: yen)
	Paid up amount	1928	1930	1931	1932	1933
Kakiage	25	25	18	18	10	5
Shimojyō	50	50	25	25	10	5

Source: "Shimojyō Archive" and "Hatta Archive".
Note: The stock of Kakiage was issued in 1927 and Shimojyō, around 1920.

did not increase despite the increase in volume. In fact, the greater the volume of trade, the greater the increase in various costs. To make matters worse, factors lost business due to the split of the association. As the next table shows, the profit of Kakiage shrank by half when the Shōwa Depression started and the plight continued during this period (Table 10.9).

Other major factors suffered from the same decline as Kakiage. Table 10.10 shows that stock prices dropped dramatically. In the case of the factor Shimojyō, the price of stocks dropped to one-tenth of the paid-up amount. In turn, this led to further deterioration in the financial condition of clothiers who had invested in the stocks.[18]

3.3. Changes in the association and weakening of financial structures

The recession led to a deterioration in the textile market in the latter half of the 1920s and the first half of 1930s. Competition with other textile regions, which adopted rayon as a material and started to supply cheaper clothes, also worsened the situation of the Isezaki weaving industry. Entrepreneurs in Isezaki had learned a lesson from the failure of the silk-cotton blends around 1910 and the association hesitated to allow Isezaki clothiers to use rayon in spite of growing demand for a new policy.

There were also other signs of dissent. It was reported that some Isezaki clothiers were producing low-quality textiles, below the standards set by the association, and marketing them under the brand names of neighboring regions. Even though the low-quality commodities did not bear the Isezaki brand, they had the same characteristics, and these "copy-cat" commodities were damaging the Isezaki brand. Mutual trust among clothiers was at the brink of collapse. In the end, the association allowed the use of rayon in 1932. After the adoption of rayon, clothiers succeeded in inventing a new attractive product.

Another issue the trade association had to address was returned products. Whenever a recession hit the textile market, many products were returned by wholesalers who were having difficulty selling them. Although clothiers had previously tolerated this practice, the recession continued so long that the clothiers could not tolerate the factors' attitude this time. One local newspaper article reported that clothiers were being forced to accept commodities that had been sent out as much as a year earlier.

At the same time, factors demanded that the association should take responsibility for the inspection system, which was run by the association. If the system functioned well, there would be no defective products. In other words, factors gave up taking responsibility concerning returned products.

In 1931, the association set up a new organization to handle returned products. However, given the difficult market conditions, it was not easy to solve this problem. According to reports, wholesalers found it easier to return unsold products.

Clothiers gradually grew frustrated with the distribution system managed by factors. Their frustration culminated in 1932 in the formation of several new organizations. First, some of the influential clothiers who produced hand-loom products decided to establish their own independent trading organization. As for the general trading association that had been in operation for several decades, members decided to set up a new trade association that excluded factors, and the Mutual Aid Association established after the Great Kantō Earthquake, was dismantled. The leading factor, Shimojyō decided to set up his own power-loom factory. It seems that the spirit of cooperation among entrepreneurs that had for so long supported the development of the Isezaki weaving industry had disappeared.

As for the financial institutions that had sustained the industry, they also had to struggle during these troubled times. Of the two main banks involved in supporting the weaving trade, the Isezaki branch of Yasuda Bank had an easier time, gathering many deposits in the midst of the financial turmoil; it was able to maintain a relatively strict policy toward local entrepreneurs. On the other hand, total deposits at the Isezaki Bank decreased, and it was forced to hold collateral in land. A former bank clerk claims that the bank took a lenient attitude toward clients, and would only confiscate property that had been put up as collateral.

After the financial turmoil of the late 1920s, many regional banks lost confidence in clients and were forced to merge. When the Isezaki Bank was forced into a merger, the price of its stock was given a relatively low evaluation, and many shareholders in the region suffered losses.

3.4. *The weakening of social capital*

Mutual trust and cooperation had been a part of Isezaki's heritage. However, the expansion of production using subcontractors outside of Isezaki destroyed this tradition. A clothier could easily increase production using power-loom factories outside the area of the association. He didn't need to maintain good relations with neighboring subcontractors and weavers. Even a newcomer could make use of the regional brand without paying a special fee. As we have seen, the increased supply changed the market balance and as a consequence, the bargaining position of Isezaki entrepreneurs was weakened. As Japan entered a recession and then was struck by the worldwide depression, market conditions became tighter and a huge volume of unsold products was returned to the producers. In the late 1920s, the financial situation of the entrepreneurs worsened, notwithstanding the fact that the volume traded in the Isezaki market was recorded as the highest in the pre-Second World War period.

During this period, big retailers such as department stores and wholesalers increased their bargaining power. Isezaki products were featured in discount sales to attract consumers. While there was still some respect for high quality goods, the continuous round of bargain sales had a long-term negative effect on the Isezaki brand name. After several years of bargain sales, it became difficult for the Isezaki clothiers to maintain a high-level brand position and to attract consumers.

4. Conclusion

The social capital that has been the subject of this essay includes a number of items, such as mutual trust, social networks, morale and management skills. Although it did not exist in a visible form, it affected the behavior of both the upper and lower-class people in Isezaki.

Our consideration of the history of the Isezaki weaving industry has shown how social capital can strengthen over time. We traced the beginning of the process to the inheritance from the political movement for popular rights and a national assembly. At that time, the leaders of the movement put the top priority on the prosperity of the people. The participants were strongly motivated and their attitude spread in the region because they were influential and many of them became leaders in the business field or bureaucrats in the local political field.

Many Japanese trade associations worked successfully to improve the quality of their products. The Isezaki weaving industry was one such association, and it represents a case where—thanks to the archives of various entrepreneurs—we can see clearly how this process worked. Leaders play a crucial role in the creation and development of mechanisms for cooperative activities. One of the tasks of the leaders is to help their communities understand the benefits of cooperation, by clarifying the goals and suggesting the range of possible steps that might be taken. The leaders of the Isezaki weaving industry successfully led their colleagues to see the merit of establishing the Isezaki brand and targeted the lower end of the market as a way to develop their industry. Regional industrial leaders, such as Shimojyō and Morimura, contributed greatly to the development of the industry. These entrepreneurs recognized the advantages of cooperation and led their regions to new forms of organization.

We have traced the history of the Isezaki industry through several business cycles. One of the first challenges came during the long recession in the early twentieth century. At that time one of the factors withdrew from the Isezaki market, and even major entrepreneurs in the region, such as the factor Kakiage and clothier Shimojyō, faced financial difficulties. In response to that crisis, entrepreneurs cooperated to make Isezaki products competitive in the textile market. Although their products were said to be lower quality during the boom in the period of the First World War, the association held to its strategy. They proved to be correct, and after the 1920 recession, Isezaki could enjoy a good market situation.

Factors adopted appropriate strategies to represent the interest of the local industry, and clothiers responded to these strategies with support for the industry and financial assistance. As a result, the industry was able to maintain a strong performance: mutual cooperation facilitated common interests. To invest in the stock of factors was not only to aid factors financially but also to receive an opportunity to accumulate assets, which could be used as collateral in times of need.

Beginning in the late 1920s, the entrepreneurs of the Isezaki weaving industry began to experience severe difficulties. While they might have been able to maintain a strong position in the market if they had limited supply and worked to maintain the Isezaki brand name, they were not able to achieve this goal in large part as the result of changes that had occurred during the 1920s boom. Until 1920, the area of putting-out was limited to the registered region of the trade association and there were very few power-looms in the region. In an age of expansion, the association had generously welcomed newcomers who wanted to set up new clothier firms. In the traditional Isezaki system, there were no specific regulations to limit the supply of Isezaki cloth. Rather, there was a natural limit on output volume as a result of the limits of labor supply within the registered production region. Clothiers working in the system had to learn how to manage relations with weavers and other subcontractors. Even the owners of power-loom factories worked to keep their workers' morale high. Ironically it was the great success of the strategy in the first half of the 1920s that led to the decline of the region: year after year of rising demand led some producers to start sub-contracting to power-loom factories outside the Isezaki region. Once that happened, the natural controls on output ceased to work, and when recession and then depression hit in the late 1920s and early 1930s, individual merchants increased volume in an attempt to sustain profits—forcing down prices and initiating a cycle that would destroy the cooperative mechanisms in the industry.

The Isezaki region with its rich history of the exploitation of social capital, was unable to maintain this good economic situation in the latter half of the 1920s and the beginning of the 1930s. The association could not find effective policies to deal with the recession in the textile market. The department stores sold Isezaki products at discounted prices to attract consumers whose income had been drastically decreased by the recession. The association was unable to control supply, and the market was flooded with products which were produced not only in the Isezaki region but also in neighboring regions. The deterioration of the clothiers' financial situation destroyed loyalty, mutual trust and social capital to the extent that cooperatives split and patterns were pirated. The social capital waned.

Social capital has a supplementary function that affects the decision-making of entrepreneurs. Entrepreneurs mainly pursue economic objectives.[19] It was impossible for them to maximize the interests of their individual firms in the long run without the help of social capital.[20]

If an entrepreneur can define correctly the factors that affect his management and if he can get enough information at reasonable cost, we can suppose that he can rationally optimize his inputs and outputs. Cooperation among entrepreneurs can be classified as collective action. The most important condition for successful implementation of such collective action is to clearly define the parameters for collective action (Ostrom 1990: 90–2). However, the network of Isezaki residents showed that such a definition was difficult. The fate of a prominent leader of the industry depended upon the content of mutual trust or the loyalty to the community of people, which included not only entrepreneurs who joined associations and had common economic objectives but also politicians and businessmen of other industries.

The importance of mutual trust was illustrated in the case of the bailout plan of Shimojyō. He himself could not anticipate his failure and did not expect such help from various people. However, when a leader shared common values with other people, he could cope with problems with their support.

Social capital can have both positive and negative effects. It can make the entry cost low and increase the supply. Isezaki entrepreneurs failed to recognize the need to control supply. Their generous attitude to new clothiers destroyed their bargaining power in the market, and led in the end to the collapse of the system that they had worked to create.

Notes

1. Imagining community ties as an exogenous factor is theoretically consistent with the traditional viewpoint that individual motivation can be explained only from privately-oriented objectives. There is a theoretical issue at this point.
2. Many scholars have analysed the rural weaving industry in Japan. My approach to the Isezaki weaving industry utilizes a unique perspective emphasizing social capital and an empirical study based on rich primary sources. The main players of the industry, clothiers, factors and banks have left a huge volume of archives. The study tries to reproduce the dynamism of decision-making among entrepreneurs and argues for a kind of modified monism. The central motivation is maximization of profit, but it should be modified by common values among local people. The assertion is critically based upon the rich primary sources.
3. The analysis concerning the change of the market structures and production system is based not only on unpublished in-house management documents of clothiers and factors, but also on many articles of local newspapers. In those days each prefecture had its own local newspapers. *Jyōmō Shinbun* (Jyōmō Newspaper) was published in Gunma Prefecture. Although this newspaper was issued throughout the period examined in this paper, the content of the articles was not as rich and informative as that of the newspapers indicated below. *Tokyo Asahi Shinbun* (Tokyo Asahi Newspaper) is also one of national newspapers which reported local events. In addition, the town of Isezaki had its own local newspaper, *Isezaki Shinbun* (Isezaki Newspaper). Each paper had its unique opinion about the industry. Generally speaking, the Isezaki newspaper had an industrialist-oriented inclination and emphasized opportunistic perspectives, while the Tokyo Asahi newspaper had a reader-oriented inclination and analysed the various problems.
4. A local newspaper reported that 3/14 of the textiles were woven in Kiryū and Ashikaga and 7/14 were woven with power-looms around 1925.
5. The description of the policies of the association is based mainly on published materials, such as official reports on the industry and the chronicle of the association. The background and result of the policies are analysed with articles of three newspapers.
6. The Yaichirō Shimojyō family played an indispensable role in the industry. They have also left a huge volume of archives in a traditional Japanese dozō (earthen storehouse). The archives cover not only notes booked by Yaichirō, I, III and IV and their subordinates but also the diary kept by Yaichirō IV.

7. The central government held such exhibitions to encourage growth in the Japanese economy in those days.

8. Ikat textiles can be broken down into warp ikat, weft ikat and double ikat. Warp ikat and weft ikat are woven with dyed thread of warp and weft respectively. Double ikat are woven from yarn-dyed warp and weft thread. It is much more difficult to weave.

9. The relationships between factors and clothiers were strong in Isezaki. Only half of the ikat products were dealt with by dealers in another prominent ikat producing district of Nara.

10. One of major factors, Kakiage left a huge pile of documents, which are held in the collection of the Kiryū Shiritsu Toshokan [Kiryū Municipal Library]. They include semi-annual corporate reports and unpublished in-house documents concerning the overall financial situation as well as individual transactions. In addition, we can examine the minutes of the management meetings. The minutes reveal not only the controversies among employees but also the decision process for management policies.

11. Reports on Kanetani's legitimacy of rejoining the market and the clothiers' antagonism can be seen in many of the Isezaki Newspaper's articles, which put top priority on the interest of Isezaki residents. Sometimes such a policy of editors hinders supplying the accurate information to readers. In this case, their strong interest resulted in reporting the problem effectively.

12. The relation between clothiers and factors is examined through lists of stock holders of each incorporated clothier. With the lists, we also estimate how much each clothier invested.

13. We gathered the balance sheets of three local banks. Gunma Commercial Bank's archive includes semi-annual corporate reports from the establishment through the merger in the 1920s by a major bank run by the Yasuda zaibatsu. We also referred to some semi-annual reports intermittently in the case of Isezaki Bank and another defunct local bank. In addition, the Shimojyō archive includes lists of promissory notes, which tells us the destination, value and dates. By analyzing those documents, we can draw a curve showing the amount which changes in the process of time and depicts the unique loan patterns according to destination.

14. The description of the dispute is based on many primary sources. They include not only the semi-annual corporate reports of the bank, but also the minutes of the board meeting of the bank, and internal secret documents concerning soured loans. These documents were once archived at one section of the Fuji Bank, which has its origin in the Yasuda zaibatsu. With the materials we cannot not only analyse, the difference of the policies between the bank and locals, but also the financial risks of clothiers.

15. When a former bureaucrat was asked by residents to take the post of mayor, he accepted the proposal on the condition that he could appoint the socialist as a vice mayor. This anecdote also illustrates the tradition of social bonds in the region.

16. Morita and Okuno (1898), 70–1.

17. The top leader of the movement, Taizō Ishikawa, was born as a son of a blind storyteller. His mother ran a restaurant. His parents belonged to the lowest class in the feudalistic society.

18. Generally speaking, the stock prices of local companies are difficult to put a value on due to the absence of official stock markets. We, however, know the change of prices by analysing the asset notes of the Hatta archive. Mr Hatta was a handloom clothier and had an excellent perspective of capitalism. He valued his assets, including his stocks, and we get important information about asset prices in the local invisible market.

19. The decision-making process of entrepreneurs is explained from the perspective of " integrated monism" in Matsuzaki (1997).

20. People in Isezaki described the risky management of clothiers in the following expression: a clothier cannot continue operation for three generations. Many clothiers went bankrupt as the textile industry fluctuated. Long-term strategies did not guarantee good results. Consequently, such strategies were not always fruitful, and factors' loans to clothiers soured. The intention to maximize profits from a long-term perspective came from a subjective expectation rather than an objective estimation.

References

Hampden-Turner, C., and A.Trompenaars, *The Seven Cultures of Capitalism* (New York, 1993).

Koshō, Tadashi, "Ashikaga orimonogyō no tenkai to nōson kōzō" [The development of Ashikaga weaving industry and the structure of rural villages], *Tochiseidoshigaku* 86 (Tokyo, 1980), 1–17.

Matsuzaki, Hisami, "Subjective and objective elements in corporate decision-making", *Urawa Ronsō* 17 (Urawa, 1997).

——, *Chiiki Keizai no Keisei to Hatten no Genri* [The Priciples of the Formation and Development of the Regional Economy] (Tokyo, 2001).

Morita, Goichi and Masujirō Okuno, *Yamato Momen Dō Kumiai Enkakushi* [The History of Yamato Cotton Textile and the Association of this Industry] (Nara, 1898).

Ostrom, E., *Governing the Commons* (Cambridge, 1990).

Piore, M. J. and C. F. Sabel, *The Second Industrial Divide: Possibilities for Prosperity* (New York, 1984).

Putnam, R. D., *Making Democracy Work: Civic Traditions in Modern Italy* (Princeton, 1993).

Schumpeter, J. A., *The Theory of Economic Development*, (Opie, Redvers trans.) (New Brunswick, 1983).

Shinohara, Miyohei *Chōki keizai tōkei 6: Kojin shōhi shishutsu* [Estimates of Long Term Economic Statistics of Japan 6: Personal Consumption Expenditures] (Tokyo, 1969).

Tanimoto, Masayuki and Takeshi Abe "Kigyō bokkō to kindai keiei, zairai keiei" [Modern business, indigenous business in the age of the rise of the enterprises], in Miyamoto, Matao and Takeshi Abe (eds), *Nihon Keieishi 2: Keiei Kakushin to Kōgyōka* (Tokyo, 1995).

Taub, R. P., *Community Capitalism: The South Shore Bank's Strategy for Neighborhood Revitalization* (Boston, 1988).

11

Communal Action in the Development of Regional Industrial Policy: A Case Study of the Kawamata Silk Weaving Industry

FUTOSHI YAMAUCHI

1. Introduction

Local community actors and organizations played a major role in the development of the silk industry in Date-gun, Fukushima Prefecture during the Meiji period. This paper traces the development of local trade associations, the policies they promoted, and the struggles within those organizations when the interests of different kinds of producers produced clashes.

The paper begins with the founding of the first trade association in Date-gun. The trade association was first created as a mechanism for dealing with quality control problems that had appeared as the industry developed during the Meiji period. In Date-gun, as well as other areas, the implementation of quality control by local trade associations often met resistance. In many areas there were conflicts of interests with regard to market transactions (Tamura 1989, Uekawa 1984). There also were conflicts caused by the quality regulations imposed by the associations (Yasuoka 1991). Earlier studies have only touched on these issues.

In order to better understand the important roles local trade associations played in Japan's modern development, we need to explore the local politics that led to the formation of such trade associations and the activities they sponsored. This paper will consider such questions through an exploration of the different kinds of groups that participated in the trade association in one silk district in Fukushima Prefecture. Earlier studies have generally assumed that the chief actors who contributed to the formation of trade associations were prominent merchants and large-scale producers who had a vested interest in promoting a trade association. There is a question, however, as to whether such prominent individuals were the only promoters of trade associations. Further, it should also be clarified whether personal interest and economic power were the sole incentives for the development of trade associations. Research on regional industrial policy of Masana Maeda has shown that members of the rural elite also promoted regional industrial policy with the intent of achieving regional revitalization (Soda 1980: 138). This study will re-examine the question of who promoted regional trade associations through a careful examination of all of the actors in the trade association in the Kawamata silk district.

The time frame for our study begins with the period immediately after the Russo–Japanese war, a period when we can see a major structural shift in the silk industry. In the aftermath of the Russo–Japanese war, the silk industry in Date—which was primarily producing for the export market—was faced with increasing competition. In this situation, the quality control problems became a major issue. The increasing competition provided stimulus for organization. Earlier studies of the textile industry during this period have noted other initiatives for change designed to deal with the same problems: textile producers tried to implement a comprehensive product inspection system, to expand marketing activities, and to introduce new production technologies including the use of power looms (Kiyokawa 1995, Ōmori 1991). It has also been shown that the silk industry interacted closely with external organizations, most importantly prefectural and national governments, in its industrial promotion campaign (Tamura 1984, Koshō 1965). This paper will add to that mixture the very important role played by local community organizations in the reorganization of the silk industry. To investigate this role of the local community, it is necessary to take a close look at how members of the rural elite, including wealthy farmers and local notables, viewed and tackled the issue. It is also necessary to consider the relation between such individuals and those involved in the silk business.

This paper thus attempts to analyze local industrial policy in the textile industry by placing it within the broader framework of local community. In doing so, it focuses on two groups of actors, wealthy farmers and silk traders, tracing the transformational process before and after the Russo-Japanese war.[1]

There were, of course, many silk-weaving districts in Japan. The case study in this paper draws on data from the silk industry in Kawamata, a region in Date-gun, Fukusima Prefecture. The silk industry had flourished in the town of Kawamata for a long period of time. During the pre-modern period, Kawamata was famous for its production of a special type of silk fabric known as *Hiraginu* [*flat silk cloth*]. In the modern period, Kawamata was still deeply involved in silk production, producing silk fabrics for export markets.

2. The Trade Association and the Local Community

2.1. The silk industry in Kawamata after the Sino–Japanese war

By the end of the Sino–Japanese war, total sales of silk fabrics for export surpassed those of silk products for the domestic market, making Kawamata one of Japan's major centers for the production of silk fabrics for the export market.

Although total production in Kawamata was quite large, the scale of individual production units in Kawamata was quite small. Table 11.1 shows that export silk fabric producers in Kawamata were not confined to the town area, but were also spread across nearby rural areas. The scale of these rural weavers was quite small. Silk production in Kawamata, especially in the rural areas, developed as a household industry to supplement farming income. Although weaving developed as a sideline industry, this does not necessarily mean that rural producers relied only on family labor. As we can see from Table 11.2, there were producers with more than four looms in the town area, that is, producers who we would assume used hired labor in the production process. Even the largest producer in the town area, however, owned only sixteen looms. When compared to other centres producing silk fabrics for the export market, the scale of production in Kawamata is undeniably small.[2]

Table 11.1. Weavers in Kawamata and villages in Date-gun 1894

	Weaving housholds	Looms	%	Number of workers		Output % (Rolls)	
				Female	Male		
Kawamata town	230	550	15.3	800	200	129,893	37.9
Tomita village	400	500	13.9	550	50	56,000	16.3
Iizaka associational village	256	318	8.8	318		22,540	6.6
Fukuda village	128	194	5.4	322		10,444	3
Ojima village	135	227	6.3	302	2	9,735	2.8
Iino village	200	300	8.3	300		37,000	10.8
Ōkubo village	230	230	6.4	230		38,920	11.4
Aoki village	215	230	6.4	230		6,500	1.9
Tatsukoyama village	232	348	9.7	348		7,000	2
Kote village	224	269	7.5	259	1	5,437	1.6
Kotegawa village	84	108	3	120		4,860	1.4
Moniwa village	200	200	5.5	230		1,570	0.5
Oguni village	30	30	0.8	30		400	0.1
Other villages	31	97	2.7	136		12,528	3.7
Total	2,595	3,601	100.0	4,171	253	342,827	100.0

Source: Meiji 27-nen Date-gun Tōkeisho [Statistical Yearbook of Date County] (1894).

Table 11.2. Production scale and number of weavers in Kawamata, 1899

Number of weavers in a workshop	Number of weavers	%	Number of looms	%	Number of looms per workshop
Under 4	196	78.4	341	51.1	1.7
Under 9	45	18	222	33.3	4.9
9 and over 10	9	3.6	104	15.6	11.6
Total	250	100	667	100	2.7

Sources: Meiji 24 nen Nōshōkō Shorui Tsuzuri [Document Portfolio of Agriculture, Commerce and Industry] (Kawamata Town Council Documents)* (1891).

Silk fabrics produced in Kawamata were usually traded through the local periodic market, making it difficult for silk merchants to control the trade (Nōshōkō Shorui Tsuzuri [The document portfolio of agriculture, commerce and industry] (1891). The market days in Kawamata were the second (2nd, 12th, and 22nd) and the seventh (7th, 17th, and 27th) days of each month.[3] On a market day, silk fabrics were brought to the market either by silk producers or silk factors who had gone out to rural areas to buy up fabrics. The fabrics were sold to silk fabric factors and local wholesalers who had shops in the market. Transactions were carried out with the silk before refined and were settled mostly by cash payment. Aside from transactions at the periodic market, there were also a minor number of transactions outside the market framework. On days when markets were not being held, silk wholesalers purchased fabrics either from factors or directly from producers. The fabrics collected in the Kawamata markets were shipped to the Yokohama market.

Four of the seven local wholesalers that opened shops at the market in Kawamata were local residents. Because they played an important role as intermediaries between Kawamata and Yokohama, we might imagine that they played a leadership role in the development of the Kawamata silk industry. However, data from Kawamata suggests that they did not take on such a role. One indication of their relatively minor role is the fact that their income was considerably lower than that of silk merchants in other silk-producing regions. This will become clearer when we compare the figures to those of silk wholesalers in Fukui Prefecture, the largest production center of export silk fabric in Japan. The income level of silk wholesalers in Kawamata was markedly lower than that of major silk wholesalers in Fukui Prefecture. Moreover, judging from the Income Survey Report 1897 [Dai sanshu shotoku shirabe], even within Date-gun, the income level of silk wholesalers was relatively low. Silk wholesalers in Kawamata did not belong to the high-income stratum, and from this we can assume that they were not in a position to play a leading position in the development of the silk industry in their community.

In summary, silk merchants in Kawamata operated on a small scale, and earned relatively small incomes. They were not large property owners. As a consequence, they were in a weaker position than were wealthier silk merchants in other prefectures and production centres.

2.2. Organizing the trade association

In the spring of 1895, Fukushima Minpō [The local newspaper in Fukushima] reported that the silk industry in Fukushima Prefecture was again confronted with quality control problems (29 May 1895). At the time, there was a booming demand for export silk fabric goods. Especially popular were light silk fabrics. Silk producers thus competed with others in producing light silk fabrics. Production of light fabrics required special care to assure tensile strength and a balanced number of warp and weft yarns. In the rush to fill the market demand and better their competitors, producers simply reduced the number of threads in the fabrics, resulting in the production of low quality goods. A reputation for low quality goods would, over the long run, harm the competitive position of local producers. To deal with this problem, silk industrialists in Kawamata decided to establish a trade association, which would be given responsibility for implementing a quality inspection system. Eventually, the Kawamata Silk Industry Association was established in October 1896. Members of the association included silk weavers, merchants, bleachers and other participants in the silk industry. The association was organized in line with Fukushima Prefectural regulations for the establishment of trade associations in the textile industry.

A close examination of the membership of the association suggests that communal bonds were as important as economic functions in the founding of the association. Table 11.3 shows that most of the councillors of the association were farmers-cum-silk weavers in the rural areas. Although these individuals were undoubtedly weavers, they were also rich farmers and/or individuals involved in sericulture who paid land tax of more than ten yen each year. Their incomes were largely drawn from farming or sericulture, with the income from silk weaving occupying a minor portion of their total income. This group of councillors was very different from the silk merchants who obtained their incomes mostly from silk commerce and a variety of silk product sales. Moreover, a relatively large number of rural weavers were in the upper status levels within their villages and had been elected as chairman or a member of a town assembly. In short, these councillors were wealthy farmers engaged in agriculture, sericulture and the trade in silkworm eggs; they were, at the same time, from distinguished families in their villages. We might thus assume that they were in a position to exert social and economic power within the local community. Although they engaged in silk weaving, it

Table 11.3. Councillors and presidents of the Trade Association, 1896

Name	Towns and Villages	Occupation	Title	Land Tax (yen)	Income (yen), 1895	Income (yen), 1900
Satō, Densirō	Kote village	Agriculture and silk weaving	Local assembly member	60	378	317 (3.8%) (silk weaving 5%)
Watanabe, Kazo	Kote village	Agriculture	Local assembly member	18		
Satō, Kichibei	Kote village	Agriculture, sericulture and silk weaving	Local assembly member	14		
Chiba, Eizaburō	Kotegawa village	Agriculture	Local assembly member	35		
Terashima, Senzō	Kotegawa village	[Agriculture]				
Kanetani, Kihachi	Kotegawa village	[commerce]				
Satō, Chujirō	Oguni village	Agriculture	Local assembly member	20		300 (15.3%)
Endō, Zensuke	Ishido village	Agriculture	Local assembly member	48	322	550 (0%)
Sugano, Zenbei	Ojima village	Agriculture and silk weaving	Local assembly member	21		
Saitō, Sawauemon	Otsunaki village	Agriculture and sericulture	Local assembly member	13		
Sugano, Heizaburō	Tomita village		Local assembly member			
Miura, Tamesuke	Tomita village	Agriculture and silk weaving		17		
Abe, Tajiuemon	Fukuda village	[Agriculture]		23		
Sakuta, Torazaburō	Fukuda village	Agriculture and silk weaving [Agriculture]				306 (11.7%)
Sato, Isaburō	Fukuda village					
Sato, Genji	Fukuda village					
Sato, Kanesuke	Fukuda village	Agriculture, sericulture and silk weaving		22		313 (11.5%)
Sugano, Zenemon	Fukuda village		Local assembly chairman	120	480	2614 (0.9%) (silk weaving 8%)
Takahashi, Ryūzō	Iino village		Local assembly member	28		485 (8.2%)
Asō, Kichinojyō	Iino village					

Sugano, Motozō	Iino village	(commerce) Agriculture and reed manufacturing		28		891 (81.7%)
Ouchi, Katsunosuke	Iino village					374 (26.7%)
Asakura, Tetuzō	Tatsukoyama village		Local assembly Chairman	250	961	2,324 (0%)
Abe, Zenkichi	Tatsukoyama village	[Agriculture]	Local assembly member	26		
Suda, Jyōzaburō	Aoki village	Agriculture, sericulture and silk weaving	Local assembly Chairman		31	312 (9.0%)
Takano, Kisaku	Okubo village	Agriculture [commerce]				489 (4.9%)
Takano, Tōsaburō	Okubo village					
Satō, Raisuke	Iizaka village					
Ohashi, Isaburō	Kaketa village					
Kumasaka, Rokurobei	Hobara village	Commerce		100	448 (commerce 54%)	1,317 (57.6%)
Satō, Kiichi	Kawamata town					
Kōno, Geijirō	Kawamata town	[Silk weaving]			317 (silk weaving 20%)	864 (74.3%)
Sugano, Kozō	Kawamata town	Commerce		35		440 (11.8%)
Satō, Seiichirō	Kawamata town				341 (commerce 74%)	
Tanizaki, Matahachi	Kawamata town	[Commerce]				
Ouchi, Yasobei	Kawamata town	[Commerce]			458 (commerce 75%)	1,803 (17.0%)
Miura, Ujyūrō	Kawamata town	[Commerce]			376 (commerce 84%)	918 (91.8%)

Sources: Meiji 27-nen Date-gun Tokeisho [Statistical Yearbook of Date County].
Fukushima-ken Shidatsu Ni-gun Meike-kagami (1895) [Who's who in the two Shidatsu counties of Fukushima].
Meiji 28-nen Dai Sanshu Shotokukin-daka Shitashirabe-sho (1895/1900) [The Income Survey Report 1895/1900] (Nakagis' Archives).
Meiji 33-nen Dai Sanshu Shotoku Shirabe (1894) [The Survey Report of Third kind of Income 1894] (Kameoka Masamotos' Archives).

Notes: Occupation, title and land tax data were drawn from "Who's Who". An entry of occupation in parentheses was drawn from a resumé submitted to the prefectural government in 1894 (Fukushima prefectural document no. 3361). At the time of the association's reorganization in 1900, association members were required to submit their resumés to the prefectural government. A figure of 1895 income in parentheses indicates the percentage of silk weaving/commerce income to total annual income. The figure for 1900 income in parentheses indicates the percentage of miscellaneous sales income to total annual income.

was not a major source of income for them. Their involvement in the silk industry was meant to set an example, as they worked to introduce new industry and technology, as a sort of *noblesse oblige*. Therefore, I have assumed that rapid accumulation of capital was not their main motivation for silk weaving.

The president of the association, Zen'emon Sugano, reflects the distinctive characteristics of the councillor elected from the rural area. His income, one of the highest among the councillors, came mostly from agriculture and sericulture, not from silk weaving. Sugano was the chairman of a local assembly in Fukuda village at the time, was also a member of the prefectural office, and was later to be elected as a member of the House of Representatives. It would seem that his willingness to serve as the president of the association, therefore, was not for the purpose of pursuing personal profit out of the position, but was rather the result of his political and social activities as a member of a distinguished family in the local community.

The Kawamata Silk Industry Association, which started out with councillors drawn from wealthy farmers and local notables, was soon to confront a problem that would shake the very foundation of the association: a protest by weavers and merchants against the inspection system (Fukushima Minpō, 1 Jun., 1897). Silk weavers believed that the inspection system was not doing an effective job, arguing that it took a great deal of time, yet the results were neither understandable nor accurate. They further claimed that the mechanical, automatic inspection procedure undervalued the efforts of skilled female workers who produced high-quality goods. As a result, they proclaimed, the inspection blindly determined the selling price of silk products, failing to differentiate high quality products from low quality ones. For silk weavers, the inspection promoted by the Association was both incomprehensible and unfair. At the same time, the silk merchants disregarded the inspection results and traded goods in line with their own quality judgement. The standardized inspection, therefore, was accepted by neither weavers nor merchants; rather it was often ignored by both.

2.3. Market conflicts

The growing scepticism among silk weavers and merchants forced the Association to take measures to restore confidence in the inspection system, and to gain compliance. On 25 December 1896, the council passed a resolution supporting the Silk Fabrics Administration Regulation (Kinu orimono torishimari kisoku), aimed at tighter control of market activity. At the time, the silk trade in Kawamata was centered on two markets: Shin-Nakamachi market and the central market. These were periodic markets, with trading in silk fabrics taking place on the second (2nd, 12th, and 22nd) and seventh (7th, 17th and 27th) days of each cycle every month. Silk goods were also traded outside the periodic markets. In order to limit trade within the central market on the market days and to bring it under the tight control of the Association, the Regulations stipulated that the Shin-Nakamachi market was to be closed and that trade outside the marketplace was prohibited (Nōshōkō Shorui Tsuzuri, 1896). By limiting the trade to the central market, which had greater organizational infrastructure, the association attempted to tighten its administrative control over the silk trade and at the same time enforce the inspection system and various other regulatory procedures (Kenchō monjyo [Fukushima Prefectural document] No. 3360).

Kawamata residents who lived near the Shin-Nakamachi market strongly protested. Local residents believed that the attempt of the association to reinforce the inspection system and administrative control over the silk trade conflicted with agreed upon practices in the local community. In spite of this, the prefectural government decided to give priority to the association's decision (Nōshōkō Shorui Tsuzuri, 1897). The only recognition of the legitimacy of the residents' complaints came in some government-sponsored measures to deal with the negative economic impact caused by the closing of the market.

Following approval by the prefectural government, trade in silk fabrics was centralized at the central market on 17 May 1897 (Kenchō monjyo, No. 3360). Trade, soon fell into a state of utter confusion. The central marketplace was crowded with silk producers and merchants, and buying and selling was in turmoil.

Market confusion, caused by the rush on limited facilities at the central market, led silk wholesalers and dealers to make a move to mitigate the situation. Their solution was to trade on days outside the regular periodic market schedule: thus merchants began to purchase goods, at their shops or residences, on the first, sixth, third and eighth days of the ten-day cycles.

The association did not approve of this strategy, which it believed was intended to evade the regulations. Zen'emon Sugano, President of the association, submitted a proposal to the prefectural government on 30 May (Kenchō monjyo, No. 3360). In the letter, Sugano proposed revising the Silk Fabrics Administration Regulations so that the association would be empowered to penalize those who evaded the regulations.[4]

As we can see from these events, the initial conflict centering on the location of the market had been transformed. In the first stage the conflict was one between those who lived near the market and the councillors of the Association. At this stage there was a clear clash between the interests of those who lived in the vicinity of the market that was slated for closure and those of the Association. The residents were trying to maintain the economic prosperity of the district and also to preserve the customary practices within the community; the Association, with initiatives taken by members of the rural elite, was attempting to develop the silk industry by reinforcing quality control measures. In this new stage of the conflict, different sets of actors had begun to play central roles. On one side stood those actually involved in, or those who heavily depended upon, the silk industry and on the other, the councillors of the association.

In this case, the prefectural government eventually threw its support behind the official policy of the Association, declaring that 'the trade of goods within the community should be limited to the specified market days (Kenchō monjyo No. 3360). But these new municipal regulations caused a tremendous stir among silk weavers and merchants in Kawamata, and soon there was further strong protest against the regulations (Fukushima Minpō, Aug. 1897). The swiftness and magnitude of the protest reflects how badly the regulations hit the financial interests of the small manufacturers: before the regulations came into force, these manufacturers tried to secure a constant cash flow by trading outside the market.

Our consideration so far has revealed a number of distinctive features in the development of the silk industry in Kawamata. First, a majority of the councillors of the Association—wealthy farmers and local notables— headed by Zen'emon Sugano and supported by the prefectural government attempted to solve the quality control problem by implementing an inspection system and concentrating trade in only one market. Those deeply involved in the silk industry, especially the silk merchants, shared the wider goal of developing the silk industry in principle; however, in practice, the Association's implementation of the new regulations quickly became an obstacle to their daily business and they turned to open opposition. As a result, while the council, mainly comprised of wealthy farmers, tried to pursue a formulaic and rigid policy, those engaged in daily trade wanted an inspection procedure that did not hinder business. The difference between the two positions eventually surfaced as conflicts centering on the market.

2.4. *Reorganization of the association*

In April 1897, when the association was still struggling with the problems described above, Jyūyō Yushutsu-hin Dōgyō Kumiai Hō (the Trade Association Act for Strategic Export Commodities) was promulgated by the Meiji government. Associations like that in the Kawamata silk industry were covered by the new Act, and it was necessary for the association to be reorganized to meet the new national regulations. Reorganization, at a time when the Association was already under considerable stress because of the earlier conflict, was not an easy task. One of the largest stumbling blocks was the fact that the new law required that four-fifth's of the members of any association approve its reorganization.

In February 1898, Zen'emon Sugano, who thought it impossible to obtain consensus within the Association, asked the chairman of Date assembly to order the establishment of a trade association based on the Act (Kenchō monjyo, No. 3360). The chairman, in turn, petitioned the prefectural governor, asking him to issue the order. Finally, the prefectural government asked the Ministry of Agriculture to issue an order compelling the participants in the local industry to establish a Kawamata silk trade association. The response from the Ministry of Agriculture, however, stated that the compulsory establishment of the trade association should be considered only as a last resort, and that further discussions should be held among the relevant parties in Kawamata.

The moves by the chairman of the Date assembly and by the president of the Association suggest that they wanted to retain a mixed trade association that integrated all parties to the industry, including silk weavers, merchants and others. Our investigation must now turn to the question as to why the Association's leaders felt they would not be able to achieve consensus. In Chairman Date's view, the main problem was the silk industrialists, especially silk merchants, who evaded prefectural regulations, and refused to agree to the proposal for the reorganization. He openly criticized them, arguing that their stubborn attitude would hinder the future development of the silk industry.

This harsh view of silk merchants reflected the views of Chairman Date who represented the association leaders. Silk merchants, on the other hand, quite naturally had a different view of the situation. They were not convinced by the logic of the majority of the Association, and did not accept the managerial policy of the association. The silk merchants believed that the Association's leaders had neglected the practical problems of the silk trade, and that they jumped too easily at the ideal solution, without due consideration for the views of the silk merchants. Silk merchants thus looked at the association leaders with suspicion. The silk merchants believed that the rural elite who made up the leadership of the Association threatened their business interests. As a result of these clashes, the silk merchants decided to establish a separate trade association comprised only of silk merchants.

The campaign for the new trade association, brought to a standstill by the protest of silk merchants, resumed again a few months later when the quality control problem re-emerged and threatened to destroy the reputation and market for silk fabrics from Kawamata (Fukushima Minpō, 14 Feb., 1899). The prime promoter for the revived campaign for a new trade association was Tetsuzō Asakura. Asakura was a wealthy farmer who was engaged in agriculture and sericulture; he was also a prominent landowner in Tatukoyama village. Moreover, just like Zen'emon Sugano, he had occupied a variety of governmental positions in the local community, and was at the time a member of the prefectural assembly. He was later elected as speaker of the local assembly and, finally, as a member of the House of Representatives (Asakurake monjyo [Asakuras' document]). He was thus not just a wealthy farmer, but also an aggressive political and social activist in the local community. The initial success of the new campaign, under Asakura's leadership, suggests the important role played by individuals who were in a position to exert political and social power within the community. Finally in November 1899, the inaugural assembly was held to establish the Kawamata Silk Industry Association, an association that was in compliance with the Trade Association Act for Strategic Export Goods (Kenchō monjyo, No. 3363).

This section has shown that the reorganization of the Trade Association was finally realized as a result of a combination of strong supervision by the prefectural government and aggressive promotion by a man like Tetsuzō Asakura, who had broad influence in the local community. These factors, supervision of the local government and communal influence exerted by the promoter, were necessary to overcome the opposition on the part of the silk merchants. However, we should not assume that the silk merchants were fully content with the reorganization scheme. Their true feelings of discontent are amply illustrated in the turmoil at the inaugural assembly: silk merchants such as Matahachi Tanizaki submitted a proposal to revise the articles of the association (Kenchō monjyo, No. 3363). When the assembly voted against the proposal, he walked out of the assembly. Also in the following year, those involved in the silk industry—silk merchants such as Matahachi Tanizaki and silk weavers in Kawamata town—filed a petition with the Ministry of Agriculture and Commerce, stating that the new industrial cooperative was established by force by promoters not deeply involved in the silk business.

The conflicts triggered by the reorganization campaign cannot be fully understood if we only look at a framework that stresses opposition between producers and merchants. It should rather be perceived as a conflict between the industrialists (those who were heavily dependent on the silk industry) and the wealthy farmers (those promoters for the trade association who were not deeply committed to the silk industry as their main source of income).

3. Regional Industrial Policy after the Russo–Japanese War

3.1. Structural shifts in silk production

The export silk fabric industry in Kawamata went through a structural transformation after the Russo–Japanese war. As we can see from Fig. 11.1 which shows the volume of production, the total production figures bottomed out during the period of the post-war recession, then steadily recovered, and finally increased thereafter. Sales figures tell quite a

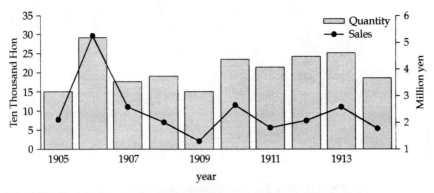

Fig. 11.1. Export silk production in Date-gun (quantity and sales).
Source: Fukushima-ken Tōkeisho [Statistical Yearbook of Fukushima Prefecture].

different story. If we look first at the sale of export silk fabric we will see that trade volume showed a slight recovery soon after the war, but then stagnated. The price of export silk fabric tended to fall after the Russo-Japanese war. At one point the situation was so bad that the price of export silk fabric was lower than that of silk thread, hindering both silk weavers and merchants from making any profit on the trade in export silk fabric. The silk industry in Kawamata, one of the local newspapers reported, was having a very hard time due to the post-war recession.

Fig. 11.2 further demonstrates the two opposing trends: on the one hand the volume of production in the town area of Kawamata consistently increased; on the other hand, the figures for other areas, such as Date-gun, consistently decreased. The production base for export silk fabric in Date-gun shifted from rural areas to the town of Kawamata and its immediate vicinity. This structural shift of the silk industry in Kawamata may be attributed to the introduction of power-loom weaving in the area of the town. The number of power looms, no more than 30 to 40 around 1907 in Kawamata town, rapidly increased to more than 1,000 in 1910, and reached 1,500 in 1913 (Senshokugakkou Shorui Tsuzuri [The document of the silk-weaving industry school]).

One of the distinctive features of machine weaving in Kawamata town, as illustrated by Table 11.4, is that the majority of power-loom weavers were small-scale producers, possessing fewer than twenty looms. The looms owned by the small-scale producers took up more than half of the total machines in Kawamata. Table 11.5 shows that most of these producers belonged to the middle income stratum, a range of income brackets from 16 to 22, according to the categorization of per household payment of prefectural tax (kenzei-kosūwari). It should further be noted that 25 percent of the power-loom owners belonged to the lower stratum of the categorization. There were 16 "factories"—workshops with more

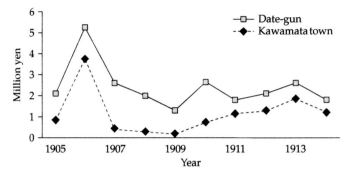

Fig. 11.2. Export silk in Date-gun and Kawamata town.

Sources: Date-gun Tōkeisho [Statistical Yearbook of Date County].
Sho-gakkō Kyōdo-shi (1907–11) [Local History of Primary Schools] (Kawamata Town 1907–11).
Gensei Chousa-bo (1912–14) [Census report] (Kawamata Town 1912–14).

Table 11.4. Distribution of power looms among the workshops in Kawamata town (1912)

Number of power looms in a workshop	Number of weavers	%	Number of power looms	%
Under 7	69	58.5	414	29.4
Under 13	27	22.9	324	23.0
Under 19	5	4.2	90	6.4
Under 25	9	7.6	216	15.3
Under 31	2	1.7	60	4.3
Under 37	4	3.4	144	10.2
Under 43	1	0.8	42	3.0
120	1	0.8	120	8.5
Total	118	100.0	1410	100.0

Sources: Taishō Gan-nen Kawamata-machi Denryoku Jyukyū Jinmei Shirabe [The Survey Report of Electricity Users in Kawamata] (October 1912). Quoted from Kawamata-cho-shi [History of Kawamata Town] Vol. 3, 339.

than 10 workmen—in Kawamata. Of these, 13 were small "factories" with fewer than 20 workmen. These small "factories" were not founded by local notables; rather, their proprietors belonged to the relatively lower income brackets from 13 to 19. Moreover, about half of these "factories" were founded by silk merchants who specialized in the trade in silk fabrics for export.

3.2. Dissolution of the Kawamata Trade Association

The structural shift in the Kawamata silk industry inevitably had a substantial impact on the Association. This impact can be seen most directly in the movement to split and dissolve the Association that occurred in

Table 11.5. Income brackets of export silk cloth weavers

	Households with power looms	%
Income bracket special 1–6	2	1.9
Income bracket 7–15	8	7.6
Income bracket 16–22	68	65.3
Income bracket 23–	26	25.0
Total	104	99.8

Sources: Income bracket category based on the prefectural tax amount per household.
Names drawn from the same source as in Table 11.4.
Income brackets drawn from Chō-kai Giji-roku [Minutes of Town Assembly Meetings] (1914).

Notes: A household in income bracket 1–15 belongs to a higher income class, i.e., a prefecture tax payer equivalent to or more than five average prefectural tax payers; a household in income bracket 22 is an average prefectural tax payer.
Tax payers in this figure are selected from the tax payers in the previous figure that were also indentified in the income prefectural income classification.
The total number of taxpayers in this figure and that of the previous figure do not match.

December 1914. The movement originated in a motion submitted at the special assembly of the Association on 3 December (Fukushima Minpō, 8 Dec., 1914). The motion proposed an increase in the association's certification fee. The motion gave rise to a fierce debate that split the Association into two opposing parties: the Association faction supported the proposal and the reformist faction flatly rejected it. The certification fee, the Association faction claimed, should be increased to increase the Association's revenue, which had been reduced by the recession resulting from the outbreak of the World War. The measure, the Association faction emphasized, would improve the management of the Association and allow the association to pay back its loans on time. In response to these claims, the reformist faction insisted that priority should be given to cost reduction, not to an increase of the certification fee. An easy solution such as this one, they claimed, would place an extra burden, on top of the protracted recession, on those involved in the silk industry, especially power-loom weavers.

Even though the tension between the two factions was at a high level, the association faction proceeded with its plan and passed the resolution for the increase. The decision led the reformist faction to petition the prefectural government, stating their desire to withdraw from the Association and seeking permission to form a new, separate trade association. In the petition the reformists claimed that the present Association, which included members with conflicting interests, was no longer functioning as a vehicle to unite all the relevant parties in the silk industry (Fukushima Minpō, 9 Dec., 1914). According to the reformist faction, the Association was controlled by councillors who were not directly involved in the silk industry and consequently it was run inefficiently. As a result, the petition concluded, the present Association did not serve to promote the silk industry in Kawamata.

Eventually, the association should be "voluntarily" dissolved. In the meantime, power-loom weavers attempted to organize a new and exclusive trade association as a locus for exchange of industrial information; its membership was limited to power-loom weavers who were involved in the production of silk goods for export (Nōshōkō Shorui Tsuzuri, 1914). Excluding the hand-loom weavers, who were usually only engaged in the silk industry as a sideline, they eventually formed the Fukushima Export Textile Industry Association, which incorporated all the power loom weavers within Fukushima Prefecture who were producing silk for export.

To understand what this conflict means, we must consider the membership of the two factions. Table 11.6 confirms that most of the members of the reformist faction were silk producers, especially machine-silk weavers, in Kawamata town and Iino village. Most of the members of the Association faction were hand-loom weavers and silk merchants in surrounding villages. The configuration of the factions indicates that the split of the Association emerged out of the conflict between silk producers in the town and silk producers plus wealthy farmers/villagers in the rural area. It may also be seen as a conflict between power-loom weavers in town and those living in the rural area.

We can identify two processes at work in the events that led up to dissolution of the Association. On the one hand, silk producers, mostly power-loom weavers in Kawamata town and Iino village, excluded hand weavers and small-scale producers in rural areas. At the same time, the conventional structure of the Association ruptured; creating the possibilities for a new prefecture-wide organization that included only power-loom weavers. In short, the post-war recession placed machine weavers in a dominant position in the production of silk for export. Power-loom weavers in the town consequently took over the association's leadership, or the leadership in the silk industry in general, from members of the rural elite. Put another way, power-loom weavers in town usurped the leadership from the rural elite. In other words, the overall structural change in the export silk fabric industry in Date district gave rise to a parallel transition in the leadership of the industry.

3.3. *Regional industrial policy after the Russo–Japanese war*

The previous section examined how the leadership role in the export silk fabric industry shifted from the rural elite to the rising silk producers and merchants. This did not mean, however, that the emergent class could operate without any support from the local community, or that it could survive without protection and supervision from local leaders. In fact, we shall see that they needed the support of the local community. This section

Table 11.6. Two opposing factions of the Trade Association in 1914

	Name	Towns and Villages	Occupation
	Katō, Jyōsuke	Kawamata town	Retail
	Oukōchi, Sukeshichi	Ōkubo village	Retail
	Mutō, Yasoji	Kohata village	Weaving
	Satō Shirō	Oguni village	Weaving
	Takahashi, Sōkichi	Tatsukoyamamura village	Weaving
Association	Ochiai, Tonosuke	Ojima village	Weaving
Faction	Shii, Suekichi	Harimichi village	Weaving
	Hasebe, Yomozō	Kote village	Weaving
	Koga, Sakujirō	Tomita village	Retail
	Saitō, Keizō	Tomita village	Weaving
	Shishido, Kesamatu	Fukuda village	Weaving
	Tashiro, Genjirō	Kotegawa village	Reed manufacture
	Itō, Mansirō	Aoki village	Retail
	Takahashi, Chūsuke	Aoki village	Retail
	Ishikawa, Masajyū	Kawamata town	Power Loom Weaving
	Ujiie, Takeo	Kawamata town	Power Loom Weaving
	Saitō, Seiichirō	Kawamata town	Power Loom Weaving
	Ōuchi, Toyozō	Kawamata town	Retail
	Ōsawa, Kurakichi	Kawamata town	Reed manufacturing
	Sugano, Torakichi	Kawamata town	Weaving
Reformist	Satō, Uichi	Kawamata town	Retail
Faction	Munakata, Kōnosuke	Kawamata town	Retail
	Tanizaki, Matahachi	Kawamata town	Retail
	Takahashi, Kisaku	Kawamata town	Retail
	Watanabe, Torakichi	Iino village	Power Loom Weaving
	Sugano, Kameji	Iino village	Weaving
	Sugano, Motozō	Iino village	Weaving and Retail
	Saito, Umekichi	Iino village	Retail

Sources: Fukushima Minpō, 8 December. 1915.
Taishō 3 nen Nōshōkō Shorui Tsuzuri [Portfolio of Agriculture, Commerce and Industry] (1915).

will investigate regional industrial policy with regard to the export silk fabric industry after the Russo–Japanese war.

One of the factors that strongly influenced the development of the silk industry in Date-gun was the development of the Kawamata Electric Company. Kawamata Electric Company was established in 1907 and started operations the following year. From the outset, one of the company's major functions was support of the silk industry; it was assumed that electric service would help to reduce the costs of production, and make it easier to standardize product quality (Kawamata Chō, 1979: 361).

When the Electric Company was first established, many local residents were reluctant to participate. However Yasobei Ōuchi who became President of the company set up the largest export silk fabric factory in Kawamata in 1909 on his own (Yamane 1926: 67). The Electric Company's board of directors included local notables such as Mohei Mutō, the largest landowner in Kawamata, and Tokubei Kimura, the biggest cloth merchant in town (Nōshōkō Shorui Tsuzuri [Document Portfolio of Agriculture, Commerce and Industry] 1913). As we have noted above, the introduction of electricity promoted the shift to power looms in Kawamata. In doing so, Kawamata Electric Company played an epoch-making role. In that case, I want to pay attention to the participation of the local leaders.

Another development, outside the framework of the association, which had a major impact on the development of the silk industry was the establishment of Kawamata Production Assistance Company (Kawamata Seisan-sha). The Company aimed at supporting capital-short silk producers by loaning more than 400 looms (Fukushima Minpō, 2 March, 1910). Kawamata Production Assistance Company was established in 1910 as an unlimited partnership with the prominent family of Yashichi Watanabe as a primary partner. It should be noted that other local notables, such as Tameichirō Ōuchi and Yasobei Ōuchi, were also involved in the establishment of the company. The family of Yashichi Watanabe also established other related companies including Tamariya Silk Manufacturing Company (Tamariya kinukase seizōjyo), a company that supplied silk materials to capital-short weavers, established in 1910; and the consignment sales department of Tamariya founded in 1913 that sold the weaving of silk fabric on commission (Hyōshō kankei shorui [The document portfolio of Commendation]).

Tamariya was not the only company that commissioned silk production. Kawamata Commissioning Company, initially established as Kawamata Commissioning and Trading in 1909 and reorganized as a larger entity in 1911, also provided a wide variety of services ranging from the commissioning service of sales and purchase of silk threads and fabrics, warehousing and delivery (Nihon Ginkō 1915). In addition, the company extended credit to small-scale silk producers. If we look at the original stockholders of the company (Kawamata Chō 1979: 361), we can see that it was established by local notables; about half of the shares were held by Mohei Mutō, Matajirō Ujiie, the third largest landowner-cum-sake brewer in Kawamata, and Yaheiji Watanabe, the fourth largest landowner-cum-sake brewer in Kawamata. Moreover these three local notables played a crucial role in the establishment of the company. Mohei Mutō served as President of the company, the others as directors.

Aside from the establishment of these companies, the establishment of Sangyō Kumiai (industrial cooperative) was of no less importance as a promotional policy for the silk industry. Among the five industrial

cooperatives in Kawamata, the oldest was the Kawamata Credit
Cooperative for Purchasing and Production, a limited liability organization. With a large number of cooperative members and a vast network
spreading through the whole spectrum of various classes in the town, the
cooperative provided loans to silk producers for the purchase of the
weaving machine.

A closer look at the cooperative's activities may suggest that those
activities functioned to promote silk production in the local community.
The cooperative's establishment was originally proposed in the town
assembly. The rationale for establishing the cooperative was restoration
of the silk industry's position as a key industry. Although a majority of
its 69 members were silk producers, more than half of its operational
funds came from farmers. The cooperative's activity, which was eventually limited to lending only, made a substantial profit every year from the
interest on loans and the interest on saving funds from other financial
institutions (Jigyō houkokusho [Project report] 1912). An examination of
the major investors in the cooperative, as shown in Table 11.7, reveals that
about half of the total investment was obtained from people in the upper
social strata, such as local notables. Most of those who borrowed from the
cooperative were those who had only a minimum investment, and most
of them belonged to the middle-income bracket. Most of the borrowers,
in other words, were small-scale silk producers. The cooperative thus
served as a vehicle to allocate capital resources within the local community: it was established jointly by a group of the rural elite and a group
of middle-class silk producers. The First Project Report 1909 says the most
of the capital backing came from those in the upper social strata, and most
of the capital was loaned to silk producers to purchase power looms for
weaving.

This analysis of what I have collectively termed "industrial policies"
looked at organizations other than the Cooperative, particularly focusing
on the role people in the upper social strata played in promoting the silk
industry in Kawamata. At that time the silk industry, which was seen as
the key industry in town, was on the verge of decline. Instead of establishing large factories on their own, local notables set up various companies and industrial cooperatives that supplied funds to silk producers.
Through these financing activities, they provided both protection and
support to small-scale silk producers for the purpose of streamlining, and
consequently reinvigorating, the silk industry in the community.

While local notables were willing to undertake activities to promote the
silk industry, they were only willing to get involved in activities that
involved limited risks; if their efforts failed, the losses would still be quite
small. The records of the companies they supported show that many of the
ventures did involve risk. While the substantial profit made by the electric
company was shared among the investors and put aside as a reserve fund,

Table 11.7. Major investors in the Kawamata Credit Cooperative of Production and Sales 1911

Investor	Investment Unit	Income Bracket	Title	Occupation
Watanabe, Yashichi	10	1	Member of prefectural assembly/Member of local assembly/Owner of Tamariya	Land owner/Sake-brewer/Moneylender
Ōuchi, Tameichirō	10	5	Member of Prefectural assembly	Weaving factory owner/Merchant/Land owner
Ujiie, Matajirō	10	1	Member of local assembly/Director, Kawamata Commissioning Company	Land owner/Sake-brewer/Moneylender
Watanabe, Yaheiji	10	1	Member of local assembly/Director, Kawamata Commissioning Company	Land owner/Sake-brewer/Moneylender
Kimura, Tokubei	10	4	Member of local assembly/Director, Kawamata Power Utility Company	Land owner/Merchant/Moneylender
Mutō, Toraji	10	8	Chief financial officer of local assembly	Land owner/Moneylender
Ōuchi, Senpachi	10	13	Member of local assembly	Weaving factory owner/Silk merchant
Takahashi, Kisaku	10	19	Member of local assembly/Director, Kawamata Commissioning Company/Director, Kawamata Power Utility Company	Weaving factory owner/Silk merchant
Mutō, Mohei	10	special 1	Member of local assembly/Director, Kawamata Commissioning Company/Director, Kawamata Power Utility Company	Land owner/Sake-brewer/Merchant
Satō, Genkichi	10	20	Town mayor	Land owner/Merchant

Sources: Taishō Gan-nen Daiyon-kai Jigyō Hōkokusho [Fourth Project Report] (Meiji 42-nen Sōkai Kankei Shorui [General Meeting Documents] (1909)). Town assembly meeting minutes 1911 [Meiji 44-nen chōkai gijiroku], the document portfolio of agriculture, commerce and industry 1891 [Meiji nijyuyo-nen Nōshōkō Shorui Tsuzuri].

Notes: Major investors with more than ten investment units. Income brackets according to the prefectural tax amount per household. Listed titles of local assembly are at 1911.

other companies such as Kawamata Production Assistance Company, Tamariya Silk Manufacturing Company and the commissioning department of Tamariya suffered huge losses and were finally dissolved. These losses occurred during the period when the silk industry declined. A similar pattern can be observed in the activities of industrial cooperatives. As we can see from Table 11.8, the percentage of secured loans provided by the cooperatives increased in 1909, and was still higher in 1910. However, in 1911, when the deepening recession drastically reduced the outstanding loan volume, unsecured loans exceeded the secured ones. And in 1912, an overwhelming majority of the outstanding loan total was in secured loans. One of the distinctive features of the cooperatives' loan strategy was that, in most cases, looms were offered as security for loans (Jigyō hōkokushō, 1911, 1912). Second, an increasing number of loans were given to the wealthier class: 60 percent—six out of eleven—of the loans made from 1911 to 1912 were given to those who had invested in more than five "shares" or those who belonged to the income brackets of fifteen or higher; more than 70 percent of the unsecured loans went to the wealthier class in town. Moreover, some of the unsecured loans were provided to those who were not identified as power-loom weavers. These facts seems to indicate that the cooperatives' loan strategy had shifted its target from loans to medium-scale silk producers, to loans given to a relatively wealthier class of silk producers and to those not directly involved in the silk industry.

This conclusion is also supported by a number of facts. First, the cooperative made a profit every year; second, few of the small-scale silk producers took part in the cooperatives; and third, that Jyūzō Hikichi, the only small-scale silk producer who borrowed from the cooperative, turned out to be the largest delinquent at the time of the dissolution of the cooperative (Jigyō hōkokushō, 1912). The industrial cooperatives, therefore, were not established to provide funds to the smallest-scale producers, but to support a wealthier class of silk producers. In other

Table 11.8. Outstanding loans of Kawamata Cooperative of Credit, Purchase and Sales

	New Loan				Outstanding			
	Unsecured		Secured		Unsecured		Secured	
Year	Amount (yen)	Project	Amount (yen)	Project	Amount (yen)	Project	Amount (yen)	Project
1909			2,000	7			2,000	7
1910	900	4	1,100	4	900	4	3,100	11
1911	700	3	300	1	1,600	7	3,400	12
1912	1,722	6	300	1	3,322	13	3,700	13

Sources: Jigyō Hōkoku [The Project Report] in Meiji 42-nen Nōshōkō Shorui Tsuzuri [The Document Portfolio of Agriculture, Commerce and Industry 1909].

words, the cooperatives provided funds to silk producers, but only under conditions where there was minimal risk. As a result, when the silk market delined, the funds available to small-scale silk producers were in very short supply.

This section has pointed out that a wealthier class in town was committed to supporting the silk industry only to a limited extent, and reluctant to get involved in activities that involved higher financial risks. In the meantime, power loom weavers needed, and actually demanded, further commitment from the wealthier class. The dependence of these silk producers on the wealthier class was manifested increasingly at the beginning of the Taishō period. The next section will examine this phenomenon.

3.4. Establishment of the Kawamata Credit, Purchase and Sales Cooperative

One of the biggest issues in Kawamata at the beginning of Taishō period, the establishment of the Kawamata Credit, Purchase and Sales Cooperative, intensified the involvement of the wealthy class with the silk industry.

Kawamata Credit, Purchase and Sales Cooperative was an a institution that was established to share liability for debts in the silk industry. In the summer of 1912, Kawamata obtained approval for a low-interest financing scheme. The scheme was to cover two of the silk-producing regions in Fukushima Prefecture, Kawamata and Odaka (Fukushima Minpō, 29 Sep., 1912). Two conditions were attached to distribution of the funds for Kawamata. First, the five existing industrial cooperatives in Kawamata were to be combined into a single entity. Second, a wealthier class of people in Kawamata were asked to take responsibility for the redemption of the loan. To obtain the government low-interest loan, it was necessary for Kawamata to set up an industry-wide cooperative incorporating the wealthier class of people who would be held responsible for the repayment of the funds. Getting the agreement of the wealthier individuals was not an easy task.

The first obstacle emerged in the resistance of the wealthier class to the requirement that they assume the liability. The conditions placed by the government, requiring them not only to bear the burden of the investment but also to guarantee the repayment of the loan, was intimidating. Silk producers, greatly frustrated by the passive attitude of the wealthier class, held a conference of silk producers and harshly criticized them (Fukushima Minpō, 18 Jan., 1913).

The loan procedures were the second obstacle. The council of the cooperative, mainly made up of the upper class in Kawamata, issued a notice stating that a silk producer needed to have two or more guarantors in

order to apply for a loan (Fukushima Minpō,16 July, 1913). This regulation soon met with strong protest. The conflict that arose around this issue
may be perceived as one caused by differences in the understanding of
the cooperative between councillors and silk producers. For silk producers, the cooperative was an institution incorporating both large- and
small-scale businesses, and was founded on the basis of mutual help. Its
primary purpose was to bail out those silk producers who suffered from
the recession, by providing cheaper funds supported by resources within
the local community. The requirement of loan guarantors (silk producers
emphasized), should be generated by the cooperative itself. The councillors, on the other hand, attempted to strengthen the managerial basis of
the cooperative. This was a natural response the requirement of the
Ministry of Finance that the councillors make silk producers repay the
loans given to them and secure the redemption of the government low-
interest loan.

Faced with the protracted struggle over this issue, silk producers
judged that the councillors of the cooperative were not likely to take any
drastic action, and that they themselves should start campaigning for the
cooperative's new financial operation (Fukushima Minpō, 30 July, 1913).
Pressed by the move of the silk producers, the cooperative finally settled
the issue of loan procedures. Although they were able to finally reach
agreement on this issue, a new dispute delayed its implementation.
Moreover, seven councillors including local notables such as Mohei Mutō,
Yaheiji Watanabe, Tokubei Kimura and Matajirō Ujiie, submitted their
resignations as councillors, creating a new stalemate (Fukushima Minpō,
29 Aug., 1913).

The course of the events may suggest that internal conflicts were caused
by the conflict between two factions of the councillors. Those who still
held the position of councillor, lead by Yashichi Watanabe, insisted on
sticking to the original loan procedures, following the agreement with the
prefectural government. Another group of councillors, represented by
Mohei Mutō, attempted to extend the original loan requirement that
requested the cooperative members to secure the loan.

Finally the resignations were withdrawn, in November 1913, the
Kawamata Credit Cooperative held an inauguration ceremony and began
operations. But the cooperative's operations were extremely vulnerable.
The situation caused an internal conflict to surface again, triggered by a
dispute concerning the revision of the articles of cooperative.

The articles of the cooperative originally stipulated that the cooperative
was responsible for consignment sale, not the purchase, of silk products.
But in reality, the cooperative purchased the products and took responsibility for sale. While those councillors and silk producers who supported
the revision tried to improve the efficiency of management among the silk
producers, those who opposed feared that the revision would have a

detrimental effect on the management of the cooperative, and insisted that the interests of the cooperative members other than silk producers and of those who received no benefit from the silk industry should also be represented (Kenchō Monjyo No. 3483).

The various struggles over the establishment and operation of the cooperative may illustrate the dynamism of power struggles between local notables, which included the wealthier class, and silk producers in Kawamata town. Local notables wanted, on one hand, to avoid financial risks in the promotional activities for the silk industry and, on the other, to encourage silk producers to stand on their own feet. Silk producers in turn tried to gain support from the local notables in order to strengthen and stabilize their firms.

4. Conclusion

This chapter has examined "industrial policies" in Kawamata town, Date gun, Fukushima Prefecture. The silk industry in Kawamata had a long history dating back to the pre-modern period. In earlier times small- and medium-scale merchants and producers had dominated the industry. The examination of the industry in this chapter has clarified a number of characteristics of the regional industrial policy.

First we have examined the conditions that supported the organization of the trade association. Pressed by problems of quality control that emerged after the Sino–Japanese war, founding of a trade association to deal with the problem became an urgent issue in Kawamata. The task was not easy since an intricate web of interests impeded the endeavour. The dominant faction that pushed through the scheme included members of the rural elite who used their economic, social and political power to establish and sustain the trade association. They tackled the quality control problem by implementing a compulsory inspection system, over the protests of small-scale producers and merchants. Their economic, social and political influence, and occasional harsh measures, helped give shape to the early phase of the trade association in Kawamata.

The second point concerns the relations between industrial transformation and the shift of power relations in Kawamata. The severe economic plunge after the Russo–Japanese war led to a transformation of the export silk fabric industry. The most conspicuous aspect of the transformation was the introduction of machine weaving by silk producers and merchants in the town area. These machine weavers gradually took control of the silk industry. As a result, they also came to play a more important role in determining local "industrial policy" with regard to the silk industry. One of the results, the dissolution of the trade association, reflects this change. In the process of the struggles over the association, the opposition that previously divided members of the rural elite and silk producers/merchants disappeared. The nature of the conflict was changed, with the new lines differentiating the interests of members of the rural elite who were allied with the small-scale silk producers in the rural areas from those of the power-loom operators in the town. The shift may indicate that, as export silk fabric production in rural areas stagnated, the influence of wealthy farmers and villagers had waned. As rural production declined, silk producers in the town gained a more influential position. Through the industrial transformation in Kawamata, silk producers in town took over control of the industry from members of the rural elite.

The third point deals with the process through which the role of the rural elite was transformed during and after the industrial transformation. Although silk producers in the town had come to play the leading role in the industry, they could not afford to promote "regional industrial policy" on their own. For example, silk producers in town did not have sufficient capital resources to fund the purchase of all of the power looms. They therefore had to rely on support from local notables. And indeed a number of initiatives were supported by such local notables. Their commitment to such initiatives, however, was constrained. They hesitated to become fully responsible for the management risk of the association and insisted on the managerial independence of silk producers. The reluctance of the notables to undertake support activities with high levels of economic risk led to fierce struggles between the local notables and the silk producers who needed the low-interest loans supplied by the association in order to stabilize the management of their individual firms.

This chapter revealed that the local community with its economic, social and political structures played a vital role in shaping regional industrial policy in Kawamata. The organization of trade associations during the Meiji period involved a variety of players: silk merchants, bleachers, part-time silk producers and full-time "factory" owners. Different kinds of silk industrialists, gathered together in response to the initiatives of members of the rural elite, promoted a local "industrial policy" that included measures to improve quality control through an inspection system. In the case of quality control measures, we can see that the trade association contributed to the development of the silk industry because of the active participation of members of the rural elite. Rural elites, immune from the conflict of interests in the silk industry, became actively involved in the for mulation and initiation of local policy.[5] Their role, however, was transformed after the Russo-Japanese war. In the post-war period, the initiative in the formation of regional industrial policy shifted to silk producers heavily involved in the export silk fabric business. Machine weavers in town gradually took control over the industry policy. To expand the policy, however, they still had to rely on economic, social and political resources within the local community, namely support from members of the rural elite. Silk producers in town thus criticized wealthy farmers and villagers, and tried to persuade them to support initiatives to improve management of the silk industry. While rural elites responded to such requests by contributing to various organizations, they also demanded that small-scale producers exercise greater independence. As silk producers gained increasing autonomy and control over the infrastructure shaping their industry, a fierce bargaining went on over the degree of commitment of the rural elite.

The development of local industrial policy for the export silk fabric industry during the Meiji period should not be seen as an autonomous movement, but as a movement heavily influenced by the economic transformation and deeply embedded in social dynamics within the local community.

Notes

1. E. Pratt already has paid attention to a role of rural elites (Gōnō) in Japan's proto industrialization. In terms of the following period of the industrial development, however, he has only pointed out the fall of the rural elites and ignored their political influences (E. Pratt 1999). This chapter observes their significant influences on the local industrial development plan at the end of nineteenth century and try to clarify the roles of elites as sponsors and risk-takers for local industrial development at the beginning of the twentieth century.
2. Kandatsu has shown that Nanjō-gun, Fukui Prefecture's biggest export silk fabric producing center in 1901, had an average of 9.9 looms per household; the largest scale of production was in the form of a "factory," having more than 32 workmen. Moreover, he has shown that the prefectural average for loom ownership was 5.1 per household, and there were five big "factories" that had more than 100 workmen in the prefecture (Kandatsu 1974 Table 79). The average production scale in Fukui Prefecture at that time was far larger than that in Kawamata town.
3. The market was opened in Aza Shin-Nakamachi market on the 2nd, 12th and 22nd day in each month, and in the Central market of Aza Teppō-machi on the 7th, 17th, and 27th day in each month.
4. Silk merchants shrewdly took advantage of the loophole in the association's regulations. While the regulations stipulated that the trade should be limited to the central market on the market days, it failed to specify the trade exercised outside the market days.
5. I would like to add a number of points regarding the nature of the trade association in its early years. It is not uncommon in a silk industrial region for dominant producers and merchants within a community to take the initiative

in establishing and orienting the trade association. There remains, however, the question of whether their business experience and capability alone account for this role. It should be pointed out that it may take political, social and economic influence to unite miscellaneous parities with conflicting interests for the establishment and management of the trade association. Without communal influence or power within the community, the trade association, just like any other trade association in Japan, would have been torn apart by the fierce internal conflicts. To establish a trade association and stabilize its operation, therefore, it may have been necessary to have someone who had a sort of mediating or coordinating capability within the community. Other regions' histories also tell us that many association leaders in the early years were local notables who had long been involved in the textile business. Their commitment to the industry over many generations gave them a foundation for credibility and social, economic and political influence within the community, which enabled them to play an organizing role. Just as rural elites in Kawamata played a vital role in establishing and administrating the trade association, it may have also been necessary in other regions to have key persons with various forms of communal influence or with coordinating capability within the local community.

References

Kandatsu, Haruki, *Meijiki Nōson Orimonogyō no Tenkai* [The Development of the Rural Weaving Industry in Meiji Japan] (Tokyo, 1974).

Kawamata Chō [Town], *Kawamata Chō-shi*, Vol. 3 [History of Kawamata Town] (Fukushima, 1979).

Kiyokawa, Yukihiko, *Nihon no Keizai-hatten to Gijyut-u-fukyū* [The Spread of Technology in Japan's Economic Development] (Tokyo, 1995).

Koshō, Tadashi, "Yushutsu habutae kōgyō ni okeru kindaika katei no tokushitu" [The characteristics of the modernizing process in the export silk fabric industry], *Kenkyū Ronshū* 6 (Tokyo, 1965), 150–73.

Nihon Ginkō Chōsa-kyoku [Investigation Section of the Bank of Japan], *Kawamata Habutae ni kansuru Chōsa* [Report on the Kawamata Habutae] (Tokyo, 1915, Reprinted in *Nihon Kinyū-shi Siryō Meiji-Taishō-hen* Vol. 23, Tokyo, 1960).

Ōmori, Kazuhiro, "Nichiro sengo kei-ei to shokusan-kōgyō" [The administration after the Russo-Japanese war and the industrial development policy], *Nihon Rekishi* 514 (Tokyo, 1991): 22–33.

Pratt, E., *Japan's Protoindustrial Elite* (Harvard, 1999).

Soda, Osamu, *Chihō Sangyō no Shisō to Undō* [The Philosophy and Movement of Local Industry] (Kyoto, 1980).

Tamura, Hitoshi, "Senzen-ki ni okeru Tokorozawa orimono-gyō no sanchi-keisei to kōzō-henka" [The formation of a textile producing center in Tokorozawa and its structural transformation during the pre-war period], in Tokorozawa-shi hensan-shitsu (eds), *Tokorozawa Orimono-sanchi no Keisei to Hatten* (Tokorozawa, 1989).

Tamura, Hitoshi, "Nō-son orimono kōgyō no tenkai to kangyō seisaku" [The development of the rural textile industry and the industrial development policy], *Bungaku Ronsō* 90 (Aichi, 1984), 1–28.

Uekawa, Yoshimi, "Nishijin orimono-gyō kumiai to orimono shijō mondai" [Nishijin Textile Association and Textile Market Issues], *Kyoto Gakuen Daigaku ron-shū* 13–1 (Kyoto, 1984), 47–81.

Yamane, Shōichi, *Kote Fūdo Jinbutsushi* [The Portrait of Great Men in Kote] (Fukushima, 1926).

Yasuoka, Shigeaki, "Shijō kakudai to dōgyō-kumiai no hinshitsu-kisei" [The market expansion and the quality regulation by the trade association], *Dōshisha Shōgaku* 42-4/5 (Kyoto, 1991), 166–83.

12

Capital Accumulation and the Local Economy: Brewers and Local Notables

MASAYUKI TANIMOTO

1. Introduction

Brewing occupies an important place in Japanese industrial history. Market-oriented production developed in the brewing industry from the early part of the Tokugawa era and, supported by domestic demand, continued on a broad scale after the Meiji Restoration of 1868. According to Japan's first national survey of production conducted in 1874, total output in the brewing industry was worth approximately 34,326,000 yen (Naimu-shō 1874). The main products were alcoholic beverages (sake), which accounted for 18,605,000 yen of the total, soy sauce (shōyu), which accounted for 6,338,000 yen, and soy paste (miso), which accounted for 6,137,000 yen. Production levels in the brewing industry were the highest in the non-agricultural sector and easily surpassed those of weaving (approximately 17,159,000 yen) and raw silk (approximately 6,165,000 yen). Moreover, among the brewing businesses of the late nineteenth century were some that have survived until today. Indeed, many of today's major brewing companies trace their origins as far back as the Tokugawa era. Brewing is almost the only sector in which such continuity of firms can be seen. Both its importance in industrial production in the second half of the nineteenth century and its continuity of firm suggest that brewing can be seen as one of Japan's so-called "traditional" industries.

Within the group of traditional industries, a high level of per-enterprise labor and capital accumulation distinguished brewing. Even in the latter part of the Tokugawa era, sake brewers and soy-sauce manufacturers who employed dozens of workers could be seen as influential producer prototypes. In this sense, the brewing industry differed significantly from the textile industry, which was organized primarily as a domestic system based on family labor. Many brewers had substantial amounts of accumulated capital. See, for example, Table 12.1, which lists the

Table 12.1. Occupational distribution of property owners with the assets of more than 500,000 yen

Occupation	1901		1911	
	(person)	(%)	(person)	(%)
Agriculture	73	15.0	122	11.5
Forestry	12	2.5	18	1.7
Fishery	0	0.0	8	0.8
Mining	15	3.1	23	2.2
Manufacturing	39	8.0	94	8.9
(Of which)				
Sake	**17**	**3.5**	**39**	**3.7**
Soy sauce	**3**	**0.6**	**21**	**2.0**
Silk reeling	3	0.6	5	0.5
Others	16	3.3	29	2.8
Commerce	213	43.8	435	41.3
Banking exective	31	6.4	63	6.0
Corporation executive	6	1.2	81	7.7
Landowner, house-owner	9	1.9	40	3.8
Salaried and professionals	1	0.2	10	0.9
Nobility	67	13.8	124	11.8
Unspecified	17	3.5	32	3.0
Others	3	0.6	4	0.4
Total	486	100.0	1054	100.0

Source: Shibuya *et al.* (1983).

wealthiest people in Japan by occupational category at the beginning of the twentieth century. Persons categorized as makers of sake, soy sauce or other brewed products together comprised 4 percent of the total in 1901 and almost 6 percent in 1911. Brewers far outnumbered persons in other manufacturing industries, including silk reeling, a growing export industry of the day. Moreover, they roughly equalled the number of directors in emerging modern enterprises such as cotton spinning. Next, Table 12.2 shows the distribution of tax payments by those engaged in commerce and industry in Niigata Prefecture around 1898. Compared with all persons engaged in commerce and industry, brewers were generally located among the higher strata of taxpayers; they also ranked high compared with persons occupied in the textile industry. By the time of this survey, more than 75 percent of brewers in Niigata Prefecture paid "income" tax, which was, in fact, primarily a tax on property (Hayashi, T. 1965, Ch. 5). This percentage was higher than the corresponding figure for all persons engaged in commerce and industry and much higher than the figure for textile manufacturers. During this period, the most influential brewers were included in the ranks of the richest people in Japan. At the same time, their strong economic resources placed them in an advantageous position in regional communities compared with manufacturers in other

Table 12.2. Distribution of traders by taxation (Niigata Prefecture 1898)

Taxation classes (Income tax and trade tax) (yen)	Number of traders				Ratio	
	Total		Brewers	Textiles	Brewers	Textiles
	A	(%)	B	C	B/A (%)	C/A (%)
500–	1	0.1				
250–300	2	0.1	1		**50.0**	
200–250	3	0.2	1		**33.3**	
150–200	7	0.4	1	1	**14.3**	14.3
100–150	27	1.5	4	6	**14.8**	22.2
90–100	6	0.3		3		**50.0**
80–90	15	0.8		6		**40.0**
70–80	15	0.8	3	8	**20.0**	53.3
60–70	23	1.3	6	7	**26.1**	30.4
50–60	47	2.6	4	17	**8.5**	36.2
40–50	49	2.7	8	15	**16.3**	30.6
30–40	118	6.6	14	36	**11.9**	30.5
20–30	226	12.6	35	66	**15.5**	29.2
10–20	625	34.7	36	208	5.8	**33.3**
−10	586	32.6	16	167	2.7	28.5
Unrecorded	50	2.8	1	20	2.0	**40.0**
Total	1,800	100.0	130	560	7.2	31.1
Number of traders with records of income tax	951		100	277		
Percentage of traders with records of income tax	52.8		76.9	49.5		

Source: Nihonzenkoku Shōkōjinmeiroku [National Directory of Traders] (1898).

Note:The bold numbers are bigger than those of total.

so-called traditional industries. In other words, brewers embodied the capital accumulation that took place in the late Tokugawa and Meiji eras.

This essay focuses on the holders of accumulated capital in the brewing industry to examine the characteristics of the capital accumulation process and the connection between accumulated capital and the start of industrialisation. The following section (section 2) provides an overview of the development of the brewing industry. It explains the emergence of a multi-layered structure in which different types of producers oriented themselves to different market sectors. This characteristic organization contributed to the overall stability of brewing businesses. Section 3 examines historical materials on particular brewery businesses [i.e., the Hamaguchi family brewery of Chōshi] in an attempt to clarify the characteristic features of producers' capital accumulation and investment activities. One of the main factual findings is that brewers dared to invest their capital locally—in areas where they maintained close relationships.

Capital accumulation in "traditional" industries was thus linked to the emergence of modern enterprises, and this linkage was supported by a regional community in which "traditional capitalists" acted as "local notables" as much as entrepreneurs. The role of regional community discussed in section 4 is one of the significant issues addressed in this volume.

In this essay, discussion of the brewing industry refers primarily to soy sauce production, since this is the area for which business records were available. Of course, from the point of view of consumption, soy sauce and sake are often regarded differently. Yet, because the production process for both includes fermentation, both are categorized as part of the brewing industry. Soy sauce and sake producers shared other characteristics, and the author believes that the discussion in this essay will help to clarify the common features of the various brewing businesses in Japan. [1]

2. The Development of the Brewing Industry—the Example of Soy Sauce

The late Tokugawa era saw the emergence of specialised brewers, such as sake makers in Nada (present-day Hyōgo Prefecture) and soy sauce producers in Noda and Chōshi (present-day Chiba Prefecture). Some of those brewers, notably the soy sauce producer Kikkoman of Noda, have grown to become major commercial brewers of the present day (Fruin 1983). At the same time, however, village records offer evidence of the widespread home production of soy paste and soy sauce as well as the custom of producing and drinking home-brewed, unrefined sake (*nigori zake*). Indeed, the existence of small-scale producers in rural areas has frequently been noted. In 1885, an administrative officer from the Ministry of Finance announced that 800,000 koku (1 koku is equivalent to 180 litres) of soy sauce was produced nationally (Meiji Hōseikeizaishi Kenkyūjo 1970: 1,044). However, he also added that this figure reflected only the volume of soy sauce produced for the market, in other words, for the 3–4 million city dwellers who did not produce their own soy sauce (Japan's total population at the time was approximately 35 million). As for sake, home brewing became subject to taxation in 1883 as part of the Meiji government's policy of tax increases on alcohol; in 1898, home-brewing itself was prohibited. Such regulation, however, suggested how deep-rooted the custom of home brewing was. Even taxation statistics of the 1890s, which are thought to reflect serious under-reporting, suggested that 1 million of a total national sake production of 4 million was home brewed (Saito and Tanimoto 1989). For farmers engaged in heavy labor, alcohol consumption offered a good way of taking in additional calories. Thus, they considered sake more as a necessity for accomplishing everyday labor than as a luxury (Shinohara 1969). Since the purchasing power of farmers was limited, they supplied themselves with sake by home brewing.

The above observations suggest that neither the producers nor the consumers of brewed products in the Tokugawa–Meiji transition period should be understood too simply. One important feature of the brewing industry was that suppliers formed a multi-layered structure, with each layer of producers attempting to secure a specific market. What follows is a brief discussion of the structure of production and consumption in the soy sauce industry.

The commercialization of soy sauce production began in the early Tokugawa period, with the appearance of soy sauce producers in cities such as Kyoto. From the turn of the eighteenth century, soy sauce from surrounding areas flowed into the Kyoto market. Tatsuno, in particular, had emerged as a major brewing region by the end of the Tokugawa era (Hasegawa 1993). Together with Yuasa, it ranked as one of western Japan's 1,000-koku producing regions. In eastern Japan, Edo, a city of about one million people in the eighteenth and nineteenth centuries, originally imported soy sauce from Osaka, but by the nineteenth century was relying primarily on the Kantō region suppliers (Hayashi, R. 1986). This shift was due to the development of producers in the Kantō region who aimed directly at the Edo market. Chōshi and Noda were two of most important soy sauce-supplying regions for Edo. In the opening years of the Meiji era, Noda had soy sauce producers at the 10,000 koku-level, while in Chōshi some brewers produced as much as 3,000 koku annually.

Thus, from the latter part of the eighteenth-century, the development of the soy sauce industry was characterized by the emergence of large-scale brewers who dealt in the urban markets. Still, in the early part of the Meiji era, such large-scale enterprises were a minority. According to the Seventh Imperial Japan Annual Statistics Book (Nihonteikoku Tōkei Nenkan), the average annual production volume of an individual soy sauce producer in 1887 was just over 100 koku. In a group of several Ibaragi Prefecture villages, six brewers averaged production of 158 koku in the 1860s. Three of the six had businesses dating back to the beginning of the nineteenth century and it can be supposed that their markets lay in the surrounding farming communities (Toride-shi Kyōiku-iinkai, 1987). It may be argued that, in addition to the large brewers aiming at urban markets, the early nineteenth century also saw the emergence of small; and medium-scale producers who sold mostly in their local markets. From the late Tokugawa to the beginning of the Meiji era, one can thus see the development of a two-layered structure, comprising large-scale producers for the urban market and small- and medium-scale producers for local markets.

How was this structure transformed during the Meiji era? Figure 12.1 shows that, from the mid-1880s to 1930s, commercial soy sauce production showed relatively stable growth. Within that context of overall growth, Fig. 12.2 compares the trends for different categories of commercial brewers from 1903 through 1924. Brewers who produced less than 50 koku of soy sauce per year decreased throughout the period. Brewer numbers in all other categories increased until 1906; subsequently, producers of 50 koku and more, and 100 koku and more, fell. After 1919, however, brewers in the category of 100 koku or more once again showed an increasing trend, eventually outnumbering those whose annual output was just 50 koku or more. Overall, the line that separated increase from decline in brewer numbers was an annual production level of 100 koku: brewers who produced less than 100 koku declined in numbers; the number of brewers who produced 100 koku or more increased. Moreover, in addition to increasing their numbers, brewers who produced 500 koku or more were also able to maintain their share of production. It can thus be concluded that the rise of large-scale breweries in the opening decades of the twentieth century did not drive out all smaller competitors. Although the smallest-scale operations declined in number, medium-scale as well as large-scale breweries increased in numbers into the mid-1920s.

The above analysis suggests that a major characteristic of the marketing of brewed products in the early twentieth century was the separation between urban and rural markets, each dependent on particular sets of

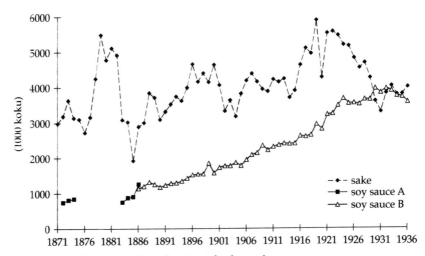

Fig. 12.1. Market oriented production of sake and soy sauce.

Source: Tanimoto (1996).

Original data: Ōkurashō [Ministry of Finance], Shuzeikyoku Nenpō [Annual Reports of the Tax Bureau], etc.

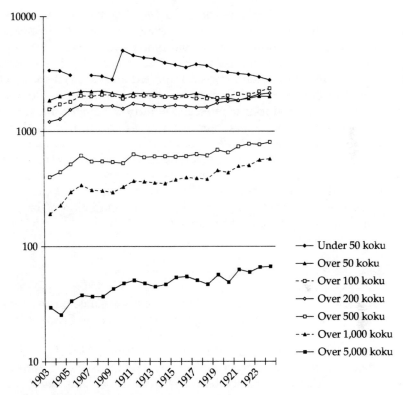

Fig. 12.2. Number of factories and workshops of brewery (Size-specific: volume of production per year).

Source: Same as Figure 1.

Note: Discontinuity between 1909 and 1910 in the production size of under 50 koku results from the change of survey criteria.

suppliers. The process of market formation may be summarized as follows. Markets for brewed products first emerged in cities, where self-sufficiency was rare and where relatively large-scale enterprises established themselves as the main suppliers. According to Tokyo Prefecture trade statistics for the latter half of 1884, 88 percent (approximately 570,000 of 650,000 barrels) of soy sauce brought into Tokyo were sold within the city rather than being re-shipped out.[2] It may be assumed that most of the sake and soy sauce brought into Edo or Tokyo were consumed in the city. In villages, by contrast, the local producer was an important supplier of brewed goods. By the late Tokugawa period, people were purchasing more goods. It was the small- and medium-scale brewers in villages and regional centres who stepped in as their suppliers, targeting the market outside cities. Out of these trends emerged a multi-layered structure of demand and supply.

Market and producer organization in the brewing industry was clearly different from that of cotton fabrics, for example. Marketing of cotton fabrics, a major sub-group of the textile industry, expanded into rural areas in the Tokugawa–Meiji transition period, creating a single market characterized by competition between imported and domestic products, and between different domestic manufacturers. In this process of competitive expansion, producers entered and withdrew from the market. The example of cotton fabrics offers a sharp contrast to the brewing industry, in which even large-scale businesses did not necessarily sell in a nation-wide market. Large-scale brewers had only limited access into rural markets, which depended, rather, on their own geographically specialized suppliers. This distinctive market structure was an important element in the entrepreneurial development and capital accumulation of brewers, and forms the focus of the next section.

3. The Case of Yamasa Shōyu[3]

Yamasa Shōyu (now Yamasa Shōyu Ltd.) was a soy-sauce business conducted by the family of Gihei Hamaguchi in what is now Chōshi City in Chiba Prefecture. "Yamasa" was the brand name of the soy sauce. The Hamaguchi family was originally from Hiro village in Kii Province, an area now part of Yuasa City in Wakayama Prefecture. Geographically there was considerable distance between Hiro village and Chōshi, but both were located close to busy fishing ports and they seem to have forged a close relationship through marine transportation. In fact, not a few Hiro village families besides that of Gihei Hamaguchi started soy-sauce businesses in Chōshi. Yuasa is included as one of the places in which soy sauce originated historically, and it is thought that the basis of Chōshi's soy-sauce industry lay in the combination of Yuasa production techniques with the wheat and soybean cultivated in Kantō plain where the soil was unsuitable for paddy fields.

Although Yamasa Shōyu was established in the late seventeenth century, it was only in the early nineteenth century that its annual production exceeded 1,000 koku. The spurt in production began in the late eighteenth century, when an increasing volume of Yamasa Shōyu reached the Edo market. By the beginning of nineteenth century, it was estimated that Edo sales accounted for over 70 percent of its production and the Edo (Tokyo) focus continued. According to the typology explained in the previous section, Yamasa Shōyu was a typical example of a large-scale brewer whose sales were directed at an urban market.

Let us consider the management of Yamasa Shōyu from the aspects of both distribution and production. For the primary ingredients of wheat and soybeans, Yamasa Shōyu relied on supplies from the dry-fields of

Shimo'osa and Hitachi provinces (later Chiba and Ibaragi Prefectures). Although employees sometimes bought the wheat and soybeans directly from producers, they usually made their purchases from market-town merchants who dealt with wheat and soybeans. It is worth noting that Yamasa Shōyu often made payments in advance. When the soy sauce was ready for sale, it was usually sent to the Kichiemon Hiroya family, relatives of the Hamaguchi family, and to a few other soy-sauce wholesalers in Edo.

Sales were handled through a kind of consignment transaction, with the wholesalers earning their income from commissions. However, the wholesalers regularly sent money to the brewer in advance. Twice a year, accounts were settled by deducting the advance payments as well as other expenses, including commissions, from the sales. Sales were calculated using an invoice price. In a genuine consignment transaction, the invoice price would have been identical with the actual sales price and any unsold soy sauce would have been returned to the manufacturer. But, in reality, unsold products were not returned and the settlement was concluded on the basis of an agreed-upon invoice price. Setting the invoice price thus became the biggest concern for both parties.

Often, the brewers were unhappy with a low invoice price and attempted to negotiate with the wholesalers. Such negotiations were organized through an association of soy-sauce brewers called the Chōshi Gumi. Similar associations also existed in Noda and in other areas of the Kantō region where soy-sauce breweries were concentrated. In the Bunsei period (1818–30), some brewers united to form the Kantō Hakkumi Soy Sauce Producers' Association and took actions such as withholding supplies. Wholesalers, for their part, formed the Kantō Soy Sauce Wholesalers' Association in the Bunka period (1804–18). It was in the opening decades of the nineteenth century that producer and wholesaler associations became exclusive, each barring non-members from participating in transactions and attempting to establish a monopolistic distribution system. The attempts on both sides to form an exclusive distribution system were a distinctive feature of the marketing process in the case of large-scale manufacturers who focused on cities. Among both Chōshi brewers and Edo wholesalers, those who were powerful in the early nineteenth century maintained or strengthened their positions as they entered the Meiji era. It is considered that, for both brewers and wholesalers, the establishment of monopolistic, relatively stable distribution systems underlay the continuity in their businesses.

Looking briefly at the production process, one finds that Yamasa Shōyu's basic labor force consisted of live-in male workers employed on the basis of yearly contracts that set out their wages and terms of employment. About 20 workers were employed on this type of contract in the early nineteenth century, and about 40 around 1890, when the company was producing 3,000 koku of soy sauce. This kind of employment structure contrasted with that of the textile industry, which depended on by-employment in peasant households. Overseeing the soy-sauce production process was the *toji* (head producer), together with another highly skilled worker known as the *kashira* (chief). Both *toji* and *kashira* wielded considerable power: they took charge of recruiting the yearly contracted employees as well as day laborers, and they established strict control over the workplace. Leaving the workplace under their management, brewery owners could expect a smooth production process.

4. Capital Accumulation and Investment Activities of Soy Sauce Producers

The previous section has shown that brewers occupied powerful positions in the distribution and production processes of the soy-sauce industry. They controlled the production process, relying especially on a full-time contract-base male labor force. In the distribution process, too, the brewers often supplied credit, and bore the risk in sales. This structure of distribution and production differed from that of the textile industry, which was formed by a combination of small-scale producers and multiple layers of distributors.

Differences in production and distribution were due primarily to the technical characteristics of brewing. Because the production process involved fermentation, it required land and buildings of a certain scale, as well as equipment such as the huge fermentation tanks. Brewing probably required the largest amount of fixed capital of all traditional industries. In the case of soy sauce, in particular, the fact that maturation took around one year meant that large amounts of floating capital were also required. Business owners in the brewing industry had to deal with structurally huge capital demands. It can be imagined that those owners capable of responding to such demands would exert a certain influence over the distribution process as well.

In other words, those entering the brewing business faced a financial barrier. However the barrier, once cleared, offered business owners a kind of stability. Probably one reason for the appearance of small- and medium-scale brewers that focused on local markets was that landlords and other property owners living in rural areas saw, and were attracted by, the relatively stable market conditions in the brewing industry. If brewers who sold to urban markets were also trying to expand their business in rural areas, the appearance of small- and medium-scale brewers in country areas would have meant the appearance of rival competitors. If the urban market were relatively stable, however, then there would be little necessity for large-scale brewers to initiate a competition over the rural soy-sauce market.

Such were the circumstances in which the structure of multi-layered (city and village) markets and suppliers was formed. It was a structure that produced wealthy brewers who ran a stable business as their family trade (or as part of it). As noted in the introduction, Japanese brewers around 1900 were often prominent property owners, both nationally and locally. But some questions remain: What kind of additional activities did brewers engage in? And how were those activities linked to the principal family trade of brewing? To answer those questions, let us consider the following individual cases of soy sauce brewers, using family archives.

As noted earlier, Yamasa Shōyu was the family business of Gihei Hamaguchi, who came originally to Chōshi from Hiro village in Ki'i Province. However, while continuing to run the soy sauce business in Chōshi, the main Hamaguchi family remained registered in Hiro village until the beginning of the twentieth century. The family head travelled between Hiro village and Chōshi or Edo, leaving routine management of the soy sauce production to a manager stationed in Chōshi. In its budget management, the Hamaguchi family kept an *oku* or "inner account" that dealt with total assets separately from household expenditures. Yamasa Shōyu received its capital investment from this *oku* account. Management of the soy-sauce operation was seen as only a part, though an important part, of the Hamaguchi family's asset operation. During the Tokugawa–Meiji transition period, due partly to the stagnant demand for soy sauce in Edo (Tokyo), Yamasa Shōyu production fluctuated around the 3,000 koku level. The relatively stable profits obtained from the soy sauce business were put first into the *oku* account and then used for other businesses such as house rental in Edo, land purchases in Ki'i Province and neighboring Izumi Province, and money lending in Edo and Chōshi. From the 1880s, the family also started to buy bonds and stocks. It can be said that, in the latter part of the nineteenth century, Hamaguchi family assets expanded into areas other than soy sauce production.

From the 1890s, however, the economic activities of the Hamaguchi family turned in a new direction, when the tenth Gihei Hamaguchi became head of the family and advocated "positive policies." In 1893, soon after succeeding as head, the tenth Gihei Hamaguchi acquired a soy-sauce factory located nearby, in Chōshi; he then embarked on a series of facility expansion projects, including construction of a new premise for production. By the turn of the century, Yamasa Shōyu was so large in scale that it was almost beyond comparison with other soy sauce producers in Chōshi. However, this discussion here will focus on the fact that Hamaguchi's "positive policies" were also clearly evident in areas outside soy sauce production. Table 12.3 shows that, despite the expansion of its Yamasa Shōyu production, the proportion of the soy-sauce business to total family assets was only around 50 percent in the late 1890s. In 1894 and 1895, the family's investment pattern was similar to what it had been

Table 12.3. Balance of Oku (Inner account) of the Hamaguchi family

(Yen)

[Assets]	1894	1895	1896	1897	1898	1899	1900	1901	1902
Lands and buildings	1,000	982	982	1,300	1,309	28,176	29,873	28,896	34,409
Soy-sauce factories	51,199	51,980	51,980	53,017	53,017	56,330	65,531	81,989	87,572
Soy-sauce business	88,103	108,960	125,646	134,836	152,561	153,412	161,538	176,546	175,121
Public bonds	33,437	39,487	40,350	15,600	5,500	5,990	5,990	5,990	5,990
Stocks	40,211	18,927	14,238	24,828	31,674	42,610	71,723	38,135	61,625
Loan	30,127	26,283	30,595	27,287	23,879	21,576	21,495	24,661	24,341
Kisaka-Hikifunegumi			33,276	41,441	46,192	27,772	32,784	44,494	44,494
Shiten (Hakodate)			50,000	50,000	59,744	59,971	55,151	63,444	59,744
Cash	870	2,168	1,895	165	939	1,490	455	48	274
Busō Bank								10,000	
Others	1,086	3,196	802	2,711	1,526	18,068	14,470	8,684	4,994
[Capital and Liabilities]									
Capital	241,945	249,759	297,991	324,599	349,202	380,839	413,858	430,763	435,182
Reserve			4,396	11,185	18,359	28,980	39,059	45,341	49,626
Deposit	1,724	2,224	2,724	3,732	4,449	5,576	6,093	6,783	6,256
Busō Bank									7,500
Others	2,364		44,653	11,669	4,331				
Total	246,033	251,983	349,764	351,185	376,341	415,395	459,010	482,887	498,564
Ratio of investment for Soy-sauce brewering (%)	56.6	63.9	50.8	53.5	54.6	50.5	49.5	53.5	52.7

Source: Archives of Yamasa Shōyu Corporation.

Note: Settlement days are the end of the year.

in the early Meiji era. But from 1897, money lending activities decreased gradually; family-owned public bonds decreased rapidly. By contrast, money was newly invested in such items listed in Table 12.3 as "Kisaka-Hikifunegumi" and "Shiten (Hakodate)", which together attracted more funds than lending and public bonds combined in 1896. It is thought that Kisaka-Hikifunegumi reflected an attempt to establish a shipping trade between Ki'i and Osaka. Between 1896 and 1901, a total of 40,000 yen was handed over as capital investment to Gen'emon Dō, an entrepreneur in Wakayama Prefecture (i.e. Ki'i Province) who had contacts with the Hamaguchi family. But the book balance of this investment remained unchanged from 1901, and in 1904 it was paid off as a loss. The word "Shiten (branch)" referred to Yamasa Shōyu's Hakodate branch, which was initially set up to handle soy sauce sales but later extended its activities to include dealing in marine products. Seiji Nakatani, a businessman from Wakayama Prefecture, managed the Hakodate branch.

The facts revealed above have shown that the Hamaguchi family started new businesses in the 1890s. Note that the family invested in local businesses such as Kisaka-Hikifunegumi, with which it had connections based on geographical contiguousness. A similar tendency was evident in the family's stock investments. Table 12.3 shows that the balance of Hamaguchi stock investments fell sharply in 1895. But it can be seen from Table 12.4 that the decline was due to the sale of shares in Nihon Yūsen, Japan's biggest marine transportation company, and Kanegafuchi Bōseki, a prominent mechanized cotton spinning company. Thus, the expansion of soy-sauce production and the new investment activities, both carried out in the 1890s, were financed by the sale of stocks and public bonds together with the sale of land in Izumi Province that was not listed in the family's accounts. From 1896, stock investments grew again. Characteristic of this new round of investment was the fact that stocks were acquired in businesses that were connected with Wakayama or Chiba Prefecture, the home bases of the Hamaguchi family. Out of the 70,000-yen stock investment balance in 1900, close to 50 percent was invested in local enterprises such as Arita Kigyō Bank (at the time Hiro village was part of Arita district), Chōshi Kisen (a steamship transportation firm), Chōshi Bank, and Busō Bank. It goes without question that subsequent sales of Nihon Railways shares and additional investment in Busō Bank and Kishū Railways brought a significant increase in the weight of Wakayama and Chiba companies in the Hamaguchi stockholdings. At one time the family was the largest shareholder of Arita Kigyō Bank, and around 20,000 yen was invested in Busō Bank every year. From 1901 the tenth Gihei Hamaguchi was president of Busō Bank. In such ways, the Hamaguchi family strengthened its connections with local business companies.

Table 12.4. Share investments in Oku (Inner account) of the Hamaguchi family.

(balance)	1894 (piece)	1896 (yen)	1897 (yen)	1900 (yen)
Nihon Railways	108	10,983	13,433	34,734
Nihon Yūsen (shipping)	300			
Kanegafuchi Bōseki (spinning)	250			
Fuji Bōseki		625	1,625	2,500
Shanghai Bōseki		1,000	1,500	
Nihon Kangyō Bank			500	500
Others				1,005
Subtotal		12,608 (88.6%)	17,058 (68.7%)	38,739 (54.2%)
(Corporations in Wakayama prefecture)				
Kishū Railways		80	180	
Arita Kigyō Bank			6,000	16,000
Wakayama Nōkō Bank				80
Subtotal		80 (0.1%)	6,180 (24.9%)	17,260 (24.1%)
(Corporations related to Chiba prefecture)				
Chōshi Kisen (shipping)		1,300	1,300	1,300
Chōshi Bank				2,630
Busō Bank				10,000
Others		250	290	1,600
Subtotal		1,550 (10.9%)	1,590 (6.4%)	15,530 (21.7%)
Total		14,238 (100.0%)	24,828 (100.0%)	71,529 (100.0%)

(increase or decrease)	1901 (yen)	1902 (yen)	1903 (yen)	1904 (yen)	1905 (yen)
Nihon Railways	− 18,743	+ 162		+ 420	+ 630
Kishū Railways		+ 1,250	+ 250		+ 2,075
Arita Kigyō Bank	− 16,000				
Chōshi Kisen	− 1,730				
Busō Bank	+ 2,357	+ 19,882	+ 23,038	+ 26,252	+ 23,985

Source: Same as previous table.

These Hamaguchi family commercial activities were supported by wealth accumulated from the Tokugawa era. As part of the "positive policies" of the 1890s, land, public bonds and shares of central corporations were sold off and the proceeds were directed to the new investments.

Further financial support came from the high rate of profit gained from soy-sauce production during this period. Boosted by its expanded scale and technical advances such as the mechanisation of compression, Yamasa Shōyu recorded an estimated return on equity (ROE) of more than 20 percent annually from the late 1890s.[4] During this time, profits from soy-sauce production accounted for more than 85 percent of Hamaguchi family income. With such a financial foundation, the Hamaguchi family began to commit itself to business activities outside of soy-sauce production, investing in local businesses that had some kind of community connection. Given that the family was selling public bonds and the shares in prominent corporations such as Nihon Yūsen and Nihon Railways (probably the top-rated shares of the day), one can be sure that the new investments were not simply a means of using idle funds. It is also important to note that the new investments, including the Wakayama businesses and Busō Bank, were not connected with soy sauce production. During this period, Yamasa Shōyu could fully support itself with its own equity capital. One can see from these examples that the accumulated wealth of the Hamaguchi family was linked with the broad development of business corporations in regional community.

Another example of active business involvement by brewers in the 1890s is offered by the house of Hachibei Sekiguchi.[5] From the early Tokugawa period the Sekiguchi family was based in Hatozaki village, Hitachi Province (Hatozaki is now part of Edosaki town in Ibaragi Prefecture). The family started making soy sauce in the middle of the Tokugawa era and became wealthy by selling it in the Edo market. By the beginning of the Meiji era, production had reached an annual level of 2,000 koku. Although it did not approach the Yamasa Shōyu level of 3,000–4,000 koku, the Sekiguchi family was one of the major soy-sauce producers of the time. In terms of its assets, moreover, the family was counted as one of Ibaragi Prefecture's wealthiest ten families in the opening years of Meiji. From the late 1880s to the 1890s, the family went on to develop active business commitments.

With regard to the basic family business, it can be noted that Sekiguchi's soy sauce was exported abroad and was often presented at exhibitions inside and outside Japan (including Japan's National Industrial Exposition and the Paris International Exposition). However, the present discussion will focus on the fact that the family started various new business activities, especially beer brewing. Through a foreign merchant's office in Yokohama the family imported hops and a German-style brewing machine. With instructions from O. Kellner, a teacher at the National Komaba Agricultural College, and H. Heckert, a technician at Kirin Beer (which was founded by a European merchant), the family was able to put its product on sale in 1888 as Jōbishi Beer. By 1889, it had exhibited the beer at the Paris exposition, receiving a bronze prize. In 1890, the brewery was enlarged and beer production seems to have reached an annual level of between 1,000 and 2,000 koku. In that year 89 large-scale sales outlets sold at least 100 boxes, each containing four-dozen bottles of Jōbishi Beer. The outlets were located in all of the prefectures in Kantō, the area surrounding Tokyo, as well as Osaka, Aichi, Niigata, Okayama, and Hokkaido. Jōbishi Beer was also exhibited at the Chicago international exposition in 1893. This was, however, the last exposition for Jōbishi, and the Sekiguchi family's beer business ended within a relatively short period. Still, around 1890 the business was not at all small.

In addition to beer brewing, Hachibei Sekiguchi was involved in various commercial activities. Although it is not possible to cover all of those activities because of the lack of account books to show the family's assets in general, we can list some of those that appear in fragmentary sources:

• In 1886 the family planned to develop Worcestershire sauce production with a soy-sauce base. By 1889 it had succeeded in producing sauce that rivalled the standards of imported counterparts. In addition to nationwide sales, it attempted exporting to Germany through F. Retz & Co, a foreign agency located in Yokohama, and it conducted sales in the United States. Sekiguchi's Worcestershire Sauce was exhibited at the Paris International Exposition.
• Brick manufacturing began in 1889. Samples were sent to the National Industrial Exposition in 1890.
• In 1888, the family was a joint investor in a new water transportation company, established to conduct a billing and shipping business on Kasumigaura Lake. Hachibei Sekiguchi became president of the company.

In addition, the Sekiguchi family ran a tea processing business, planned to start cattle breeding and some kind of stone mining business, and organized activities to spread sericulture. It was involved in at least two other companies either as a shareholder or as an investor. Although the specific content differed, it is clear that in the 1890s, the Sekiguchi family, like the Hamaguchi family, developed new business activities within its own geographic area (all of the Sekiguchi activities were organized in the area of Edosaki).

Another common characteristic of the new business activities was that they did not necessarily obtain good results. Both the Sekiguchi and Hamaguchi families, in 1896 and 1906 respectively, adopted a corporate restructuring for their soy-sauce businesses. For each, the move was not a response to positive business developments. Rather, it was a decision to hand over the family soy-sauce business to a joint stock or unlimited partnership company established by relatives or customers. One reason for this turn of events was family investment in other business activities. Both families had continued those other investments despite the lack of steady profits, reducing their assets, expanding their debts and making it more difficult to raise funds. Such consequences indicated that the new business activities of both families involved considerable risk. In other words, both the Hamaguchi and Sekiguchi families chose to invest in local businesses with which they had some connection even though that choice carried risk. It is revealed that their investment pattern was not exceptional, but common to many local property owners in the 1890s.[6]

The question remains: why did such a pattern exist in Japan at that time? In answering this question, one additional point that deserves attention is that the Sekiguchi family was involved not only in business but also in social and political activities. In fact, a number of documents written at the time described Hachibei Sekiguchi as a person who was making an immense contribution to the regional community.[7] As far as one can learn from other contemporary records, in 1881 Hachibei Sekiguchi became the representative of the village; he was also a member of the committee for educational affairs. In 1883, he donated over one tan (approximately 0.1 hectare) of land and 500 yen for the construction of the Hatozaki primary school. Moreover, Hachibei joined the Rikken Kaishintō (Constitutional Reform Party), one of the major parties of the People's Rights Movement, and financially supported a Kaishintō-affiliated magazine called *Jōsō Zasshi* (Jōsō Magazine) that was published in the Edosaki area. He himself wrote two short essays on social systems and customs in this magazine. Finally, Hachibei Sekiguchi was a candidate in the first House of Representative election of 1890 and was elected as the only representative from the sixth constituency of Ibaragi Prefecture.

The Hamaguchi family engaged in similar political and social activities as well. When a tsunami hit Hiro village in Ki'i Province in 1856, the seventh Gihei Hamaguchi organized construction work to build an embankment; he also supplied a total of 1,500 ryō over a period of three years. During this time, the soy sauce business in Chōshi was completely entrusted to a manager, who, it was said, had to restrain Gihei's demands for money. In addition, Gihei was involved in government reforms of the Ki'i domain, was appointed a financial magistrate (*kanjō bugyō*) in 1868, and in 1869 he was given a position of responsibility in domain education. He also joined the People's Rights Movement in the early years of the Meiji era and was installed as the first chairman of the Wakayama Prefectural Assembly in 1880.

It is quite normal for those involved in politics to be property owners. Likewise, it is hardly unusual for successful entrepreneurs to enter the political sphere. The case of the Hamaguchi family was one in which a family who had been active politically and socially since the late Tokugawa era turned to promoting business activities on the basis of local connections. In the case of the Sekiguchi family, both business and political activities took off at the same time. Both examples suggest that two apparently

different spheres of activities, business on the one hand and social or political activities on the other, were not considered strictly separate by
wealthy property holders in the early Meiji era. If this is true, then one
cannot discuss the reasons for their business activities simply in terms of
economic interest. Rather, it is necessary to find the common grounds that
extend across their activities in both spheres.

In this essay, I would like to suggest the concept of "regional community (chiiki shakai)" in explaining the motivation for activities that were
related both to the economic and to the political or social spheres. As
already mentioned, both the Hamaguchi and Sekiguchi families based
their economic activities in the regions where they maintained connections. Despite enormous risk, they conducted business activities during this
period because their relationship with regional community required that
they do so. That is how the relationship between the families' investments
and regional community may be understood. But a generalized notion of
"region" is not sufficient to explain a historical phenomenon that was
specific to the 1880s. Regional community must be understood as a
historical construction with specific content.

Recent research on the regional history of the late Tokugawa era shows
the formation of regional units that extended beyond the boundaries of
individual villages (Yabuta 1992, Kurushima 1991, Hirakawa 1996). It is
becoming clear that an autonomous public space, which extended beyond
villages, emerged in the first half of the nineteenth century. In other
words, regional communities, separate from the villages of the Tokugawa
system, were formed as a historical product of this period. Attention has
been focused, moreover, on the "local notables" who carried through the
process of forming the regional communities. It has been suggested, for
instance, that there were at least two types of property owners in rural
areas at the end of the Tokugawa era: those who pursued the economic
interests of their own businesses, and those who tried to help the poor
and maintain order in their villages. The latter type is considered to be the
archetype of the "local notables" whose presence became more apparent
in the Meiji period. Research monographs have attempted to re-examine
the activities of such "local notables" and their significance within
regional communities (Watanabe 1998).

Taking those research findings into account, one can interpret the
relationship between property owners' various activities and regional
community as follows (Tanimoto 1998). The appearance of regional community towards the end of the Tokugawa era provided the Hamaguchi
family, for example, with a place for their social activities in Ki'i Province
and also encouraged the social activities of the Sekiguchi family in
Edosaki region. The concentration of power in the Meiji central government made each "regional community" a more uniform entity that could
easily be compared with others. In this process, the particular interests of

each society became more apparent and competition between regions intensified. With the appearance of new business opportunities and economic fluctuations in the years following the Meiji Restoration, "regional economy" became an important factor in the competition between regional societies and in the formation of regional interests. As "regional economy" became an important element of regional community, involvement in the regional economy became a sphere in which reputations were enhanced beyond the simple pursuit of private economic interests. Such circumstances prompted a number of property owners to engage in activities that extended beyond short-term economic interests and led to the creation of a unique pattern of regional investment.

5. Conclusion

Let us now summarize the foregoing discussion. The characteristic feature of brewing as a so-called "traditional industry" was that individual entrepreneurs accumulated a relatively large amount of capital and labor. If the industrial revolution or modern economic growth required the investment of fixed assets and the accumulation of labor force, it could be said that brewing in the Tokugawa–Meiji transition was the industry that was most typically equipped to meet such conditions. Still, brewers did not necessarily go on to carry out an industrial revolution. The main reason was that the accumulation of capital and labor in brewing developed out of the distinctive relationship between market and its production.

On the one hand, during the Tokugawa–Meiji transition period, the demand for brewed products was still largely satisfied by home production. In this respect, brewing differed from the textile industry, in which the supply source had already begun to shift from home production to market purchases. On the other hand, a relatively large amount of fixed assets and working capital were needed to produce commodities by brewing. The first condition limited the scale of the market, whereas the second condition constituted a barrier that restricted entry among would-be producers. The multi-layered structure of the brewing industry, with large-sized brewers selling to urban markets and small- and medium-sized producers supplying areas outside the cities, resulted from a combination of the relatively limited market and the limited number of producers. In these circumstances, the relationship between market and producers was relatively stable. Moreover, unlike the textile industry and some other industries, brewing experienced only a slight impact from the external changes that followed the opening of ports at the end of the Tokugawa era. And, finally, continuity of business was evident. Compared thus with the textile industry, brewing at this time could be characterized as fairly static. Although brewing was showing an industrial form that was closest to the model required by an industrial revolution, or modern economic growth, it lacked the dynamism to be the driving force of the transition. This was a significant characteristic of brewing in the Tokugawa–Meiji transition period.

Still, in terms of investment activities, "static" management played an important role in promoting an industrial revolution or modern economic growth. The 1880s was the decade in which proper modern firms made their appearance in Japan. Many of the leading firms of the modern era were established during these years. However, what needs to be emphasised here is the broadening of the base in business formation. In 1896 there were more than 4,500 companies, 80 percent of which had capital of less than 100,000 yen. Moreover, 50 percent of the total capital belonged to companies with capital of 500,000 to 600,000 yen, or less. To take the example of cotton, companies at the 500,000–600,000 yen level were not Osaka Spinning or other main companies but medium-sized regional spinning companies such as Okayama Spinning or Kurashiki Spinning. The emergence of modern firms in Japan was not the result of attempts focused on a few large cities; it was a widespread phenomenon that could be seen around the country (Tanimoto and Abe 1995). Brewing can therefore be considered as a major source in the rise of modern firms in Japan.

As explained above, the brewing industry produced entrepreneurs who had a vast amount of accumulated capital. This accumulation was a necessary condition for their investment activities. However, starting a new business carries risk, especially in the case of a new industry or new form of business. Moreover, capital as a factor of production was the least restricted by geographical limitations, and the development of a market economy after the Meiji Restoration enhanced the possibility for the capital to flow out of the regions. Therefore, the mere presence of persons with accumulated capital in a specific region was not enough to produce the rise of modern businesses in this region. Some special reason was needed for an investor to take a high level of risk by investing in a new local business. Local notables in regional societies had such a reason. In order to obtain good reputations and then enhance them, local elites needed to respond to the demands of their communities. In the 1880s and 1890s, following the institutional changes brought about by the Meiji Restoration, investment in new businesses was one of those demands. In other words, an essential condition for establishing businesses in various regions was the presence of property owners who also had the characteristics of "local notables". Such property owners had an affinity with the brewing industry in the Tokugawa–Meiji transition period. When an owner of capital, based on a stable though not necessarily expanding industry, had a close link with the regional community, there appeared a property owner with the characteristics of a "local notable". Brewing was a major "traditional industry" that produced such property owners. As can be seen in the cases of the Hamaguchi and Sekiguchi families, their business activities were not necessarily successful. Therefore, one might need an analysis from a different viewpoint to identify the factors that have promoted the success of newly established firms. However, it was significant that, in the most difficult, early period of industrial transformation, there existed a widespread movement for setting up new businesses and firms, especially for the late take-off economy.[8] The investment activities of those economic groups or entrepreneurs rooted in the regional community were the hidden driving force in initiating Japan's industrial revolution or modern economic growth.

Notes

1. For common features and differences between sake and soy sauce production, see Tanimoto (1996a).
2. "Daiichi tōkei hōkoku" [The first statistic report], investigated by Tokyo Shōkōkai (The predecessor of the Tokyo Chamber of Commerce).
3. Historical facts regarding Yamasa Shōyu and the Hamaguchi family in this essay are taken from the following chapters of Hayashi Reiko (ed.) (1990): Ch. 2 (by Toshio Shinoda), Ch. 3 (by Shigehiko Ioku), Ch. 4 (by Yuriko Suzuki) and Ch. 6 (by Masayuki Tanimoto).
4. Full-scale mechanization and the introduction of motor power, however, took place only in the 1910s.
5. Historical facts concerning the Sekiguchi family are taken from Tanimoto (1996b). For the Sekiguchi family's beer business, see Tochigi (1992).
6. Tanimoto and Abe (1995) have analysed investment activities by regional property owners in the late-1880s to the 1890s, the period in which modern firms emerged. The authors conclude that this kind of investment activity constituted a typical pattern.
7. Obviously some exaggeration can be assumed from the purposes of publishing such documents.
8. Investment in railway companies and other infrastructure can be included in these new categories.

References

Fruin, M., *Kikkoman* (Cambridge, Mass., 1983).
Hasegawa, Akira, *Kinsei Tokusanbutsu Ryūtsūshiron* [Distribution System of Specialties in the Early Modern Period] (Tokyo, 1993).
Hayashi, Reiko, "Chōshi shōyu jōzōgyō no shijō kōzō" [The market structure of Chōshi soy-sauce industry], in Yamaguchi, Kazuo and Kanji Ishii (eds), *Kindai Nihon no Shōhin Ryūtsū* (Tokyo, 1986).
—— (ed.), *Shōyu Jōzōgyō-shi no Kenkyū* [The Study on the History of Soy-sauce Industry] (Tokyo, 1990).

Hayashi, Takehisa, *Nihon ni okeru Sozei Kokka no Seiritsu* [The Formation of Tax State in Japan] (Tokyo, 1965).

Hirakawa, Arata, *Funsō to Yoron* [The Conflict and the Public Opinion] (Tokyo, 1996).

Kurushima, Hiroshi, "Kinsei kōki no 'chiiki shakai' no rekishiteki seikaku ni tsuite" [On the historical character of the regional community in the second half of the early modern period], *Rekishi Hyōron* 499 (Tokyo, 1991), 2–28.

Meiji Hōseikeizaishi Kenkyūjo (ed.), *Genrōin Kaigi Hikki, Kōki* [The Records of the Meetings of the Senate, the Second Half], Vol. 22 (Tokyo, 1970).

Naimushō [Ministry of the Interior], *Meiji 7 nen Fuken Bussan Hyō* [Table of Industrial Products by Prefecture] (Tokyo, 1874).

Saito, Osamu and Masayuki Tanimoto, "Zairai sangyō no saihensei" [The re-organization of indigenous industries], in Umemura, Mataji and Yūzō Yamamoto (eds), *Nihon Keizaishi 3: Kaikō to Ishin* (Tokyo, 1989).

Shibuya, Ryūichi, Shōjirō Ishiyama and Ken Saitō "Taishō-ki no dai-shisanka meibo" [The list of big-scale property owners in Taishō era], Chihōkinyūshikenkyū 14 (1983), 20–107.

Shinohara, Miyohei, *Chōki Keizai Tōkei 6: Kojin Shōhi Shishutsu* [Estimates of Long Term Economic Statistics of Japan 6: Personal Consumption Expenditures] (Tokyo, 1969).

Tanimoto, Masayuki, "Jōzōgyō" [The brewery industry], in Nishikawa Shunsaku, Kōnosuke Odaka and Osamu Saito (eds), *Nihon Keizai no 200-nen* (Tokyo, 1996a).

——, "Sekiguchi Hachibei/Naotarō" in Takeuchi, Johzen, Takeshi Abe and Minoru Sawai (eds), *Kindai Nihon niokeru Kigyōka no Shokeifu* (Osaka, 1996b).

——, "Nihon niokeru 'chiiki kōgyōka' to tōshikōdō" [Investment activities in regional Japanese industrialization], *Shakaikeizaishigaku* 64–1 (Tokyo, 1998), 88–114.

Tanimoto, Masayuki and Takeshi Abe, "Kigyō bokkō to kindai keiei, Zairai keiei" [Modern business, indigenous business in the age of the rise of enterprises], in Miyamoto, Matao and Takeshi Abe (eds.), *Nihon Keieishi 2: Keiei Kakushin to Kōgyōka* (Tokyo, 1995).

Tochigi, Toshio, "Meiji 20 nendai no chihō biiru" [Local beer brewery in Meiji 20s], Ibaragi Chihōshi Kenkyūkai (ed.), *Ibaragi Shirin* 16, (Mito, 1992), 85–107.

Toride-shi Kyōiku-iinkai (ed.), *Torideshi-shi: Kinsei Shiryō hen* [History of Toride City: Volume of Archives in Edo era] 2 (Toride, 1987).

Watanabe, Takashi, *Kinsei Sonraku no Tokusitsu to Tenkai* [The Particularity of the Villages in the Early Modern Period] (Tokyo, 1998).

Yabuta, Yutaka, *Kokuso to Hyakushō-ikki no Kenkyū* [The Study on the Suits and Riots in the Province] (Tokyo, 1992).

INDEX

Index

merchants:
 control over reorganization of
  production 89
 criticism of 251
 discontented 284
 evasion of prefectural regulations 283
 export 114
 foreign 81, 219, 315
 influential 250–1
 kind of agent for 90
 leading 79, 81
 managerial ability 34
 market-town 309
 protest against inspection 280
 putting-out 118
 see also wholesalers
metal processing 31, 32
Mexico 19, 21
middle-class people 245, 262, 291
middlemen 90
Milgrom, P. 201, 203
military sector 67, 78, 150–1
Minami, R. 145, 187
Minamitsugaru 169
Minato village 117
mine construction 67
Ministries:
 Agriculture and Commerce 25, 84, 107,
  145, 147, 151, 157, 160, 162, 168, 172,
  173, 176, 225, 231, 233, 235, 284
 Agriculture and Forestry 107, 168, 169,
  171, 172, 173, 176
 Commerce and Industry 157, 158, 164
 Finance 143, 146, 164, 225, 295, 304
 Foreign Affairs 25, 160, 225
 Navy 230
 Public Works 143, 148
Mino 223, 225, 227, 235
miscellaneous industries 76
Mitsubishi 140, 143, 257
Mitsubishi Paper 169, 172
Mitsubishi Shipbuilding 4
Mitsui 257
Mitsui Trading Company 169, 172
Miyata Corporation 84
Miyata Seisakusho 149
"modern industry" 3, 10
modernization 93, 181–240
Mogusa cloth 131, 136
monetary policy 250
money lending activities 311, 313
moral(e) hazard 18, 29, 207, 208
Morimura (trade association leader) 251

Morimura-gumi 221, 227, 228–9, 235
mortgages 258
motifs 219, 221, 223, 227, 228
motorization 52
multi-ends reeling machines 109, 114
multi-layered structures 61, 307, 310
munitions factories 4, 148
Muroran 169, 172
Mutō, Mohei 290, 295
Mutual Aid Association 256, 266
mutual trust 260, 261, 264, 266, 267

Nagano 56, 67, 142, 206
 origin of the day nursery system 113
 see also Suwa
Nagaoka 146
Nagasaki 4, 56, 143, 144, 149, 227
 foreign merchants 219
 pottery traders 219
 see also Arita
Nagasaki Iron Works 147
Nagoya 145, 160, 162, 223, 225, 227, 229,
 230, 231
Nagoya Pottery Manufacturers'
 Association 163
Naitō, Norikuni 150
Nakabayashi, Masaki 184, 186, 193, 195,
 196, 198, 199, 200, 201, 203, 204, 205,
 206, 207, 208
Nakaminowa village 105
Nakamura, Takafusa 10, 95, 140
Nakanishi, H. 148
Nakano, Shiyō 144
Nakatado Gun Straw Bag Local Trade
 Association 173
Nakatani, Seiji 313
Nara 56, 82, 260
Naramoto, T. 228
National industrial exposition (1890) 315,
 316
National Komaba Agricultural College 315
National Pottery and Porcelain Institute 232
needles 90
new products 249
 development of 227, 250–2
New York 187, 196, 198, 221, 229
newly industrializing economies 75
NGK (Nippon Gaishi Kaisha) 229
Nichiro Fishery 169, 172
night schools 151
night shifts 127, 131, 134
Nihon Ginkō Chōsa-kyoku 162
Nihon Railways 313, 315

Index